CHINA FINANCIAL POLICY REPORT

中国金融政策报告

2015

主　编　吴晓灵

副主编　何海峰

中国金融出版社

责任编辑：张　超
责任校对：张志文
责任印制：程　颖

图书在版编目（CIP）数据

中国金融政策报告.2015（Zhongguo Jinrong Zhengce Baogao.2015）/吴晓灵主编.
—北京：中国金融出版社，2015.5
ISBN 978 - 7 - 5049 - 7945 - 2

Ⅰ.①中… Ⅱ.①吴… Ⅲ.①金融政策—研究报告—中国—2015 Ⅳ.①F832.0

中国版本图书馆 CIP 数据核字（2015）第 093069 号

出版
发行　　**中国金融出版社**

社址　北京市丰台区益泽路 2 号
市场开发部　（010）63266347，63805472，63439533（传真）
网上书店　http：//www. chinafph. com　（010）63286832，63365686（传真）
读者服务部　（010）66070833，62568380
邮编　100071
经销　新华书店
印刷　保利达印务有限公司
尺寸　185 毫米×260 毫米
印张　20.25
字数　400 千
版次　2015 年 5 月第 1 版
印次　2015 年 5 月第 1 次印刷
定价　54.00 元
ISBN 978 - 7 - 5049 - 7945 - 2/F. 7505
如出现印装错误本社负责调换　联系电话（010）63263947
编辑部邮箱：jiaocaiyibu@ 126. com

编 委 会

The Editorial Board

前　言

　　《中国金融政策报告》是中欧陆家嘴国际金融研究院与中国社会科学院金融政策研究中心联合组织编写的年度研究报告，旨在对过去一年国际国内经济背景下中国金融政策的出台与执行情况进行总结和分析。

　　中国经济 2014 年进入了"新常态"，迎来了"三期叠加"的挑战——经济增长速度进入换挡期，经济结构调整面临阵痛期，前期刺激政策进入消化期。而中国金融业 2014 年开始了中国共产党十八届三中全会全面深化改革决定中"完善金融市场体系"的任务，这一重要任务旨在从体制、机制、体系、机构上建立大国开放经济的现代金融制度框架——在金融资源的配置中，不但要使市场发挥决定性作用，也要使政府更好地发挥相应的作用。回顾 2014 年，我们可以看到：中国人民银行不对称降息、创设中期借贷便利、定向降准，不断丰富和完善货币政策工具组合；国务院先后印发了《国务院关于进一步促进资本市场健康发展的若干意见》和《国务院关于加快发展现代保险服务业的若干意见》，前者被称为资本市场新"国九条"，后者被称为保险新"国十条"；而《存款保险条例（征求意见稿)》的公布，① 意味着中国存款保险制度开始进入了视野；沪港通开启（沪港股票市场交易互联互通机制试点正式开通），与自由贸易账户一起成为了中国上海自贸区的两大支柱；"互联网金融"首次进入政府工作报告；首批民营银行获批筹建；等等。

　　《中国金融政策报告（2015)》延续了《中国金融政策报告（2014)》的框架结构，它包括两大模块即主题报告和动态报告。具体地看，《中国金融政策报告（2015)》包括以下内容。

---

　　① 注：本报告定稿出版前，2015 年 3 月 31 日，国务院总理李克强签署第 660 号国务院令，公布《存款保险条例》，从 2015 年 5 月 1 日起正式实施。

　　第一部分是两篇专题文章——《"新怀特计划"还是"新凯恩斯计划"?》和《从互联网金融看新金融的发展空间》。第一篇文章讨论国际金融的老话题。现行国际货币体系存在的问题有其深刻的制度原因,经过反思,我们提出了"新凯恩斯计划"和"新怀特计划"的改进尝试——在经济合理性上,无疑前者具有一定优势,在体系架构上也更稳定、更有弹性。但受路径依赖和制度变迁成本影响,"新怀特计划"似乎更具现实可行性,未来的国际货币体系的优化路径很可能仍是在美元本位的基础上对其货币发行施加一定制约,并对国际收支调节机制进行一定程度的完善。第二篇文章关注中国金融的新现象。互联网金融是中国新金融的代表,包括第三方支付、P2P和众筹等。支付体系是一个国家最重要的基础设施,因此包括第三方支付在内的支付功能机构,应固守其基本职责,不宜"混业"从事金融理财产品发售。而P2P和众筹则极可能代表了中国新金融,即互联网金融发展的方向,因此前景广阔;但是,信息平台的建设与完善、小额分散原则的遵守、征信系统的多元化发展等监管政策要及时到位。

　　第二部分是年度报告的主题报告"新常态下的中国货币政策框架"。我们认为,中国经济的"新常态"与世界经济的"新平庸"密切相关;制定和实施货币政策是中国金融调控的核心,它追求符合中国经济发展运行实际的多个最终目标,在主要发挥总量调控功能的基础上,积极尝试结构调控的作用;世界主要经济体在量化宽松政策上的不同实践,为中国货币政策提供了启示;中国货币政策框架的完善,既要满足金融稳定运行的短期调控要求,还要符合中国金融改革与发展的目标。

　　第一部分和第二部分构成了《中国金融政策报告 (2015)》的上篇即主题报告模块,而《中国金融政策报告 (2015)》的下篇即另一模块"2014 年度中国金融政策动态"则由第三、第四和第五部分构成。

　　第三部分是 2014 年的"宏观金融政策"。这一部分将对 2014 年的货币政策、汇率与国际收支相关政策进行回顾、分析,并适度进行政策评价与展望。

　　第四部分是 2014 年的"主要金融市场发展政策"。这一部分全面回顾和分析了 2014 年内"银行业市场发展政策""股票市场发展政策""保险市场发展政策""债券市场发展政策""货币市场发展政策""财富管理市场发展政策""金融衍生品市场发展政策""商品期货市场发展政策""外汇市场发展政策"

和"中国黄金市场发展政策",同时也进行了相应的政策评价与展望。

第五部分是 2014 年的"主要金融监管政策"。这一部分对 2014 年"中国人民银行主要监管政策""中国银监会主要监管政策""中国证监会主要监管政策"和"中国保监会主要监管政策"进行了回顾和分析,也相应给出了政策的评价与展望。

通过对《中国金融政策报告(2015)》的编写,我们深切地感受到,2014年中国金融改革开放的全面深化与扩大正在展开,以互联网金融为代表的金融创新正在全面兴起。因此,中国金融政策的科学制定与实践,不但会加快促进中国金融的现代化,而且也将逐渐影响到世界经济和金融。

本报告作为集体研究的结果,作者主要由中欧陆家嘴国际金融研究院、中国社会科学院金融政策研究中心以及其他金融界人士构成,最后由吴晓灵、何海峰对报告全文进行了修改和定稿。先后参加各部分撰稿的执笔人是:吴晓灵、何海峰、于卫国、伍戈、储幼阳、荣艺华、刘学庆、王鑫、王敏、王琪、甘正在、朱小川。何海峰和于卫国对报告中文部分进行了校对和统编。何海峰、于卫国、余粤、周晓松、史广龙、王鑫、朱小川、吴建刚和李雪静对报告英文部分进行了校对和统编。于卫国对报告的格式进行了编辑加工。我们感谢中国金融出版社王效端主任、张超编辑认真和严谨的工作。

我们一如既往地期盼着各种批评和建议。

中欧陆家嘴国际金融研究院常务副院长
暨中国社会科学院金融政策研究中心主任
何海峰(代序)
2015 年 3 月 29 日

Foreword

China Financial Policy Report is an annual research report prepared jointly by the CEIBS Lujiazui Institute of International Finance and the Institute of Financial Policy, Chinese Academy of Social Sciences, intended to summarize and analyze the introduction and implementation of China's financial policy under the background of international and domestic economy in the past year.

In 2014, Chinese economy entered the "New Normal", faced with the "Three-period Superimposed" challenge – economic growth shifting period, structural adjustment pain period and early-stage policy digestion period. In 2014, Chinese finance started the important mission of "improving the financial market system" in fully deepening reform as required by the Third Plenary Session of the 18th CPC Central Committee, aiming to build a modern financial system framework of open economy in a great power from respects of system, mechanism, structure and institution – in allocation of financial resources, not only make the market play a decisive role, but also make the government better play the corresponding role. Looking back to 2014, we can see that, the People's Bank of China, through asymmetric interest cuts, medium-term lending facilities and directional reserve reductions, continuously enriched and improved monetary policy instrument portfolios; the State Council successively issued the *Several Opinions on Further Promoting the Healthy Development of the Capital Market*, called as "New Nine State Regulations" for the capital market, and the *Several Opinions on Accelerating the Development of the Modern Insurance Service Industry*, called as "New Ten National Rules" for insurance; the release of the *Deposit Insurance Regulations (Draft for Comments)*[①] meant that China's deposit insurance system came into view; the launch of Shanghai-Hong Kong Stock Connect [i. e. The Stock Exchange of Hong Kong Limited (SEHK) and Shanghai Stock Exchange (SSE)

---

① Note: Before publishing of this report, on March 31, Premier Li Keqiang signed the State Council Order No. 660 *Deposit Insurance Regulations* in Beijing, which will be implemented from May 1, 2015.

established mutual order-routing connectivity〕, together with free trade accounts, became two pillars of China Shanghai Pilot Free Trade Zone; "Internet Finance" was included in the government work report for the first time; the establishment of the first group of private banks was approved, etc.

China Financial Policy Report (2015) continued the framework structure of *China Financial Policy Report* (2014), consisting of two modules: thematic report and dynamic report. Specifically, *China Financial Policy Report* (2015) included the following content:

It comes first is two feature articles – " 'New White Plan' or 'New Keynes Plan'?" and "Thoughts on the Development Space of New Finance from Internet Finance Perspective". The first article discussed the old topic about international finance. Problems existing in the modern international currency system has its profound institutional reasons, and through reflection, we put forward the "New Keynes Plan" and "New White Plan" for improvements – in respect of economic rationality, the former undoubtedly is with certain advantages, and has a more stable, more flexible systemic structure. However, subject to path dependence and institutional change costs, the "New White Plan" seems to have more realistic feasibility, and the optimization path of the future international currency system is still likely to impose certain restrictions on currency issuance based on the dollar standard, and make certain improvements on the adjustment mechanism for balance of payments. The second article focused on the new phenomenon of Chinese finance. Internet finance is a representative of China's new finance, including third-party payment, P2P and crowd-funding. The payment system is the most important infrastructure for a country, so payment institutions, including third-party payment, should stick to their basic duties rather than conduct "mixed operation" by engaging in offering financial products. P2P and crowd-funding most likely represent China's new finance, i. e. direction of internet finance development, so they may have broad prospects; however, regulatory policies regarding the establishment and improvement of information platform, observance with small-amount dispersion principles and diversified development of credit reference system must be formulated in a timely manner.

Chapter 3 is the thematic report "China's Monetary Policy Framework under the New Normal". We believe that, the "New Normal" of Chinese economy and the "New Mediocre" of world economy are closely related; the formulation and implementation of monetary policy is the core of China's financial control, which pursues multiple ultimate goals in line with the actual operation of China's economic development, and on the basis of mainly playing the role of gross control, actively tries the role of structural adjustment. Different practices of major economies around the world on quantitative easing policy provide inspiration for China's monetary policy. The improvement of China's monetary policy framework should meet the short-term control requirements of stable financial operation, as well as the objectives of China's financial reform and development.

Chapter 1、Chapter 2 and Chapter 3 form the first section (i. e. thematic report module) of *China Financial Policy Report* (*2015*), while the second section (i. e. the module of "China's Financial Policies in 2014") of *China Financial Policy Report* (*2015*) is formed by Chapter 4、Chapter 5 and Chapter 6.

Chapter 4 is the "Macro Financial Policies" in 2014. This part will review and analyze monetary policy and policies regarding exchange rate and balance of payments in 2014, and will also carry out appropriate policy evaluation and outlook.

Chapter 5 is the "Highlights of Financial Market Development Policy" in 2014. This part will comprehensively review and analyze the "Banking Market Development Policy" "Stock Market Development Policy" "Insurance Market Development Policy" "Bond Market Development Policy" "Money Market Development Policy" "Wealth Management Market Development Policy" "Financial Derivatives Market Development Policy" "Commodity Futures Market Development Policy" "Foreign Exchange Market Development Policy" and "Chinese Gold Market Development Policy" in 2014, and will also carry out appropriate policy evaluation and outlook.

Chapter 6 is the "Highlights of Financial Regulatory Policy" in 2014. This part will review and analyze the "Highlights of Regulatory Policy of the PBC" "Highlights of Regulatory Policy of the CBRC" "Highlights of Regulatory Policy of the CSRC" and "Highlights of Regulatory Policy of the CIRC" in 2014, and will also carry out appropriate policy evaluation and outlook.

By preparing the *China Financial Policy Report* (*2015*), we deeply feel that, China's financial reform and opening up was fully deepening and expanding in 2014, and financial innovation represented by internet finance rose as a whole. Therefore, the scientific formulation and implementation of China's financial policy will not only accelerate the "Modernization" of Chinese finance, but also will gradually affect world economy and finance.

This report is a result of collective research, mainly authored by persons from CEIBS Lujiazui Institute of International Finance and the Institute of Financial Policy, Chinese Academy of Social Sciences, as well as other persons from the financial community, revised and finalized by Wu Xiaoling and He Haifeng. Persons successively involved in the writing of each part include: Wu Xiaoling, He Haifeng, Yu Weiguo, Wu Ge, Chu Youyang, Rong Yihua, Liu Xueqing, Wang Xin, Wang Min, Wang Qi, Gan Zhengzai and Zhu Xiaochuan. He Haifeng and Yu Weiguo proofread and compiled the Chinese version of this report. He Haifeng, Yu Weiguo, Yu Yue, Zhou Xiaosong, Shi Guanglong, Wang Xin, Zhu Xiaochuan, Wu Jiangang and Li Xuejing proofread and compiled the English version of this report. Yu Weiguo edited the format of this report. We highly appreciate the rigorous work of Director Wang Xiaoduan and Editor Zhang Chao from China Financial Publishing House.

We always look forward to various criticisms and suggestions.

He, Haifeng（**Preface**）
Executive Vice President of CEIBS Lujiazui Institute of International Finance
Director of Institute of Financial Policy of Chinese Academy of Social Sciences
March 29, 2015

目　　录

English Version

Part One Feature Articles and Thematic Reports

Part Two China's Financial Policies in 2014

上　篇

专题文章与
主题报告

专题文章一

"新怀特计划"还是"新凯恩斯计划"？

——对构建稳定与有效的国际货币体系的思考①

吴晓灵

探讨未来国际货币体系改革的方案是一个宏大的课题，也有许多专家学者做了很深入的研究，但据我所知，目前仍未达成共识。这里我也只做学术讨论，这是开放性的议题，大家可畅所欲言，各抒己见。下面我先抛砖引玉，谈谈自己的一点看法。

一、现行国际货币体系的现状与问题

2008 年国际金融危机爆发到现在已经过去了将近 6 年，但全球经济仍处于缓慢复苏中。学界普遍认为，此次危机是过去十几年来全球性失衡不断积累的总爆发，而现行国际货币体系存在的诸多不足则可能是促成全球性失衡的根源之一。但遗憾的是，这种全球性失衡问题仍未得到根本性解决，各主要国家缺乏改革现状的勇气和动力，理论界也远未就未来国际货币体系安排达成明确的共识。现行国际货币体系的问题主要体现为：

一是全球流动性管理容易失控。布雷顿森林体系崩溃以来，以全球外汇储备为典型代表的全球流动性快速增长，尤其是 2002 年以来更是飞速增长。据世界银行统计，2011 年底，全球除黄金之外的外汇储备达到 10.56 万亿美元，比 1975 年增长 52.8 倍，比 2002 年增长 3.3 倍，而同期全球 GDP 仅增长 11.0 倍和 1.1 倍，外汇储备/GDP 从1975 年的 3.38% 上升至 2011 年 15.08%，尤其是 2000 年以后该比例更是快速上升。因此，相比实际经济增长，全球流动性显得长期过剩。

二是跨境资本流动波动剧烈。随着全球流动性规模的与日俱增以及资本项目自由化的推进，跨境资本流动日益频繁，规模空前且波动剧烈。净私人资本流动与 GDP 的比

---

① 本文根据作者 2014 年 6 月 17 日在上海"国际货币体系再思考——布雷顿森林会议七十周年后"国际研讨会上的讲话整理。

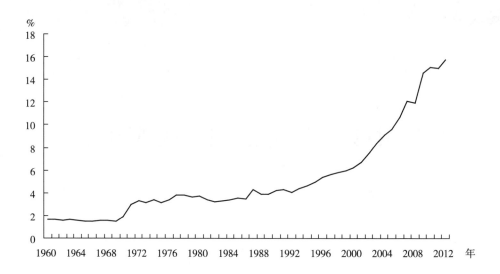

资料来源：IFS、WIND。

图1-1 全球除黄金外的外汇储备在全球 GDP 中的占比

率在过去的 20 多年中波动尤为剧烈，很多地区都经历了极短期内资本流动大进大出的变动（Darvas，2014）。其对金融稳定以及宏观经济的持续发展带来了巨大挑战。

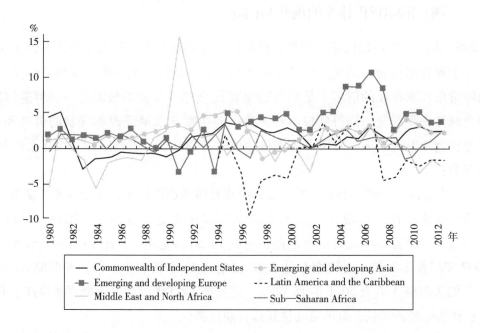

资料来源：IMF WEO，2014-04。

图1-2 净私人资本流动/GDP

三是加剧了全球失衡的进一步发展。全球失衡可能主要由非货币体系的诸多因素引发，但当前的国际货币体系进一步加剧了失衡。这集中体现在美国可以通过发行美元进行无限融资以弥补其经常项目赤字，同时现有体系又缺乏对该国际收支失衡的有效调节机制，这助长了全球失衡的持续深入发展。

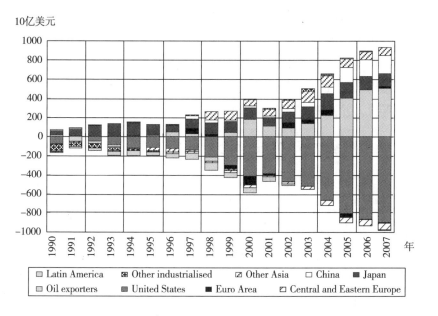

资料来源：IMF（World Economic Outlook and Direction of Trade Statistics）；欧洲央行工作人员的计算。

图1-3 全球经常账户头寸（1997—2007年年度数据）

上述现象和问题的背后有着深刻的制度原因：一是缺乏对储备货币发行的约束机制。布雷顿森林体系崩溃后，美元与黄金脱钩，货币发行彻底"去黄金化"，完全依靠信用发行。而现有的国际货币体系缺少足以代表全球整体利益的主体。虽然不乏 IMF 等国际组织，但受众所周知的制度设计与治理架构影响，它们在管理全球储备货币、约束国际货币发行等方面的作用十分有限。这就造成了在实践中虽然某些储备货币也有自己国内的"货币锚"（如通胀、就业或其他货币政策目标），但其发行均未基于全球整体状况，制度架构上缺乏对其履行全球储备货币职能的约束。从这个意义上来讲，主要储备货币的发行机制中缺乏基于全球经贸发展的"货币锚"。

二是主权货币与国际储备货币两种角色的冲突。在当前以主权国家货币作为主要国际储备货币的体系下，每一种储备货币都扮演着两种角色——首先是主权货币，然后才是储备货币。在现实中，这两种角色在很多情况下是冲突的，其背后是主权国家利益与全球整体利益之间的矛盾。但不幸的是，在现实抉择时，主权货币角色往往占有压倒性的优势。极端地说，储备货币发行当局一般不会考虑全球利益，除非该利益影响到其主权国家利益。

三是缺乏对国际收支失衡的有效调节机制。牙买加体系从本质上说是一个"无体系"的体系，除了废除黄金作为货币发行的基础之外，原则上对汇率制度、汇兑管理、国际收支状况等并未作出强制性的限定。在布雷顿森林体系下，逆差国还承担了国际收支调节责任，而在牙买加体系下，决策者过度地将希望寄托于浮动汇率的自动调节功能，并未设定任何失衡调节的强制性规则。但事实上，在金融一体化背景下，汇率很可能脱离基本面而过度波动，其对国际收支的调节作用也越来越不稳定。因此，从制度安排上来看，牙买加体系可能注定是一个失衡的体系。

综上所述，现行的国际货币体系本质上可能助长储备货币国家滥发货币的冲动，扭曲全球资源配置机制，加剧国际收支的失衡。而调节机制的缺失则进一步强化既有失衡，使其不断累积，并发展成全球性的难题。

二、国际货币体系改革的历史争论：怀特计划与凯恩斯计划

以史为镜，可以知兴替。在 70 多年前，曾发生过一场如何设计、构建国际货币体系的争论，一举奠定了此后几十年国际货币体系的基调，时至今日仍发挥着重大影响。那场争论的焦点聚集在凯恩斯计划和怀特计划之争。应该说，这两个计划的目的都是一致的——试图构建一个稳定的国际货币体系。其分歧主要体现在以下几方面：

一是基金制和银行制的区别。这是两个计划最根本的分歧。怀特计划设想建立的仅仅是一个基金——国际稳定基金。虽然怀特也提出了 unita，但其仅仅是记账单位而不是货币，实际使用流通的仍是美元等主权货币。由于一旦认购完成基金的份额就相对固定，因此其缺乏实质上的提款渠道，也就没有货币派生机制，所以，该计划自诞生之日开始就注定缺乏自动适应全球经贸增长的灵活性。换言之，国际稳定基金的总值是相对固定的，可以预期，随着经贸规模的增长，其相对全球经贸总量的占比势必下降，对汇率稳定的调节作用也势必减弱。而凯恩斯计划则设想建立一个全球中央银行——国际清算同盟，创造并发行一种新的超主权储备货币——bancor，通过要求顺差国强制将盈余存入同盟账户和向逆差国提供透支（实质上的贷款）构造了货币派生渠道，可以根据全球经贸发展提供所需的充足的支付清算媒介。

二是有关黄金非货币化的分歧。怀特计划虽然主张黄金退出货币流通，但其美元与黄金间可兑换的保证证明本质上仍是一种变形的黄金本位制，黄金仍旧是事实上的"影子货币"，美元的发行仍受制于黄金储量。与之相反，凯恩斯计划虽然规定了 bancor 的价值由黄金确定，但其与黄金间的单向兑换——可以用黄金换取 bancor，反之则不行——在事实上实现了黄金的非货币化，bancor 的发行取决于全球经贸规模。极端地讲，若去掉黄金也无损于该体系运行。

三是货币锚的差异。从上述第二点分歧可以合理地推断出，在怀特计划下，黄金仍是其货币锚；而在凯恩斯计划下，实际上的货币锚已经变成了全球贸易总量，在该计划中，各成员国将会被分配到一个初始份额，该份额由二战之前的 3 年各国进出口贸易平均额的 75% 来计算，此后，为反映全球经贸的发展，每隔 5 年重新计算一次份额。

四是国际收支失衡调节机制的区别。首先，在调节的责任分担上，怀特计划是不对

称的调整，逆差国承担几乎全部的调整责任，逆差国必须将逆差保持在份额允许的范围之内，即第一年不能超过该国份额的 150%，以后不能超过 200%；凯恩斯计划主张对称的调整，顺差国和逆差国共同承担调整责任，即当成员国清算账户顺/逆差超过其份额的 25% 时即被确定为收支不平衡，要对其超额部分收取管理费，并要求其采取相应的扩张或紧缩政策，超过份额的资金将在年底被没收作为公共储备基金。其次，在调节的方式上，两者存在着抵押贷款与贷款的区别：怀特计划采取了货币互换的方式，即逆差国用本币换取所需其他国家的货币，本质上是以本币作为抵押获取外币贷款；而凯恩斯计划则允许逆差国直接申请透支或提存。

表 1-1   怀特计划和凯恩斯计划的比较

	怀特计划	凯恩斯计划
组织方式	基金制	银行制
储备货币	美元（unita 仅为记账单位）	bancor
发行机构	美联储	国际清算同盟
分配机制	按与美国的双边国际收支状况分配	按占全球贸易的相对规模分配
货币锚	黄金	全球贸易总量
国际收支调节机制	非对称调节	对称调节
特里芬悖论	难以破解	可望破解
实施可行性	基本采用	未采用

从理论上，凯恩斯计划更具经济合理性：凯恩斯似乎真正看到了金本位制固有的缺陷，其主张使黄金非货币化，并以全球贸易总量为锚的设想使货币发行自动与全球经贸发展相匹配。但不幸的是，凯恩斯计划遭遇到二战后美国"一家独大"世界格局的现实挑战，其国际清算同盟的设想直接损害了美国货币政策独立性和铸币税，最终在与怀特计划的角逐中败北。相应地，二战后 IMF 也基本以怀特计划为蓝本设立。

三、国际货币体系的新探索："新怀特计划"还是"新凯恩斯计划"？

这次全球性的金融危机促进我们进一步反思现有的国际货币体系，探索理想货币体系的构架，思考未来转型路径的可行性。在我看来，基于历史上的争论，并结合现阶段国际经济金融的现实，我们依然可以沿着两个思路展开探索：一是借鉴怀特计划的思路（我们暂且称之为"新怀特计划"），二是借鉴凯恩斯计划的思路（我们暂且称之为"新凯恩斯计划"）。其大致思路与区别如下。

（一）国际储备货币选择：主权货币本位还是超主权货币本位？

从 18 世纪的英镑本位制开始，国际货币体系始终是以主权货币充当国际储备货币。这种安排有其方便管理的优点，同样也存在货币发行缺乏国际约束等不足，进而可能危害到国际货币体系的整体稳定。解决这个问题的方向大致有两个："新怀特计划"主张继续在主权货币充当国际储备货币的基础上对货币发行施加国际约束；"新凯恩斯计划"的思路则是创设超主权货币作为国际储备货币。

就"新怀特计划"而言，最近的例子就是考虑用 G20 提出的一些互评估指标来约束主要储备货币发行国的货币发行。2010 年 G20 首尔峰会的互评估项目曾对成员国提出过十几项财经纪律的制约指标，其中有六个核心指标极具参考价值。一旦这些指标被强制满足，可望对主要储备货币发行构成一定的财经纪律约束。但这涉及到一国经济主权的让渡和国际间的政策协调，面临的现实困难和挑战仍不少。

而在"新凯恩斯计划"的方向上，许多学者和机构都做了类似研究，如伯恩斯坦计划、特里芬计划等，包括 SDR 的创设也是超主权货币的有益尝试，当然其中最负盛名的仍属凯恩斯计划。事实上，1968 年 IMF 创设和分配 SDR 在一定程度上部分借鉴了凯恩斯当初的设想。现在看来，与怀特计划相比，凯恩斯计划无疑具有更多的合理性，其以全球贸易规模为锚的设计在处理币值稳定和流动性供给的矛盾上更具优势。但理论上的合理性与现实中的可行性并不是一回事，要实现超主权货币对主权货币的替代必然面临政治、经济、金融等诸多阻碍，必须解决如何形成和分配、如何扩大使用、如何与现有体系衔接与过渡等一系列难题。所以，从可行性上看，"新怀特计划"的做法可能更具操作性。

总之，这两个计划的背后主要是货币发行机构的差异。"新凯恩斯计划"要求成立一个全球性的中央银行来发行和管理超主权货币，维持全球货币体系稳定；而"新怀特计划"下，主权国家货币当局承担发行储备货币的职责，不需要全球央行来管理，但需要对该国货币发行施加更多国际约束。

（二）货币锚选择："外生锚"还是"内生锚"？

要使货币能充分发挥自身重要的职能，首先应保证其币值的稳定性，特别是其作为价值尺度、交易媒介和储藏等职能的稳定性。因此，未来的国际货币体系不能回避"货币锚"的问题。一个合适的"货币锚"必须能有效协调币值稳定和流动性供给之间的矛盾，这就要求：第一，具有相当的稳定性以约束货币发行，保证货币价值的相对稳定；第二，与全球经贸往来具有一定的相关性，确保满足实体经济对流动性的需求。

当前美元本位的货币体系下，美联储以美国经济状况（通胀和就业）为"锚"发行国际储备货币（美元），因此，从国际储备货币发行机制来讲，这是一个相对全球经济而言"外生"的货币锚，因为它不以全球经贸状况为参照。按照"新怀特计划"，在延续美元本位的前提下，为保持币值的稳定，对美联储货币发行进行适当约束是必要的。约束的方式可以是寻求一个具有自身独立价值的"商品锚"（如选用储量更丰富的贵金属作为货币锚，或者构造一个大宗商品篮子作为货币锚，甚至以某种形式的能源作为货币锚），也可以构造基于美国宏观经济状况的指标（如负债率、杠杆率等）来约束美联储的货币发行。但无论采用哪种形式，"新怀特计划"中的货币锚始终具有外生性。

理论上讲，既然货币最主要的职能是作为交易媒介，那么货币锚就必须与全球经贸发展及其交易相称，即具有与全球经贸发展相适应的内生性。当初凯恩斯设想的全球贸易规模作为货币锚具有一定的合理性。按照"新凯恩斯计划"的思路，鉴于当前国际资本流动已大大超越了贸易结算需求，与此相应地，必须选择更宽泛的经济指标作为货币发行的锚。例如，可以考虑选择一定的"经济指数篮子"，将反映全球通胀和经济增长状况的代表性指标纳入其中，既包括数量型指标，也包括价格型指标，这些都是比较合适的选择范围。但具体选取哪些指标，指标权重如何确定，仍是需要深入研究的问题。此外，也有学者主张将 SDR 作为货币锚，是否可行？如何推进？这些都是开放的话题，大家可以各抒己见。

（三）国际收支调节：对称调整还是非对称调整？

此次全球危机充分证明了一个有效的失衡调节机制对于货币体系的重要性。布雷顿森林体系是非对称调整机制，牙买加体系虽然也存在 IMF 第四条款磋商等机制，但在实践中缺乏约束力和执行力，因此实际上是一个调节机制缺失的体系。"新怀特计划"下的未来货币体系本质上仍属非对称调整。美元本位和各方实力不均衡的现实决定其本质上不可能实现对称。"新凯恩斯计划"则主张对称的调整。当然，调整的机制如何设计？如何保证其有效性和可执行性？这些都需要进一步研究。

（四）特里芬悖论：延续还是破解？

讨论国际货币体系就不能不提及特里芬悖论。特里芬悖论最初指的是在以主权货币（美元）作为国际货币的条件下，国际贸易和投资的发展需要美国通过经常账户逆差不断输出美元以保持充足的清偿力（支付工具），但长期逆差将影响对美元可兑换的信心，势必导致各国争相将美元兑换成黄金，从而导致美国黄金储备的枯竭，最终损害布雷顿森林体系"双挂钩"的根基。进入 21 世纪以来，美国出现了"格林斯潘困惑"，长端利率与短端利率的联动被割裂。从利率作为货币价格的意义上说，这意味着美元的价格出现了扭曲，美元的长期与短期的币值不再稳定一致，并且，随着海外美元的增加，这种价格扭曲也可能日益严重。这可谓是"价格版"的特里芬悖论。

特里芬悖论在本质上是稳定币值和流动性供给之间的矛盾。导致特里芬悖论的根本原因是储备货币发行与全球经贸发展脱节，致使稳定币值和流动性供给两者不可兼顾。金本位制保证了币值的稳定，但在流动性供给上跟不上全球经贸的扩展。牙买加体系保证了流动性的供给，但引致了长期的全球性通胀。因此，要真正破解特里芬悖论，就必须使货币的价值和供给内生化，凯恩斯计划作出了初步的尝试，可惜未能付诸实践。而在主权货币本位制下，货币发行仅取决于主权国家状况，不可能从根本上破解这个悖论。从这个意义上说，只要"新怀特计划"不放弃主权货币本位，特里芬悖论也必将是其挥之不去的梦魇。相反地，"新凯恩斯计划"继承了凯恩斯关于超主权货币的理念，有可能一劳永逸地破解这个悖论。

表1-2   "新怀特计划"和"新凯恩斯计划"的对比

	"新怀特计划"	"新凯恩斯计划"
组织方式	基金制	银行制
储备货币	主权货币	超主权货币
发行机构	主权国家货币当局	全球中央银行
分配机制	按与国际货币发行国的双边国际收支状况分配	按占世界经济的相对规模分配
货币锚	外生锚（如对货币发行国施加 G20 互评估等更多约束）	内生锚（如通胀、增长等世界经济总量指标）
国际收支调节机制	非对称调节	对称调节
特里芬悖论	难以破解	可望破解
实施难度	相对较小	相对较大

综观"新凯恩斯计划"和"新怀特计划"，在经济合理性上，无疑前者具有一定优势，在体系架构上也更稳定、更有弹性。但受路径依赖和制度变迁成本影响，"新怀特计划"似乎更具现实可行性，未来的国际货币体系的优化路径很可能仍是在美元本位的基础上对其货币发行施加一定制约，并对国际收支调节机制进行一定程度的完善。

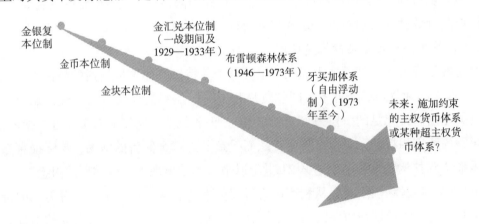

图1-4   国际货币体系的演进图

（五）市场选择还是人为设计？

最后，我还想谈一个貌似有点题外的问题，涉及对市场力量和人类理性的看法，即，人为设计出来的机制能否保证比通过市场自由选择出来的机制更具有效率。这是长期困扰理论界的难题。

例如，马克思在论述货币时说过："金银天然不是货币，但货币天然是金银。"这从一个侧面说明了在确定货币材质时市场竞争所起的作用。哈耶克在《货币的非国家化》中集中论述了市场竞争在货币发行中的作用，他主张废除政府对货币发行的垄断权，允许私人部门自由发行不同的货币，而市场竞争的力量足以制约货币滥发的冲动，保持稳定、有效的货币体系。

与布雷顿森林体系相比，牙买加体系的形成似乎更多地反映了市场竞争与选择的力量。1973 年布雷顿森林体系正式崩溃后，许多人预言美元将失去中心货币的地位。但在路径依赖或网络外部性的影响下，美元依然保持了其在国际经贸往来中的主导地位。反观日本，在上世纪八九十年代"人为"设计了包括推动建立离岸市场、建立协利基金、加大日元对外援助等一系列制度，试图大力推动日元国际化。诚然，在一段时间内，日元在全球储备中的占比确实有所上升，但随着日本经济停滞的十年，日元占比马上回落。因此，在未来国际货币体系构建中，如何看待市场选择和人为设计的关系是一个重大的问题。如何确保人为主动设计的货币体系优于市场选择？我们是否有必要进行这种设计？是否能协调这两者的关系，取长补短？这都是值得深思的问题。

我认为，危机促进改革。人为设计不是凭空设计而是面对危机时形成的市场共识。"新怀特计划"有路径依赖的优势，但愿它能适应危机后的新国际形势。如果不能适应将会引致更深刻的世界经济金融危机，那时的人为设计可能会更多地依赖有弹性的货币供给制度。我不希望看到后者，那个代价是沉重的，但我们应该对此有所研究。

专题文章二

从互联网金融看新金融的发展空间①

吴晓灵

一、互联网金融与第三方支付

我的第一个观点是，互联网跨界金融中的直接融资是未来新金融发展的重要方向。互联网金融是利用互联网技术和移动通信技术为客户提供服务的新型金融业务模式，既包括传统金融机构通过利用互联网开展的金融业务，也包括互联网企业利用互联网技术开展的跨界金融业务。

经过 2013 年这一年的互联网金融爆炸式的增长，社会逐渐地统一了一种认识，就是互联网金融其实包括了两个方面，一个方面就是我们传统的金融业务更多地运用了互联网技术和新型的移动通信技术；而另一个方面，就是我们现在的互联网企业，它们从事着金融的业务。最近，大家看到报纸上有一个经常出现的题目和名词，叫做互联网跨界金融，这个就是我们现在所讲的互联网金融的一个方面，也就是狭义的互联网金融。

传统金融业仍将是互联网金融的主体，市场的竞争将迫使其强化互联网技术和多种通信技术在金融业务中的运用。2013 年是互联网金融元年，但是，在这个元年当中，受到极大冲击和震撼的是我们传统的金融。大家看到了互联网企业利用互联网技术为很多的过去不能够享受到金融服务的群体提供了金融服务，而创造了很多奇迹，包括阿里金融，他们通过支付宝来销售天弘增利基金，起名叫余额宝，给金融带来的震撼使传统金融界开始思考自己的服务模式和怎么样更好地与互联网技术和移动通信技术结合。应该说，在未来一段时期，我们传统的金融机构会在产品的销售、风险控制还有业务创新方面更多地运用互联网技术和移动通信技术。

面对广义的互联网金融，传统金融会在互联网企业的冲击下奋起直追，改变自己的业务模式和服务的方式，未来在传统金融自我变革之后，留给互联网企业的是什么样的发展空间呢？我认为互联网跨界金融中的直接融资是未来发展的主要方向。

---

① 本文根据作者在 2014 年 6 月 29 日 "第一届新金融联盟峰会" 上的讲话整理。

首先，我们看一下第三方支付，第三方支付会向专业领域支付进行返归。我们现在的第三方支付的互联网企业，刚开始的时候是在专门的领域当中进行的，包括发展比较好的支付宝，也是在淘宝上的企业和商户进行交易的时候发挥支付功能。但是从销售基金开始，支付宝已经突破了商品交易服务，而走向了金融产品的买卖，有很多其他第三方支付企业也开始在第三方支付上开展更多的支付业务。

但是，我们应该看到，支付业务是银行业务的核心，为了保证支付的安全，保证在支付业务当中不出现洗钱等犯罪行为，监管当局会对第三方支付业务进行比较严格的管理。

我们都说银行是创造信用货币的机构，而银行的存款、贷款和结算业务三结合，是它创造信用货币的基础。从去年风生水起的互联网金融我们可以看到，在这三项业务中，核心是支付结算，因为支付结算的账户本身就是货币存在的形态，账户资金的移动就是交易媒介职能完成的结果。而且我们所有的经济活动最终能够顺利地进行，交易能够顺利地进行，都取决于货币的支付结算。

我们也可以看到，当今世界上开展金融方面的竞争或者说货币战争的时候，大家最主要看的是支付结算。凡是对一个国家进行经济制裁的时候，所制裁的其实就是支付结算网络。因而支付结算是金融业非常关键的核心业务，它既是银行的核心业务，也是所有金融产品、金融交易的命脉。这样一项业务应该受到严格的监管。

过去央行在发放第三方支付牌照的时候，非常清晰地要求第三方支付仅仅是完成小额支付，而且要求第三方支付的资本金要和它的客户的沉淀资金有一定的比例，是它的十分之一。对连接的银行也有一定的限制，需是五家银行，超出五家银行之外则要增加对资本金和备付金的要求。这些要求之所以提出来，就是要保证支付结算客户资金的安全，防止有人利用支付结算来进行犯罪活动和洗钱。

如果我们现在要第三方支付严格地执行央行发牌照的初衷，那么第三方支付逐渐地都会回归到专业领域的支付当中去，因为它是小额的，并要真实地实现客户实名制、真实身份和可追溯。

另外，第三方支付销售金融产品会由于传统金融业务加强网上销售而失去强劲的扩张势头。去年我们看到的互联网金融的强劲势头表现在余额宝和各种"宝宝"们，它们的本质就是在第三方支付平台上销售金融产品、理财产品。传统金融机构掌握着更加健全的支付结算系统和几亿的客户账户，当它们认识到这个问题时，凭借着它们的支付能力和众多的账户数量，在网上销售金融产品应该说是有强大的竞争优势的。因而，第三方支付在网上的基金销售方面也没有特别大的发展余地，我认为余额宝已经基本上做到极致了。

二、网络借贷与众筹发展前景广阔

我的第二个观点是，网络借贷和众筹资金会有广阔的发展前景，它的融资量不会高于传统金融，但它服务的人群会有极大的扩展空间。

首先，我想分析一下网络借贷。征信体系的缺失，使得 P2P 很难健康发展，很多公司都走向了间接融资的误区，只有具备征信能力的公司，才能最终走向正确的方向。我们现在的 P2P 公司在国内风生水起的有很多，据说是有上千家 P2P 公司，但是，我们国家到目前为止真正做到点对点的 P2P 业务的公司，如果我说得夸张一点的话，几乎没有。

但是，也有几个做得比较好的公司，但是他们都遇到了一个瓶颈制约，就是我们的投资者总希望自己的本金能够有人来替他担保。我从市场上看，有两类对他们的本金承诺担保的模式。一种是借助第三方的担保，一种是靠风险准备金的提取来保证对投资人本金的担保。

这两种模式都有它业务的局限性。如果是第三方担保的话，随着 P2P 业务的增加，担保机构资本金的存量是会要求很大的，就算是拿银行 12 倍的杠杆率来做担保的话，那么它的资本金也顶多是 12 倍。10 个亿的资本金只能够做到 120 亿的业务量，应该说担保机构的资本筹措量决定了 P2P 平台所发展的业务量。

这其中有一个悖论，担保公司的资金本越来越大的时候，它可以担保的量是越来越大的，但是怎么保证它的资本金安全？把钱放在银行吃存款利息，买国债吗？这些途径是安全的，但是，收益是很少的，要想支撑担保公司的发展是非常困难的，这也使很多的担保公司最后不得不走向变相自营放贷和投资的歧路。因而，通过第三方担保公司让 P2P 平台业务更多地发展，这条路是难以为继的。

通过提取风险准备金的方式来保障客户的本金安全，随着不良贷款的产生，风险准备金的提取比例也要上升。什么才能够准确地提取存款准备金呢？是对客户信用的分析。因而，这种方式它也要受制于信用征信的发展。

在中国征信体系缺失的情况下，我们很难对借款人的资信进行比较好的分析，我们国家也缺少完备的财产登记制度，我们对出借人的资产情况和他是不是有风险承受能力也难以做出准确的判断，因而，这两条是制约我们 P2P 发展的很大的瓶颈。而基于电商平台的网上借贷，有其特有的征信体系保证其健康发展。如果在那些能够看得到客户行为的平台能够建立独立的征信体系，那么 P2P 就能够比较健康地发展。

我再谈下众筹。众筹模式大家知道其实是有多种的，最初的众筹是大家筹钱来办一些事情，有的是有偿的，有的是捐献的。而现在我们国家更多的人是通过众筹的方式做债权众筹和股权众筹，债权众筹基本上就是我们刚才说的 P2P，现在有更多的人在做股权众筹。在我国多层次资本市场发展还不够健全的情况下，应该说股权的众筹有它广阔的发展前景。本次《证券法》的修法也借鉴了国际经验，各方也希望通过修法给股权众筹留下空间。

三、网络借贷与众筹融资的监管建议及发展方向

第三个问题，我想讲一下对网络借贷和众筹融资的监管建议。第一，纯信息平台应该是 P2P 和众筹监管的基本底线。现在很多 P2P 公司最大的风险点就在于它们有资金池，而且资金池的资金是可以动用的。现在很多希望健康发展、稳健发展的 P2P 公司主动提出来要把他们的资金在第三方去存管，由第三方对他的资金进行监督，我想这是防止风险非常好的措施。但是这仅仅是防止卷款逃跑的风险，而不能够很好地控制出借人的风险，真正要控制出借人的风险，还有赖于征信系统的建立。

第二，小额分散是保护投资人的重要方法。信息真实披露是对融资方的基本要求，需要对借款人的信息认真地披露，尤其是对于股权众筹来说。同时，另一方面，限制投资方的金额也是降低信息披露成本的重要前提。如果投资方的投资金额比较低、比较少，那么这时候即便是出现了风险，对他的影响也不大。因为他的金额小，风险对自己的影响小，这种情况下我们对于信息披露就可以适当地降低一些标准。这不是说我们主观上想降低标准，而是说我们现在的征信系统使得我们难以真正完全地把信息充分地披露出来。在我们不能够真实、完全地披露所有信息的时候，对投资人最好的保护就是让他少投一点。投成了他就获得收益，投不成，损失了，对他的损害也不会太大。

在财产登记制度不健全的情况下，用较低额度与财产比例相结合的方式较为现实。大家都知道，国外的 P2P 和众筹对投资人都有一个投资的金额不能够超过可支配的财产的一定比例的限制，这个意思就是说一旦投资失败了，投资者也不会受到很大的伤害。但是我国的财产登记制度是缺失的，我们很难知道一个人的真实财产总额。因而，从法规上说，从平台的规则上说，可以规定一定的财产比例，但是从现实上来说，规定一个额度比较小的绝对额来说，可能更安全一些。

财产比例可适当扩大，但也应该有封顶的金额。财产比例在国外可能占整个财产的 5%，或者百分之几。有些人就说这样的话我的金额太小了，所以希望在指定财产比例的时候能够高一些。但我认为从有效控制风险的角度出发，还是应该有一个封顶的绝对额度。所以，我们在讨论法规时，在《证券法》修法过程当中，尽管会给众筹留下一定的法律空间，但是，可能也会从财产的比例和绝对的金额上面来做一定的控制。这是大家在修法时的建议。

第三，鼓励民间建立征信公司，有利于促进直接融资的发展。现在大家都在呼吁，希望央行管的信贷登记系统能够对社会开放，能够对 P2P 小贷公司开放。但是大家也应该知道，这个系统开放了以后，因为借款人及业务数量众多，且往往金额很小，数据成本是非常高的，而且仅仅查询借贷的金额，也不能完全控制一个人的信用风险，因此发展民间征信公司是非常重要的。在国家规定政务信息要以公开为一般、不公开为特例的情况下，很多违反纪律和法规的行为都会在网上查询到。在这样的情况下，鼓励民间征

信公司的发展，让他们整理众多的负面信息，对个人信用情况作出报告，对于发展民间各种金融活动来说是非常有利的。

所以，我想一方面我们应该呼吁央行的信贷登记系统向社会开放，但另一方面我们更要着力于建立民间的征信系统。央行已经开始在准备发放这方面的牌照，网络公司有众多的信息、有大数据处理的能力，我们应该利用这些能力和信息来建立民间的征信公司，帮助金融业更健康地发展。

这就是我对互联网金融新金融发展方向的几点意见，我说得可能比较保守——新金融真正的发展余地，我认为是直接融资的P2P和众筹。传统金融应该说是互联网金融最大的一块，但是，新金融要想进入到这块去是不太容易的。而且传统的金融机构一旦他们意识到了这个问题，改变起来以后，对于其他的新来竞争者都是一个巨大的压力。

而刚才我说到的一般银行所没有做到的一些小的P2P和众筹，虽然量小，但是人数众多，也可以集腋成裘。单就拿余额宝为例，从一块钱销售起，成就了它5 000多亿的销售量。如果我们的民间力量能够在13亿人口的小额借贷和股权投资方面做一些事情的话，我想空间也还是要比向传统金融进军大一些。

以上是我的一些不成熟的意见，谢谢大家批评指正。

主题报告：新常态下的中国货币政策框架

何海峰①　于卫国②

随着中国经济改革开放的持续和深入，以及同期国际经济和金融运行发生的新变化，中国货币政策框架在不断得到完善。一方面，它要与中国经济金融的体制和机制相适应；另一方面，也要在中国经济转型中发挥宏观金融调控的主要功能。新常态下，中国正在全面深化经济体制、政治体制、文化体制等改革，货币政策框架也在发生一些积极变化。

一、世界"新平庸"与中国"新常态"

从 2008 年以来，各国为应对国际金融危机付出了很多努力和代价，最坏的时期似乎已经过去；但是，全球经济前景仍不容乐观。从数据上看，除 2009 年全球经济出现强劲反弹外，从 2010 年到 2014 年，全球经济增长一路下行，全球经济增速跌至 3.3%，低于 2000 年至 2007 年平均的 4.7%，更低于 2004 年至 2007 年繁荣时期平均的 5.2%。

2014 年，世界经济在低增长和高失业中陷入"新平庸"，中国经济则以新策略进入"新常态"。2014 年，全球经济仍然处在艰难曲折的复苏之中，复苏极不平衡，美国经济一枝独秀，一年来低开高走。全球的高收入经济体，尤其是欧元区高收入经济体表现依旧疲软，IMF 估计欧元区 2014 年经济增长 0.8%。日本的经济复苏乏力也十分明显，IMF 估计 2014 年日本经济增长 0.9%，在安倍经济学的三张牌打完后，经济仍难以乐观。新兴经济体最近两年也逐渐整体减速。最大的新兴经济体中国已经从高速增长进入中低速增长的"新常态"，拉美、俄罗斯经济表现都不理想。许多国家经济减速，货币动荡，改革进展缓慢，有的国家已经步入衰退。俄罗斯、巴西、阿根廷、土耳其、印尼等新兴市场国家的货币都不同程度遭遇贬值危机，金融和经济稳定受到冲击。

自国际金融危机以来，全球经济的结构性矛盾，诸如金融过度虚拟化、高杠杆、各

---

① 何海峰，中欧陆家嘴国际金融研究院常务副院长，中国社科院金融政策研究中心主任。
② 于卫国，经济学博士，中欧陆家嘴国际金融研究院研究员，特华博士后科研工作站博士后。

国发展不平衡等，一直未得到根本的缓解和改善；面对经济增长一路下行的现状，主要经济体先后推行了"非常规货币政策"，而经济改革却一再缺位。按照经济学理论，长期中来看，货币仅是实体经济上的一层面纱；因此，单独依靠"非常规货币政策"不能解决任何实质性问题，反而会导致全球经济潜在增长速度的下降。债务危机和信心不足导致全球需求和投资不足，需求不足又导致高失业，投资不足又导致生产效率下降，如此循环往复，最终导致了资本、劳动和全要素生产率的整体下降。

近年来全球经济持续呈现出的不均衡发展态势和低增长、高失业相伴的特点被国际货币基金组织的总裁拉加德称为"新平庸（New Mediocre）"：就业的创造和经济包容性处在不可接受的低水平，当前欧洲（及世界）经济疲软，缺少活力，投资缓慢，内需不振，政府对策既不够勇敢也难以落实。

世界经济的"新平庸"，不可避免地影响到了中国经济。

改革开放以来，特别是2001年加入世贸组织后，中国通过投资扩张和货币超发，实现了20多年的经济快速增长。但是，在这一过程中，中国也积累了亟须通过改革解决的若干问题：生态恶化、资源枯竭、产能过剩、内需不足等，这些都对经济可持续发展产生了制约。在持续20多年的高增长后，中国经济增速开始放缓。

2014年5月，习近平在河南考察时说："中国发展仍处于重要战略机遇期，要增强信心，从当前中国经济发展的阶段性特征出发，适应新常态，保持战略上的平常心态。"这是中国首次提及"新常态"。2014年11月9日，习近平在亚太经合组织（APEC）工商领导人峰会上，首次系统阐述了"新常态"。他表示："新常态将给中国带来新的发展机遇。"习近平指出，中国经济呈现出新常态，有几个主要特点：一是从高速增长转为中高速增长；二是经济结构不断优化升级，第三产业消费需求逐步成为主体，城乡区域差距逐步缩小，居民收入占比上升，发展成果惠及更广大民众；三是从要素驱动、投资驱动转向创新驱动。更重要的是，他强调"中国经济的强韧性是防范风险的最有力支撑"。

中国经济新常态将给中国带来四方面发展新机遇：第一，新常态下，中国经济增速虽然放缓，实际增量依然可观。2013年一年中国经济的增量就相当于1994年全年的经济总量，可以在全世界排到第17位。第二，新常态下，中国经济增长更趋平稳，增长动力更为多元。中国正在协同推进新型工业化、城镇化、信息化、农业现代化，这有利于化解各种成长的烦恼。中国经济更多依赖国内消费需求拉动，避免过于依赖出口的外部风险。第三，新常态下，中国经济结构优化升级，发展前景更加稳定。2014年前三个季度，中国最终消费对经济增长的贡献率为48.5%，超过了投资。服务业增加值占比46.7%，继续超过第二产业。高新技术产业和装备制造业增速分别为12.3%和11.1%，明显高于工业平均增速。单位国内生产总值能耗下降4.6%。第四，新常态下，中国政府大力简政放权，市场活力进一步释放。

中国经济的"新常态"很可能将深刻地改变中国和世界的关系。2010年，中国取代日本，成为全球第二大经济体。2014年，中国的GDP超过10万亿美元，成为除美国之外第二个GDP跨过10万亿美元门槛的国家。同时，中国对全球经济增长的贡献依然高居第一，据IMF测算，2014年中国经济增长对世界经济增长的贡献率为27.8%，美国则仅为15.3%。目前，消费取代投资成为中国经济增长的最大引擎，"中国需求"和"中国市场"逐渐取代"中国制造"。2014年全年，中国社会消费品零售总额名义增长12%，市场规模居全球第二。据商务部和国家外汇管理局统计，2014年，中国对外总投资规模已超过实际使用外资金额，历史上首次成为资本净输出国，这标志着中国已进入在全球范围内进行资源配置的新时代。在新常态之下，中国加快构建开放型经济，通过资本和产业结合，为全球提供长期基建等公共产品，从金砖银行到亚投行和丝路基金，从大力推动"一带一路"建设到推进贸易便利化，中国正不断增强与世界经济的"粘合力"。

二、传统视角下的中国货币政策框架

中国经济新常态可以简化理解为"三期叠加"——经济增速换挡期、结构调整阵痛期和前期政策消化期。进入新常态后，需要从经济发展规律和新常态视角观察和分析中国经济运行。目前中国经济增速总体符合预期，就业和价格形势较为稳定，结构调整步伐有所加快，但经济内生增长动力尚待增强，增长对债务和投资依赖过高等结构性矛盾仍然突出，结构调整过程中经济下行压力和风险暴露有所增大，资源环境的过度承载和约束也更加凸显。受债务率高、风险溢价上升以及结构扭曲等复杂因素影响，企业融资难、融资贵问题引起各界广泛关注。

近年来，受货币和信用快速膨胀的影响，中国金融资产过度膨胀、企业杠杆率过高、房地产泡沫等问题凸显，经济金融系统内生脆弱性增强。在这种情况下，一旦资产价格泡沫破裂，可能出现"资产负债表衰退"，这是影响货币政策调控效果的重要因素。

在这一背景之下，主动适应经济发展新常态，构建货币政策新框架，建立有效的宏观金融调控机制，具有十分重要的意义。

（一）中国货币政策的目标

除美联储实行低通胀和充分就业的双重目标外，发达国家和许多市场化程度较高的新兴市场国家，尤其是在金融危机前的二十多年时间里，货币政策目标大多是单一化的，即通货膨胀目标制。在2008年金融危机前的二十年里，实施通胀目标制的主要经济体在控制通胀方面都做得比较成功，同时经济也维持着一定的增长。欧央行、日央行、英格兰银行等都实行稳定物价的单一目标。

中国货币政策的目标一直是多元化的。《中华人民共和国中国人民银行法》第三条明确规定："货币政策目标是保持货币币值的稳定，并以此促进经济增长。"币值稳定包括两方面的内涵，一方面是指对内的物价稳定，另一方面是指对外的汇率稳定。由此可见，中国货币政策目标的多元化是源自于《中国人民银行法》。改革开放以来，中国从计划经济体制转向市场经济体制，长期面临国际收支双顺差格局，国内流动性被动投放较多，这使中央银行不得不关注国际收支等问题，货币政策的制定需要统筹考虑物价、就业、增长以及国际收支等目标之间的关系。所以，具体来说，中国货币政策的最终目标包括：保持适度的经济增长，物价稳定，充分就业，保持国际收支平衡。除此之外，由于金融稳定和货币政策有一定的协调关系，金融稳定也是中国央行管理的一个重要内容。

（二）货币政策传导机制

货币政策传导机制，是指从运用货币政策到实现货币政策目标的过程，货币传导机制是否完善及提高，直接影响货币政策的实施效果以及对经济的贡献。

市场化程度较高的经济体，货币政策传导机制主要通过价格（利率）渠道，传导途径一般有三个基本环节，其顺序是：（1）通过金融市场实施公开操作来调节短期市场利率；（2）短期利率通过金融市场影响长期利率、资产价格和汇率；（3）金融市场传导到实体经济，影响企业和个人的投资、储蓄和消费等经济活动，进而影响通胀、产出和就业等。

过去，中国的货币政策传导机制主要通过数量（基础货币、准备金率和信贷供给）渠道，其中，信贷渠道在中国货币政策传导机制中发挥主要作用。主要原因在于：地方政府和国有企业预算软约束导致它们对资金价格不敏感，价格（利率）工具难以发挥作用，银行信贷却能直接影响地方政府和国有企业的投资行为；人民币汇率并非自由浮动，央行通过外汇市场的干预，会影响基础货币的投放。

货币政策传导机制决定了货币政策的中介目标。中国货币政策的中间目标包括货币供应量、利率水平和信贷额。1996 年，中国人民银行采用货币供应量 M_1 和 M_2 作为货币政策的调控目标，标志着中国开始引入货币政策中介目标。1998 年以来，随着信贷规模控制的逐渐弱化，货币供应量作为中介目标的地位更是无可争议。目前，中国的货币供应量指标在很大程度上仍被看做是货币政策取向的风向标。

（三）货币政策工具

中国的货币政策工具主要包括数量型工具、价格型工具、公开市场操作和窗口指导。数量型工具包括法定存款准备金和超额存款准备金利率，价格型工具包括存贷款基准利率、再贷款（再贴现）利率，公开市场操作则作为日常流动性管理的重要工具发挥作用。值得强调的是，窗口指导在我国的作用不容忽视，人民银行不定期召开窗口指导会议。由于我国金融体系仍保持一定程度的行政色彩，窗口指导在某些情况下无疑发挥了更直接、更有效的作用。

三、非常规货币政策：理论与实践

（一）非常规货币政策的理论

所谓常规货币政策是指，在经济低迷时，央行通过调整基准利率进行价格性调控或通过公开市场操作、调整法定存款准备金率进行数量性调控来释放流动性，达到预定目标。然而，在2008年全球金融危机的冲击下，银行受到重创，银行体系功能下降，货币政策传导机制严重受阻，货币供应量急剧紧缩，同时，央行的操作目标——短期利率接近于零，单纯下调利率已不足以恢复市场信心，在这样的情况下，常规的货币政策陷入困境，非常规货币政策便成为央行进行危机救助的主要工具。

非常规货币政策是在没有降息空间或利率的市场传递机制严重受阻的情形下，比如，短期名义利率下限接近于零或单纯下调利率已不足以恢复市场信心时，央行通过调整资产负债表的结构或膨胀资产负债表的规模直接向市场注入流动性的行为，以保证在利率极低的情况下继续维持市场的流动性。

非常规货币政策主要分为承诺效应、信贷宽松和量化宽松三种类型。

承诺效应，是指中央银行通过与公众的沟通，向公众提供清晰的承诺，承诺短期利率在相当长的时期内维持在零利率或较低的水平，从而改变市场利率预期。承诺效应通常为有条件的承诺，即中央银行承诺，在实现经济复苏的某种既定目标之前，不会撤出宽松的货币政策。承诺效应使公众能够准确地判断货币当局未来的货币政策，在承诺效应下，公众确信短期低利率的长期存在必然引起市场长期利率的下降。因此，承诺效应可以改变市场利率预期，避免消费、支出的延后，刺激需求的增加。

信贷宽松，是指在中央银行资产负债表总规模基本不变的前提下，通过购买私人部门流动性较差或风险较高的资产，从而改变中央银行资产负债表的资产方结构，在这一过程中，私人部门所持有的各类资产的比例及相对价格也发生了变化，进而对实体经济产生影响。

量化宽松政策，是指中央银行通过购买证券增加商业银行在央行的超额储备存款的规模而使自身资产负债表得到扩张，使其超过维持零利率所需的水平，从而影响金融市场上的资产价格和经济产出。中央银行通过购买政府或金融机构所持有的长期国债，使得长期国债的价格上涨，从而降低长期国债的收益率。国债收益率是各类金融资产的基准利率，长期国债收益率的下降，市场长期利率也将随之下降。中央银行购买金融机构的证券，相当于将等额的资金存入金融机构的存款准备金账户，这意味着基础货币的扩充。

（二）非常规货币政策的实践

2008年金融危机爆发后，在常规货币政策失效的情况下，世界主要经济体纷纷实施了非常规货币政策。

1. 美联储实施的非常规货币政策措施

在承诺效应方面，美联储作出了无条件承诺，确保利率将持续保持在零利率边界。继续将联邦基金目标利率维持在 0~0.25% 的水平不变，并在 2009 年 3—12 月的 7 次例会后发表的政策声明中承诺将在相当一段时间内维持该利率水平不变。在信贷宽松和量化宽松方面，从 2008 年 11 月开始，美联储先后开展了几轮大规模资产购买，2008 年 11 月宣布实施 5 000 亿美元抵押贷款支持证券和 1 000 亿美元联邦机构债券的资产购买计划；2009 年 3 月 18 日，美联储宣布将实施三项非常规货币政策措施：一是将在今后 6 个月内购进最多 3 000 亿美元的长期国债；二是再购入 7 500 亿美元联邦机构以抵押贷款支持的证券，使此类证券购入总规模于年内达 1. 25 万亿美元；三是再购买 "两房" 发行或担保的 1 000 亿美元债券，使年内总规模达 2 000 亿美元。2010 年 11 月宣布 6 000 亿美元长期国债购买计划，2011 年 9 月实施一项典型的资产负债表结构变动措施，宣布购买 4 000 亿美元 6 年至 30 年长期国债，同时卖出同等金额的 3 年及更短期的国债，以降低长期利率水平，被称为 "扭转操作"，2012 年 9 月宣布每月购买 400 亿美元的抵押贷款支持证券，直至经济出现满意状况为止。

2. 日本央行的非常规货币政策

日本利用新政府执政的稳定性，通过日本式量化宽松政策，以通胀逆转通缩的方式，既救日本经济于危机当前，也希望将日本经济拉出十余年的经济停滞状态。日本央行于 2010 年 10 月开始实施广泛宽松政策，购买了范围广泛的各类资产，不仅包括政府债券，还有信用产品（如商业票据和公司债券）、股权金融产品（如交易所交易基金）和日本不动产投资信托，目的是直接压低 3 年期限以内的部分收益率曲线，同时压缩各种风险溢价。2012 年 2 月，日本央行引入了 "中长期价格稳定目标"，并宣布制定一个当前目标，即 CPI 同比增长 1%。虽然这些政策通过提供宽松的金融环境支持了经济发展，但并未改变家庭和企业根深蒂固的通货紧缩预期。2013 年 4 月，日本央行引入了量化和质化宽松政策，即 QQE 政策，这一政策涵盖了量化和质化两种元素。为强化稳定价格的承诺，政策明确且坚定地承诺在 2 年内实现 2% 通胀目标，并且直接作用于私人实体的通胀预期。为了巩固这一承诺，日本央行决定采取新一轮大胆的宽松货币政策，既包括质的宽松，也包括量的宽松。通过该政策，日本央行在年内把基础货币（央行直接提供的货币）扩大一倍，并且购买大量日本政府债券，包括剩余期限更长的债券。该政策与过去的政策的不同之处在于，它力图积极影响私人实体的预期形成（黑田东彦，2014）。

3. 欧央行的 "加强信贷支持" 和证券购买

欧洲央行在 2009 年 6 月 24 日宣布以目前 1% 的政策利率向商业银行提供无限量抵押贷款，期限长达 1 年。2010 年，欧元区政府债券市场急剧恶化，5 月 10 日，欧央行宣布实施 "证券市场计划"，从二级市场购买政府债券。2011 年 10 月 6 日实施 400 亿欧元的第二轮担保债券购买计划。2011 年末，欧债危机蔓延到欧元区核心国家，欧央行分别于 2011 年 12 月 21 日和 2012 年 2 月 29 日执行了两个三年期再融资操作，共向银行发放了 10 187 亿欧元贷款。

4. 中国的非常规货币政策

面对 2008 年的金融危机，中国的非常规货币政策主要包括：2008 年 9 月开始，中国人民银行开始转向适度宽松的货币政策：5 次下调存贷款基准利率，4 次下调存款准备金率，放松对金融机构信贷规划的约束，加大金融支持经济发展力度。

（三）非常规货币政策的效果

2009 年初开始，全球非常规货币政策的效果开始显现。从反映实体经济的各项主要经济指标如工业产出指数、零售业指数、世界 GDP 增长率、PMI（制造业采购经理人指数）和世界贸易指数指标来看，非常规货币政策在相当程度上发挥了应有的积极作用：及时拯救了一些濒临破产的金融机构和企业，有效地防范了系统性金融风险的再次发生；向金融市场注入大量的流动性和资金，逐渐恢复市场信心等。

当然，非常规货币政策的实施也有不少负面效应。首先，央行的独立性受到削弱。在金融危机中，央行购买私人部门发行的证券和长期国债，导致了财政货币化，削弱了其制定和实施货币政策的独立性。其次，非常规货币政策使得央行的资产负债表规模迅速膨胀，风险激增，加大了整个经济和金融体系的脆弱性。第三，全球流动性激增，埋下了未来通胀的隐患。

四、改革发展的新要求

世界经济进入新平庸，以及中国经济进入新常态，对中国以货币政策为主的宏观金融调控提出了新挑战，中国货币政策框架也在发生积极改变。

（一）中国宏观金融调控面临的新挑战

首先，随着影子银行和金融创新的快速发展，货币的运行规律发生了变化，表现出更加复杂的结构化特征，金融监管的有效性降低。中国金融业中以银行理财、信托计划、民间金融等为代表的金融创新业务自 2009 年迎来了发展高潮，受此影响，新增贷款在社会融资总量中的占比从 2009 年的 75.7% 快速下降到 2012 年的 57.9%。

其次，长期依赖高投资的增长模式，导致货币信贷总量较多、杠杆率总体较高，进一步扩张的空间有限。2014 年末金融机构本外币贷款余额已经达到 86.8 万亿元，与当年 GDP 的比例为 136.5%。2014 年末 M_2 更是达到 122.8 万亿元，无论历史纵向比较，还是与其他国家进行横向比较，都是相当高的比例。2013 年末，中国企业债务约为 68 万亿元，占 GDP 之比达 120%（美国不到 80%），A 股非金融企业资产负债率由 2000 年的 40% 上升至 2013 年的 60% 以上。从国际比较而言，2013 年中国非金融企业部门债务率水平（相当于 GDP 的 120%）居于 OECD 国家最高水平区间。对成熟的经济体而言，企业债务一般会达到 GDP 的 50%～70%，而中国是这个数字的 2 倍。

再次，随着金融创新和金融市场加快发展，数量型调控面临的挑战增大，而健全和完善价格型调控机制的任务还十分繁重，转型期的货币政策须兼顾"量"与"价"平衡，转换难度上升，从而对引导和稳定预期的要求更高。

最后，中国经济金融体系逐渐融入全球，美元走强以及主要经济体宏观政策分化将进一步加剧外部环境的复杂性和不确定性。

（二）中国货币政策的目标、机制和工具在发生变化

从货币政策目标上看，除了四大传统目标外，与新常态密切相关的动态性目标得到重视。首先，新常态下，为结构调整和转型升级创造中性适度的货币金融环境或将成为货币政策目标的重点。新常态的核心是经济发展方式和经济结构的改变，所以，必须处理好经济结构调整和宏观总量政策之间的关系。其次，稳增长在货币政策多目标中的分量正在下降。2014 年中国 GDP 增长 7.4%，2013 年增长 7.7%，2012 年增长 7.8%，2011 年增长 9.2%。2011 年以来 GDP 增速逐年下滑，但就业形势却没有明显恶化。同时，各级政府正在下调 GDP 增长目标并淡化 GDP 考核，2015 年李克强的政府工作报告将 GDP 增长目标定在 7% 左右，势必降低稳增长在货币政策多目标中的分量。第三，房地产泡沫和企业杠杆居高不下，维护金融稳定显得愈发重要。金融稳定在传统货币政策框架中的分量并不大，但 2008 年的金融危机使得各国央行意识到，资产泡沫对金融稳定意义重大。除了房地产泡沫，中国企业杠杆率居高不下且仍在继续上升，企业债务对 GDP 比例的快速上升也是影响金融稳定的一个重要的潜在因素。第四，融资难、融资贵问题日益紧迫，货币政策责无旁贷。近年中国的人口结构与储蓄率已经发生了深刻变化，而囿于金融体制和体系结构性缺陷，企业实际利率和融资成本仍居高不下。2014 年国务院常务会议连续 8 次（3 月 25 日、5 月 21 日、7 月 2 日、7 月 16 日、7 月 23 日、9 月 17 日、1 月 24 日、11 月 19 日）提及融资问题，降低企业融资成本已形成政策共识，货币政策责无旁贷。

从货币政策传导机制上看，中国经济进入"新常态"，为货币政策传导机制从数量渠道转为价格渠道创造了条件。一是货币供给量和债务增长对经济增长的贡献日益下降，从 M_2 与 GDP 以及 CPI 的相关性看，2000—2007 年 M_2 增长率与 CPI 的相关性达到 0.67，而 2008—2013 年该比率下降为 0.19；M_2 增长率与 GDP 增长率的相关性也从 0.32 下降到 0.24。[①] 二是经常项目顺差占 GDP 的比重回落，新增外汇占款趋势下降，过去基础货币投放主要来源于外汇占款的情况发生变化，随着汇率市场化改革，从 2014 年开始，汇率从一路单边升值变成双向浮动，经常账户差额占 GDP 的比重从 2006 年的 10% 下降为现在的 2% 左右。[②] 三是商业银行风险偏好降低，资产扩张意愿下降，经济增长

---

① 《中国央行货币政策框架转型大幕开启》，载《武汉金融》，2014（11）。
② 《中国央行货币政策框架转型大幕开启》，载《武汉金融》，2014（11）。

由高速转向中高速，失业率持续低位，客观上也为货币政策传导机制从数量渠道转为价格渠道创造了条件。

从货币政策中介目标上看，过去，信贷渠道是中国货币政策最重要的传导机制，因此货币政策中介目标是信贷额度、M_2 增速等数量指标，货币政策操作也离不开窗口指导和准备金率调节等数量操作。新常态下，央行试图更多地发挥利率在货币政策传导中的作用，实现货币政策从数量调控向价格调控的转型，这就要求央行将银行间市场利率视为货币政策中介目标，货币政策的操作也主要集中于银行间市场。

从货币政策操作工具上看，中国人民银行在 2013、2014 年开始强调，货币政策要从数量型工具更明显转为价格型工具。实际上，转变并不明显。主要原因在于，为了实现汇率改革的渐进性、持续性和连续性，央行曾经一度大量购买外汇。2014 年 5 月，周小川行长在清华大学五道口全球金融论坛上明确提出："未来中国货币政策要走'利率走廊'模式，短期利率有一个区间。到了下限后，金融机构就可以向央行融资；到了上限时候，央行会减少这样的融资。而这个中间值就是央行的短期政策利率，我们会向这个方向来发展。"实际上，央行已经开始借鉴"利率走廊"系统，具体表现就是 SLO（公开市场短期流动性调节工具）和 SLF（常备借贷便利）两大工具的设立。央行于 2013 年开始采用 SLF，2014 年又使用了 PSL（抵押补充贷款）。2014 年 1 月 20 日，央行向部分地方法人金融结构开展 SLF 操作试点，就被市场视为中国版"利率走廊"的小规模实验。随后，央行又引入了 7 天以内的短期流动性调节工具（SLO）。

（三）积极探索货币政策对宏观经济的结构性调节功能

一般地，货币政策主要发挥总量调控的功能。对于当前中国经济来说，可能需要积极探索结构调节的功能。中国人民银行坚持宏观政策要稳、微观政策要活的总体思路，统筹稳增长、促改革、调结构、惠民生和防风险，继续实施稳健的货币政策，保持政策的连续性和稳定性，坚持"总量稳定、结构优化"的取向，保持定力、主动作为，更加注重松紧适度，适时适度预调微调，促进经济健康可持续发展。同时，寓改革于调控之中，把货币政策调控与深化改革紧密结合起来，更充分地发挥市场在资源配置中的决定性作用。进一步完善调控模式，疏通传导机制，通过增加供给和竞争改善金融服务，提高金融运行效率和服务实体经济的能力。从中国人民银行此前的相关实践中看，差别准备金动态调整措施和信贷政策指导，已经发挥了结构性调控的功能。

（四）建立审慎管理政策与货币政策的有效配合机制

货币政策主要发挥总量调控上的逆周期调节和结构引导作用，而审慎管理政策则更加关注金融系统的稳定。进入新常态，中国经济运行规律和结构将发生变化，中国金融体制和运行机制也更加强调市场化改革的原则，货币政策调控作用的更好发挥更加需要金融体系的稳健运行。审慎管理政策既包括宏观审慎管理政策，也包括微观审慎管理政策。特别是随着中国利率市场化改革的深入，金融业对内对外的进一步开放，单体金融机构和日益多样化的金融体系将面对更加复杂的潜在金融风险，宏微观审慎管理政策的组织框架、运行机制、工具手段等都需要与货币政策等调控政策建立有效的联动配合机制。

国际金融危机为货币政策的理论与实践提供了新案例，提出了新问题，同时也促进了货币政策理论与实践的新发展。中国货币政策既需要借鉴成熟理论与国际经验，更需要从中国改革开放和中国经济发展新阶段的实践出发，开阔视野，不断创新，建立新常态下的框架体系和运行机制。

参考文献

[1] 周小川：《2008 年金融危机以来货币政策框架的演变》，清华大学五道口金融学院演讲，2014 - 05。

[2] 张晓慧：《新常态下的货币政策》，载《中国金融》，2015（2）。

[3] 赵扬、边泉水、刘鎏、吴杰云：《利动天下：货币政策框架转型》，中金公司宏观经济分析报告，2014 - 09 - 21。

[4] 何德旭：《货币政策新框架》，载《中国经济报告》，2015（1）。

[5] 本刊特约评论员：《中国央行货币政策框架转型大幕开启》，载《武汉金融》，2014（11）。

[6] 厉大业、张海阳：《货币政策框架的新思路》，载《中国金融》，2014（20）。

[7] 陈敏强：《2009 年美、欧、英、日央行非常规货币政策及其效应比较分析》，载《国际金融研究》，2010（7）。

[8] 李亮：《非常规货币政策的理论与实践》，载《金融发展评论》，2013（6）。

[9] 王亮亮、李明星、苗永旺：《非常规货币政策：理论、实践、效果与退出机制》，载《上海经济研究》，2010（5）。

[10] 中国人民银行货币政策分析小组：《中国货币政策执行报告——2014 年第三季度》，2014 - 11 - 06。

[11] 张茉楠：《当前环境下非常规货币政策可能的取向》，载《上海证券报》，2014 - 04 - 15。

[12] 黑田东彦：《非传统型货币政策的理论与实践》，日本央行行长黑田东彦在国际经济协会举办的第十七届世界大会上的演讲，载《金融发展评论》，2014（9）。

下　篇

2014年度中国金融
政策动态

宏观金融政策

一、货币政策①

（一）2014 年度主要货币政策的制定和颁布情况

2014 年，中国人民银行全年制定和颁布的主要货币政策如表 4 -1 所示。

表 4 -1   2014 年中国人民银行相关货币政策操作汇总表

时　间	主要政策
1 月 17 日	中国人民银行发布《关于开展常备借贷便利操作试点的通知》（银发〔2014〕19 号），在北京、江苏、山东、广东、河北、山西、浙江、吉林、河南、深圳开展分支机构常备借贷便利操作试点，主要解决符合宏观审慎要求的地方法人金融机构流动性需求，稳定市场预期，促进货币市场平稳运行
1 月 30 日	中国人民银行发布《关于调整再贷款分类的通知》（银发〔2014〕36 号），将再贷款由三类调整为四类，即将原流动性再贷款进一步细分为流动性再贷款和信贷政策支持再贷款，金融稳定再贷款和专项政策性再贷款分类不变
3 月 1 日	中国人民银行放开中国（上海）自由贸易试验区小额外币存款利率上限。自贸区的先行先试，将为在全国推进小额外币存款利率市场化积累可复制、可推广的经验，并为下一步深入推进利率市场化改革打好坚实基础
3 月 5 日	中国人民银行增加支农再贷款额度 200 亿元，支持金融机构做好春耕备耕金融服务
4 月 22 日	中国人民银行决定从 4 月 25 日起下调县域农村商业银行人民币存款准备金率 2 个百分点，下调县域农村合作银行人民币存款准备金率 0.5 个百分点
4 月 25 日	为贯彻落实国务院第 43 次常务会议精神，中国人民银行创设抵押补充贷款，（PSL）为开发性金融支持棚改提供长期稳定、成本适当的资金来源
6 月 9 日	中国人民银行决定从 6 月 16 日起对符合审慎经营要求且"三农"和小微企业贷款达到一定比例的商业银行（不含 4 月 25 日已下调过准备金率的机构），下调人民币存款准备金率 0.5 个百分点，对财务公司、金融租赁公司和汽车金融公司下调人民币存款准备金率 0.5 个百分点

---

① 执笔：于卫国。

时　　间	主要政策
9月	中国人民银行创设中期借贷便利（Medium－term Lending Facility，MLF），对符合宏观审慎管理要求的金融机构提供中期基础货币，中期借贷便利利率发挥中期政策利率的作用，促进降低社会融资成本
11月22日	中国人民银行采取非对称方式下调金融机构人民币贷款和存款基准利率。其中，金融机构一年期贷款基准利率下调0.4个百分点至5.6%；一年期存款基准利率下调0.25个百分点至2.75%。同时结合推进利率市场化改革，将金融机构存款利率浮动区间的上限由存款基准利率的1.1倍调整为1.2倍；其他各档次贷款和存款基准利率相应调整，并对基准利率期限档次作适当简并
12月23日	中国人民银行印发《关于存款口径调整后存款准备金政策和利率管理政策有关事项的通知》（银发〔2014〕387号）。中国人民银行于2015年起对存款统计口径进行调整，将存款类金融机构吸收并原在同业往来项下统计的证券及交易结算类存放、银行业非存款类存放、SPV存放、其他金融机构存放以及境外金融机构存放纳入各项存款统计范围。上述新纳入各项存款口径的存款计入存款准备金交存范围，适用的存款准备金率暂定为零。上述存款的利率管理政策保持不变，利率由双方按照市场化原则协商确定

资料来源：中国人民银行。

（二）2014年度货币政策分析及评价

1. 2014年主要货币政策制定的背景

中国经济进入"新常态"，处在增速换挡、结构调整和前期政策消化三期叠加阶段。总体上，中国经济继续在合理区间平稳运行，第三产业增加值比重继续提高，消费对经济增长的贡献提高。消费价格温和上涨，就业形势较为稳定，进出口平稳增长。2014年全年国内生产总值（GDP）同比增长7.4%，居民消费价格（CPI）同比上涨2.0%。同时，经济增长对债务和投资依赖过高等结构性矛盾仍然突出，结构调整过程中经济下行压力和风险暴露有所增大，资源环境的过度承载和约束也更加凸显，企业融资成本居高不下。

从国际上看，国际金融危机爆发以来，全球经济进入深刻的再平衡调整期，各经济体宏观政策出现分化，美国的货币政策可能出现较大调整，欧日经济复苏存在较大不确定性，国际主要货币汇率波动和跨境资本流动可能进一步加大，这些都增大了宏观政策面临的挑战和实施的难度。

2. 2014年主要货币政策操作及评价

中国人民银行继续实施稳健的货币政策，不断补充和完善货币政策工具组合，用调结构的方式适时适度预调微调。在外汇占款投放基础货币出现阶段性放缓的情况下，综合运用公开市场操作以及短期流动性调节工具、常备借贷便利等多种货币政策工具，保持流动性合理充裕，创设中期借贷便利（MLF）和抵押补充贷款工具（PSL），引导金融机构向国家政策导向的实体经济部门提供低成本资金。非对称下调存贷款基准利率，两次实施定向降准，存款利率浮动区间上限扩大至基准利率的 1.2 倍，简并基准利率期限档次；《存款保险条例（征求意见稿）》向全社会公开征求意见。

灵活开展公开市场操作。2014 年上半年，针对外汇占款增长前快后慢、春节等季节性因素对流动性影响较大的特点，以正回购操作为主、逆回购操作为辅，搭配使用短期流动性调节工具（SLO）灵活开展公开市场操作；进入下半年之后，综合考虑流动性总量仍较为充裕，但外汇占款增长进一步放缓、影响流动性供求的不确定因素有所增多的实际情况，逐步降低公开市场正回购操作的力度和频率，并通过正回购和央行票据到期、开展 SLO 操作等适时适度投放流动性。全年公开市场累计开展正回购操作 30 210 亿元，开展逆回购操作 5 250 亿元；开展 SLO 操作累计投放流动性 10 210 亿元，回笼流动性 1 000 亿元。年末公开市场正、逆回购操作余额均为 0；SLO 投放流动性操作余额为 1 000 亿元，回笼流动性操作余额为 0；央行票据余额为 4 222 亿元。

适时开展常备借贷便利操作，创设中期借贷便利。为加强和改善银行体系流动性管理，保持流动性合理适度，促进货币市场平稳运行，2014 年 1 月，中国人民银行在 10 个省（市）开展分支机构常备借贷便利操作试点，向符合宏观审慎要求的地方法人金融机构提供短期流动性支持。中国人民银行于 2014 年 9 月创设中期借贷便利，向符合宏观审慎管理要求的商业银行、政策性银行提供中期基础货币。2014 年，人民银行累计开展中期借贷便利操作 1.14 万亿元，年末余额为 6 445 亿元，期限均为 3 个月，利率为 3.5%。总体看，在外汇占款渠道投放基础货币出现阶段性放缓的情况下，中期借贷便利起到了主动补充基础货币的作用。

实施定向降准。中国人民银行于 2014 年 4 月和 6 月，分别下调县域农村商业银行和农村合作银行人民币存款准备金率 2 个和 0.5 个百分点，对符合审慎经营要求且"三农"或小微企业贷款达到一定比例的商业银行下调人民币存款准备金率 0.5 个百分点。此外，下调财务公司、金融租赁公司和汽车金融公司人民币存款准备金率 0.5 个百分点。

下调金融机构存贷款基准利率。针对"融资难、融资贵"问题，结合物价等变动趋势，中国人民银行决定于 2014 年 11 月 22 日采取非对称方式下调金融机构人民币贷款和存款基准利率。其中，金融机构一年期贷款基准利率下调 0.4 个百分点至 5.6%；一年期存款基准利率下调 0.25 个百分点至 2.75%。

推进利率市场化改革。金融机构利率管制有序放开。2014 年 3 月 1 日，放开中国（上海）自由贸易试验区小额外币存款利率上限。11 月 22 日，在下调存贷款基准利率的同时，将人民币存款利率浮动区间的上限由存款基准利率的 1.1 倍调整为 1.2 倍，并对基准利率期限档次作适当简并，金融机构自主定价空间进一步扩大。市场利率定价自律机制不断健全。自律机制成员范围逐步扩大，新增93家金融机构作为自律机制成员，进一步发挥自律机制的激励约束作用。

上述稳健货币政策的实施，为经济社会发展创造了良好的金融环境，货币信贷和社会融资平稳增长，贷款结构继续改善，企业融资成本高问题有一定程度缓解。2014年末，广义货币供应量 M_2 余额同比增长12.2%，人民币贷款余额同比增长13.6%。全年社会融资规模为16.46万亿元。12月份非金融企业及其他部门贷款加权平均利率为6.77%，比年初下降0.42个百分点。

（三）下一阶段货币政策展望

中国经济发展进入新常态，核心是经济发展方式和经济结构的改变。在这样的宏观经济大背景下，必须处理好经济结构调整和宏观总量政策之间的关系。宏观总量政策要把握好取向和力度，要在基础条件出现较大变化时适时适度调整，防止经济出现惯性下滑，同时也要注意防止过度"放水"固化结构扭曲、推升债务和杠杆水平。在保持总量稳定的同时，要进一步促进结构优化，用调结构的方式有针对性地解决经济运行中的突出问题，盘活存量、优化增量，支持经济结构调整和转型升级。

中国人民银行将继续按照宏观政策要稳、微观政策要活的思路，统筹稳增长、促改革、调结构、惠民生和防风险，继续实施稳健的货币政策，坚持"总量稳定、结构优化"的取向，根据经济基本面变化适时适度预调微调，增强调控的灵活性、针对性和有效性，为经济结构调整与转型升级营造中性、适度的货币金融环境，促进经济科学发展、可持续发展。同时，寓改革于调控之中，把货币政策调控与深化改革紧密结合起来，更充分地发挥市场在资源配置中的决定性作用。

一是利用数量、价格工具组合，健全宏观审慎政策框架，实现货币信贷和社会融资规模合理增长。根据经济金融形势变化以及金融创新对银行体系流动性的影响，灵活运用公开市场操作等多种货币政策工具，完善中央银行抵押品管理框架，调节好流动性水平，保持货币市场稳定。

二是盘活存量、优化增量，支持经济结构调整和转型升级。实施和落实"定向降准"的相关措施，发挥好信贷政策支持再贷款和再贴现政策的作用，引导金融机构优化信贷结构。继续通过保持货币信贷合理增长、完善多层次资本市场、增加金融供给、加大改革和结构调整力度，标本兼治，着力降低社会融资成本。

三是推进利率市场化改革。进一步健全市场利率定价自律机制，提高金融机构自主定价能力。继续培育上海银行间同业拆放利率（Shibor）和贷款基础利率（LPR），建设较为完善的市场利率体系。建立健全中央银行的利率调控框架，强化价格型调控和传导机制。

四是完善金融市场体系，切实发挥好金融市场在稳定经济增长、推动经济结构调整和转型升级、深化改革开放和防范金融风险方面的作用。加强市场基础性建设，为经济结构调整和转型升级提供高效的投融资市场。大力发展直接融资，推动多层次资本市场建设。

五是防范系统性金融风险，维护金融体系稳定。加强宏观审慎管理，引导金融机构稳健经营，督促金融机构加强流动性管理、内控和风险管理。加强对同业业务和理财业务发展中的潜在风险的监测与防范。加强对地方政府性债务和偿债能力的跟踪监测，防控债务风险。加快建立存款保险制度，完善金融机构市场化退出机制。采取综合措施维护金融稳定，守住不发生系统性、区域性金融风险的底线。

二、汇率与国际收支相关政策①

（一）2014 年主要汇率及国际收支政策制定情况

表 4 – 2 　　　　　　　　2014 年主要汇率政策和国际收支政策汇总

时　间	政　策
3 月 15 日	中国人民银行宣布自 2014 年 3 月 17 日起，银行间即期外汇市场人民币兑美元交易价浮动幅度由 1% 扩大至 2%，外汇指定银行为客户提供当日美元最高现汇卖出价与最低现汇买入价之差不得超过当日汇率中间价的幅度由 2% 扩大至 3%
3 月 18 日	经中国人民银行授权，中国外汇交易中心宣布在银行间外汇市场开展人民币对新西兰元直接交易
4 月 25 日	中国人民银行与新西兰储备银行续签双边本币互换协议，互换金额仍为 250 亿元人民币/50 亿新西兰元。有效期三年，经双方同意可以展期
5 月 30 日	中国人民银行使用中韩本币互换协议下 4 亿韩国圆（约合 240 万元人民币）资金支持企业贸易融资，这是中国人民银行首次在双边本币互换协议下动用对方货币
6 月 18 日	为促进中国与英国之间的双边贸易和投资，便利人民币和英镑在贸易投资结算中的使用，满足经济主体降低汇兑成本的需要，经人民银行授权，中国外汇交易中心宣布在银行间外汇市场完善人民币对英镑的交易方式，发展人民币对英镑直接交易
7 月 1 日	为进一步完善人民币汇率市场化形成机制，中国人民银行发布《关于银行间外汇市场交易汇价和银行挂牌汇价管理有关事项的通知》（银发〔2014〕188 号），取消银行对客户各币种挂牌买卖价差管理
7 月 18 日	中国人民银行与阿根廷中央银行续签了双边本币互换协议，互换规模为 700 亿元人民币/900 亿阿根廷比索，有效期三年，经双方同意可以展期
7 月 21 日	中国人民银行与瑞士国家银行签署了双边本币互换协议，互换规模为 1 500 亿元人民币/210 亿瑞士法郎，有效期三年，经双方同意可以展期

───────────

① 执笔：于卫国。

续表

时　间	政　　策
8 月 21 日	中国人民银行与蒙古银行续签了双边本币互换协议，互换规模扩大为 150 亿元人民币/4.5 万亿蒙古图格里克，有效期三年，经双方同意可以展期
9 月 16 日	中国人民银行与斯里兰卡中央银行签署了双边本币互换协议，互换规模为 100 亿元人民币/2 250 亿斯里兰卡卢比，有效期三年，经双方同意可以展期
9 月 29 日	为促进中国与欧元区成员国之间的双边贸易和投资，便利人民币和欧元在贸易投资结算中的使用，满足经济主体降低汇兑成本的需要，经人民银行授权，中国外汇交易中心宣布在银行间外汇市场完善人民币对欧元的交易方式，开展人民币对欧元直接交易
10 月 11 日	中国人民银行与韩国银行续签了双边本币互换协议，互换规模为 3 600 亿元人民币/64 万亿韩国圆，有效期三年，经双方同意可以展期
10 月 13 日	中国人民银行与俄罗斯联邦中央银行签署了双边本币互换协议，互换规模为 1 500 亿元人民币/8 150 亿卢布，有效期三年，经双方同意可以展期
10 月 27 日	为促进中国与新加坡之间的双边贸易和投资，便利人民币和新加坡元在贸易投资结算中的使用，满足经济主体降低汇兑成本的需要，经中国人民银行授权，中国外汇交易中心宣布自 10 月 28 日起在银行间外汇市场开展人民币对新加坡元直接交易
11 月 2 日	中国人民银行发布《关于跨国企业集团开展跨境人民币资金集中运营业务有关事宜的通知》（银发〔2014〕324 号）
11 月 3 日	中国人民银行与卡塔尔中央银行签署了规模为 350 亿元人民币/208 亿里亚尔的中卡双边本币互换协议。同日，双方签署了在多哈建立人民币清算安排的合作备忘录
11 月 8 日	中国人民银行与加拿大中央银行签署了双边本币互换协议，互换规模为 2 000 亿元人民币/300 亿加元，有效期三年，经双方同意可以展期。同日，双方签署了在加拿大建立人民币清算安排的合作备忘录
11 月 22 日	中国人民银行与香港金融管理局续签了双边本币互换协议，互换规模为 4 000 亿元人民币/5 050 亿港元，有效期三年，经双方同意可以展期
12 月 14 日	中国人民银行与哈萨克斯坦国家银行续签了双边本币互换协议，互换规模为 70 亿元人民币/2 000 亿哈萨克斯坦坚戈，有效期三年，经双方同意可以展期
12 月 22 日	中国人民银行与泰国银行续签了双边本币互换协议，互换规模为 700 亿元人民币/3 700 亿泰铢，有效期三年，经双方同意可以展期。同日，双方还签署了在泰国建立人民币清算安排的合作备忘录
12 月 23 日	中国人民银行与巴基斯坦国家银行续签了双边本币互换协议，互换规模为 100 亿元人民币/1 650 亿巴基斯坦卢比，有效期三年，经双方同意可以展期

资料来源：国家外汇管理局。

（二）2014年汇率及国际收支主要政策操作及作用

2014年3月15日，中国人民银行宣布将银行间即期外汇市场人民币兑美元交易价浮动幅度由1%扩大至2%。7月2日，中国人民银行取消银行对客户美元挂牌买卖价差管理。让市场供求在汇率形成中发挥更大作用，人民币汇率弹性增强，汇率预期分化，央行基本退出常态外汇干预，建立有管理的浮动汇率制度。

为促进双边贸易和投资，中国人民银行继续采取措施推动人民币直接交易市场发展。2014年，在银行间外汇市场先后推出人民币对新西兰元、英镑、欧元以及新加坡元直接交易，推出人民币对哈萨克斯坦坚戈银行间市场区域交易。银行间外汇市场人民币直接交易成交活跃，流动性明显提升，降低了微观经济主体的汇兑成本。

2014年，在中国人民银行与境外货币当局签署的双边本币互换协议下，境外货币当局共开展交易11 305.50亿元人民币，共实际动用380.07亿元人民币，动用余额为158.01亿元人民币，对促进双边贸易投资发挥了积极作用。

2014年取消5项行政审批项目，共废止外汇管理法规88件。深化贸易外汇管理改革，推进边贸和个人贸易便利化，取消边贸账户行政许可，简化个人贸易单证要求，促进外贸多元化发展。全国22家试点企业累计办理跨境收付已超过10亿美元，支持电子商务等新型服务业发展。

允许200余家国有、民营和外资跨国企业集中管理其境内外外汇资金，切实降低大型企业和跨国公司的财务成本。

按照负面清单的思路，在上海自贸区、天津滨海新区等17个国家级经济金融改革试验区开展资本金意愿结汇改革试点，赋予企业资本金结汇的自主权和选择权。

大幅简化返程投资外汇管理，允许购付汇用于境外特殊目的的公司设立及营运，取消对特殊目的的公司的境外放款限制。简化人民币合格境外机构投资者额度管理，支持部分地区开展合格境内有限合伙人（QDLP）试点。

取消全部跨境担保事前审批，统一中外资企业外保内贷政策；取消外债转贷款在相关环节的核准；在部分地区开展外商投资企业外债比例自律试点，降低企业融资成本。

2014年，人民币对美元汇率中间价最高为6.0930元，最低为6.1710元，245个交易日中107个交易日升值、138个交易日贬值，最大单日升值幅度为0.37%（225点），最大单日贬值幅度为0.18%（111点）。

人民币对欧元、日元等其他国际主要货币汇率有所升值。2014年末，人民币对欧元、日元汇率中间价分别为1欧元兑7.4556元人民币、100日元兑5.1371元人民币，分别较2013年末升值12.92%和升值12.46%。从2005年人民币汇率形成机制改革以来至2014年末，人民币对欧元汇率累计升值34.32%，对日元汇率累计升值42.22%。

2014年，我国国际收支经常项目顺差13 148亿元人民币，资本和金融项目逆差5 939亿元人民币，国际储备资产增加7 209亿元人民币。按美元计价，2014年，我国国际收支经常项目顺差 2 138 亿美元，其中，货物贸易顺差 4 719 亿美元，服务贸易逆差 1 981 亿美元，收益逆差 298 亿美元，经常转移逆差 302 亿美元。资本和金融项目逆差 960 亿美元，其中，直接投资净流入 1 985 亿美元。国际储备资产增加 1 178 亿美元，其中，外汇储备资产增加 1 188 亿美元，特别提款权及在基金组织的储备头寸减少 11 亿美元。

人民银行基本退出常态化外汇干预，人民币汇率保持合理均衡水平上的基本稳定，双向浮动弹性增强，年末人民币对美元汇率中间价为 6.1190 元，比上年末贬值 0.36%。

（三）政策展望

国内外仍存在许多不确定、不稳定因素。在贸易和直接投资继续维持较大规模顺差的基础上，我国国际收支可能呈现双向波动的振荡走势。如果美联储加息，可能引起全球范围内国际资本流动的大幅振荡，境内企业也将面临债务去美元化压力。欧洲和日本经济形势尚不明朗，新兴经济体仍面临较大下行压力，外部环境依然较为复杂。此外，地缘政治冲突等突发事件也将给我国跨境资本流动带来较大不确定性。

面对全面深化改革的新任务、新要求和极其复杂的国内外形势，外汇管理部门将继续贯彻落实党的十八大、十八届三中全会精神，紧紧围绕促进国际收支基本平衡这一战略目标，大力推动贸易和投资便利化，不断提升外汇管理防范风险和服务实体经济的能力。一是推进外汇管理改革创新，坚持简政放权、转变职能，积极推进事中事后管理，大力发展外汇市场，管好用好外汇储备。二是夯实统计监测基础，不断完善统计制度，改进统计方法，完善数据采集和综合利用，加快监测分析系统建设整合步伐，不断提高监测分析能力和水平。三是坚守不发生系统性、区域性金融风险底线，加快完善跨境资本流动监测预警和风险应对机制，探索建立宏观审慎框架下的跨境资本流动管理体系，加强外汇检查的针对性和有效性。

主要金融市场发展政策

一、银行业市场发展政策①

(一) 银行业市场发展政策概述

2014 年，世界经济温和复苏，国内经济平稳发展，中国继续实施积极的财政政策和稳健的货币政策，商业银行资产和负债规模稳步增长，盈利水平、准备金水平和资本充足水平持续较好。然而受经济增速下行、利率市场化、互联网金融等因素影响，银行业景气度有所下降。但总体来看，国内银行业经营态势依然保持稳健。

根据银监会数据，截至 2014 年 12 月末，我国银行业金融机构境内外本外币资产总额为 172.3 万亿元，负债总额为 160.0 万亿元，净利润为 1.56 万亿元，资本充足率为 13.18%，不良贷款率 1.25%。

表 5 - 1　　　　　　　　　　2014 年银行业金融机构发展主要情况　　　　　　单位：亿元，%

主要指标	2010 年	2011 年	2012 年	2013 年	2014 年
总资产	94.26 万	111.5 万	133.6 万	151.3	172.3 万
总负债	88.43 万	104.3 万	125.0 万	141.1	160.0 万
净利润	7 637	10 412	12 386	14 180	15 548
资产利润率	1.10	1.30	1.28	1.27	1.23
资本利润率	19.20	20.40	19.85	19.17	17.59
净息差	2.50	2.70	2.75	2.68	2.70
非利息收入占比	17.50	19.30	19.83	21.15	21.47
成本收入比	35.30	33.40	33.10	32.90	31.62
核心一级资本	42 985	53 367	64 340	75 793	90 739
资本充足率	12.20	12.70	13.25	12.19	13.18
核心一级资本充足率	10.10	10.20	10.62	9.95	10.56
流动性比例	42.20	43.20	45.83	44.03	46.44
存贷比	64.50	64.90	65.31	66.08	65.09
人民币超额备付金率	3.20	3.10	3.51	2.54	2.65
不良贷款余额	4 336	4 279	4 929	5 921	8 426
不良贷款率	1.10	1.00	0.95	1.00	1.25
贷款损失准备	9 438	11 898	14 564	16 740	19 552
拨备覆盖率	217.70	278.10	295.51	282.70	232.06

资料来源：银监会。

---

① 执笔：王敏。

表 5 – 2   2014 年对银行业发展产生影响的主要政策列表

政策及主要内容	颁布机构
《中华人民共和国外资银行管理条例》	国务院
《国务院办公厅关于多措并举着力缓解企业融资成本高问题的指导意见》	国务院
《关于规范金融机构同业业务的通知》	人民银行
《关于加强商业银行存款偏离度管理有关事项的通知》	人民银行
《关于开展常备借贷便利操作试点的通知》	人民银行
《中国人民银行办公厅关于做好 2014 年信贷政策工作的意见》	人民银行
《关于进一步做好住房金融服务工作的通知》	人民银行
《存款保险条例（征求意见稿）》	人民银行
《关于存款口径调整后存款准备金政策和利率管理政策有关事项的通知》	人民银行
《中国银监会关于进一步促进村镇银行健康发展的指导意见》	银监会
《中国银监会　中国证监会关于商业银行发行优先股补充一级资本的指导意见》	银监会
《商业银行杠杆率管理办法》	银监会
《商业银行流动性风险管理办法（试行）》	银监会
《中国银监会关于调整商业银行存贷比计算口径的通知》	银监会

资料来源：人民银行、银监会。

（二）银行业市场发展政策分析

1. 银行业资产规模持续增长，贷款增速进一步趋缓

截至 2014 年末，商业银行总资产达 172.3 万亿元，新增 21 万亿元，同比增长 13.87%，增速企稳回升。但商业银行贷款增速进一步回落。截至 12 月末，商业银行各项贷款余额为 67.47 万亿元，新增 8.24 万亿元，同比增速由 2013 年的 14.62% 进一步回落至 13.9%。

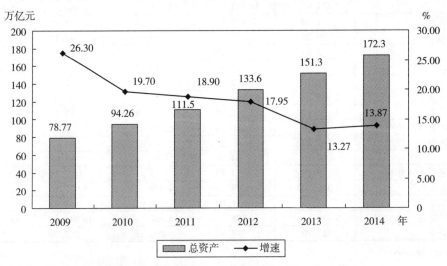

资料来源：银监会。

图 5 – 1　2009—2014 年商业银行总资产规模和增速变化

2014年，面对经济下行压力，央行实施了两次定向降准。4月央行下调县域农村商业银行人民币存款准备金率2个百分点，下调县域农村合作银行人民币存款准备金率0.5个百分点；6月央行对符合审慎经营要求且"三农"和小微企业贷款达到一定比例的商业银行下调人民币存款准备金率0.5个百分点，对财务公司、金融租赁公司和汽车金融公司下调人民币存款准备金率0.5个百分点。定向降准政策旨在引导商业银行有针对性地加强对"三农"和小微企业的支持，增强信贷支持实体经济的能力。其着眼点是，在货币信贷存量较大和增速保持较高水平的情况下，不适合采取大幅扩张总量的方式解决结构性问题。

同时，央行通过扩大常备借贷便利操作（SLF）试点和创设中期借贷便利，保持银行体系中性适度的流动性水平。1月，在北京、江苏、山东等10省市，由当地人民银行分支机构向符合条件的中小金融机构提供SLF短期流动性支持。SLF试点范围扩大，有利于改善中小银行流动性，维护金融市场稳定，提升中小银行的流动性管理能力。9月和10月，央行通过中期借贷便利向银行体系等分别投放基础货币5 000亿元和2 695亿元。中期借贷便利的创设有利于保持市场中性、适度的流动性水平，也利用于引导商业银行降低贷款利率和社会融资成本，支持实体经济增长。

2. 银行业负债规模持续增长，存款流失压力上升

截至2014年末，商业银行总负债规模达160万亿元，比上年末增加18.9万亿元，同比增长13.35%，增速企稳回升。

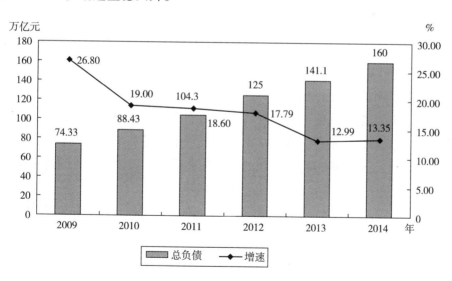

资料来源：银监会。

图5-2 2009—2014年商业银行总负债规模和增速变化

值得关注的是，商业银行存款流失压力加大，存贷款增速差距进一步扩大。受利率市场化、互联网金融、股市回暖分流、不规范的同业业务收缩、"冲存款"行为减少导

致存款派生相应缩减等因素影响，商业银行存款业务增速明显下降。根据银监会数据，2014 年商业银行各项存款余额为 98.34 万亿元，全年增加 8.61 万亿元，增幅 9.6%，较 2013 年全年 10.52 万亿元的增长和 13.29% 的增速分别下降 1.91 万亿元和 3.69 个百分点。同时，存款增速明显慢于贷款，特别是下半年，贷款和存款的增速差距进一步扩大。2014 年 6 月末存款增速为 14.3%，至 2014 年 12 月末已逐步降至 9.6%，而同期贷款增速相应为 14.2% 和 13.1%，增速差距逐步拉大。

为促进存款业务健康发展，国内出台了两项政策：一是中国银监会下发了《中国银监会关于调整商业银行存贷比计算口径的通知》。通知规定，支农再贷款、支小再贷款所对应的贷款和"三农"专项金融债所对应的涉农贷款等 6 项，不再计入贷存比（贷款）计算的分子，银行对企业或个人发行的大额可转让存单、外资法人银行吸收的境外母行一年期以上存放净额两项计入分母（存款）。此次存贷比计算口径调整有利于缓解银行的存贷比达标压力，也有助于银行把更多的信贷资源投入实体经济，尤其是"三农"和小微企业领域。虽然在过去存贷比监管在管控流动性风险、控制信贷过快增长和维护银行体系稳定方面发挥了一定的积极作用，但也扭曲了商业银行经营行为，催生了一系列资金掮客"买存款"的现象，不利于流动性管理和金融稳定。因此，从未来发展看，应尽快启动《商业银行法》的修订工作，取消存贷比限制，用流动性覆盖比例和净稳定资金比例替代存贷比例，以更好地适应我国银行业资产负债结构多元化发展的趋势。

二是银监会、财政部和央行联合发布了《关于加强商业银行存款偏离度管理有关事项的通知》。文件要求商业银行应加强存款稳定性管理，不得设立时点性存款规模考评指标，不得采取高息揽储、非法返利、以贷转存手段违规吸收和虚假增加存款，对月末存款偏离度超过 3% 的商业银行采取限制准入、降低评级、限制业务、提高稳定存款比例等监管纠正与处罚措施。偏离度管理新规有助于约束商业银行时点性冲存行为，降低商业银行存款的波动，稳定存款成本，平抑季末货币市场利率大幅波动，但在存贷比管控下，要从根本上改变商业银行冲时点的存款拓展模式仍需要一定时间的调整和过渡。

3. 银行业利润水平持续提升，盈利能力有所下滑

2014 年，中国银行业面临了来自多方面的挑战，经营压力较往年有明显上升，利润增长出现明显放缓。根据银监会数据，2014 年，商业银行全年累计实现净利润 1.55 万亿元，比 2013 年增加 1 369 亿元，同比增长 9.7%，增速较 2013 年下降 4.8 个百分点；平均资产利润率为 1.23%，同比下降 0.04 个百分点；平均资本利润率为 17.59%，同比下降 1.58 个百分点。

分析商业银行净利润变动的原因，主要有以下几个方面。一是利率市场化改革深入推进，银行业负债成本有所上升。11 月央行将金融机构存款利率浮动区间的上限由存款基准利率的 1.1 倍调整为 1.2 倍。国内五大行采取有条件上浮的存款定价策略，股份制

银行基本上将存款利率一浮到顶，银行吸收存款的成本有所上升。二是中间业务增长出现减速。2014 年，受到减轻企业负担政策的影响，往年增长较快的财务顾问收入出现回落，使商业银行中间业务收入增速与 2013 年相比出现较大幅度的回落。根据银监会数据，2014 年，商业银行非利息收入 9 022 亿元，比上年增加 1 455 亿元，同比增长19.2%，增速下滑 1.5 个百分点。三是拨备支出的增加是盈利增速下降的最主要原因。受国内经济增速放缓、小微企业和部分产能过剩行业不良贷款持续增长等因素影响，2014 年商业银行信用风险压力增大，拨备支出大幅增长消耗了商业银行大量的拨备前利润。截至 2014 年末，商业银行不良贷款余额为 8 426 亿元，比上年末增加 2 506 亿元；不良贷款率为 1.25%，比上年末上升 0.25 个百分点。

4. 同业业务在监管新规下规范发展

近年来，商业银行同业业务发展迅速，部分银行利用同业业务绕过监管部门对银行的存贷比管理、资本监管、信贷投向管理等，为企业提供融资。此类业务在为银行带来利润的同时，也造成了一定的金融风险隐患，并存在抬高社会融资成本、发展不规范、信息披露不充分、规避金融监管和宏观调控等问题。2014 年 5 月，人民银行、银监会、证监会、保监会、国家外汇局联合印发了《关于规范金融机构同业业务的通知》，引导商业银行同业业务规范健康发展，维护银行体系稳健运行。在新政影响下，2014 年商业银行同业资产负债持续上升的趋势减缓，通过同业业务对接非标准债权资产并进行监管套利的模式得到有效遏制，同业业务逐步规范发展。

5. 优先股发行和资本高级法实施，银行业资本更为充实

2014 年，优先股的推广、资本管理高级方法实施等措施，推动银行业资本充足率有所提升。截至 2014 年末，商业银行加权平均一级资本充足率为 10.76%，比上年末上升0.81 个百分点；加权平均资本充足率为 13.18%，比上年末上升 0.99 个百分点。

3 月，证监会和银监会分别发布了《优先股试点管理办法》和《中国银监会 中国证监会关于商业银行发行优先股补充一级资本的指导意见》。根据新规，优先股募集资金可以纳入核心资本，补充一级资本金。优先股发行扩大了商业银行融资渠道，有助于纾缓银行面临的资本压力，提升资本质量，缓解银行资本亲周期性。截至 2014 年 12 月末，农业银行、中国银行分别完成了银行业首单 400 亿元境内优先股和 70 亿美元的境外优先股发行，平安银行、光大银行、民生银行、宁波银行等 10 余家银行也公布了优先股发行计划。

4 月，银监会核准了工商银行、农业银行、中国银行、建设银行、交通银行、招商银行等六家银行实施资本管理高级方法。由于高级法相比现行权重法能有效降低风险加权资产，尤其是按揭贷款的风险权重系数，从而提升银行各口径下的资本充足水平。从实施效果看，六家被核准的商业银行资本充足率在扣除其他因素后，均有不同幅度的提升。更为重要的是，高级方法的实施将对商业银行转型产生深远的影响，有助于推动银

行风险管理向定性与定量相结合模式转变，促进银行完善全面风险管理框架和内部资本充足评估程序，推动银行逐渐形成以内源资本积累为主、外源资本补充为辅的资本积累新模式。

6. 银行业改革开放新策出台，有效促进民营和外资银行发展

9月末，前海微众银行、天津金城银行、温州民商银行、浙江网商银行、上海华瑞银行等首批5家民营银行全部获得银监会批准筹建。民营银行首批试点破冰获批，不仅意味着民营资本在市场经济当中获得平等的地位，而且有利于民营银行通过错位竞争，向社会提供更好的金融服务，激发金融活力，提高金融资源配置效率。

12月，国务院公布《国务院关于修改〈中华人民共和国外资银行管理条例〉的决定》，新规放宽了外资银行准入和开办人民币业务的条件，对外商独资银行、中外合资银行在中国境内设立的分行，不再要求其总行无偿拨给营运资金的最低需达到1亿元；外商独资银行、中外合资银行可以根据自身的实际业务需求，在其分行之间有效配置营运资金，不再将已经在中国境内设立代表处作为外国银行初次设立分行的条件。同时，在申请经营人民币业务的条件方面，外资银行营业性机构在中国境内的开业年限要求由3年以上改为1年以上，不再要求申请前2年连续盈利。外资银行新规意在逐渐去除双重标准，加速中国银行业的市场化和国际化进程，有利于更好地发挥外资银行的积极作用，促进国内外金融业在资金、技术、产品和管理方面进一步融合，提升国内银行业服务和管理水平。

(三) 银行业市场发展政策展望

2015年，商业银行依然面临经济增长稳中趋缓、利率市场化深入推进、互联网金融强势冲击等因素的影响，但稳增长政策、积极的财政政策、中性偏松的货币政策和银行监管政策的调整将使得商业银行经营环境有所改善。

1. 积极的财政政策和中性偏松的货币政策有助于银行资产增长

2015年国内经济工作的首要任务仍然是保持经济稳定增长，积极的财政政策将加力增效，财政赤字扩大至16 200亿元，比2014年增加2 700亿元。基建投资持续发力，"一带一路"战略带动对外直接投资快速发展，京津冀协同发展、长江经济带等区域战略重点实施，这些因素将拉动贷款需求。同时，在信贷、税收、取消限购和降息等政策的综合刺激下，房地产市场有望在2015年上半年触底之后企稳，住房按揭贷款需求、开发贷款需求都将有所回升。此外，在中性偏松的货币政策下，M_2增速目标在12%左右，全年新增贷款在11万亿元左右，进而推动商业银行资产稳步增长。

2. 受正反两方面因素影响，负债业务增速仍将略有放缓

受货币创造放缓、金融脱媒、互联网金融等因素影响，2015年商业银行存款分流、增速下滑的大趋势仍将持续。不过存款业务也面临三方面的政策驱动：一是存贷比口径可能进一步放宽，这将为银行带来一定的信贷投放派生存款。二是准备金率适度下调概

率较大，有利于银行提升存款规模。随着人民币单边升值预期打破，外汇占款增速下滑，预计2015年全年存款准备金率仍有可能下调，这有利于银行存款的增长。三是在流动性宽松的格局下，余额宝等货币市场基金收益率将有所下降，有利于缓解银行存款被持续分流的压力。

但是同业负债将在2015年保持高速增长。2014年央行同业新规将部分同业存款纳入各项存款，并规定同业存款不缴纳存款准备金，这将促进商业银行发展同业负债业务。从长远看，随着资产证券化业务推广、资本市场深化以及由此带来的直接融资模式发展和金融脱媒加剧，被分流的银行存款在进入资本市场后将以同业负债的形式回归银行体系，商业银行同业负债占银行负债的比重不断提升是长期趋势，预计2015年商业银行同业负债将保持高增长态势。

3. 商业银行盈利增速缓中趋稳，净息差仍然面临较大的压力

由于资产增长平稳、利率市场化程度加深、资产减值损失准备增加、同业跨业竞争加剧等负面因素影响，2015年商业银行营业收入增速将较2014年下降，净利润增速进一步放缓。特别是2015年银行净息差面临较大的结构性压力。一是2014年末非对称降息的重定价过程在2015年将对银行存量存贷款息差形成显著影响。2014年11月，中国人民银行采取非对称方式下调金融机构人民币贷款和存款基准利率。其中，金融机构一年期贷款基准利率和存款基准利率分别下调0.4个百分点、0.25个百分点至2.75%，非对称降息将给银行净息差带来负面影响。二是利率市场化进程持续推进，低成本存款负债增速总体较缓，银行负债成本有持续的上升压力。三是2015年存款利率浮动区间有进一步放松的可能性，存贷款基准利率也有经历再次下调的可能性，这将给商业银行净息差带来不利影响。四是民营银行业务的经营模式和发展速度是影响2015年银行净息差收窄幅度的不确定因素。以拓展市场份额为目的的过度竞争，会对行业净利差水平形成一定冲击。综合以上多重因素，2015年银行业净息差收窄幅度要明显大于2014年，收窄幅度可能在15～30个基点。

4. 存款保险制度的推出，有利于促进银行业持续健康发展

2014年，国务院审议通过了《存款保险制度实施方案》《存款保险条例（征求意见稿）》，并完成社会公开征求意见工作，2015年存款保险制度有望正式实施。根据该征求意见稿，存款保险制度将覆盖在境内设立的商业银行、农村合作银行、农村信用合作社等吸收存款的银行业金融机构，并对不同类型的机构采取差别费率。在赔付金额方面实行限额偿付，每位存款人在同一家银行的最高偿付金额为50万元。存款保险制度的推出有助于保护存款人的合法权益，及时防范和化解金融风险，减少政府隐性担保，促进金融机构健康发展，维护金融稳定和推动我国金融系统健康、稳定、持续发展。

二、股票市场发展政策①

(一) 2014 年中国股市主要发展政策一览

表 5 - 3   **2014 年中国股市主要发展政策**

发布日期	政策名称	发文单位
1 月 7 日	《关于保险资金投资创业板上市公司股票等有关问题的通知》	中国保监会
2 月 10 日	《证券交易数据交换协议》《证券交易数据交换编解码协议》和《证券期货业非公开募集产品编码及管理规范》	中国证监会
3 月 21 日	《优先股试点管理办法》	中国证监会
3 月 24 日	《国务院关于进一步优化企业兼并重组市场环境的意见》	国务院
3 月 25 日	国务院常务会议确定,积极稳妥推进股票发行注册制改革,加快多层次股权市场建设,鼓励市场化并购重组	国务院
3 月 25 日	《关于私募投资基金开户和结算有关问题的通知》	中国证券登记结算有限公司
4 月 4 日	中国证监会发布上市公司发行优先股相关信息披露准则,包括《发行优先股申请文件》《发行优先股发行预案和发行情况报告书》和《发行优先股募集说明书》	中国证监会
4 月 10 日	中国证券监督管理委员会、香港证券及期货事务监察委员会联合发布公告,批准上海证券交易所、香港联合交易所、中国证券登记结算有限责任公司、香港中央结算有限公司开展沪港股票市场交易互联互通机制试点	中国证监会、香港证券及期货事务监察委员会
4 月 22 日	《国务院办公厅关于金融服务"三农"发展的若干意见》	国务院
5 月 9 日	《国务院关于进一步促进资本市场健康发展的若干意见》	国务院
5 月 9 日	《上海证券交易所优先股业务试点管理办法》	上海证券交易所
5 月 15 日	《关于进一步推进证券经营机构创新发展的意见》	中国证监会
6 月 12 日	《深圳证券交易所优先股试点业务实施细则》	深圳证券交易所
6 月 13 日	《沪港股票市场交易互联互通机制试点若干规定》	中国证监会
6 月 20 日	《关于上市公司实施员工持股计划试点的指导意见》	中国证监会
8 月 5 日	《国务院办公厅关于多措并举着力缓解企业融资成本高问题的指导意见》	国务院
9 月 19 日	《关于统一账户平台上线安排的通知》	中国证券登记结算有限责任公司
9 月 26 日	《上海证券交易所沪港通试点办法》	上海证券交易所
10 月 17 日	《关于证券公司参与沪港通业务试点有关事项的通知》	中国证监会

---

① 执笔:王鑫。

续表

发布日期	政策名称	发文单位
11月26日	《国务院关于创新重点领域投融资机制鼓励社会投资的指导意见》	国务院
12月16日	《公开募集证券投资基金运作指引第1号——商品期货交易型开放式基金指引》	中国证监会

资料来源：课题组整理。

（二）2014年股票市场主要发展政策分析

1. 新"国九条"绘制资本市场顶层设计

2014年5月9日，国务院印发了《国务院关于进一步促进资本市场健康发展的若干意见》，该意见被许多市场人士称为新"国九条"。该意见从顶层设计的层面全面绘制了包括股票市场、债券市场、期货市场在内的资本市场发展蓝图，明确了股权市场的层次结构、基本要求和发展债券市场、期货市场的政策措施。提出要加快建设多渠道、广覆盖、严监管、高效率的股权市场，规范发展债券市场，拓展期货市场，着力优化市场体系结构、运行机制、基础设施和外部环境，实现发行交易方式多样、投融资工具丰富、风险管理功能完备、场内场外和公募私募协调发展。到2020年，基本形成结构合理、功能完善、规范透明、稳健高效、开放包容的多层次资本市场体系。

2. "沪港通"试点开始启动

2014年4月10日，中国证券监督管理委员会、香港证券及期货事务监察委员会联合发布公告，批准上海证券交易所、香港联合交易所、中国证券登记结算有限责任公司、香港中央结算有限公司开展沪港股票市场交易互联互通机制试点。2014年6月13日，证监会发布了《沪港股票市场交易互联互通机制试点若干规定》，该规定共19条，明确了上海证券交易所、香港联合交易所，证券交易服务公司及中国证券登记结算公司、香港中央结算公司开展沪港通业务应当履行的职责，对境内证券公司开展沪港通业务提出原则性要求，明确了沪港通的业务范围、外资持股比例、清算交收方式、交收货币等相关事项，对投资者保护、监督管理、资料保存等内容提出了相关要求。[①] 2014年9月26日，上海证券交易所发布了《上海证券交易所沪港通试点办法》。沪港通是我国资本市场对外开放的重要内容，有利于加强两地资本市场联系，推动资本市场双向开放，在增强我国资本市场的综合实力、巩固上海和香港两个金融中心的地位、推动人民币国际化等方面具有积极意义。

3. IPO年内重启

2014年1月17日，在时隔一年多后，纽威股份在上交所公开上市交易，成为本次

---

① 新华网：《证监会发布〈沪港股票市场交易互联互通机制试点若干规定〉》，http://news.xinhuanet.com/fortune/2014-06/13/c_1111139985.htm，2015-02-01。

IPO 重启后上市的首只新股。1 月 21 日，3 家中小企业板、5 家创业板共 8 家公司股票在深交所上市交易，这是此次发行制度改革进程中深市首批新股上市。随后，沪深证券交易所分别修改了 IPO 网上按市值申购实施办法，中国证券业协会也修订发布了《首次公开发行股票承销业务规范》。2014 年 6 月 9 日，中国证监会核准了 10 家企业的首发申请，沪深交易所各 5 家。上述企业及其承销商将分别与沪深交易所协商确定发行日程，并陆续刊登招股说明书，这标志着备受市场关注的 IPO 重新开闸。本次 IPO 重启伴随着新股发行机制改革的步伐，这一方面重新恢复了中国股市的融资功能，同时也意味着 IPO 注册制改革正在逐步接近。

4. 上市公司员工持股试点启动

2014 年 6 月 20 日，中国证监会发布了《关于上市公司实施员工持股计划试点的指导意见》（以下简称《指导意见》）。《指导意见》明确，上市公司可以根据员工意愿实施员工持股计划，通过合法方式使员工获得本公司股票并长期持有，股份权益按约定分配给员工。实施员工持股计划，相关资金可以来自员工薪酬或以其他合法方式筹集，所需本公司股票可以来自上市公司回购、直接从二级市场购买、认购非公开发行股票、公司股东自愿赠予等合法方式。《指导意见》还就员工持股计划的实施程序、管理模式、信息披露及内幕交易防控等问题作出规定。中国证监会新闻发言人指出，在上市公司中推进员工持股计划试点，有利于建立和完善劳动者与所有者的利益共享机制，改善公司治理水平，提高职工凝聚力和公司竞争力。[①]

5. 证监会发布《优先股试点管理办法》

2014 年 3 月 21 日，中国证监会发布《优先股试点管理办法》（以下简称《办法》）。《办法》共九章，七十条，包括总则、优先股股东权利的行使、上市公司发行优先股、非上市公众公司非公开发行优先股、交易转让及登记结算、信息披露、回购与并购重组、监管措施和法律责任、附则等。根据《办法》，上市公司可以公开发行优先股，非上市公众公司可以非公开发行优先股。上市公司发行优先股，可以申请一次核准，分次发行。非公开发行优先股仅向《办法》规定的合格投资者发行，每次发行对象不得超过二百人。中国证监会新闻发言人表示，优先股试点是我国资本市场的一项重大改革创新，涉及面广，利益关系复杂，证监会将在总结试点经验的基础上，不断改进和完善优先股制度。

6. 新三板试点范围进一步扩容

2014 年 1 月 24 日，全国股转系统在北京举行新三板全国扩容后首批企业集体挂牌仪式，共有 285 家企业参加，其中 266 家公司于当日正式挂牌。这是国务院发布《关于全国中小企业股份转让系统有关问题的决定》之后，全国股份转让系统的首场集体挂牌

---

① 中国证监会网站：《中国证监会制定并发布〈关于上市公司实施员工持股计划试点的指导意见〉》，http://www.csrc.gov.cn/pub/newsite/zjhxwfb/xwdd/201406/t20140620_256427.html，2015 - 02 - 04。

仪式。证监会表示，全国股份转让系统试点范围扩大至全国，拓宽了资本市场的服务覆盖面和渠道，改变了原来只有交易所上市一条路的状况。企业可以根据自身实际需求，自由选择在证券交易所上市或全国股份转让系统挂牌，这将有利于减轻A股市场的发行上市压力，缓解A股市场的扩容预期。总体来看，全国股份转让系统大规模公司挂牌不会对A股市场产生资金分流效应。[①]

（三）政策评价与展望

2014年是中国股票市场加快推进改革的一年，出台了大量重要的改革措施和发展政策，如新"国九条"的出台、沪港通的试点与IPO的重启等，这对我国资本市场的市场化、法制化与国际化改革具有重要的意义，许多改革举措可以称得上中国证券市场对外直接对接和开放的里程碑。展望2015年，贯彻落实各项指导意见，加快完善资本市场的国际化和体系化的建设步伐将会是推进改革的重中之重，同时，资本市场的制度创新、业务创新和产品创新的力度应该会进一步加大，资本市场的创新将会在金融领域改革中充分发挥先行先试的重要作用。

三、保险市场发展政策[②]

（一）2014年保险市场主要发展政策一览

表5-4　　　　　　　　　2014年中国保险市场主要发展政策

日期	文件名称	发布单位
3月3日	《关于加快推动北京保险产业园创新发展的意见》	保监会、北京市人民政府
3月21日	《中国保监会关于保险业对口支援江西省赣州市定南县等原中央苏区振兴发展的指导意见》	保监会
3月25日	《保险业服务新型城镇化发展的指导意见》	保监会
5月15日	《中国保监会办公厅关于进一步简化行政审批支持中国（上海）自由贸易试验区发展的通知》	保监会办公厅
6月17日	《中国保监会关于开展老年人住房反向抵押养老保险试点的指导意见》	保监会
7月28日	《中国保险监督管理委员会 浙江省人民政府关于在浙江省宁波市建设保险创新综合示范区的通知》	保监会、浙江省人民政府
8月10日	《国务院关于加快发展现代保险服务业的若干意见》	国务院
10月27日	《国务院办公厅关于加快发展商业健康保险的若干意见》	国务院办公厅

资料来源：课题组整理。

---

① 资料来源：凤凰财经网站，http://finance.ifeng.com/a/20140124/11549144_0.shtml，2015-02-21。

② 执笔：刘学庆。

（二）2014 年保险市场主要发展政策分析

保监会主席项俊波在 2015 年全国保险监管工作会议上指出，在经济下行的环境下，通过改革推动、需求拉动、政策驱动三管齐下，2014 年，保险业扭转了行业发展乏力的势头，行业驶入发展的快车道。一是业务增速持续提高。2014 年全国保费收入突破 2 万亿元大关，保险业总资产突破 10 万亿元大关。保险业增速达 17.5%，是国际金融危机以来最高的一年。财产险保费收入 7 203 亿元，同比增长 16%；人身险保费收入 1.3 万亿元，同比增长 18.2%。二是结构调整走向深入。与实体经济联系紧密的保证保险同比增长 66.1%，与民生保障关系密切的年金保险同比增长 77.2%，保障性较强的健康保险同比增长 41.3%。10 年期以上新单期交占比同比提高 5.9 个百分点。三是行业经营效益显著提升。保险公司利润总额约 2 046.6 亿元，同比增长 106.4%，是历史上最好的一年。保险资金运用实现收益 5 358.8 亿元，同比增长 46.5%，创历史新高。保险资金投资收益率 6.3%，综合收益率 9.2%，比上年分别提高 1.3 个和 5.1 个百分点，均创五年来最高水平。四是行业资本实力明显增强。截至 2014 年底，全行业净资产 1.3 万亿元，较年初增长 56.4%。同时，保险业服务经济社会大局的能力进一步提升。2014 年保险业为全社会提供风险保障 1 114 万亿元，同比增长 25.5%，保险业赔款与给付 7 216.2 亿元，同比增长 16.2%。保险业完善社会保障的作用、参与社会管理的作用、服务"三农"的能力、支撑经济发展的能力显著增强。

2014 年保险业发展的成绩得益于国家和保险监管部门出台或实施的一系列重要发展政策。这些改革政策和创新措施激发了保险业发展的内生动力，对保险业服务经济社会发展具有重大影响，也为保险业未来的发展打下了坚实的基础。

1. 国务院发布新"国十条"，全面部署新时期保险业改革、发展和监管

2014 年 8 月 10 日，国务院发布《国务院关于加快发展现代保险服务业的若干意见》（以下称新"国十条"）。新"国十条"着眼于服务国家治理体系和治理能力现代化，明确了加快发展现代保险服务业的指导思想、基本原则、发展目标，对新时期保险业改革、发展和监管进行了全面部署。

一是明确了保险业的发展目标。新"国十条"提出，到 2020 年，基本建成保障全面、功能完善、安全稳健、诚信规范，具有较强服务能力、创新能力和国际竞争力，与我国经济社会发展需求相适应的现代保险服务业，努力由保险大国向保险强国转变。保险成为政府、企业、居民风险管理和财富管理的基本手段，成为提高保障水平和保障质量的重要渠道，成为政府改进公共服务、加强社会管理的有效工具。保险深度（保费收入/国内生产总值）达到 5%，保险密度（保费收入/总人口）达到 3500 元/人。保险的社会"稳定器"和经济"助推器"作用得到有效发挥。

二是拓宽了保险业的服务领域和服务功能。新"国十条"要求，通过把商业保险建成社会保障体系的重要支柱、创新养老保险产品服务和发展多样化健康保险服务，构筑

保险民生保障网，完善多层次社会保障体系；通过运用保险机制创新公共服务提供方式和发挥责任保险化解矛盾纠纷的作用，发挥保险风险管理功能，完善社会治理体系；通过将保险纳入灾害事故防范救助体系、建立巨灾保险制度，完善保险经济补偿机制，提高灾害救助参与度；大力发展"三农"保险，创新支农惠农方式；发挥保险资金长期投资的独特优势、促进保险市场与货币市场、资本市场协调发展、推动保险服务经济结构调整和加大保险业支持企业"走出去"力度，拓展保险服务功能，促进经济提质增效升级。

三是完善了保险业发展的支持政策。新"国十条"根据保险行业发展需要提出了一系列支持保险业发展的新政策措施。具体包括：建立保险监管协调机制；鼓励政府通过多种方式购买保险服务；研究完善加快保险业发展的税收政策；加强养老产业和健康服务业用地保障；完善对农业保险的财政补贴政策等。

四是深化了保险业的改革开放。明确了深化改革的主攻方向，包括加快建立现代保险企业制度，全面深化寿险和商业车险费率市场化改革，深入推进保险市场准入退出机制改革，加快完善保险市场体系，支持保险公司境内外上市。提出了对外开放的主要任务，包括鼓励中资保险公司"走出去"，为我国海外企业提供风险保障，通过国际资本市场筹集资金，努力扩大保险服务出口；引导外资保险公司将先进经验和技术植入中国市场。同时，鼓励保险产品服务创新，加快发展再保险市场，充分发挥保险中介市场的作用。

五是确定了行业基础建设的重点内容。包括要推进保险业信用体系建设；加快建立风险数据库，组建资产托管中心、资产交易平台、再保险交易所、防灾防损中心等基础平台；加强宣传教育，提升全社会保险意识。

六是要求进一步加强和改进保险监管。加快建设以风险为导向的保险监管制度，加快建设第二代偿付能力监管制度，完善保险法规体系，推进监管信息化建设，发挥保险行业协会等自律组织作用，加强基层保险监管工作，推进监管体系和监管能力现代化。加强保险消费者合法权益保护，完善保险消费者合法权益保护法律法规和规章制度，探索建立保险消费纠纷多元化解决机制，监督保险机构全面履行对保险消费者的各项义务。加强保险业全面风险管理，强化责任追究，加强金融监管协调，防范风险跨行业传递，健全保险保障基金管理制度和运行机制，守住不发生系统性、区域性金融风险的底线。

新"国十条"将保险业的发展从行业意愿上升到国家意志，成为我国经济社会发展总体布局中的重要一环。新"国十条"各项政策的落实，将引领保险业进入更高水平的快速发展通道。

2. 国务院发布加快商业健康保险发展意见，商业健康险再获政策红利

经过30多年的发展，我国的商业健康保险取得了比较大的成效。但与世界一些发

达国家和地区比较，我国商业健康保险发展仍然相对滞后，健康保险保费占卫生总费用的比重仍较低，产业规模较小、服务供给不足。2009 年，中共中央、国务院发布《关于深化医药卫生体制改革的意见》，提出要积极发展商业健康保险。2013 年 9 月，国务院发布《关于促进健康服务业发展的若干意见》，进一步为商业健康保险的发展指明方向。2014 年 8 月，国务院发布的《关于加快发展现代保险服务业的若干意见》也提出要发展多样化的健康保险服务。

为进一步落实中共中央、国务院的上述政策，持续推进商业健康保险发展，国务院办公厅于 2014 年 10 月 27 日发布《国务院办公厅关于加快发展商业健康保险的若干意见》（以下简称《商业健康险意见》）。这是国家第一次从深化医药卫生体制改革、发展健康服务业、促进经济提质增效升级的高度定位商业健康保险的功能，是第一次全面部署商业健康保险发展的专项文件。《商业健康险意见》主要包括以下内容：

清晰界定了商业健康保险的具体概念。《商业健康险意见》指出，商业健康保险是由商业保险机构对因健康原因和医疗行为导致的损失给付保险金的保险，主要包括医疗保险、疾病保险、失能收入损失保险、护理保险以及相关的医疗意外保险、医疗责任保险等。

明确提出了商业健康保险的发展目标。《商业健康险意见》提出，到 2020 年，基本建立市场体系完备、产品形态丰富、经营诚信规范的现代商业健康保险服务业。实现商业健康保险运行机制较为完善、服务能力明显提升、服务领域更加广泛、投保人数大幅增加，商业健康保险赔付支出占卫生总费用的比重显著提高。

鼓励扩大商业健康保险供给。鼓励商业保险机构丰富商业健康保险产品；鼓励延伸产业链，从费用报销和经济补偿等方面向病前、病中、病后的综合性健康保障管理方向发展；鼓励开设残疾人康复、托养、照料和心智障碍者家庭财产信托等商业保险。促进提高医疗执业保险覆盖面。支持健康产业科技创新。

推动完善医疗保障服务体系。全面推进并规范商业保险机构承办城乡居民大病保险，并具体对提供一站式服务、提高统筹层次、建立健全独立核算、医疗费用控制等提出了要求。要求加大政府购买服务力度，稳步推进商业保险机构参与各类医疗保险经办服务。完善商业保险机构和医疗卫生机构合作机制，并开展以下合作：确定商业健康保险定点医疗机构，缓解医患信息不对称和医患矛盾，通过商业健康保险费率调节机制降低不合理医疗费用支出，商业保险机构对城乡居民大病保险定点医疗机构进行医疗费用监督、控制和评价等。

要求加强商业健康保险专业化能力建设。《商业健康险意见》要求商业保险机构加强管理制度建设、切实提升专业服务能力、努力提供优质服务、提升信息化建设水平，提升管理和服务水平。同时，要加强和完善监督管理，规范商业健康保险市场秩序。

完善了发展商业健康保险的支持政策。《商业健康险意见》提出，要加强组织领导和部门协同，促进商业健康保险服务业持续健康发展；要引导保险机构投资健康服务产业，要加强对公益性的商业健康保险用地的保障；要完善财政税收等支持政策；要通过加大知识普及、宣传力度等工作，营造商业健康保险发展的良好社会氛围。

《商业健康险意见》的出台，是国务院从战略高度创新改革思路，运用市场机制深入推进医改、积极破解经济社会发展难题、保障和改善民生的有力举措，势必会为我国商业健康保险发展带来巨大的政策机遇和改革红利，对于保险业的发展和服务经济社会全局都具有十分重要的意义。

3. 加大试点推广力度，巨灾保险制度建设迈出新步伐

我国是世界上自然灾害最严重的国家之一，地震、洪涝、干旱、台风等自然灾害发生频繁，亟须建立巨灾保险制度，分散巨灾风险。继 2013 年十八届三中全会通过的《中共中央关于全面深化改革若干重大问题的决定》要求"完善保险补偿机制，建立巨灾保险制度"，以及保监会推动巨灾保险在深圳等地方层面破题开局后，2014 年巨灾保险制度建设迈出了若干新步伐。

一是开展巨灾保险制度顶层设计，明确路线图和时间表。2014 年 8 月，国务院出台的保险业 新"国十条"，首次为巨灾保险制度确定了具体框架，明确了顶层设计，提出"逐步形成财政支持下的多层次巨灾风险分散机制"。中国保监会副主席周延礼 10 月在北京披露建立巨灾保险制度三步走的路线图和时间表。第一步，在 2014 年底前完成"建立巨灾保险制度"专题研究工作，明确巨灾保险制度框架；第二步，在 2017 年底前完成巨灾保险立法工作，推动出台《地震巨灾保险条例》，研究建立巨灾保险基金；第三步，在 2017—2020 年进入全面实施阶段，逐步将巨灾保险制度纳入到国家防灾减灾综合体系中。

二是推进制度框架和立法进程。2014 年，中国保监会完成"建立巨灾保险制度"重点课题，构建巨灾保险制度总体框架；推动《地震巨灾保险条例》立法进程，完成《地震巨灾保险条例》初稿；制定地震巨灾保险制度试运行方案，开发城乡住宅地震保险产品，推动组建地震保险共保体。

三是加大巨灾保险试点推广力度。继 2013 年通过《深圳市巨灾保险方案》、正式实施巨灾保险制度后，深圳市民政局与保险公司签订《深圳市巨灾保险协议》，并于 2014 年 6 月 1 日起正式生效，标志着全国首单巨灾保险合同生效。深圳在全国首推巨灾保险，无疑是深圳保险业的一大创新，可以为国内其他城市建立巨灾保险制度提供借鉴。2014 年 11 月 11 日，巨灾保险在宁波正式实施。宁波成为国内继深圳以后的第二个巨灾保险试点城市，针对居民损失、救灾等提供了相对应的保险。上海、浙江、四川等地也正在积极筹划建立地区性的巨灾保险机制。

巨灾保险是一个世界性的难题。保监会在 2014 年积极开展课题研究、顶层设计、

政策立法和试点推广，必将有力推动建立适合我国国情的巨灾保险制度。

4. 开展先行先试，探索保险业全面深化改革新途径

为深入贯彻党的十八届三中全会精神，2014 年，保监会在上海自贸区、深圳前海深港现代服务业合作区、北京保险产业园和宁波保险创新综合示范区推出一系列先行先试、简政放权的措施，积极探索保险业全面深化改革新途径，加快保险业改革创新，进一步提升保险服务实体经济和社会和谐稳定的能力。

推出上海自贸区保险监管简化行政审批三项举措。中国保监会在 2013 年出台支持中国（上海）自由贸易试验区建设 8 项政策的基础上，于 2014 年 5 月 15 日下发《中国保监会办公厅关于进一步简化行政审批　支持中国（上海）自由贸易试验区发展的通知》，推出与当前上海自贸试验区保险市场发展紧密相关、利在长远、能够立即落地实施的三项举措：允许上海航运保险协会试点开发航运保险协会条款，报备后由会员公司自主使用；取消在沪航运保险营运中心、再保险公司在自贸区内设立分支机构的事前审批，由上海保监局实施备案管理；取消自贸区内保险支公司高管人员任职资格的事前审批，由上海保监局实施备案管理。这是中国保监会支持中国（上海）自由贸易试验区建设、落实国务院总体方案中有关简化事前准入、强化事中事后监管制度的具体实践，是进一步创新制度、简政放权的重大举措。

发布支持深圳保险创新发展的 8 项措施。为加快深圳保险创新发展试验区建设，支持前海金融保险先行先试，中国保监会于 2014 年 8 月印发关于深化深圳保险创新发展试验区建设，加快前海开发开放的 8 条政策措施。具体为：（1）支持前海开发开放和深化深港合作作为深圳保险创新发展试验区建设的重要内容。（2）支持在前海设立自保公司、相互制保险公司等新型保险组织以及航运保险、责任保险、健康保险、养老保险等专业保险机构。推动前海建设再保险中心。（3）支持深港保险融合发展，积极探索深港两地保险市场在产品、服务、资金、人才等领域互联互通的方式和途径。（4）研究在《内地与香港关于设立更紧密经贸关系的安排》（CEPA）框架下适当降低香港保险公司在前海设立机构和开展业务的准入要求，积极支持符合条件的香港保险经纪公司在前海设立保险代理公司；支持更多保险机构利用香港市场拓宽资本补充渠道，在境外设立机构并开展人民币保险业务。（5）支持深圳保险机构开展保险资金运用创新，探索保险资金境外投资试点，进一步拓宽保险资金运用渠道和范围。（6）支持在前海开展互联网保险业务创新，鼓励开展与互联网金融特点相适应的保险产品、营销、服务以及交易方式创新，培育互联网保险新业态和新型要素交易平台。（7）支持试点开展短期出口信用险业务，为实体经济发展和进出口贸易提供融资便利和风险保障。（8）支持在前海探索保险监管创新。

推进北京保险产业园创新发展。2014 年 3 月 3 日，中国保监会和北京市人民政府发布《关于加快推动北京保险产业园创新发展的意见》，提出在石景山国家服务业综合改

革试点区统筹谋划、科学布局，稳妥有序推进保险业"产业核心区""产业辐射区"和"产业拓展区"建设，打造以保险产业为龙头的国家级金融创新示范区，努力将保险产业园建设成为全国保险创新试验区、保险产业聚集区和保险文化引领区。该意见提出，园区的产业导向上要牢牢把握首都发展的阶段性特征和城市功能定位，聚焦保险业改革创新，吸引增量，突出经营总部、区域总部建设；引导创新型保险业态发展，完善保险主产业和上下游全产业链；稳步推进保险交易所试点建设，加快形成现代市场体系；支持监管机构、行业组织和研发机构进行业务布局，打造全国保险政策智库；积极建设全国保险"数字特区"；建立市场化的准入退出机制。同时，还明确了一系列支持保障措施。

推动宁波保险创新综合示范区建设。2014年7月28日，中国保监会和浙江省人民政府发布《关于在浙江省宁波市建设保险创新综合示范区的通知》。2014年9月，宁波保险创新综合示范区建设启动，全国首个保险创新综合示范区项目正式落地。中国保监会将把一些具有全国性重大示范带动作用的改革创新项目安排在宁波先行先试。宁波拟从六个方面重点展开示范区建设：一是坚持制度创新引领，构建创新自育平台；二是推动保险组织创新，集聚保险产业要素；三是开展保险产品创新，促进经济发展提质增效，针对宁波海洋经济、外向型经济特点及小微企业等保险需求，开发特色性保险产品，保障地方实体经济发展；四是创新政府公共服务，完善社会治理体系；五是发展健康和养老保险，完善社会保障体系建设；六是创新保险资金运用，支持产业转型升级。宁波保险创新综合示范区的落地有助于促进宁波在保险组织和产品技术创新、丰富保险市场体系、加强和改善经济社会薄弱领域保险服务、加大保险政策扶持力度等方面的先行先试。

5. 探索保险业服务新型城镇化，促进保险业服务实体经济发展

为贯彻落实《国家新型城镇化发展规划（2014—2020年）》相关要求，保监会于2014年3月25日印发《保险业服务新型城镇化发展的指导意见》。

该指导意见坚持以人为本、改革创新、市场主导、政府引导的原则，提出了六项重点措施。一是要统筹发展商业养老和医疗健康保险，完善城乡多层次社会保障体系，缓解新型城镇化建设过程中人口转移带来的社保压力。二是进一步深化资金运用改革，创新资金运用形式，支持城镇基础设施建设、运营以及养老健康产业、保障性住房等民生项目发展。三是从服务开放型经济发展、改善小微企业融资环境、为技术创新提供保险保障、服务低碳经济等方面提出要求，推动城市产业结构优化升级。四是推进政府采购保险产品和服务，提升公共服务资源配置效能。大力发展与公众利益密切相关的责任保险，辅助政府创新公共管理方式。推动建立国家政策支持的巨灾保险制度，增强防灾减灾救灾应急能力。五是健全农业保险服务体系，促进新型城镇化与农业现代化协调发展。六是深化改革创新，逐步建立以保险企业为主体、新型城镇化市场需求为导向，适

度监管、政策激励为推动的保险创新机制，不断激发保险业服务新型城镇化的内在动力和活力。

保险服务新型城镇化将探索保险业服务新型城镇化的体制机制和有效模式，逐步使保险业成为统筹发展多层次城乡保障体系的重要支柱，成为新型城镇化建设的重要融资渠道，成为完善社会治理和改进公共服务的重要工具，成为新型城镇化过程中应对灾害事故风险的重要手段。

6. 开展住房反向抵押养老保险试点，丰富养老保障方式

2013 年 9 月 6 日，国务院发布《国务院关于加快发展养老服务业的若干意见》，为我国养老服务业的发展描绘了蓝图，提出要开展老年人住房反向抵押养老保险试点，丰富养老保障方式。为落实上述要求，保监会于 2014 年 6 月 17 日发布《中国保监会关于开展老年人住房反向抵押养老保险试点的指导意见》（以下简称《反向抵押养老保险指导意见》）。

住房反向抵押养老保险是一种将住房抵押与终身养老年金保险相结合的创新型商业养老保险业务，即拥有房屋完全产权的老年人，将其房产抵押给保险公司，继续拥有房屋占有、使用、收益和经抵押权人同意的处置权，并按照约定条件领取养老金直至身故；老年人身故后，保险公司获得抵押房产处置权，处置所得将优先用于偿付养老保险相关费用。这种养老方式被视为完善养老保障机制的一项重要补充，对促进我国多层次养老保障体系的建立、保护养老保险市场的健康发展具有积极的意义；也有利于保险业发挥在风险管理、资金管理等方面的优势，更好地参与养老服务业发展。

《反向抵押养老保险指导意见》确定了 2 年的试点期间，并选择北京、上海、广州、武汉四个城市作为住房反向抵押养老保险试点城市。《反向抵押养老保险指导意见》还规定了参与试点的保险公司的资格条件，要求申请试点资格的保险公司应开业满 5 年，注册资本不少于 20 亿元；满足保险公司偿付能力管理规定，申请试点时上一年度末及最近季度末的偿付能力充足率不低于 120%；具备开展反向抵押养老保险所必需的专业技术、管理能力和各类专业人员等。

为保护老年人合法权益，《反向抵押养老保险指导意见》对业务宣传、销售人员管理、销售过程管理、信息披露等方面作出了严格规定：一是要求保险公司客观公正地开展业务宣传，业务宣传材料应由总公司统一制作并严格管理。二是保监会将适时指导中国保险行业协会建立反向抵押养老保险销售人员资格考试制度。在该制度建立前，保险公司应主动建立销售人员管理制度，明确资格条件，建立培训及考核制度，并在公司网站公布取得资格的销售人员。三是要求保险公司明确参保客户的范围和条件，不得向不符合相关要求的客户推介业务。房产价值应当聘请具有一级资质的房地产估价机构进行评估，费用由保险公司和消费者共同负担。保险公司应当对消费者进行签约前辅导，并通过录音、录像，或第三方见证等方式增强合同签订过程的公平性、公正性。四是规定

老年人住房反向抵押养老保险产品的犹豫期为 30 个自然日，保险公司应当在犹豫期内再次向投保人介绍反向抵押养老保险产品，确认投保人的真实购买意愿。五是要求保险公司定期向客户披露反向抵押养老保险相关信息。六是鼓励保险公司在服务领域延伸、服务内容多样化和服务手段创新等方面积极探索，完善与反向抵押养老保险相关的养老服务链条。七是要求保险公司高度重视客户投诉，做好解释沟通和后续处理。

（三）政策评价与展望

2014 年，中国保险业在复杂困难的形势下，坚持抓服务、严监管、防风险、促发展，各项工作扎实推进，行业发展驶入快车道，改革发展实现重大跨越，保险业站在了新的发展起点上。中国保监会主席项俊波在 2015 年 1 月召开的全国保险监管工作会议上明确，2015 年，保险业要深入理解、主动适应经济新常态，抓住我国保险业发展的黄金机遇期，勇于推进改革创新，加快转变发展方式，切实转换发展动力，推动我国从保险大国向保险强国转变，确保新"国十条"提出的发展目标顺利实现。具体来说，2015 年将重点抓好以下促进保险业发展的工作：

首先，要重点推动三项重大政策落地。一是推动巨灾保险加快发展。在近两年巨灾保险试点和制度建设方面取得了重大突破的基础上，按照建立巨灾保险制度"三步走"的规划，进入"第二步"，重点是推进立法保障、建立核心机制，要推动《地震巨灾保险条例》等巨灾保险立法，研究建立巨灾保险基金，推动实施住房地震保险制度，指导巨灾保险共保体运行，总结并推广巨灾保险试点。二是推动养老险和健康险税优政策落地。启动个人税延商业养老保险试点，推动健康险税优政策尽快出台；抓紧做好健康险、养老险相关监管制度、标准产品、业务流程和信息平台等配套建设，确保税优政策出台后尽快实施。三是推动大病保险全面铺开。要落实国务院办公厅《关于加快发展商业健康保险的若干意见》和六部委联合发布的《关于开展城乡居民大病保险工作的指导意见》的要求，不断提高大病保险保障面，争取全国各省份及各地市全覆盖；要修订大病保险业务管理制度，规范财务核算、招投标管理和市场准入退出等环节，确保大病保险依法合规开展。

其次，要围绕国家战略和民生领域，提升服务经济社会全局的能力。一是创新保险业服务国家重大战略的机制和手段，为"一带一路"等国家重大战略服务。二是完善和发展农业保险制度和农险产品，推动农业再保险业共同体运行机制和农业巨灾风险分散机制建设，为农业现代化服务。三是力争出台加快商业养老保险发展政策意见，争取保险机构参与基本养老保险基金的运营和管理，拓展企业年金业务，有序推进住房反向抵押养老保险试点，贯彻落实《关于加快发展商业健康保险的若干意见》，推进保险机构经办新农合等各类医保服务，修订《健康保险管理办法》等，强化健康险业务监管，为健全社会保障体系服务。四是加快责任险发展，为完善社会治理体系服务。五是推广保险业支持小微企业经验，缓解小微企业"融资难"问题。

另外，保监会明确，在 2015 年还将着力推进深化行政审批制度改革、完善保险市场体系等工作，加强行业基础建设。

四、债券市场发展政策①

2014 年，从制度建设、基础设施推进、产品创新、投资者丰富等层面，各项政策稳步推出，债券市场保持了良好的发展势头，规模继续增长，公司信用类债券发行量大幅上升，市场对外开放水平进一步提高，中国债券市场在国民经济发展中的作用和地位进一步增强。

（一）债券市场政策

1 月 28 日，人民银行发布《中国人民银行关于建立场外金融衍生产品集中清算机制及开展人民币利率互换集中清算业务有关事宜的通知》，以促进中国场外金融衍生产品市场健康规范发展，建立场外金融衍生产品集中清算机制。该通知要求全国银行间债券市场参与者达成的人民币利率互换等场外金融衍生产品交易应按要求进行集中清算，银行间市场清算所股份有限公司提供集中清算服务。

3 月，人民银行发布公告〔2014〕第 3 号，增加商业银行柜台债券业务品种，由记账式国债扩大至国家开发银行金融债券、政策性金融债券和中国铁路总公司等政府支持机构债券，这是商业银行柜台自 2002 年开展记账式国债交易后首次引入新券种。该公告同时取消商业银行承办记账式国债柜台交易审批的行政许可，人民银行对该事项的市场主体准入不设准入条件、不存在实质性约束。并且，公告指出，承办银行可以通过其营业网点、电子银行等渠道向投资者分销债券，与投资者进行债券买卖，并办理债券托管与结算。

4 月 9 日，人民银行发布《关于银行间债券市场招标发行债券有关事宜的通知》（银市场〔2014〕16 号），调整了非金融企业使用招标系统发行债券的门槛要求，为鼓励非金融企业招标发行债券提供了制度支持。该通知放宽了对发行人主体信用等级、发行规模和投标参与人数量的要求，并对发行人和中介机构在招标结束后需公开披露和上报人民银行的相关信息作出具体要求。

4 月 24 日，国家发展和改革委员会发布《企业债券簿记建档发行业务指引（暂行）》和《企业债券招标发行业务指引（暂行）》，以加强企业债券发行制度建设，进一步规范企业债券簿记建档和招标发行行为，保护参与各方的合法权益。

5 月，财政部发布《2014 年地方政府债券自发自还试点办法》，决定在上海、浙江、广东、深圳、江苏、山东、北京、江西、宁夏、青岛等十省市进行地方债自发自还试点。为有效防控风险，该办法中提出了引入债券评级机制，并要求地方政府按规定披露

---

① 执笔：荣艺华。

债券基本情况、财政经济运行情况、地方债务情况等相关信息。这是自 2011 年底推出地方政府自行发债试点以来，深入加强地方政府性债务管理的又一举措。

5 月 8 日，中国人民银行、中国银行业监督管理委员会公告〔2014〕第 8 号发布，鼓励符合条件的金融租赁公司、汽车金融公司、消费金融公司发行金融债券，将消费金融公司作为新的金融债券发行主体引入银行间债券市场，同时降低了金融租赁公司、汽车金融公司申请金融债券发行的条件，并对报送文件、募集资金用途等作出了规定。

6 月，全国银行间同业拆借中心发布《银行间债券市场尝试做市业务规程》，进一步完善了银行间债券市场做市商制度，有利于更充分地发挥尝试做市商机构的积极作用。

9 月 26 日，国家发展和改革委员会发布《关于全面加强企业债券风险防范的若干意见》，通过严格规范发债准入、加强债券存续期监管、强化偿债保障以及规范和约束承销商、信用评级机构行为等措施，形成系统化的防范企业债券风险的政策体系。

10 月 15 日，国家发展和改革委员会发布《企业债券审核新增注意事项》。这是根据《关于全面加强企业债券风险防范的若干意见》制定的细则，它明确了申请发行企业债需要补充的资料和数据，进一步提高了企业债发行的门槛，规范企业债券发行行为。

10 月 17 日，人民银行发布《中国人民银行金融市场司关于非金融机构合格投资人进入银行间债券市场有关事项的通知》（银市场〔2014〕35 号），允许符合条件的非金融机构合格投资人通过非金融机构合格投资人交易平台进行债券投资交易，明确了相应的监管机构、自律组织及市场平台的职责定位，并对交易结算基本流程和主承销商连续报价及有条件换券问题作出了具体要求。

11 月 28 日，人民银行下发《中国人民银行金融市场司关于做好部分合格机构投资者进入银行间债券市场有关工作的通知》（银市场〔2014〕43 号），允许符合条件的农村商业银行、农村合作银行、农村信用社和村镇银行等农村金融机构，信托产品、证券公司资产管理计划、基金管理公司及其子公司的特定客户资产管理计划、保险资产管理公司资产管理产品等非法人投资者进入银行间债券市场。

12 月 18 日，人民银行发布《全国银行间债券市场债券预发行业务管理办法》（中国人民银行公告〔2014〕第 29 号），提高债券发行定价的透明度和竞争性，完善债券收益率曲线，活跃二级市场交易。此办法对预发行券种范围、交易和结算方式等作出要求，并提出了相应的风险控制措施。

（二）政策评估

与往年相比，2014 年出台的中国债券市场政策较多，从发行市场、交易市场、投资者队伍建设、产品创新、基础设施建设等多层面、全角度地推出改革发展措施，既重规范，又有创新，有效地激发了市场的活力，促进了债券市场健康发展。

　　国家发展和改革委员会出台了多项规范措施，进一步加大企业债券发行管理力度，发布的《关于全面加强企业债券风险防范的若干意见》及下发的《企业债券审核新增注意事项》进一步提高了企业债发行的门槛，规范了企业债券发行行为。

　　在提高债券发行定价透明度方面，人民银行发布的《关于银行间债券市场招标发行债券有关事宜的通知》放宽了对发行人主体信用等级、发行规模和投标参与人数量的要求，并对发行人和中介机构在招标结束后需公开披露和上报人民银行的相关信息作出具体要求，鼓励非金融企业招标发行债券。在此基础上，发布的《全国银行间债券市场债券预发行业务管理办法》进一步提高了债券发行定价的透明度和竞争性。为加强企业债券发行制度建设，进一步规范企业债券簿记建档和招标发行行为，保护参与各方的合法权益，国家发展和改革委员会在与市场各方协商基础上制定并发布《企业债券簿记建档发行业务指引（暂行）》和《企业债券招标发行业务指引（暂行）》，进一步规范了企业债券的发行。

　　尝试做市业务在为选拔做市商发挥积极作用的同时，也体现出机构数量较多、类型丰富、做市规模逐年上升等特点，已经成为做市商制度的重要组成部分。《银行间债券市场尝试做市业务规程》的发布进一步完善了银行间债券市场做市商制度，有利于更充分地发挥尝试做市商机构的积极作用，提高二级市场活跃度。

　　商业银行柜台金融债券具有投资门槛低、风险小、收益高、灵活性强等优点，为普通投资者合理的资产配置提供了更多选择。人民银行〔2014〕第3号公告发布后，截至2014年末，国家开发银行和进出口银行已分别通过商业银行柜台分销债券67亿元和30亿元。增加商业银行柜台债券业务品种，不仅为社会公众投资金融债券开辟了新的渠道，也有助于提高市场流动性和社会资金使用效率，改善债券产品的投资者结构，进一步扩大债券市场发展空间，加大债券市场发展深度。

　　2014年，人民银行采取多种措施，增加银行间债券市场投资者种类，丰富市场主体层次。《中国人民银行金融市场司关于非金融机构合格投资人进入银行间债券市场有关事项的通知》允许符合条件的非金融机构合格投资人通过非金融机构合格投资人交易平台进入银行间债券市场，有利于完善多层次债券市场体系，进一步夯实银行间债券市场投资人基础。《中国人民银行金融市场司关于做好部分合格机构投资者进入银行间债券市场有关工作的通知》允许符合条件的农村商业银行、农村合作银行、农村信用社和村镇银行等农村金融机构，信托产品、证券公司资产管理计划、基金管理公司及其子公司的特定客户资产管理计划、保险资产管理公司资产管理产品等非法人投资者进入银行间债券市场，有效地满足了农村类金融机构、多类型资产管理产品的投资需求，进一步丰富了投资者类型。

　　2014年虽然没有出台具体的产品创新政策，但在前几年发行制度逐步完善的基础上，监管部门大力支持市场创新，顺应经济发展需求，满足国家调结构、促转型的需求，银行间债券市场先后引入了碳收益票据、并购票据、定向可转票据和项目收益类票据等重要创新型债券品种，丰富了债券市场产品结构，为发行人和投资人提供了更多产品选择。5月，中广核风电有限公司在银行间市场成功发行首单与节能减排紧密相关的绿色债券——碳收益票据，有效衔接了国内碳交易市场与资本市场。6月，首只用于支付并购价款的债务融资工具——贵州开磷控股（集团）有限责任公司10亿元并购票据成功发行。截至2014年末，累计有9家企业发行9只并购票据，发行金额156.38亿元。7月，首只定向可转票据——杨凌本香农业产业集团有限公司2014年第一期定向可转票据成功发行，既兼顾了不同类型投资者的风险收益偏好，又最大限度地满足企业融资需求，降低企业融资成本。7月，国内首只项目收益票据——14郑州地坤PRN001正式发行，体现了债券市场支持新型城镇化建设的重要作用，并且引导地方融资平台逐步剥离政府融资职能，探索建立透明规范的城市建设投融资体制。

金融支持实体经济发展是金融业发展的使命和根本目的，2014年在债券市场有效支持实体经济发展的基础上，有关部委继续出台政策切实加大对地方政府、小微企业和消费的支持力度。

在支持地方政府发展方面，财政部发布的《2014年地方政府债券自发自还试点办法》，允许上海、浙江、广东、深圳、江苏、山东、北京、江西、宁夏、青岛等十省市进行地方债自发自还试点，即试点省市在国务院批准的发债规模限额内，自行组织本地区政府债券发行、支付利息和偿还本金。该办法正式公布后，广东省于6月23日发行首单自发自还地方债，随后其余试点省市的发行工作相继顺利推进。本轮试点共计发行自发自还地方政府债券1 092亿元。地方政府债券自发自还试点的启动是探索建立规范的地方政府举债筹资机制的重要一步，对于缓解地方政府偿债压力、化解债务风险、提高地方财政透明度等都具有积极意义。在8月31日全国人大常委会表决通过修改后的《中华人民共和国预算法》后，未来地方政府债券自发自还以及地方政府债券市场规模有望逐步扩大。

为支持商业银行发行金融债券专项用于小微企业贷款，人民银行发布了《关于金融债券专项用于小微企业贷款后续监督管理有关事宜的通知》，有利于确保相关债券募集资金全部用于小微企业贷款，进一步改善小微企业金融服务。

中国人民银行、中国银行业监督管理委员会的〔2014〕第8号公告首次将消费金融公司作为新的金融债券发行主体引入银行间市场，降低了金融租赁公司、汽车金融公司申请金融债券发行的条件，加大了金融对消费的支持力度。

在进一步健全反映市场供求关系的国债收益率曲线方面，11月2日，财政部在其网站首次发布了中国关键期限国债收益率曲线，主要内容包括1年、3年、5年、7年、10年等关键期限国债及其收益率水平形成的图表，由中央结算公司编制及提供。此次财政部发布的国债收益率曲线有利于进一步推进财政信息公开工作，对于提高国债管理政策透明度、发挥国债市场化利率的定价基准作用、健全国债收益率曲线，以及促进国债市场持续稳定健康发展具有重要意义。

在构建高效透明规范的金融市场基础设施方面，2014 年，人民银行与中国证券监督管理委员会以《金融市场基础设施原则》为标准，联合开展相关评估，启动对我国金融市场基础设施评估工作，监督管理国内金融市场基础设施。目前，已有序地开展了基础设施自评、交叉评估和监管部门外部评估等一系列扎实有效的评估工作。

在与国际自律组织及国际基础设施接轨方面，上海清算所 8 月与欧清银行集团签署合作意向书，探讨业务和技术方面的合作方式，9 月与芝加哥商品交易所（CME）签署合作备忘录，在产品开发、平台技术、员工交流等方面开展全方位合作。9 月，银行间交易商协会参加了第六次中英经济财金对话系列活动中的中英金融圆桌会，就加强两国金融市场自律组织层面的合作达成共识。10 月，中央国债登记结算有限公司承办了第十八届亚太中央托管组织（ACG）年会，发布了《西安倡议》，提出：所有 ACG 成员承诺相互畅通交流，中央托管机构等核心金融基础设施共同培育建立稳健、高效、包容、系统的亚洲金融基础设施合作圈，以推动亚太证券市场的发展；要发挥中央托管机构的规模经济优势，促进市场高效有序，发展跨境互联；要坚持平等、互助、开放、共赢的原则，有效顺应市场多样性，广泛寻求境内外利益攸关方的参与。

（三）债券市场发展展望

2015 年是全面深化改革开放的关键之年，是债券市场在经济新常态下改革开放、大发展的关键之年。在稳增长、调结构、促改革的新常态下，市场的活力进一步释放，各项创新动力将不断增强，债券市场将迎来新常态式的发展，市场进一步扩容，产品创新不断加快，投资者群体进一步拓宽，基础设施建设继续完善，对外开放程度进一步提升。

五、货币市场发展政策[①]

2014 年，在我国全面深化改革和实施稳健货币政策的背景下，监管部门采取多种措施，促进货币市场规范、健康发展，市场主体不断丰富和增加，市场规模继续稳步扩大，利率中枢下移，波动幅度减少，货币市场有效发挥了传导货币政策、促进利率市场化及加强流动性管理的功能。

（一）同业拆借市场

2014 年，全国银行间同业拆借市场并无新的、大的政策出台，在 2007 年《同业拆借管理办法》的制度框架下，市场管理的灵活性加大，从注重事前管理到强调事中、事后管理，更加突出信息披露管理，加强市场透明度建设。在此基调上，2014 年，同业拆

---

① 执笔：荣艺华。

借市场主体大幅增加，交易规模稳步增长，利率中枢有所下行，波动幅度逐步收窄，对外开放程度不断提高，流动性管理功能进一步增强。

人民银行积极促进同业拆借市场健康发展，2014 年新增了 97 家金融机构进入全国银行间同业拆借市场，市场成员共有九大类，总计 1 219 家。其中，银行业金融机构 902 家，财务公司 129 家，证券公司 87 家，信托公司 54 家，保险公司 10 家，资产管理公司 4 家，金融租赁公司 18 家，汽车金融公司 13 家，其他机构 2 家。

同业拆借市场在 2007 年经历了近 400% 的跨越式增长后，稳步增长，但 2013 年出现了明显回落，从上年的 46.74 万亿元下降至 35.52 万亿元，降幅达 24.00%。2014 年同业拆借市场恢复增长势头，全年累计成交 37.66 万亿元，日均成交 1 506.51 亿元，同比增长 6.04%。

同业拆借市场利率呈现两头高、中间低的走势，同业拆借全年加权平均利率为 2.96%，比 2013 年下降了 71 个基点。以 7 天期利率为例，春节前后，市场利率从 1 月中旬开始快速上升，至 1 月 20 日达到全年最高点 6.64%；随后单边下降至全年最低点——3 月 12 日的 2.34%；4 月开始，市场利率小幅波动，波动区间在 3%~4%，且波幅逐渐缩小；临近年末，市场利率明显上升，至 12 月 22 日出现年内次高点 6.26%，之后小幅回落，至 12 月 31 日收于 4.89%。从利率波动幅度来看，较上年有所收窄，全年拆借利率极差为 430 个基点，同比缩小 540 个基点。

同业拆借市场交易期限继续以短期为主。2014 年同业拆借交易中，7 天期以内交易占比 94.53%。

同业拆借市场交易结构中，银行业金融机构的交易占比继续维持在 80% 以上。2014 年，银行业金融机构同业拆借交易占比为 82.58%，非银行金融机构交易占比为 17.42%。股份制银行的交易量最大，占整个市场的 36.33%，接下来依次为城市商业银行和政策性银行，交易量占比分别为 13.58% 和 8.89%。非银行金融机构全年成交 13.12 万亿元，同比增长 53.27%。其中，最为活跃的机构是证券公司和财务公司，交易量分别占整个市场的 10.84% 和 4.88%。

货币市场融资格局继续保持银行业金融机构融出，非银行金融机构融入的特点。其中，净融出量最大的是政策性银行，累计净融出 47.40 万亿元，同比增长 53.40%；其次是四大行，累计净融出 37.02 万亿元（2013 年净融入接近 2 000 亿元）；此外，股份制商业银行也净融出 14.43 万亿元，同比增长 232.49%。这三类机构在同业拆借市场净融出资金 13.67 万亿元，占资金净融出总量的 83.51%。货币市场上资金融入最多的依次是城市商业银行、证券公司和农村金融机构，全年分别净融入 33.97 万亿元、27.52 万亿元和 21.49 万亿元，在资金净融入方占比为 31.35%、25.41% 和 19.84%。三类机构在同业拆借市场净融入资金 13.09 万亿元，占资金净融入总量的 79.95%。非银行金融机构除资产管理公司、信托公司和金融租赁公司有少量资金融出外，其他均为净融入，其中，证券公司资金净融入量最大，为 27.52 万亿元，同比增长 75.29%。

2014 年，中国工商银行新加坡分行和中国银行台北分行进入银行间同业拆借市场。这是继 2009 年、2010 年中国银行（香港）有限公司和中国银行澳门分行进入境内银行间同业拆借市场后，市场新增的两家境外人民币清算行。与此相伴，境外人民币清算行在境内同业拆借市场交易规模大幅增长，交易量从 2009 年的 177.4 亿元增长至 2014 年的 4 788.6 亿元，增长了 27 倍，有力地支持了人民币跨境使用。

2015 年，同业拆借市场的管理将更加注重事中、事后管理，更加突出信息披露管理，加强市场透明度建设。在我国改革开放的大背景下，利率市场化将进一步推进，汇率形成机制不断完善，资本项目可兑换和金融对外开放有序进行，自贸区等区域金融改革继续深入，人民币国际化步伐加快，金融市场创新会更加显著。这些金融改革和开放的推进，将进一步激发银行间同业拆借市场的活力，市场成员将进一步丰富和增加，市场规模继续扩大，市场对外开放力度加大，市场的流动性管理功能进一步增强。

（二）回购市场

自 1997 年银行间债券市场成立以来，以银行间债券回购市场为主体的债券回购市场经历了 10 多年的快速发展，市场广度和深度不断扩大，银行间债券回购市场交易规模继 2011 年首次达到 100 万亿元后，2014 年突破 200 万亿元。回购市场不仅对金融机构资产负债管理和流动性管理发挥着越来越重要的作用，而且也逐渐成为人民银行公开市场操作的重要平台，及货币市场短期利率的重要参考。

2014 年，没有出台与回购市场有关的政策。银行间债券回购市场在 2013 年回购主协议推出之后，市场健康快速发展，交易规模大幅增加，交易期限结构继续呈现短期化特征，回购利率总体下行，政策性金融债在回购标的中占比最大，大型商业银行和政策性银行表现为资金净融出。

银行间债券回购市场全年累计成交 224.42 万亿元，日均成交 8 976.9 亿元，同比增长 41.89%。其中，质押式回购成交 212.42 万亿元，日均成交 8 496.76 亿元，同比增长 39.77%；买断式回购成交 12.00 万亿元，日均成交 480.14 亿元，同比增长 93.97%。

回购市场利率呈现两头高、中间低的走势，但回购利率及波动幅度均较 2013 年有所下降。质押式回购加权平均利率为 2.98%，比 2013 年下降 56 个基点。最高点为 1 月 29 日的 5.90%，最低点为 3 月 11 日的 1.93%，利率极差为 397 基点，比 2013 年下降 570 个基点。买断式回购日加权平均利率为 3.44%，比 2013 年下降 52 个基点，利率极差为 399 个基点。

在交易期限结构方面，7 天以下的质押式回购交易占比达 92.72%，其中，隔夜品种成交 166.91 万亿元，占质押式回购总成交量的 78.57%。14 天以上期限回购交易占比有所下降，其中 14 天品种成交量占比为 4.52%，21 天及以上的交易成交占比为

2.76%。买断式回购交易期限结构重新呈现短期化，7 天以下的交易占总成交量比重达 87.31%，较 2013 年增加 4.29 个百分点。

在回购标的中，以国债、央行票据和政策性金融债为标的的质押式回购占比为 79.09%，比 2013 年增加了 1.13 个百分点。其中，以央行票据作为回购标的的交易占比由 2013 年的 4.11%进一步减少至 0.76%，但以政策性金融债作为回购标的的交易占比为 40.70%，上升了 4.55 个百分点。同时，以短期融资券、超短期融资券、中期票据、集合票据和企业债为标的的质押式回购占比为 15.86%，比 2013 年下降了 0.79 个百分点。在买断式回购标的中，以国债、央行票据和政策性金融债为标的的占比为 45.44%，比 2013 年增加 0.28 个百分点。以短期融资券、超短期融资券、中期票据、集合票据和企业债为标的占比由 2013 年的 49.28%上升到 51.30%。

在融资结构中，城市商业银行、农村商业银行和农村合作银行、股份制商业银行分列融入资金的前三位，占正回购总量的比重分别为 30.13%、14.89%和 14.40%；大型商业银行、政策性银行、城市商业银行分列融出资金的前三位，占逆回购总量的比重分别为 21.56%、19.08%和 17.03%。

随着我国利率市场化改革的持续推进，以及金融市场改革开放力度的不断加大，银行间债券回购市场也将继续稳步快速发展，产品结构将会进一步丰富，各项制度建设和基础设施建设不断完善，银行间债券回购市场作为人民银行进行公开市场操作的重要平台，将为引导货币市场利率走势和调节市场流动性创造良好的实施条件。

（三）票据市场

2014 年票据市场总体运行平稳，银行承兑汇票业务持续平稳增长，票据融资总量先降后升，同比实现增长较快，机构活跃度继续保持高位。其中，第一季度，受年初一般性信贷需求旺盛影响，票据融资余额小幅下降；第二季度起，市场资金面总体充裕，票据承兑和融资余额双双实现稳步增长。在降息、降准等货币政策实施后，在公开市场、再贴现、再贷款利率引导下，票据市场利率总体呈震荡下跌和季末回升的波动运行态势，跌幅逐季收窄和年末小幅回升。

2 月，国家发展改革委和中国银监会联合发布《关于印发商业银行服务政府指导价政府定价目录的通知》（发改价格〔2014〕268 号），其中明确：商业银行为银行客户提供的基础金融服务实行政府指导价、政府定价管理。实行政府指导价、政府定价的基础金融服务包括部分转账汇款、现金汇款、取现和票据等商业银行服务项目。与 2003 年的《商业银行服务价格管理暂行办法》相比，"银行承兑汇票"定价方式已调出原政府指导定价范围。

4 月，中国人民银行、银监会、证监会、保监会、国家外汇局联合印发《关于规范金融机构同业业务的通知》（银发〔2014〕127 号），就规范同业业务种类和会计核算、加强和改善同业业务内外部管理、推动开展规范的资产负债业务创新等方面提出了十八条规范性意见。其中明确：买入返售（卖出回购）业务项下的金融资产应当为银行承兑汇票，债券、央票等在银行间市场、证券交易所市场交易的具有合理公允价值和较高流动性的金融资产，但不包括商业承兑汇票。同业投资项下的金融资产包括金融机构购买或委托其他金融机构购买的金融债、次级债等在银行间市场或证券交易所市场交易的同业金融资产，以及商业银行理财产品、信托投资计划、证券投资基金、证券公司资产管理计划、基金管理公司及子公司资产管理计划、保险业资产管理机构资产管理产品等特定目的载体，不包括银行承兑汇票和商业承兑汇票。

5月，银监会办公厅下发《中国银监会办公厅关于规范商业银行同业业务治理的通知》（银监办发〔2014〕140号），文件规定：商业银行应具备与所开展同业业务规模和复杂程度相适应的同业业务治理体系，由法人总部对同业业务进行统一管理，将同业业务纳入全面风险管理；商业银行开展同业业务实行专营部门制，由法人总部建立或指定专营部门负责经营；商业银行同业业务专营部门对可以通过金融交易市场进行电子化交易的同业业务，不得委托其他部门或分支机构办理；并建立健全同业业务授权管理体系、授信管理政策、交易对手准入机制等。

5月，中国人民银行上海总部印发《中国（上海）自由贸易试验区分账核算业务实施细则（试行）》和《中国（上海）自由贸易试验区分账核算业务风险审慎管理细则（试行）》（见银总部发〔2014〕46号），其中规定：机构自由贸易账户可使用电子商业汇票，银行业金融机构应对自由贸易账户签发和转让的电子商业汇票进行相应的审核。

8月，为贯彻落实国务院常务会议关于"加大支农、支小再贷款和再贴现力度"的要求，提高金融服务"三农"、小微企业等国民经济薄弱环节的能力，人民银行对部分分支行增加再贴现额度120亿元，要求全部用于支持金融机构扩大"三农"、小微企业信贷投放，同时采取有效措施，进一步完善再贴现管理，引导金融机构扩大对"三农"、小微企业信贷投放，促进降低社会融资成本。

2014年，人民银行实施稳健的货币政策，通过各种货币政策工具的组合，将总量和结构调节有机结合，有效调节市场流动性，引导金融支持实体经济。其中，通过加大支农、支小再贷款和再贴现力度，引导金融机构扩大对"三农"、小微企业信贷投放，促进降低社会融资成本。

各项定向宽松货币政策的预调微调，为市场提供了充裕流动性的同时，也为商业银行票据业务的发展提供了有利的市场环境，金融机构票据承兑和融资余额持续增长，票据转贴现业务交易活跃，充分发挥了票据业务在支持实体经济、助力结构调整、促进中小企业信用增级和融资支持方面的重要作用。另一方面，在人民银行存贷款利率、再贴现利率、公开市场操作利率等基准利率的引导下，票据市场利率总体出现震荡下行，有助于降低社会融资成本。

近年来，同业业务的功能从原来的调剂资金头寸，逐步转向了绕过表内信贷行业限制、化解资本约束、降低存贷比和扩大资产负债表的有效途径，金融机构将同业业务演变为实质上的信贷类业务。票据业务的转贴现和回购业务则是银行同业业务的重要组成部分。2014年4月，为规范商业银行同业业务，减少资金中间环节，促进资金流向实体经济，人民银行等五部委联合下发了《关于规范金融机构同业业务的通知》，银监会随后下发《中国银监会办公厅关于规范商业银行同业业务治理的通知》，两份文件对同业业务种类和会计核算、同业业务内外部管理等方面都作出了明确的规定。对票据市场来说，上述规定一方面使得商业承兑汇票无法作为回购业务标的，减少了商业银行票据资产摆布空间，另一方面促使商业银行票据业务向总行上收，降低了票据回购市场的交易活跃度。通知下发以来，票据回购交易意愿和成交量均出现同比明显下降。

此外，10月和12月，银监会发布《关于开展银行业金融机构同业新规执行情况专项检查的通知》和《中国银监会关于全面开展银行业金融机构加强内部管控遏制违规经营和违法犯罪专项检查工作的通知》。前者涉及票据、资本计提、理财、信贷资产转让和同业专营公司治理等14项法律法规；后者重点排查违规经营和违法犯罪高发的信贷业务、存款业务、票据业务、同业业务、理财业务、财务管理等领域。两次检查重点关注商业银行的票据回购业务、票据管理体制改革和票据业务合规性等方面，短期内各项票据业务的规模增长速度出现小幅下降，但对票据业务的专业化管理和规范发展将有积极作用。

《商业银行服务政府指导价政府定价目录》的下发，意味着延续了20年的万分之五的银行承兑汇票承兑手续费定价终于迎来了市场化改革。对于票据市场发展来说，银行承兑汇票的市场化定价机制一方面增加了银行中间收入渠道，另一方面，票据承兑业务的风险承担实质有助于培养银行的自主定价能力，有利于票据市场的稳健发展。

作为《中国（上海）自由贸易试验区分账核算业务实施细则（试行）》的配套规定，《中国（上海）自由贸易试验区分账核算业务风险审慎管理细则（试行）》允许机构自由贸易账户使用电子商业汇票，为区内企业的支付结算和贸易融资提供便捷有效的途径，同时也对电子票据业务的发展起到积极的推动作用。此外，自贸区先行先试会进一步推动票据市场的业务创新和跨市场发展。

未来几年，我国经济发展"新常态"特征逐步显现，在产业升级、结构调整的背景下，票据市场将继续拥有良好的发展机遇，但票据业务在价格、渠道和资产运用等方面将面临着更加激烈和广泛的竞争。电子票据、交易互联网化、票据资金化运作、跨市场创新等或将成为今后的市场亮点。

六、财富管理市场发展政策[①]

2015年1月20日，国家统计局发布的数据显示，2014年全年全国居民人均可支配

---

① 执笔：王琪。

收入 20 167 元，比 2013 年名义增长 10.1%，扣除价格因素实际增长 8.0%。农村居民人均可支配收入 10 489 元，比上年增长 11.2%，扣除价格因素实际增长 9.2%。2014 年居民收入增幅超过 GDP。

居民收入增加是财富管理市场发展的有力保障。2014 年，我国财富管理市场规模保持增长态势，但各类机构之间的竞争更加激烈，理财产品收益出现分化现象。商业银行理财产品仍处于领先地位，信托产品紧随其后，券商集合理财产品虽规模不大，但得益于股市的良好表现，其收益表现较好。

（一）银行理财产品市场

中国社科院金融所财富管理研究中心统计的数据显示：2014 年全年，银行理财产品发行市场持续平稳增长，291 家商业银行发行银行理财产品共计 6.85 万款，募集资金规模约达 43.0 万亿元人民币，产品数量和募集资金规模同比分别增长 57.1% 与 49.7%（见图 5–3）。银行理财市场依然在国内财富管理市场中保持着领军地位。银行理财产品市场的持续膨胀不仅依赖于商业银行谋求转型发展的主动创新，更依赖于社会融资客观需求的推动。

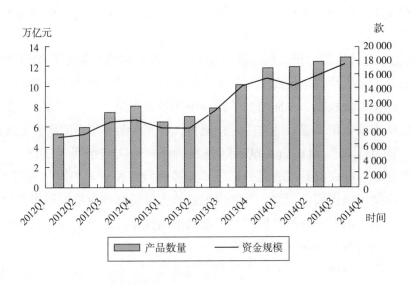

资料来源：中国社科院金融所财富管理研究中心。

图 5–3　2012—2014 年银行理财产品发行数量和募集规模

规模继续增长，但银行理财收益却未能继续上涨。2013 年，在"调结构、去杠杆"的政策背景下，融资环境趋紧，市场利率高企，尤其是下半年以来，银行理财产品收益率节节攀升，并出现"钱荒"现象。进入 2014 年，银行理财产品收益率出现趋势性反转，进入下行通道，主要缘于相对宽松的货币政策以及同业业务的收紧。伴随着以恒丰银行为代表的兑付危机事件的发生，金融机构的风险偏好明显下降，对于银行理财产品的发行设计和风险管控也更加严格。鉴于国内经济存在下行压力，央行采取多种措施引导利率下行，为银行理财产品的预期收益率下行奠定基调。

2014年11月，银行理财产品收益率创年内新低，1个月产品的平均收益率为4.40%，3个月产品的平均收益率为4.92%。令人意外的是，11月22日央行降息后银行理财产品收益率不降反升，12月份，理财产品收益率出现反弹。这一方面是年末效应的体现，另一方面，这是因为股市向好对商业银行形成"存款外流"压力，商业银行希望通过提升产品收益留住客户资金。

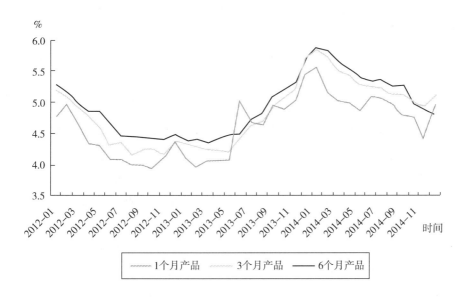

资料来源：中国社科院金融所财富管理研究中心。

图5－4 银行理财产品月度收益率走势

在监管方面，探索银行理财业务服务实体经济的新产品和新模式，鼓励直接投资，化解理财业务潜在风险，推动理财业务向资产管理业务转型是2014年理财业务监管的主旋律。

遵循这一主线，银监会于2014年2月下发《中国银监会办公厅关于2014年银行理财业务监管工作的指导意见》（"39号文"），对全年的理财监管工作提出八大重点。与"107号文"一脉相承，"39号文"重点关注信息披露、刚性兑付、风险传递等问题，探索理财业务服务实体经济的新模式。在信息披露方面，主要强化理财业务非现场监管，落实理财信息登记系统相关规定。在风险控制方面，以管理架构调整为基础，从资金投向、风险控制、会计核算、信息披露等多角度推动理财业务风险隔离机制的确立。对银行理财业务实现事业部改革，统一产品设计、成本核算和风险控制。在业务创新方面，积极鼓励银行理财业务探索新的产品和模式，进行真实投资，更好地直接服务于实体经济。

理财事业部制改革。2014 年 7 月，银监会发布《中国银监会关于完善银行理财业务组织管理体系有关事项的通知》（"35 号文"），继续落实银行理财事业部改革，要求银行业金融机构应按照单独核算、风险隔离、行为规范、归口管理等要求开展理财业务事业部制改革，设立专门的理财业务经营部门，负责集中统一经营管理全行理财业务，并要求将理财业务风险纳入全行风险管理体系，建立风险缓释机制。此外"35 号文"明确要求银行不得提供含有刚性兑付内容的理财产品介绍，从推出理财直接融资工具和银行理财管理计划到明确表示不得提供刚性兑付的介绍，这些举措彰显了监管部门推动理财业务转型的决心。但从观念上改变投资者对理财产品刚性兑付的观念并非易事。

存款偏离度管理。2014 年 9 月，银监会联合财政部、人民银行下发《中国银监会办公厅 财政部办公厅 人民银行办公厅关于加强商业银行存款偏离度管理有关事项的通知》（"236 号文"），对商业银行月末、季末存款"冲时点"行为进行约束，规定商业银行月末存款偏离度不得超过 3%，明确规定不得通过理财产品倒存，即，理财产品期限结构设计不合理，发行和到期时间集中于每月下旬，商业银行往往于月末、季末等关键时点将理财资金转为存款。受"236 号文"影响，理财产品的到期日分布或将更加平均，银行理财产品的期限分布及收益类型分布也可能有所变化，商业银行将通过长期限产品和保本型产品的发行，提升日均存款余额。

重新修订《管理办法》。2014 年 12 月，银监会下发《商业银行理财业务监督管理办法（征求意见稿）》，向商业银行征求意见，明确将"更好化解银行理财业务的潜在风险，推动理财业务回归资产管理业务本质"作为总体目标，主要涵盖如下五方面内容：

其一，化解风险，推动理财业务合理转型。重点在于破除"隐性担保"和"刚性兑付"，落实风险承担主体。按照"实质重于形式"的原则计算风险资产，计提风险准备。保本型产品及预期收益型产品中的"非标"资产部分需计入表内核算。净值型开放式产品投资的"非标"资产及无期限错配的项目融资类产品的"非标"资产无须回表。"有保有压"的政策导向旨在推动银行理财产品由预期收益型产品向开放式净值型和无期限错配的项目融资类产品转型。

其二，对接企业融资需求，直接服务实体经济。明确了理财产品的独立性与破产隔离的法律效果，允许理财产品独立开设资金账户和证券账户，鼓励理财产品开展直接投资，以"去杠杆""去链条""去通道"为目标，实现理财资金与企业真实融资项目直接对接，降低企业融资成本。

其三，强化风险匹配，更好保护投资者利益。细化风险评级标准，实现销售分层，项目融资类、股权投资类及另类投资产品仅能面向高净值客户、私人银行客户和机构客户销售。

其四，主动调整，适应统一监管标准。努力实现与其他资产管理行业中其他金融产品统一监管标准。

其五，实现市场化与专业化。明确银行理财产品主要类型包括结构性产品、开放式和封闭式净值型产品、预期收益率型产品、项目融资类产品、股权投资类产品、另类投资以及其他创新产品。

回顾近两年来的监管动作，从2013年"8号文"对非标资产的规范，到银行理财管理计划和理财直接融资工具的试点，再到独立的理财事业部制改革，最后到近段时间的商业银行法修订启动，它们都为银行理财业务指出了一个关键发展方向——回归资产管理本质。随着银行理财管理计划的参与银行逐渐增多，理财直接融资工具的发行量和交易量将稳步增长，这将促进非标投资"去通道化"以及理财产品的开放式、基金化转型。

2015年，开放式净值型理财产品或将成为市场主流，这也是监管层试图打破刚性兑付的重要工具。净值型理财产品最大的优点在于赎回条款的灵活性。传统的滚动型理财产品只能在开放期内办理申购及赎回，而净值型理财产品在资金灵活性上有了很大突破，任何时间客户都可预约申购或赎回本产品，银行于每月产品开放日受理客户预约申请。由于银行每日公布产品净值，因此，净值型理财产品具备信息透明的特点，方便客户随时随地掌握产品净值走势。

理财产品的收益率无疑是投资者最关注的指标之一。由于净值型理财产品属于非保本浮动型理财产品，在资产管理计划推出之前，市场普遍担心其预期收益率是否波动较大。但实际情况却是，净值型理财产品不但实际年化收益率普遍高于同类理财产品，并且每期公布的收益率非常稳定。这要归功于目前市场上的净值型理财产品投资标的多为债权类标的，主要投资于高流动性资产及债权类资产，如债券及债券基金、货币市场基金、同业存款等，资产组合的安全系数较高且收益较稳定。

数据显示，2014年上半年，开放式净值型产品发展速度最快，共募集资金1.17万亿元，同比增长174.53%，占全部理财产品的募集金额比例从2013年上半年的1.27%增长至2.37%。未来，净值型理财产品数量与占比或将进一步提升。

（二）券商集合理财产品市场

2015年3月6日，基金业协会公布的数据显示，截至2014年底，证券公司资管业务管理资产规模为7.95万亿元，较2013年底增加2.74万亿元，增幅为53%。从主动管理、被动管理产品规模以及占比来看：证券公司主动管理规模占比较小，仅为17%；被动产品规模占比较大，占比为83%。

得益于A股市场与债券市场双结构性牛市，2014年，券商集合理财产品业绩靓丽。全年业绩可查的1 631只券商集合产品（剔除清盘及成立未满一年的产品）平均收益率达13.22%，呈现普涨局面，其中，1 534只集合理财产品获得正收益，占比超过九成，其中，25 只产品收益率超过 100%，几乎都被分级产品 B 端占据，这 25 只集合理财产品中有 13 只债券型产品，9 只混合型产品，3 只股票型产品。

2014 年，证监会辖下资产管理机构迎来新一轮制度红利。2014 年 5 月 9 日，国务院出台新"国九条"明确了资本市场改革的总体方向。证监会于 5 月 13 日、6 月 12 日相继推出《关于进一步推进证券经营机构创新发展的意见》与《关于大力推进证券投资基金行业创新发展的意见》（以下简称"两项创新发展意见"），明确提出：加快建设现代资产管理机构、支持产品创新、推进监管转型的三大目标。2014 年 9 月，监管层下发《证券期货经营机构资产管理业务管理办法（征求意见稿）》（以下简称《意见稿》）和《关于规范证券公司、基金管理公司及其子公司从事特定客户资产管理业务有关事项的通知（征求意见稿）》（以下简称《通知》），重塑了证监会所辖资产管理机构的监管框架和业务边界。

监管框架的调整折射出资产管理业务由"机构分类监管"向"业务分类监管"的突破。重塑监管框架首先体现为统一监管部门和监管准则。2014 年 4 月，证监会调整内设部门，将此前分别监管券商资管和基金子公司的原机构部、基金部合并成立"证券基金机构监管部"，资管业务纳入统一监管；《意见稿》统一了证券公司、基金管理公司、期货公司及相应资管子公司的监管细则，并授权证券投资基金业协会对证券公司、基金管理公司及其子公司进行登记，对其资产管理计划实施备案，期货业协会负责期货公司资管业务的登记和备案。此外，"两项创新发展意见"明确了将转变监管方式、放宽行业准入作为创新发展的重要内容。转变监管方式的要义在于建立适应创新发展的监管模式，统一监管尺度，从重事前审批向加强事中、事后监管转变，简化行政程序，探索"负面清单"管理模式。放宽行业准入，侧重于实施牌照管理，探索功能监管。

业务边界的调整首先体现在拓宽投资范围，投资范围的扩大将提升券商、期货、基金资产管理业务的市场竞争力，重塑行业格局。《意见稿》将资产管理业务区分"一对一"和"一对多"两种形式，将"未通过证券期货交易所、全国中小企业股份转让系统或银行间市场转让的股权、债权及其他财产权利，证监会认可的其他财产"正式纳入投资范围，并命名为"另类资产管理计划"，而此前券商集合资产管理计划不能投资于此，基金公司则须通过专门的子公司设立专项资产管理计划方可投资。此外，与《意见稿》配套发布的《通知》对资产管理业务作出诸多细节性规范，严控风险，内容涵盖：健全投资者适当性制度和销售机构遴选机制；鼓励开发主动管理产品，禁止为特定多客户开展通道业务；分级资产管理计划的杠杆设计与风险收益相匹配；禁止多个产品间的期限错配、资金池以及关联交易等操作；要求资管机构设立专门的合规风控部门等。

上述资管新政为证监会所辖机构的资产管理业务带来直接红利。同时，证券行业在其他业务领域的创新发展也为资管业务带来间接红利，最具影响力的是沪港通与资产证券化。根据证监会发布的《关于证券公司参与沪港通业务试点有关事项的通知》，证券公司资产管理业务可参与沪港通交易，可设立专门投资于香港股票或者同时投资于内地股票和香港股票的资产管理计划，有利于拓展投资范围并推动券商资管业务升级。南方基金拟推出首只沪港通基金——南方恒指 ETF，沪港通基金的推出将降低投资者参与沪港通的门槛。2014 年 11 月 19 日，证监会发布《证券公司及基金管理公司子公司资产证券化业务管理规定》及配套工作指引，取消事前行政审批，实行基金业协会事后备案和基础资产负面清单管理。资产证券化从非标资产到标准资产的转变正式开始，证券公司有发展资产证券化的前期经验——专项资产管理计划和企业资产证券化，在盘活存量的大背景下，金融体系和企业累积的庞大的存量资产将推动资产证券化成为券商资产管理业务的一大亮点。

2015 年，券商集合理财市场或将延续 2014 年的良好走势，第一季度或将突破 8 万亿元大关。A 股市场的整体表现是券商集合理财收益表现好坏的基础。券商资管产品有望成为除两融、股票质押融资之外的又一放量业务。

（三）信托产品市场

2014 年，在经济下行和竞争加剧的双重挑战下，信托业结束了自 2008 年以来的高速增长阶段，步入了转型发展的阶段。

中国信托业协会公布的数据显示：截至 2014 年末，信托行业管理的信托资产规模为 13.98 万亿元（平均每家信托公司 2 055.88 亿元），较 2013 年末的 10.91 万亿元，同比增长 28.14%，但增幅明显回落；从营业收入看，截至 2014 年末，信托业实现经营收入 954.95 亿元（平均每家信托公司 14.04 亿元），相比 2013 年末的 832.60 亿元，同比增长 14.69%，但较 2013 年末的 30.42% 的同比增长率，同比增幅回落了 15.73 个百分点。

与信托公司经营效益增速下滑的情况相反，2014 年度，信托业给受益人实现的信托收益却稳中有升。就已清算信托项目为受益人实现的信托收益总额而言，据银监会统计，2014 年，信托行业共为受益人实现 4 506 亿元的收益，相比 2013 年度的 2 944 亿元，增加了 1 562 亿元，增幅达 53.06%，远高于信托业自身业绩的增幅。

在风险控制方面，严控信托风险传导，保持信托业稳健发展成为 2014 年信托行业的主要任务。从年初的"诚至金开 1 号"兑付风波到年末《信托业保障基金管理办法》的颁布实施，2014 年信托业的转型发展紧扣"风险"这一主题。

2014 年 4 月 8 日，中国银监会办公厅发布了《中国银监会办公厅关于信托公司风险监管的指导意见》（银监办发〔2014〕99 号，下称"99 号文"），总结下来，该文主要围绕"尽责、清理、转型"三方面进行监管。

1. "尽责"

（1）项目经理尽责。"99 号文"明确了对所有信托项目，尤其是高风险项目，应安排专人跟踪，责任明确到人。（2）股东尽责。信托公司股东应承诺或在信托公司章程中约定，当信托公司出现流动性风险时，给予必要的流动性支持。信托公司经营损失侵蚀资本的，应在净资本中全额扣减，并相应压缩业务规模，或由股东及时补充资本。（3）信托公司尽责。信托公司必须从产品设计、尽职调查、风控监管、产品营销、后续管理、信息披露和风险处置等环节入手，全方位、全过程、动态化地进行管理。尤其针对项目的投后管理方面，要时时跟进和风险监测，对于房地产等重点风险领域需要定期进行压力测试。对于风险的处置方式必须市场化。（4）销售人员尽责。"坚持合格投资人标准"和"坚持私募标准"，准确划分投资人群，坚持把合适的产品卖给适合的对象，承担售卖的责任。（5）监管部门尽责。对信托公司业务范围实行严格的准入审批管理，对业务范围项下的具体产品实行报告制度，凡是入市的产品都必须按程序和统一要求在入市前10天逐笔向监管机构报告。

2. "清理"

（1）信托资金池的清理。规定"信托公司不得开展非标准化理财资金池等具有影子银行特征的业务"。同时要求对于已经开展的非标准化理财资金池业务，需提供具体情况和说明，并提出整改方案，于2014年6月30日前报送监管机构。（2）理清各个层面的职责权限及相对应的薪酬激励和处罚机制。理清信托公司股东（大）会、董事会、监事会、经营层的职责权限，各司其职，结合自身特点制定恢复与处置机制。（3）完善监管机制。厘清监管责任边界，对于融资平台、房地产、矿业、产能过剩行业、影子银行业务等风险隐患进行重点监控。

3. "转型"

"99号文"中非常重要的内容是关于信托未来的业务方向在哪里。2013年，自基金资管的产品逐步被市场所接收和认可之后，信托产品的优势不再那么突出。银监会在"99号文"中鼓励信托公司的差异化发展，提出了真正的股权投资业务、并购业务、收费类业务、信贷资产证券化业务、家族财富管理、公益信托等。

针对狂奔的信托资产规模和不断暴露的信托产品风险，2014年8月，银监会向信托公司下发最严信托评级办法——《信托公司监管评级与分类监管指引》（以下简称《指引》）。根据《指引》，评级要素包括风险管理、资产管理和合规管理三个方面。风险管理分为四个部分，分别是公司治理、内部控制、信托业务风险管理和净资本情况；资产管理要素分为五个部分，分别是综合经营能力、信托业务经营和盈利能力、研发与创新能力、营销能力、公司声誉；合规管理要素分为七个部分，分别是合规管理体系、固有业务合规性、信托业务合规性、信息披露合规性、关联交易合规性、运行效果评价以及限制性条款。

2014年底，作为总结，监管层在2014信托业年会上明确提出信托行业的"八大责任"，进一步规范和促进信托行业稳健发展与转型。第一，明确受托责任，划分买者和卖者的责任界限。下一步，银监会将制定信托尽责指引，促进信托公司更好地履职尽责，进而实现担责问责。第二，明确经纪责任。经纪责任是信托公司接受委托成立信托计划后必须明确的内部责任，可以称之为"三人行"制度，实行分权制衡。每一个信托计划的经营团队必须由项目发起人、项目营运人、项目报告人这"三人"构成。发起人是最先发现或提出信托项目的人，明确其尽责调查、立项和产品设计责任；营运人负责组织产品销售、资金归集、划付使用及全流程管理；报告人跟踪项目营运过程，按信息披露的约定，真实报送信息情况。第三，明确维权责任。目前，我国实行单一产权制度，信托法规定信托财产仅仅是由委托人委托给受托人，从而带来信托财产的模糊。这就需要引入信托财产登记制度，通过登记制度来解决信托财产转移不足的问题。第四，明确核算责任。信托公司应分账核算、分账管理，并明确告知信托相关人，受托财产及其收益在信托公司有真实的原始会计记录。第五，明确机构责任。机构责任的量化体现是机构评级，通过对一系列指标的考核，把信托公司的等级评出来。为此，银监会将出台机构评级制度，每年评一次，评级结果与业务范围挂钩，与董事会高管团队的去留挂钩。评级指标涵盖实力指标、合规指标、风险指标和社会责任指标等四个方面内容。第六，明确股东责任。股东责任可以进一步细化为四个责任，即维护公司独立性，看管好公司董事会、监事会，承担风险损失以及恢复与处置计划安排。第七，明确行业责任。设立信托业保障基金，该基金具有互助性、投资性、有偿性和惩戒性。信托保障制度是一种全新的制度安排，也是构建市场化维稳机制的有效尝试。第八，明确监管责任，防范化解风险。一是从准入开始防范风险；二是发现风险；三是评估风险；四是处置风险。

预计 2015 年我国信托市场一方面规模还将有所扩大，但增幅明显回落；另一方面，信托资产的风险积累与暴露还将沿袭上升趋势，风险项目处置将很有可能成为行业焦点问题，甚至不排除部分信托公司因自有资金消耗殆尽而陷入财务困境的可能性。防范风险依然是 2015 年监管工作的重中之重。

七、金融衍生产品市场发展政策[①]

（一）2014 年金融衍生产品市场新政或政策调整一览

2014 年 1 月 28 日，中国人民银行发布《中国人民银行关于建立场外金融衍生产品集中清算机制及开展人民币利率互换集中清算业务有关事宜的通知》（银发〔2014〕29 号）。

2014 年 1 月 28 日，市场利率定价自律机制发布《金融机构合格审慎评估实施办法》（市率发〔2014〕1 号）。

2014 年 3 月 18 日，中国外汇交易中心发布《关于开展人民币对新西兰元直接交易的公告》（中汇交公告〔2014〕20 号）。

---

① 执笔：储幼阳。

2014 年 6 月 23 日，国家外汇管理局下发《国家外汇管理局关于印发〈银行对客户办理人民币与外汇衍生产品业务管理规定〉的通知》（汇发〔2014〕34 号）。

2014 年 10 月 27 日，全国银行间同业拆借中心发布《关于推出标准利率衍生产品的通知》。

2014 年 10 月 30 日，全国银行同业拆借中心下发《关于发布〈全国银行间同业拆借中心报价商与非金融机构合格投资人债券交易规则〉的通知》（中汇交发〔2014〕255 号）。

2014 年 10 月 31 日，全国银行同业拆借中心下发《关于发布〈全国银行间同业拆借中心标准利率衍生产品交易规则〉的通知》（中汇交发〔2014〕260 号）。

2014 年 12 月 26 日，全国银行同业拆借中心下发《关于发布〈全国银行间同业拆借中心本币市场数据接口服务管理办法〉的通知》（中汇交发〔2014〕328 号）。

（二）2014 年中国金融衍生产品市场主要金融政策

1. 促进和规范外汇衍生产品市场发展

2014 年 6 月 23 日，为规范外汇衍生产品市场发展，提高政策透明度和便利化，更好地满足市场主体管理汇率风险的需求，国家外汇管理局制定了《银行对客户办理人民币与外汇衍生产品业务管理规定》，并以汇发〔2014〕34 号文印发了《国家外汇管理局关于印发〈银行对客户办理人民币与外汇衍生产品业务管理规定〉的通知》，通知中所称"人民币与外汇衍生产品"（以下简称衍生产品），包括人民币外汇远期、掉期和期权。该规定从以下几个方面规范了银行 OTC 人民币及外汇衍生产品交易，对于规范发展我国银行 OTC 市场具有深远意义。该规定自 2014 年 8 月 1 日起施行。

第一，规定了银行开展人民币及外汇衍生产品交易的基本原则。银行对客户办理衍生产品业务，应当坚持实需交易原则。实需交易，是指客户办理衍生产品业务具有对冲外汇风险敞口的真实需求背景，并且作为交易基础所持有的外汇资产负债、预期未来的外汇收支按照外汇管理规定可以办理即期结售汇业务。与客户达成衍生产品交易前，银行应按照"了解你的客户""了解你的业务"和"尽职审查"原则，确认客户办理衍生产品业务符合实需交易原则，并获取由客户提供的声明、确认函等能够证明其真实需求背景的书面材料。

第二，规定了国家外汇管理局对银行开办代客衍生产品业务的监管权。根据国际收支和外汇市场状况，国家外汇管理局可以对银行开展衍生产品业务采取必要的应急管理措施，保障外汇市场平稳运行。国家外汇管理局对银行开办代客衍生产品业务实行总行（部）统一备案管理；全国性商业银行、政策性银行开办衍生产品业务，向国家外汇管理局提交申请材料，由国家外汇管理局办理备案；其他银行向所在地外汇局分支局提交申请材料，由所在地外汇局分支局（外汇管理部）办理备案，备案结果抄报国家外汇管理局。国家外汇管理局或外汇局分支局（外汇管理部）自收到符合本规定要求的完整申请资料之日起 20 个工作日内予以备案；银行应按照国家外汇管理局的规定报送与衍生产品业务相关的报表和资料，具体统计报告制度另行规定；国家外汇管理局可以定期或不定期核查银行有关衍生产品业务的资料和报表、风险管理制度、内部控制制度和业务处理系统是否与"了解你的客户""了解你的业务"和"尽职审查"展业原则相适应，对管理不到位的银行将予以风险提示或警示；国家外汇管理局组织银行等外汇市场参与者建立市场自律机制，完善衍生产品的客户管理、风险控制等行业规范，维护外汇市场公平竞争环境。

第三，规定了银行开办代客衍生产品业务的市场准入资格。取得即期结售汇业务资格；有健全的衍生产品交易风险管理制度和内部控制制度及适当的风险识别、计量、管理和交易系统，配备开展衍生产品业务所需要的专业人员；符合银行业监督管理部门有关金融衍生产品交易业务资格的规定。

第四，规定了银行可以开办代客衍生产品业务的种类以及具体操作要求。一是规定了银行可以开办远期、期权、外汇掉期和货币掉期等四种具体的衍生产品业务。二是银行对客户办理衍生产品业务的币种、期限、价格等交易要素，由双方依据真实需求背景按照商业原则协商确定，对于虚构真实需求背景开展衍生产品业务、重复进行套期保值的客户，银行应依法终止已与其开展的交易，并通过信用评级等内部管理制度，限制此类客户后续开展衍生产品业务。三是期权业务采用差额结算时，用于确定轧差金额使用的参考价应是境内真实、有效的市场汇率。四是银行办理衍生产品业务的客户范围限于境内机构，个体工商户视同境内机构。境内个人开展符合外汇管理规定的对外投资形成外汇风险敞口，银行可以按照实需交易原则为其办理衍生产品业务。五是银行应当高度重视衍生产品业务的客户管理，在综合考虑衍生产品分类和客户分类基础上，开展持续、充分的客户适合度评估和风险揭示。六是银行应确认客户进行衍生产品交易已获得内部有效授权及所必需的上级主管部门许可，并具备足够的风险承受能力。七是银行应将客户办理衍生产品业务的单证资料留存备查，保存期限不少于 5 年。八是银行开展衍生产品业务应遵守结售汇综合头寸管理规定，准确、合理计量和管理衍生产品交易头寸。银行分支机构办理代客衍生产品业务应由其总行（部）统一进行平盘、敞口管理和风险控制。

2. 建立场外金融衍生产品集中清算机制及开展人民币利率互换集中清算业务

2014 年 1 月 28 日，为促进场外金融衍生产品市场健康规范发展，建立场外金融衍生产品集中清算机制，中国人民银行发布《中国人民银行关于建立场外金融衍生产品集中清算机制及开展人民币利率互换集中清算业务有关事宜的通知》（以下简称《通知》），《通知》中提到的人民币利率互换集中清算业务是指市场参与者将其达成的人民币利率互换交易，提交上海清算所进行集中清算，由上海清算所作为中央对手方（CCP）承继交易双方的权利及义务，并按照多边净额方式计算市场参与者在相同结算日的利息净额，建立相应风险控制机制，保证合约履行、完成利息净额结算的处理过程。该通知确立了以下几项制度：

第一，全国银行间债券市场参与者达成的人民币利率互换等场外金融衍生产品交易，应按要求进行集中清算，上海清算所提供集中清算服务。《通知》中要求，人民币利率互换交易应通过全国银行间同业拆借中心交易系统确认，上海清算所为市场参与者提供人民币利率互换交易的集中清算服务，市场参与者参加人民币利率互换集中清算业务，应与上海清算所签订《人民币利率互换集中清算协议》，由上海清算所进行集中清算的人民币利率互换交易，适用市场参与者与上海清算所签订的《人民币利率互换集中清算协议》。另外自 2014 年 7 月 1 日起，金融机构之间新达成的，以 FR007、Shibor_ON 和 Shibor_3M 为参考利率的，期限在 5 年以下（含 5 年）的人民币利率互换交易，凡参与主体、合约要素符合上海清算所有关规定的，均应提交上海清算所进行集中清算。不能进行集中清算的，应向中国人民银行说明。

第二，上海清算所应按《通知》要求建立集中清算的制度体系。《通知》要求上海清算所制定集中清算业务参与者标准，建立参与者信用风险监测和评估体系；建立保证金、清算基金、风险准备金等风险管理制度，合理测算集中清算参与者头寸的盯市价值和风险敞口，定期开展回归测试和压力测试；建立集中清算业务参与者违约处理机制，落实银行授信等流动性支持措施，确保清算业务安全平稳运行；上海清算所应将人民币利率互换集中清算参与机构提交的保证金、清算基金与自有资产相隔离，严禁挪作他用；市场参与者因参与集中清算业务而向上海清算所提交的保证金、清算基金等，属于所提交的机构所有，应仅用于履行集中清算所产生的债权债务及其违约处理；人民币利率互换集中清算参与机构应确保相应的资金账户有足够余额用于资金结算和保证金结算；处于结算过程中的资金或保证金只能用于该笔结算，结算一旦完成不可撤销。

第三，明确了中国人民银行在集中清算工作中的具体监管职权。《通知》中规定，中国人民银行将按照《金融市场基础设施原则》等规定的合格中央对手方的标准，对上海清算所进行持续有效的监督和管理；市场成员应根据有关监管要求，对由上海清算所集中清算的人民币利率互换交易，按照合格中央对手方标准计算相应的风险加权资产；上海清算所应定期向中国人民银行上海总部，各分行、营业管理部、省会（首府）城市中心支行、副省级城市中心支行提供其辖区内机构参与人民币利率互换集中清算的有关信息；中国人民银行各分支机构应加强对辖区内机构参与人民币利率互换集中清算业务的日常管理。中国人民银行将根据场外金融衍生产品的风险敞口情况、交易活跃程度、定价机制完善情况、标准化程度及指定集中清算机构的准备充分性等情况，决定其他场外金融衍生产品进行集中清算的类别及具体品种。

第四，明确了同业拆借中心、上海清算所在集中清算工作中的具体职责分工。同业拆借中心、上海清算所应加强协调配合，分别做好人民币利率互换交易、清算的日常监测工作，并于每月前 10 个工作日内，将上月人民币利率互换集中清算业务相关情况以书面方式向中国人民银行报告，抄送中国银行间市场交易商协会。发现异常情况应及时处理并报告；同业拆借中心、上海清算所应根据本通知要求制定具体的交易、清算业务规则，报中国人民银行批准后实施。

3. 市场利率自律机制完善与扩围

2014 年 1 月 28 日，为有序推进利率市场化改革，经人民银行备案，"遴选市场利率定价自律机制"（以下简称自律机制）制定并发布《金融机构合格审慎评估实施办法》（市率发〔2014〕1 号），自律机制的成员被赋予更多市场化定价权，这有利于促进金融机构强化财务约束、提高自主定价能力、完善市场供求决定的利率形成机制。遴选市场利率定价自律机制是由金融机构组成的市场定价自律和协调机制。市场利率定价自律机制在符合国家有关利率管理规定的前提下，对金融机构自主确定的货币市场、信贷市场等金融市场利率进行自律管理，维护市场正当竞争秩序，促进市场规范健康发展。市场利率定价自律机制成员分为基础成员和核心成员。基础成员是指经合格审慎评估，符合财务硬约束条件和宏观审慎政策框架要求且经营较为稳健的金融机构。核心成员是指在基础成员中，经综合实力评估，系统重要性程度高、市场影响力大、自主定价能力强等综合实力显著的金融机构。

作为利率市场化的"基础设施"，市场利率定价自律机制 2014 年 7 月首次扩围。中国外汇交易中心公告显示，根据《金融机构合格审慎评估实施办法》，按照自愿参与原则，经自律机制的金融机构合格审慎评估，93 家银行日前被吸收为基础成员。这 93 家银行包括民生银行、平安银行、光大银行、华夏银行等股份制银行及北京银行、南京银行、重庆银行等城商行，部分农商行、农合行、联社、外资行也在扩围名单之中。此次新加入的 93 家银行属于基础成员，目前，工行、农行、中行、建行、交行、国开行、中信、招行、兴业、浦发这 10 家银行是市场利率定价自律机制中的核心成员。

公告显示，自律机制基础成员可申请参与上海银行间同业拆借利率（Shibor）和贷款基础利率（LPR）场外报价、发行同业存单等涉及市场基准利率培育的金融产品，并享有参与其他相关业务的权利，同时应履行遵守自律机制各项规章制度、执行自律机制决议、完成自律机制交办的工作等义务。

健全市场利率定价自律机制是我国利率市场化最迫近的目标之一。中国利率市场化将采取"三步走"战略，第一步目标是，着力健全市场利率定价自律机制，提高金融机构自主定价能力；做好贷款基础利率报价工作，为信贷产品定价提供参考。第二步目标是，注重培育形成较为完善的市场利率体系，完善央行利率调控框架和利率传导机制。第三步目标是，全面实现利率市场化，健全市场化利率宏观调控机制。

4. 标准利率衍生产品交易规则的制定与交易推出

2014 年 10 月 27 日，全国银行间同业拆借中心发布《关于推出标准利率衍生产品的通知》，该通知称全国银行间同业拆借中心定于 2014 年 11 月 3 日推出标准利率衍生产品，并同时发布《标准利率衍生产品要素表》。10 月 31 日，全国银行间同业拆借中心制定发布了《全国银行间同业拆借中心标准利率衍生产品交易规则》（中汇交发〔2014〕260 号）。11 月 3 日，为满足市场成员需求，全国银行间同业拆借中心推出标准利率衍生产品。所谓标准利率衍生产品就是对利率互换、远期利率协议等利率衍生产品的到期日、期限等产品要素进行了标准化设置。首批一共推出四个品种：1 个月标准隔夜指数互换、3 个月标准 Shibor1W 利率互换、3 个月标准 7 天回购利率互换和 3 个月标准 Shibor3M 远期利率协议。标准利率衍生产品交易制度包括：

（1）参与机构。银行间利率衍生产品市场成员均可参与标准利率衍生产品交易。

（2）交易方式。标准利率衍生产品在 X－Swap 系统上采用双边授信方式通过匿名点击达成交易，现阶段与 X－Swap 系统利率互换产品共用授信额度。

（3）交易确认。交易达成后交易双方在交易中心交易后处理服务平台完成确认，确认流程与现有利率互换一致。距最后交易日不足 4 个工作日达成的交易，应在最后交易日中午 12 点前完成交易确认。

（4）清算与交割。市场成员可选择双边自行清算和中央对手方清算两种清算方式。合约交割日交易双方根据交易后处理服务平台生成的交割单进行现金交割。

（5）节假日调整。全国银行间同业拆借中心根据国务院公布的节假日安排，发布相关合约的到期日、起息日调整公告，参与机构据以自行调整内部系统成交数据，已达成的交易无须再进行确认。

标准化利率衍生产品与原有的银行间利率互换（IRS）的主要区别在于其期限固定，交割日确定。在 IRS 滚动到期机制下，套利者已有的净头寸可以通过反向操作平仓，但如果不在当天平仓，则已有的风险敞口无法完全通过反向操作消除；标准化互换合约采取集中到期后，头寸对冲后不遗留风险敞口，便于投资者进行回购养券＋互换、多个互换组合等交易策略的市场风险管理。

此次标准化产品的品种设置覆盖了已有利率互换主要品种的标的 FR007，Shibor_0/N 和 Shibor_3M，虽然期限并不完全匹配，但可以通过每个品种不同月份到期日的合约组合得到所需期限，有利于提高现有互换和远期的关注度和参与度。

提出标准化利率衍生产品的初期可能成交遇冷，甚至可能对现有品种存在一定分流的效应，但长期来看仍带来正面效应。

5. 完善多层次债券市场体系建设，增加市场交易品种

为落实中国人民银行关于完善多层次债券市场体系的要求，提高银行间债券市场流动性，2014 年 10 月 30 日，全国银行间同业拆借中心发布《全国银行间同业拆借中心报价商与非金融机构合格投资人债券交易规则》，允许非金融机构合格投资人进入银行间债券市场实现报价、成交、行情及信息查询等功能。

为促进中国与新西兰之间的双边贸易和投资，便利人民币和新西兰元在贸易投资结算中的使用，满足经济主体降低汇兑成本的需要，经中国人民银行授权，自2014年3月19日起银行间外汇市场开展人民币对新西兰元直接交易。

（三）政策展望

2015年的金融衍生产品市场的政策动向可能集中在以下几个方面：

随着场外人民币衍生产品发展步伐不断加快，场内标准化人民币利率衍生产品如十年期国债期货、三十年期国债期货、一年期国债期货可能会陆续推出，这有利于弥补目前仅有五年期国债期货的局面，有利于形成更为完整的国债收益率曲线，为机构投资者的套期保值提供更多的金融对冲工具。

利率市场化的过程中将有更多的企业加入到使用人民币利率衍生产品来对冲风险的行列当中，银行间市场投资者群体将不断推出，与其配套的政策也将不断发布。

随着本届政府加快市场化改革"简政放权"的不断深入，在金融领域内政府的职能定位将从监管逐步向宏观调控转型，从政府直接制定政策更多地向市场自发形成规则转移，未来出台的政策可能将更多是着眼于推动市场自律，建立并完善利率市场定价机制、利率市场竞争机制。

八、商品期货市场发展政策[①]

（一）2014年商品期货市场主要政策

表5-5　　　　　　　　　　商品期货市场主要政策一览

日　期	主要政策	发文单位
1月2日	《关于调整云南天然橡胶交割仓库异地贴水的通知》（上期办发〔2014〕1号）	上海期货交易所
2月19日	《关于公布施行〈大连商品交易所聚丙烯期货合约〉和相关实施细则修正案的通知》（大商所发〔2014〕33号）	大连商品交易所
2月26日	《关于增加指定期货保证金存管银行的通知》（大商所发〔2014〕40号）	大连商品交易所
3月10日	《关于调整线型低密度聚乙烯和聚氯乙烯指定交割仓库的通知》（大商所发〔2014〕47号）	大连商品交易所
3月17日	《关于印发上海期货交易所热轧卷板期货标准合约及相关规则的公告》（上期办发〔2014〕2号）	上海期货交易所
3月17日	《关于热轧卷板期货交割商品补充规定的通知》（上期办发〔2014〕26号）	上海期货交易所
3月17日	《关于热轧卷板期货升贴水及仓储费用的通知》（上期办发〔2014〕27号）	上海期货交易所

---

① 执笔：甘正在。

日 期	主要政策	发文单位
3 月 17 日	《关于公布实施〈上海期货交易所钢材交割商品注册管理规定〉（修订案）的公告》（上期办发〔2014〕3 号）	上海期货交易所
3 月 20 日	《关于调整部分品种交易手续费收取标准的通知》（上期办发〔2014〕32 号）	上海期货交易所
4 月 2 日	《关于公布黄大豆 1 号指定交割仓库散粮入出库费用最高限价的通知》（大商所发〔2014〕65 号）	大连商品交易所
4 月 10 日	《关于调整部分品种交易手续费收取标准的通知》（大商所发〔2014〕71 号）	大连商品交易所
4 月 18 日	《关于公布施行〈大连商品交易所保税交割实施细则（试行）〉的通知》（大商所发〔2014〕81 号）	大连商品交易所
4 月 18 日	《关于开展期货保税交割业务试点的通知》（大商所发〔2014〕82 号）	大连商品交易所
4 月 18 日	《关于调整黄大豆 2 号指定交割仓库的通知》（大商所发〔2014〕84 号）	大连商品交易所
5 月 4 日	《关于扎实做好白糖期权业务准备工作的通知》（郑商发〔2014〕90 号）	郑州商品交易所
5 月 9 日	《国务院关于进一步促进资本市场健康发展的若干意见》（国发〔2014〕17 号）	国务院
6 月 13 日	《关于修改会员管理办法相关规则的通知》（大商所发〔2014〕130 号）	大连商品交易所
6 月 13 日	《关于调整线型低密度聚乙烯交割质量标准的通知》（大商所发〔2014〕131 号）	大连商品交易所
6 月 13 日	《关于甲醇期货合约及部分品种业务细则修改事项的通知》（郑商发〔2014〕115 号）	郑州商品交易所
6 月 20 日	《关于公布〈郑州商品交易所期货交易风险控制管理办法〉（修订案）的通知》（郑商发〔2014〕116 号）	郑州商品交易所
6 月 26 日	《关于发布施行夜盘交易相关合约、实施细则的通知》（大商所发〔2014〕142 号）	大连商品交易所
7 月 4 日	《关于公布郑州商品交易所晚籼稻期货合约及相关业务细则的通知》（郑商发〔2014〕135 号）	郑州商品交易所
7 月 11 日	《关于调整交割流程相关合约规则的通知》（大商所发〔2014〕153 号）	大连商品交易所
7 月 15 日	《关于增加指定期货保证金存管银行的通知》（大商所发〔2014〕154 号）	大连商品交易所
7 月 30 日	《关于开展豆粕集团内厂库仓单串换试点的通知》（大商所发〔2014〕171 号）	大连商品交易所
8 月 1 日	《关于公布郑州商品交易所铁合金期货合约及相关业务细则的通知》（郑商发〔2014〕155 号）	郑州商品交易所

续表

日　　期	主要政策	发文单位
8月19日	《关于下调热轧卷板交易手续费标准的通知》（上期办发〔2014〕91号）	上海期货交易所
8月20日	《关于在胶合板品种中增加厂库交割制度的通知》（大商所发〔2014〕190号）	大连商品交易所
8月22日	《关于发布〈中国证券期货市场场外衍生品交易主协议（2014年版）〉和〈中国证券期货市场场外衍生品交易权益类衍生品定义文件（2014年版）〉的通知》（中期协字〔2014〕68号）	中国期货业协会
8月26日	《关于发布〈期货公司设立子公司开展以风险管理服务为主的业务试点工作指引（修订）〉及配套文件的通知》（中期协字〔2014〕73号）	中国期货业协会
8月27日	《关于发布〈期货公司信息技术管理指引〉及检查细则修订版的通知》（中期协字〔2014〕75号）	中国期货业协会
9月10日	《关于修改风险管理办法等业务规则的通知》（大商所发〔2014〕211号）	大连商品交易所
9月16日	《关于进一步推进期货经营机构创新发展的意见》	中国证券监督管理委员会
9月26日	《关于调整白银期货交割手续费的通知》（上期办发〔2014〕103号）	上海期货交易所
9月26日	《关于调整白银指定交割库收费标准的通知》（上期办发〔2014〕104号）	上海期货交易所
9月26日	《关于调整天然橡胶指定交割仓库收费标准的通知》（上期办发〔2014〕105号）	上海期货交易所
9月29日	《关于调整广东铅期货交割地区升贴水的通知》（上期办发〔2014〕106号）	上海期货交易所
10月20日	《关于调整广东铅期货交割仓库库容的通知》（上期办发〔2014〕117号）	上海期货交易所
10月22日	《关于调整相关品种质量争议复检机构规则的通知》（大商所发〔2014〕243号）	大连商品交易所
10月22日	《关于修改黄大豆2号交割预报定金清退流程的通知》（大商所发〔2014〕245号）	大连商品交易所
10月29日	《期货公司监督管理办法》（中国证监会令第110号）	中国证券监督管理委员会
11月4日	《关于开展豆油、棕榈油集团内仓单串换试点的通知》（大商所发〔2014〕255号）	大连商品交易所
11月21日	《关于公布夜盘交易细则及业务实施细则修订案的通知》（郑商发〔2014〕229号）	郑州商品交易所
11月24日	《关于减收铜品种交易手续费的通知》（上期办发〔2014〕135号）	上海期货交易所
12月3日	《关于棉花期货相关业务细则修改事项的通知》（郑商发〔2014〕229号）	郑州商品交易所

续表

日　期	主要政策	发文单位
12 月 4 日	《关于强麦及普麦期货业务细则修改事项的通知》（郑商发〔2014〕240号）	郑州商品交易所
12 月 4 日	《关于早籼稻及粳稻期货业务细则修改事项的通知》（郑商发〔2014〕241号）	郑州商品交易所
12 月 4 日	《关于调整优质强筋小麦、早籼稻仓储费标准的通告》（郑商发〔2014〕40号）	郑州商品交易所
12 月 4 日	《关于发布〈期货公司资产管理业务管理规则（试行）〉的通知》（中期协字〔2014〕100 号）	中国期货业协会
12 月 5 日	《关于公布部分合约修订事项的通知》（郑商发〔2014〕243 号）	郑州商品交易所
12 月 8 日	《关于公布施行〈大连商品交易所玉米淀粉期货合约〉和相关实施细则修正案的通知》（大商所发〔2014〕276 号）	大连商品交易所
12 月 10 日	《关于公布交割细则相关修改事项的通知》（郑商发〔2014〕254 号）	郑州商品交易所
12 月 11 日	《关于进一步加强期货经营机构及其从业人员自律管理的通知》（中期协字〔2014〕102 号）	中国期货业协会
12 月 15 日	《关于发布〈期货公司资产管理业务申报材料规范〉的通知》（中期协字〔2014〕107 号）	中国期货业协会
12 月 16 日	《公开募集证券投资基金运作指引第 1 号——商品期货交易型开放式基金指引》（证监会公告〔2014〕51 号）	中国证券监督管理委员会
12 月 18 日	《关于调整早籼稻指定交割仓库入出库费用标准的通告》（郑商发〔2014〕第 46 号）	郑州商品交易所
12 月 22 日	《关于印发螺纹钢、天然橡胶两个期货合约修订案的公告》（上期办发〔2014〕8 号）	上海期货交易所
12 月 22 日	《关于螺纹钢、热轧卷板、天然橡胶和石油沥青连续交易上线运行有关事项的通知》（上期发〔2014〕173 号）	上海期货交易所
12 月 24 日	《关于调整线材和燃料油期货交易保证金标准的通知》（上期发〔2014〕182 号）	上海期货交易所
12 月 26 日	《期货交易数据交换协议》（证监会公告〔2014〕55 号）	中国证券监督管理委员会

（二）2014商品期货市场政策主要内容及分析

1. 期货交易监管政策的实施与调整

面对2013年中国期货市场的低迷，中国证监会、中国期货业协会以及上海、郑州、大连三家商品期货交易所在2014年不断探索，勇于创新，在完善原有政策、规则的基础上，以新"国九条"以及《关于进一步推进期货经营机构创新发展的意见》为导向，相继推出一系列政策促进期货行业迅速复苏。

（1）调整合约设计理念，提升市场认可度。为全面贯彻落实《国务院关于进一步促进资本市场健康发展的若干意见》，更好地贴近市场需求、便利交割，国内各商品交易所在加大新品种上市的同时，相继对甲醇、塑料、棉花、小麦、早籼稻、粳稻、螺纹钢、橡胶、白银等品种的合约及其结算细则、交割细则进行了修订，同时调整了多数品种的交割仓库及交割品牌，使其更好地被市场认可，吸引更多的企业客户参与其中，提升服务实体经济能力。

（2）严把风控关，进一步完善交易规则。完善交易规则，加强风险管理，是期货市场发展的基本保障。2014年期货市场的发展平稳，未出现严重风险事件，与期货市场日趋完善的交易规则密不可分。2014年4月18日，《大连商品交易所保税交割实施细则（试行）》正式施行；2014年6月20日，郑州商品交易所对《郑州商品交易所期货交易风险控制管理办法》进行了修订完善；2014年10月22日，大连商品交易所对黄大豆2号交割预报定金清退流程予以修改。

（3）降低期货品种交易手续费，助力期货行业复苏。2014年手续费减免政策得到延续，且形式更趋于多样化，主要体现在上海期货交易所。上海期货交易所自2014年4月1日起，铝、锌、铅、螺纹钢期货合约当日平今仓免收交易手续费；自2014年8月25日起，热轧卷板期货合约的交易手续费标准从成交金额的万分之零点八下调为成交金额的万分之零点四；自2014年11月26日至2015年3月31日，铜品种交易手续费减半收取。

（4）夜盘品种体系逐步完善，商品期货迎来连续交易模式。自2013年上海期货交易所成功推出黄金、白银、铜、铝、铅、锌夜盘连续交易之后，2014年大连、郑州交易所也相继推出夜盘交易品种，夜盘品种体系得到逐步完善，为保证行情的连续、提高品种活跃度作出了重要贡献。截至2014年底，连续交易品种由2013年的6个扩大到23个，其中上海期货交易所在原有品种基础之上，增加螺纹钢、热轧卷板、天然橡胶和石油沥青4个品种；大连商品交易所先后两批共增加棕榈油、焦炭、大豆系列、焦煤、铁矿石等8个品种；郑州商品交易所白糖、棉花、菜粕、甲醇和PTA 5大品种开启夜盘模式。自此，中国三大商品交易所均完成夜盘交易上线试点，中国商品期货迎来连续交易模式。

（5）放松管制，鼓励创新。为积极响应新"国九条"号召，中国期货业协会正式对外发布《期货公司资产管理业务管理规则（试行）》，自 2014 年 12 月 15 日起实施。管理规则放开了"一对多"业务，即期货公司及子公司从事资产管理业务包括为单一客户办理资产管理业务和为特定多个客户办理资产管理业务。"一对多"业务为期货行业打开了财富管理的空间，为期货公司向资产管理和风险管理方向转型提供了强大支撑。其他规则还包括期货公司资产管理业务准入门槛降低，净资本和分类评级均有所下调；采取登记备案制，需向中国期货业协会和私募基金登记备案系统进行备案；不得聘用第三方个人作为投资顾问等。

此外，证监会在放松管制的同时，积极鼓励业务创新。2014 年 9 月，证监会发布《关于进一步推进期货经营机构创新发展的意见》，制定了今后一段时期推进期货经营机构创新发展的总体原则和具体措施，对期货经营机构创新发展重点提出了八大举措。

2. 期货新品种创新和业务模式创新继续推出

（1）新品种创新。2014 年，我国期货市场新推出聚丙烯、热轧卷板、晚籼稻、铁合金等新合约；商品期权、冷冻猪肉等新品种的征求意见稿以及仿真交易等紧锣密鼓地开展；原油期货正式获批，相关配套政策和管理办法有序推进；商品期货 ETF 指引正式发布，期货市场引入源头活水。这些新品种的陆续推出，不仅进一步丰富了期货产品线，为市场发展扩容了空间，也为相关实体企业提供了更多的避险工具，使得期货市场服务实体经济的功能得到进一步发挥。特别是证监会 12 月发布的《公开募集证券投资基金运作指引第 1 号——商品期货交易型开放式基金指引》，对商品期货 ETF 的定义、投资范围、风险控制、相关主体责任、监管要求等内容进行了规范。开放商品期货基金将打通证券和商品两个市场，引入机构投资者参与商品期货投资，提高商品期货的流通性。

（2）业务模式创新。为了更好地促进豆粕、豆油以及棕榈油期货市场功能的有效发挥，提高期货市场服务产业的能力，进一步降低交割成本，更好地促进期现货市场结合，大连商品交易所积极推陈出新，经过深入调研，先后推出豆粕、豆油、棕榈油集团内仓单串换试点业务，并取得良好效果。

（3）鼓励发展场外衍生品业务。为进一步完善证券期货市场衍生品交易主协议及相关配套文件，促进证券期货市场场外衍生品交易业务发展，中国证券业协会、中国期货业协会、中国证券投资基金业协会于 2014 年 8 月在《中国证券市场金融衍生品交易主协议（2013 年版）》的基础上，制定了《中国证券期货市场场外衍生品交易主协议（2014 年版）》及补充协议、《中国证券期货市场场外衍生品交易权益类衍生品定义文件（2014 年版）》，为积极探索场外衍生品业务奠定了基础。

3. 完善制度建设，夯实期货市场发展的基础

2014 年 10 月，证监会正式发布《期货公司监督管理办法》（以下简称《办法》）。此次发布的《办法》落实了《国务院关于进一步促进资本市场健康发展的若干意见》

中关于提高证券期货服务业竞争力的有关意见，以及《国务院关于第六批取消和调整行政审批项目的决定》和《国务院关于修改〈期货交易管理条例〉的决定》的相关内容，体现了功能监管及适度监管的理念，有利于提升期货公司服务能力和国际竞争力。

正式发布的《办法》主要包括以下八方面的内容：一是落实简政放权要求，贯彻监管转型精神；二是降低准入门槛，优化期货公司股东条件；三是完善期货公司业务范围；四是明确期货公司多元化经营的相关要求；五是完善监管制度，着力维护投资者合法权益；六是强化期货公司信息披露义务；七是完善期货公司监管措施与法律责任；八是配合境外交易者从事特定品种期货交易作出相应制度安排。

（三）2014年期货市场政策实施评估及2015年展望

1. 2014年期货市场政策实施评估

（1）品种活跃度显著提高。根据中国证监会披露的数据显示，2014年大连商品交易所成交76 963.71万手，同比增长9.87%；上海期货交易所成交83 745.20万手，同比增长30.35%；郑州商品交易所成交67 634.33万手，同比增长22.97%。

虽然2014年我国期货市场交易量较2013年有了较为明显的增长，但由于连续交易品种多为2014年12月上线，所以品种活跃度在2015年1月体现得更加明显。根据上海期货交易所提供的数据显示，截至2015年1月26日收盘，螺纹钢、热轧卷板、天然橡胶、石油沥青4个品种连续交易期间共成交2 875.57万手和1.01万亿元。其中，螺纹钢成交2 604.44万手和6 623.34亿元，占该品种全天比重分别为31.35%和31.34%；热轧卷板成交4.70万手和12.90亿元，占该品种全天比重分别为29.46%和29.41%；天然橡胶成交262.84万手和3 422.80万手，占该品种全天比重分别为19.93%和19.96%；石油沥青成交3.61万手和10.49亿元，占该品种全天比重分别为57.52%和57.06%。其间，螺纹钢品种连续交易日均成交量144.69万手，成为仅次于白银的第二活跃的连续交易品种。持仓量方面，除热轧卷板持仓量下降外，其余新增连续交易品种持仓规模均上升。

（2）机构参与热情显著提高。连续交易品种上线首月，相关品种价格跳空明显收窄，价格平滑度显著增强。螺纹钢、热轧卷板、天然橡胶、石油沥青日均价格跳空分别环比减小3.83%、21.81%、26.67%、37.47%。价格跳空的减小显著改善了相关期货品种价格的连续性，强化了品种的价格发现功能。

价格平滑度增加也提升了客户参与交易的意愿，相关品种市场参与的广度和深度得到加强。如螺纹钢日均参与客户数环比增加7.41%、热轧卷板日均参与客户数环比增加56.12%。此外，单位客户参与螺纹钢、热轧卷板、天然橡胶、石油沥青均分别环比增加161.44%、10.93%、19.51%、28.29%。

2. 商品期货市场政策展望

2014年5月，国务院颁布了《国务院关于进一步促进资本市场健康发展的若干意见》（新"国九条"）。根据新"国九条"要求，将继续推出大宗资源性产品期货品种、发展商品期权、商品指数、碳排放权等交易工具、放宽对机构投资者和企业市场的利用限制、提高证券期货服务业竞争力、提高证券期货行业对外开放水平、推进证券期货监管转型、保护投资者特别是中小投资者合法权益等，为优化外部环境，为市场创新发展完善提供更为强大的动能。9月，证监会发布《关于进一步推进期货经营机构创新发展的意见》，制定了今后一段时期推进期货经营机构创新发展的总体原则和具体措施。

一是 ETF 期权、商品期权上市交易。自 2013 年末起，各大交易所纷纷开展面向全市场的期权仿真交易。2015 年 2 月 9 日，上证 50ETF 期权正式上市，期权的上市将对我国商品期货市场产生长远而深刻的影响。

二是原油期货挂牌上市。2014 年 12 月 15 日，内地首个国际化的商品期货品种——原油期货获得上市批准。这意味着在履行完必要程序后，原油期货有望最早于 2015 年上半年在上海自贸区面向全球开始交易，正式加入到亚太时区原油定价基准的竞争中。上海期货交易所相关负责人表示，下一步将会全面支持子公司上海国际能源交易中心与各方进一步协商，在配套政策出台的情况下，做好市场组织、规则制定、技术系统、投资者教育等工作，确保原油期货顺利推出和平稳运行。

三是连续交易调整优化工作。在总结去年连续交易成功经验的基础之上，三大交易所将继续丰富连续交易品种，同时进一步优化连续交易时间，完善与国际市场的联动机制，促进期货市场服务实体经济功能的发挥。同时，持续深入开展投资者教育，针对期货公司、产业客户、特殊单位客户等投资者群体开展广泛的业务培训，提高培训的专业性和针对性。

四是逐步放宽监管管制。包括支持期货经营机构提供风险管理服务，进一步扩大风险管理公司业务试点，拓宽子公司业务范围；明确期货经营机构的基本定位，支持期货公司做优做强，推进期货公司业务转型升级；加快发展期货公司资产管理业务；鼓励外资参股境内期货经营机构；支持期货公司为境外机构参与境内期货市场提供交易结算服务；支持期货经营机构在境外设立、收购公司等内容。

五是探索交易商制度，培育专业交易商队伍。探索建立以套期保值和风险管理为目的的专业交易商制度，积极鼓励证券期货经营机构发展成为专业交易商，依法合规开展场内做市业务，以及通过设计非标准化产品并作为对手方从事场外衍生品交易，满足实体企业个性化风险管理需求。

六是推动期货公司并购重组，提高行业集中度。近年来，期货公司数量从 2006 年的 183 家减少到目前的 154 家。尽管如此，期货行业"小、弱、散"的特点仍然在一定程度上存在，行业集中度低于国内其他金融行业，更低于境外成熟市场的期货行业，制约了期货行业服务能力的提高。2015 年将坚持市场化导向，加大政策支持力度，简化审批流程，完善配套措施，引导期货公司开展境内外并购重组，支持符合条件的境外机构依法参与境内期货公司的兼并整合，进一步提高行业集中度。

七是实现网上开户，积极探索互联网金融。随着"东航事件"的落幕，以及互联网金融的崛起，在《关于进一步推进期货经营机构创新发展的意见》的指引下，实现网上开户，积极探索互联网金融为期货公司拓展市场提供了方向和渠道。但互联网金融对于期货业来说仍然是个新生事物，蕴含了许多未知的契机和风险。期货公司试水互联网金融，严控风险和提升专业化服务能力是前提。期货公司以服务著称，但客户存在个性化定制的需求，这是互联网期货公司将要克服的问题。因此，走专业化发展道路，是应对互联网介入期货业的前提。

八是完善政策规则，为创新发展提供制度保障。引导期货经营机构建立与创新发展相适应的风险责任机制，开展负责任的创新，严格落实期货经营机构风险防范的主体责任，实现创新发展与风险防范的动态均衡。

九、外汇市场发展政策[①]

（一）2014 年新政或政策调整一览

1 月 10 日，中国外汇交易中心《关于在外汇交易系统增加货币掉期本金交换形式的通知》（中汇交发〔2014〕5 号）。

3 月 14 日，中国人民银行决定扩大外汇市场人民币兑美元汇率浮动幅度（中国人民银行公告〔2014〕第 5 号）。

6 月 11 日，《中国人民银行关于贯彻落实〈国务院办公厅关于支持外贸稳定增长的若干意见〉的指导意见》。

6 月 22 日，中国人民银行发布《银行办理结售汇业务管理办法》（中国人民银行令〔2014〕第 2 号）。

7 月 1 日，《中国人民银行关于银行间外汇市场交易汇价和银行挂牌汇价管理有关事项的通知》（银发〔2014〕188 号）。

7 月 10 日，《中国外汇交易中心关于发布〈银行间外汇市场职业操守和市场惯例指引〉等的通知》（中汇交发〔2014〕173 号）。

10 月 17 日，中国银行间市场交易商协会发布《中国人民银行金融市场司关于非金融机构合格投资人进入银行间债券市场有关事项的通知》（银市场〔2014〕35 号）。

12 月 5 日，《国家外汇管理局关于调整金融机构进入银行间外汇市场有关管理政策的通知》（汇发〔2014〕48 号）。

12 月 22 日，中国外汇交易中心《关于调整银行间人民币外汇市场即期竞价交易收费方案的通知》（中汇交发〔2014〕308 号）。

---

① 执笔：储幼阳。

12月25日，国家外汇管理局发布《国家外汇管理局关于印发〈银行办理结售汇业务管理办法实施细则〉的通知》（汇发〔2014〕53号）。

12月25日，中国外汇交易中心发布《关于推出人民币对林吉特、俄罗斯卢布和新西兰元远期和掉期交易的通知》（中汇交发〔2014〕321号）。

12月26日，中国外汇交易中心《关于调整银行间人民币外汇市场准入指引的通知》（中汇交发〔2014〕327号）。

（二）政策影响

1. 央行允许非金融机构合格投资人进入银行间债券市场

2014年10月17日，中国银行间市场交易商协会发布《中国人民银行金融市场司关于非金融机构合格投资人进入银行间债券市场有关事项的通知》（银市场〔2014〕35号），允许非金融机构合格投资人通过非金融机构合格投资人交易平台进行债券投资交易，非金融机构合格投资人交易平台正式上线。

非金融机构合格投资人交易平台以服务实体经济、完善多层次债务资本市场为核心，以满足非金融机构等机构投资人需求为立足点，为资金短缺的实体经济和资金充裕的投资人搭建直接融投资的平台，从而降低实体经济融资成本。该平台主要面向有真实交易需求的非金融机构以及经中国人民银行同意的其他机构投资人。为进一步防范市场风险，该平台对投资人资质、交易前券款检查、结算方式等设置了明确安排。

2. 扩大外汇市场人民币兑美元汇率浮动幅度

当前我国外汇市场健康发展，交易主体自主定价和风险管理能力不断增强。为顺应市场发展的要求，加大市场决定汇率的力度，建立以市场供求为基础、有管理的浮动汇率制度，中国人民银行决定扩大外汇市场人民币兑美元汇率浮动幅度（中国人民银行公告〔2014〕第5号）。

自2014年3月17日起，银行间即期外汇市场人民币兑美元交易价浮动幅度由1%扩大至2%，即每日银行间即期外汇市场人民币兑美元的交易价可在中国外汇交易中心对外公布的当日人民币兑美元中间价上下2%的幅度内浮动。外汇指定银行为客户提供当日美元最高现汇卖出价与最低现汇买入价之差不得超过当日汇率中间价的幅度由2%扩大至3%，其他规定仍遵照《中国人民银行关于银行间外汇市场交易汇价和外汇指定银行挂牌汇价管理有关问题的通知》（银发〔2010〕325号）执行。中国人民银行将继续完善人民币汇率市场化形成机制，进一步发挥市场在人民币汇率形成中的作用，增强人民币汇率双向浮动弹性，保持人民币汇率在合理、均衡水平上的基本稳定。

3. 进一步贯彻落实支持外贸稳定增长

为贯彻落实《国务院办公厅关于支持外贸稳定增长的若干意见》（国办发〔2014〕19号），支持外贸稳定增长，中国人民银行发布《中国人民银行关于贯彻落实〈国务院办公厅关于支持外贸稳定增长的若干意见〉的指导意见》。

（1）优化企业融资环境，加大信贷支持力度。进一步拓宽企业融资渠道。鼓励银行业金融机构积极创新金融产品和服务，进一步扩大出口信用保险保单融资，灵活运用流动资金贷款、进出口信用贷款、保理贷款、票据贴现、押汇贷款、对外担保等方式，加强对有订单、有效益的进出口企业和外贸综合服务企业的信贷支持，促进小微企业出口。支持符合条件的企业发行非金融企业债务融资工具，推动中小企业集合票据、中小企业区域集优票据、信用增进等多种创新相互配合，拓宽包括中小企业在内的进出口企业融资渠道。

充分发挥政策性金融对外贸的支持作用。鼓励中国进出口银行增加优惠出口买方信贷和优惠贷款投放，简化优买、优贷项目和资金审批程序，加大对企业"走出去"特别是中小企业进出口信贷的支持力度。鼓励政策性金融机构加大对服务贸易的扶持力度，支持服务贸易重点项目建设。

积极发展融资租赁。积极发展以有形动产为标的的融资租赁业务，支持大型设备进出口。积极支持符合条件的金融租赁公司等非银行业金融机构，通过发行金融债券、参与信贷资产证券化试点等方式，扩大融资渠道。

（2）推进跨境贸易结算，开展跨境人民币资金集中运营业务。简化跨境贸易和投资人民币结算业务流程。银行业金融机构可在"了解你的客户""了解你的业务"和"尽职审查"三原则基础上，凭境内企业提交的收付款指令，直接办理经常项下和直接投资项下人民币跨境结算业务。

开展跨境人民币资金集中运营业务。跨国企业集团可以根据中国人民银行有关规定开展跨境人民币资金集中运营业务，包括跨境双向人民币资金池业务、经常项下跨境人民币集中收付业务等。跨国企业集团总部可以指定在中华人民共和国境内依法注册成立并实际经营或投资、具有独立法人资格的成员企业（包括财务公司），作为开展跨境人民币资金集中运营业务的全国性或区域性主办企业。主办企业在办理经常项下跨境人民币集中收付业务时，可采用轧差净额结算方式，按照经常项下企业集团收付总额轧差或成员企业收付额逐个轧差结算。跨境人民币资金集中运营业务应按照国际收支申报相关规定履行国际收支申报义务。

开展个人跨境贸易人民币结算业务。银行业金融机构可为个人开展的货物贸易、服务贸易跨境人民币业务提供结算服务。银行业金融机构在"了解你的客户""了解你的业务""尽职审查"三原则的基础上，可凭个人有效身份证件或者工商营业执照直接为客户办理跨境贸易人民币结算业务，必要时可要求客户提交相关业务凭证。

支持银行业金融机构与支付机构合作开展跨境人民币结算业务。银行业金融机构可与依法取得"互联网支付"业务许可的支付机构合作，为企业和个人跨境货物贸易、服务贸易提供人民币结算服务。银行业金融机构应与支付机构签订跨境电子商务人民币结算业务协议，并报当地中国人民银行分支机构备案。

（3）进一步完善人民币汇率形成机制，丰富汇率避险工具。继续完善人民币汇率市场化形成机制，加大市场决定汇率的力度，促进国际收支平衡。根据外汇市场发育状况和经济金融形势，增强人民币汇率双向浮动弹性，保持人民币汇率在合理均衡水平上的基本稳定。进一步发挥市场决定汇率的作用，完善以市场供求为基础的、有管理的浮动汇率制度。继续推动人民币对其他货币直接交易市场发展。

加大外汇产品创新力度，增加外汇市场交易品种，研究外汇期权组合产品和期货业务创新，形成即期、远期、期货、期权等多种产品结合，汇率产品和利率产品结合的产品体系。丰富外汇市场参与主体，降低商业银行外汇衍生产品准入门槛，适当放宽中小银行开办远期结售汇业务资格条件。完善交易、清算、信息等基础设施建设，更好地满足企业和居民基于实需原则的汇率避险需求。

4. 完善银行结售汇业务监管

为了完善银行结售汇业务监管制度，保障外汇市场平稳运行，中国人民银行对《外汇指定银行办理结汇、售汇业务管理暂行办法》（中国人民银行令〔2002〕第4号，以下简称《暂行办法》）进行了修订，于2014年6月22日发布了《银行办理结售汇业务管理办法》（中国人民银行令〔2014〕第2号，以下简称《管理办法》），自2014年8月1日起施行。原《暂行办法》同时废止。

《管理办法》的出台是适应结售汇业务发展和外汇管理职能转变现实需求的重要举措，体现了简政放权、构建合理监管体系的改革思路。《管理办法》主要修订内容包括：一是将结售汇业务区分为即期结售汇业务和人民币与外汇衍生产品业务，分别制定管理规范；二是降低银行结售汇业务市场准入条件，简化市场准入管理；三是转变银行结售汇头寸管理方式，赋予银行更大的自主权，以充分发挥市场主体在外汇业务发展中的主观能动性；四是取消部分行政许可和资格要求，实现以事前审批为重向事后监管为重的转变；五是根据外汇实践发展，修订部分罚则内容。

《管理办法》的出台不影响银行已经取得的结售汇业务资格。

为便利银行办理结售汇业务，12月25日，国家外汇管理局发布了《国家外汇管理局关于印发〈银行办理结售汇业务管理办法实施细则〉的通知》（汇发〔2014〕53号，以下简称《细则》）。

《细则》贯彻落实简政放权的改革思路，整合了银行结售汇市场准入、即期结售汇业务管理、人民币与外汇衍生产品管理、银行结售汇综合头寸等方面的相关法规，并调整了部分管理内容。主要包括内容：整合银行即期结售汇、人民币与外汇衍生产品业务的市场准入管理，简化银行结售汇信息变更备案程序；取消设置个人本外币兑换统一标识的要求，明确银行办理对私结售汇业务应在醒目位置设置个人本外币兑换标识；将银行结售汇综合头寸按日考核调整为按周考核，取消结售汇综合头寸与外汇贷存比挂钩的政策；下放银行资本金（营运资金）本外币转换审批权限，取消银行代债务人结售汇审批；明确银行办理结售汇业务"了解客户、了解业务、尽职审查"的原则性要求。《细则》自 2015 年 1 月 1 日起实施。

5. 进一步完善人民币汇率市场化形成机制

为进一步完善人民币汇率市场化形成机制，2014 年 7 月 1 日，中国人民银行发布《中国人民银行关于银行间外汇市场交易汇价和银行挂牌汇价管理有关事项的通知》（银发〔2014〕188 号），就银行间外汇市场交易汇价和银行挂牌汇价管理有关事项作出如下规定：

中国人民银行授权中国外汇交易中心于每个工作日上午 9:15 对外公布当日人民币对美元、欧元、日元、港元、英镑、马来西亚林吉特、俄罗斯卢布、澳大利亚元、加拿大元和新西兰元汇率中间价，作为当日银行间即期外汇市场（含询价交易方式和撮合方式）交易汇率的中间价。中国人民银行授权中国外汇交易中心公布的当日汇率中间价适用于该中间价发布后到下一个汇率中间价发布前。

人民币对美元汇率中间价的形成方式为：中国外汇交易中心于每日银行间外汇市场开盘前向银行间外汇市场做市商询价，并将做市商报价作为人民币对美元汇率中间价的计算样本，去掉最高和最低报价后，将剩余做市商报价加权平均，得到当日人民币对美元汇率中间价，权重由中国外汇交易中心根据报价方在银行间外汇市场的交易量及报价情况等指标综合确定。

人民币对欧元、港元和加拿大元汇率中间价由中国外汇交易中心分别根据当日人民币对美元汇率中间价与上午 9：00 国际外汇市场欧元、港元和加拿大元对美元汇率套算确定。人民币对日元、英镑、澳大利亚元、新西兰元、马来西亚林吉特和俄罗斯卢布汇率中间价由中国外汇交易中心根据每日银行间外汇市场开盘前银行间外汇市场相应币种的直接交易做市商报价平均得出。

每日银行间即期外汇市场人民币对美元的交易价可在中国外汇交易中心对外公布的当日人民币对美元汇率中间价上下 2% 的幅度内浮动。人民币对欧元、日元、港元、英镑、澳大利亚元、加拿大元和新西兰元交易价在中国外汇交易中心公布的人民币对该货币汇率中间价上下 3% 的幅度内浮动。人民币对马来西亚林吉特、俄罗斯卢布交易价在中国外汇交易中心公布的人民币对该货币汇率中间价上下 5% 的幅度内浮动。人民币对其他非美元货币交易价的浮动幅度另行规定。

银行可基于市场需求和定价能力对客户自主挂牌人民币对各种货币汇价，现汇、现钞挂牌买卖价没有限制，根据市场供求自主定价。银行应建立健全挂牌汇价的内部管理制度，有效防范风险，避免不正当竞争。

本通知自发布之日起施行。《中国人民银行关于银行间外汇市场交易汇价和外汇指定银行挂牌汇价管理有关事项的通知》（银发〔2005〕183 号）、《中国人民银行关于进一步改善银行间外汇市场交易汇价和外汇指定银行挂牌汇价管理的通知》（银发

〔2005〕250 号)、《中国人民银行关于银行间外汇市场交易汇价和外汇指定银行挂牌汇价管理有关问题的通知》(银发〔2010〕325 号)同时废止,中国人民银行和国家外汇管理局其他文件中涉及银行间外汇市场交易汇价和银行挂牌汇价管理规定的有关事项以本通知为准。

6. 调整金融机构进入银行间外汇市场

为进一步简政放权,丰富市场参与主体,促进外汇市场发展,根据《中华人民共和国外汇管理条例》,2014 年 12 月 5 日,国家外汇管理局发布《国家外汇管理局关于调整金融机构进入银行间外汇市场有关管理政策的通知》(汇发〔2014〕48 号),就境内金融机构进入银行间外汇市场有关管理政策作出如下调整:

境内金融机构经国家外汇管理局批准取得即期结售汇业务资格和相关金融监管部门批准取得衍生产品交易业务资格后,在满足银行间外汇市场相关业务技术规范条件下,可以成为银行间外汇市场会员,相应开展人民币对外汇即期和衍生产品交易,国家外汇管理局不实施银行间外汇市场事前入市资格许可。

金融机构应将本机构在银行间外汇市场进行人民币对外汇即期和衍生产品交易的内部操作规程和风险管理制度送中国外汇交易中心(以下简称交易中心)备案。

金融机构在银行间外汇市场开展人民币对外汇交易,应基于对冲代客和自身结售汇业务风险、在结售汇综合头寸限额内开展做市和自营交易、从事符合规定的自身套期保值等需要,并遵守银行间外汇市场交易、清算、信息等法规、规则及有关金融监管部门的规定。

经银行业监督管理部门批准设立的货币经纪公司(含分支机构),可以在银行间外汇市场开展人民币对外汇衍生产品交易、外汇对外汇交易、外汇拆借等外汇管理规定的外汇经纪业务,国家外汇管理局不实施事前资格许可。货币经纪公司开展外汇经纪业务,应遵守银行间外汇市场有关法规、规则。

交易中心和银行间市场清算所股份有限公司(以下简称上海清算所)应根据本通知要求,相应调整有关业务规则及系统,做好技术支持与服务工作。交易中心和上海清算所负责银行间人民币对外汇交易、清算的日常监控工作,发现异常交易、清算情况应及时向国家外汇管理局报告。

金融机构应遵守职业操守和市场惯例,促进外汇市场自律管理和规范发展。

本通知自 2015 年 1 月 1 日起实施。《国家外汇管理局关于中国银行在银行间外汇市场开展人民币与外币掉期交易有关问题的批复》(汇复〔2006〕61 号)、《国家外汇管理局关于推出人民币对外汇期权交易有关问题的通知》(汇发〔2011〕8 号)、《国家外汇管理局关于调整银行间外汇市场部分业务管理的通知》(汇发〔2012〕30 号)、《国家外汇管理局关于调整人民币外汇衍生产品业务管理的通知》(汇发〔2013〕46 号)同时废止,其他文件中涉及银行间外汇市场准入管理规定的有关事项以本通知为准。

2014年12月26日，中国外汇交易中心发布《关于调整银行间人民币外汇市场准入指引的通知》（中汇交发〔2014〕327号），对银行间人民币外汇市场相关准入规则进行了调整，自2015年1月1日起正式实施。

7. 丰富外汇业务品种，调整市场交易收费方案，规范外汇市场职业操守

2014年1月10日，中国外汇交易中心发布《关于在外汇交易系统增加货币掉期本金交换形式的通知》（中汇交发〔2014〕5号）。该通知决定，中国外汇交易中心于2014年1月13日起在外汇交易系统人民币外汇货币掉期业务中增加"生效日不实际交换本金、到期日实际交换本金"的本金交换形式。

2014年12月25日，中国外汇交易中心发布《关于推出人民币对林吉特、俄罗斯卢布和新西兰元远期和掉期交易的通知》（中汇交发〔2014〕321号），决定自2014年12月29日起推出人民币对林吉特、俄罗斯卢布和新西兰元的远期和掉期交易。

2014年12月22日，中国外汇交易中心发布《关于调整银行间人民币外汇市场即期竞价交易收费方案的通知》（中汇交发〔2014〕308号）。该通知决定，自2015年1月1日起，对银行间人民币外汇市场即期竞价交易收费方案作出调整：降低人民币外汇即期竞价交易费率（不包含清算费率）至十万分之三；取消人民币外汇即期竞价交易费用累进折扣优惠。

为维护公平、诚信、有序的市场环境，在国家外汇管理局的指导下，中国外汇交易中心于2014年7月10日发布《中国外汇交易中心关于发布〈银行间外汇市场职业操守和市场惯例指引〉等的通知》（中汇交发〔2014〕173号）。银行间外汇市场做市商已签署该指引，承诺遵守相关条款诚信交易。该指引是银行间外汇市场自律性文件，自发布之日起实施。中国外汇交易中心将在国家外汇管理局的指导下组织协调银行间外汇市场会员进一步推进银行间外汇市场自律工作。

（三）外汇市场政策展望

2015年是全面深化改革的关键之年，也是全面完成"十二五"规划的收官之年。外汇管理部门要主动适应经济发展新常态，狠抓改革攻坚，有序提高跨境资本和金融交易可兑换程度，大力发展外汇市场，强化风险防控。

囿于国际环境的复杂多变，强势美元以及世界经济仍处于深度调整期，国际金融市场波动加剧。在此背景下，如何应对双向开放后的跨境资本流动冲击，主动适应经济发展新常态的国家外汇管理局面临较大挑战，包括在外汇储备对外投资收益波动性加大的情况下如何实现外汇储备保值增值，是2015年外汇市场管理工作的主要挑战。

改革创新与防风险并重，进一步提升服务实体经济的能力，依然是2015年国家外汇管理局的工作主线。扩大资本市场的双向开放几乎是大势所趋，因为中国已经明确要加快实现人民币资本项目可兑换。那么，开放以后的跨境资金快进快出可能会成为一种

常态。外汇管理局既要增加对跨境资本流动的容忍度，又要练好内功；同时，建立宏观审慎的跨境资本流动管理体制机制，但前提是顺利推进改革，解决价格上的扭曲。因此，这一年的政策看点是，简政放权，促进贸易投资便利化，推进资本项目可兑换；同时，加强跨境资金流动检测预警和风险应对。

十、中国黄金市场发展政策[①]

（一）2014 年新政或政策调整一览

1 月 2 日，上海黄金交易所推出了 Mini 黄金延期合约［mAu（T + D）］。

6 月 10 日，上海黄金交易所与上海期货交易所建立合作关系。

6 月 18 日，人民银行上海总部举行自由贸易账户业务启动仪式。上海黄金交易所与人民银行上海总部签署了合作备忘录。

7 月 25 日，平安银行和上海银行通过上海黄金交易所询价交易系统完成首笔黄金拆借交易。

8 月，交通银行和上海银行通过上海黄金交易所询价交易系统完成黄金询价业务现金差额交割品种首笔交易。

9 月 18 日，上海黄金交易所举办国际板上线启动仪式。

9 月 19 日，上海黄金交易所与香港金银业贸易场在上海举行了合作签约仪式。

11 月 10 日，上海黄金交易所和芝加哥商业交易所集团（CME Group）在上海签订《谅解备忘录》。

（二）2014 年中国黄金市场主要政策评估

1. 改善黄金市场交易运行机制

（1）推出黄金现货交易新品种。2014 年 1 月 2 日，上海黄金交易所推出了 Mini 黄金延期合约［mAu（T + D）］，其交易单位为 100 克/手，同时下调 Au99.99 品种的交易单位，由原来的 100 克/手降为 10 克/手。这两项业务上线以来，投资者积极参与，市场各方反响良好。

（2）上海黄金交易所黄金拆借平台达成首笔交易。2014 年 7 月 25 日，平安银行和上海银行通过上海黄金交易所询价交易系统完成首笔黄金拆借交易，标志着银行间黄金拆借市场的实质性启动。银行间黄金拆借市场是上海黄金交易所根据中国人民银行整体部署，为金融机构提供的黄金实物融通新渠道；同时，黄金拆借市场也是为推进黄金场外市场交易平台建设，促进银行间黄金拆借利率曲线形成而进行的基础设施建设项目之一。该市场以各类金融机构为主，定位为黄金实物融通的"批发"市场，重点体现批发融通、价格形成、做市套利等市场服务和交易性功能。

---

① 执笔：储幼阳。

黄金拆借业务（下称黄金拆借交易）是指上海黄金交易所（以下简称交易所）核准的市场参与机构，通过交易所询价系统以双边询价方式进行拆入、拆出的黄金融通业务。黄金拆借交易时间为每周一至周五9:00—11:30及13:30—17:00（交易所公告休市日除外），11:30—13:30为暂停交易状态。交易所可根据市场发展需要调整并公告交易时间。交易所询价系统挂牌的黄金拆借交易品种包括LAU99.95、LAU99.99，分别对应成色不低于99.95%和不低于99.99%的黄金交易标的。新增其他黄金、白银等贵金属拆借品种的挂牌根据交易所的公告执行。

上海黄金交易所将根据市场需求及后续反馈对黄金拆借平台不断完善，进一步满足银行间黄金实物融通需求，丰富询价市场产品线，推进黄金基准利率体系建设，更好地服务整个拆借市场的发展。

（3）上海黄金交易所黄金询价业务现金差额交割品种达成首笔交易。2014年8月，交通银行和上海银行通过上海黄金交易所询价交易系统完成黄金询价业务现金差额交割品种首笔交易，该交易首次采用上海黄金交易所黄金基准价作为现金差额交割参考价格，并顺利完成清算交割。现金差额交割业务的启动标志着黄金询价市场的产品线得到进一步拓展和完善。黄金询价业务是指上海黄金交易所核准的市场参与者，通过交易所提供的询价交易系统以双边询价方式达成的交易，或者经交易所核准的市场参与者通过中国外汇交易中心外汇交易系统以双边询价方式进行的交易，交易品种为交易所指定在交易中心外汇交易系统挂牌的交易品种。现金差额交割是国际金融市场通行的清算交割方式之一，是指在询价交易到期时，交易双方无须进行黄金实物和全额资金的对付，而是根据约定的参考价格与交易价格的差额，通过现金支付差额的方式替代履行黄金实物交割义务。上海黄金交易所根据中国人民银行整体部署，顺应市场需求，推出黄金询价业务现金差额交割品种，是推进黄金场外市场标准化、规范化建设，完善、丰富人民币计价的询价市场产品线，提升黄金场外市场登记清算服务水平的重要举措。交易所将根据市场需求及后续反馈对黄金询价系统不断完善，推进黄金场外市场体系建设，更好地服务整个黄金市场的发展。

2. 上海国际金融中心建设与黄金市场国际化

（1）上海黄金交易所国际黄金业务结算正式纳入自由贸易账户体系。2014年6月18日，人民银行上海总部举行自由贸易账户业务启动仪式。启动仪式上，上海黄金交易所理事长许罗德代表交易所与人民银行上海总部签署了合作备忘录，标志着交易所正式接入人民银行上海总部系统，依托自贸区自由贸易账户体系为国际投资者参与黄金交易提供便利。交易所还分别与工行、建行、中行上海市分行，浦发上海分行等4家银行现场签订了《结算银行合作协议》。根据协议，符合条件的境外和自贸区内客户可在签约银行分账核算单元内开设自由贸易账户，参与黄金交易。

自由贸易账户是在上海自贸区内金融开放体系的重要组成部分。试验区内的居民可通过设立本外币自由贸易账户实现分账核算管理，开展投融资创新业务；非居民可在试验区内银行开立本外币非居民自由贸易账户，按准入前国民待遇原则享受相关金融服务。中国人民银行 2013 年 12 月 2 日发布的《关于金融支持中国（上海）自由贸易试验区建设的意见》提出，条件成熟时，试验区内的居民和金融机构将能够设立本外币自由贸易账户，并能够在这些账户上进行人民币的自由兑换。所谓自由贸易账户体系，体现了分账管理、离岸自由、双向互通、有限渗透的核心。根据人民银行的《中国人民银行关于金融支持中国（上海）自由贸易试验区建设的意见》，试验区内的居民可通过设立本外币自由贸易账户（以下简称居民自由贸易账户）实现分账核算管理，开展一部分投融资创新业务；非居民可在试验区内银行开立本外币非居民自由贸易账户（以下简称非居民自由贸易账户），按准入前国民待遇原则享受相关金融服务。具体而言，居民自由贸易账户与境外账户、境内区外的非居民账户、非居民自由贸易账户以及其他居民自由贸易账户之间的资金可自由划转；同一非金融机构主体的居民自由贸易账户与其他银行结算账户之间因经常项下业务、偿还贷款、实业投资以及其他符合规定的跨境交易需要可办理资金划转；居民自由贸易账户与境内区外的银行结算账户之间产生的资金流动视同跨境业务管理。在跨境资金监管体系中，自由贸易账户在较大程度上被视同为境外账户。通过构建自由贸易账户体系，实质上在试验区内形成了一个与境内其他市场有限隔离、与国际金融市场高度接轨的金融环境，以服务于更加广泛的涉外经济活动需求。上海地区金融机构可根据人民银行规定，通过设立试验区分账核算单元的方式，为符合条件的区内主体开立自由贸易账户，并提供相关金融服务。

上海国际黄金交易中心将在签约银行分账核算单元开立自由贸易账户，为区内和国际投资者提供参与国际业务相关的结算和清算服务。

（2）黄金国际板开业启动。9 月 18 日晚，上海黄金交易所举办国际板上线启动仪式。全国政协副主席、中国人民银行行长周小川，中共上海市委副书记、市长杨雄共同为国际板开市并分别讲话。中国人民银行副行长刘士余和中共上海市委常委、副市长艾宝俊共同为上海国际黄金交易中心揭牌。启动仪式由上海黄金交易所理事长许罗德主持，人民银行相关司局、上海市政府相关部门、交易所国内外会员单位及相关机构的代表共同见证了国际板启动。在启动仪式现场，黄金国际板完成了首笔交易，瑞士 MKS 金融公司及工行、中行、交行、汇丰等几家银行成为首批参与者，标志着我国黄金市场对外开放迈出实质性的一步，"上海金"正式走向全球。启动国际板，是上海黄金交易所主动融入全球市场、顺应全球发展趋势的战略选择。伴随国际板上线，上海黄金交易所将实现四个突破：

一是会员国际化。此次交易所首批吸收了 40 家国际会员。这些会员既包括国际上最著名的商业银行和专业投资机构，也包括顶尖的黄金精炼企业，未来还会有更多国际会员加入。国际会员可以自主参与交易所所有合约交易，也可以代理国际投资者参与交易所交易。国际投资者包括了上海自由贸易区内注册的投资者，更包括了境外的投资者。

二是交易资金国际化。国际板引进离岸资金参与交易。离岸资金可以是自贸区内的离岸资金，也可以是境外的离岸资金；既包括离岸的人民币，也包括离岸的可兑换货币。这些资金将在自由贸易账户的框架下参与人民币报价的黄金等贵金属交易。

三是定价国际化。交易所所有产品以人民币计价，随着参与者更广泛、交易量更大，随着在岸投资者、在岸资金和离岸投资者、离岸资金的深度融合，将会推动交易所交易价格从区域性的价格逐步向国际性的价格转变，形成有国际影响力的人民币黄金计价基准。我们将这一定价机制和相应的产品、实物交割标准称为"上海金"。"上海金"的推出，将有助于提升黄金市场人民币价格发现功能，加强中国市场和国际市场的有效联动，有效发挥我们第一实物黄金消费国、生产国、进口国在国际市场上应有的作用，也有助于提升人民币国际影响力，助推人民币国际化。

四是储运和交割国际化。国际板启动后，客户可根据需要选择在交易所自贸区仓库交割实物黄金，由于自贸区有"一线放开"的政策，这些实物黄金既可以由交易所委托符合条件的机构进口到境内，也可以自由转口至全球其他国家，这将为亚太投资者提供更为便捷高效的转口服务，助推上海成为亚太黄金转口中心。为此，交易所上线了三个在自贸区交割的现货黄金合约，分别是交易单位100克和1千克、成色99.99的iAu100、iAu99.99，交易单位12.5千克、成色99.5的iAu99.5，在自贸区设立了一个千吨级的、现代化的黄金库，为进口和转口黄金提供一系列的交割、仓储、物流等配套服务。

3. 加强黄金市场国际合作

2014年，上海黄金交易所与香港金银业贸易场、芝加哥商品交易集团建立合作关系。

（1）上海黄金交易所与香港金银业贸易场建立合作关系。2014年9月19日下午，上海黄金交易所与香港金银业贸易场在上海举行了合作签约仪式。上海黄金交易所理事长许罗德、副总经理沈刚与香港金银业贸易场理事长张德熙、副理事长陈尚智等参加了签约仪式。双方约定，未来将以交易所国际板为契机，进一步加强合作，共同推动中国黄金市场的发展和对外开放。

（2）上海黄金交易所与芝加哥商品交易集团建立合作关系。2014年11月10日，上海黄金交易所和芝加哥商业交易所集团（CME Group）在上海签订《谅解备忘录》。CME Group终身名誉主席利奥·梅拉梅德和上海黄金交易所理事长许罗德参加签约仪式，并代表各自交易所签署了《谅解备忘录》。与CME Group建立合作伙伴关系，是交易所实行对外开放和国际化战略的重要举措之一。未来，双方将在《谅解备忘录》的框架下，本着"互惠互利、合作共赢"的原则，积极探索国内外市场合作的新模式，大力拓展服务境内外投资者的新路径，共同推动全球黄金市场的健康、平稳、有序发展。

（三）政策展望

在当前国际经济发展形势出现分化、美国经济回暖迹象逐步明朗、欧洲增长乏力、新兴经济体面临较大困难、我国经济呈现新常态、国内金融市场改革开放进一步深入的情况下，从国内外两个方面来分析，中国黄金市场均处于新的发展机遇期。展望2015年黄金市场的各项政策将继续沿着推动国内黄金交易市场机制进一步改革、加快黄金市场开放和国际合作、加强黄金国际板建设这三方面发展目标展开。

1. 推动黄金市场机制进一步改革

从推动上海国际金融中心建设的角度，出台各项政策引导黄金市场与外汇市场、资本市场良性互动，构建多层次的金融市场体系。

从上海自贸区扩容和中国资本项目加快开放的角度，出台各项政策，推动黄金市场更多参与自贸区制度建设和人民币国际化进程，在黄金投资和交易方面实现资本项目完全可兑换。

2015年，交易所将扩大国内投资者和国外投资者的范围，更多地引入非银行金融机构和境外合格投资者参与黄金市场，打造"上海金"，非银行金融机构的引入将为中国黄金市场发展提供另一个战略发展机遇，可以预见更多的贵金属业务创新开放将不断涌现。

2. 加快黄金市场开放和国际合作

2015年，中国的交易所将进一步加强与世界黄金协会、各大主要黄金交易所等国际同业的合作力度，为全球投资者提供更全面、更专业的市场服务，推动中国黄金市场和全球黄金市场的繁荣发展。

3. 加强黄金国际板建设

2015年，上海黄金国际板建设将在2014年取得的成绩上稳步推进：

应把黄金国际板建设提高到树立我国黄金市场国际地位的高度，出台各项政策，以上海黄金交易所国际板为平台整合黄金市场国内国外的资源，力争使国际板上新台阶。

重视黄金国际板具体制度设计创新，学习国外先进经验，出台更加具体的交易规则和鼓励政策，进一步完善投资主体结构、产品体系、系统建设、风控合规体系、市场推广及服务、场外市场建设、人才队伍建设和内部管理，力争在国际板交易规模、客户数量、交易产品、市场服务和国际交流合作等方面取得新进展，创新驱动，加快转型，全面提升市场化水平。

在与国内外各大交易所的市场竞争中，借助移动互联网的东风，推出具有互联网基因的黄金产品和业务。互联网与金融的联姻催生了一批互联网理财产品，但这样的互联网理财产品大多集中在货币基金领域，对于投资标的多元化以分散风险和长线投资战略来说，这些产品并不足够。而实物黄金投资的互联网化则为投资者提供了多元化、长线投资的可能，对目前较为单一的理财标的是一种有益补充。未来我国可能会出台鼓励发展互联网黄金理财产品的政策，通过移动互联网应用提供实物黄金产品，这将大大改善我国黄金市场上的参与主体以商业银行、珠宝原料商、加工制造商等黄金企业为主的单一局面，提高实物黄金市场资源的配置效率，进而推动我国黄金市场与国际市场接轨。

主要金融监管政策

一、中国人民银行主要监管政策[1]

（一）2014 年中国人民银行主要监管政策一览

表 6 – 1 　　　　　　　2014 年中国人民银行的主要监管政策

发布时间	文件名	文　号
1 月	人民银行、科技部、银监会、证监会、保监会、知识产权局联合发布《关于大力推进体制机制创新扎实做好科技金融服务的意见》	银发〔2014〕9 号
1 月	《涉及恐怖活动资产冻结管理办法》	中国人民银行、公安部、国家安全部令〔2014〕第 1 号
2 月	《中国人民银行关于建立场外金融衍生产品集中清算机制及开展人民币利率互换集中清算业务有关事宜的通知》	银发〔2014〕29 号
2 月	《关于做好家庭农场等新型农业经营主体金融服务的指导意见》	银发〔2014〕42 号
3 月	《关于加快小微企业和农村信用体系建设的意见》	银发〔2014〕37 号
3 月	人民银行、财政部、银监会、证监会、保监会、扶贫办、共青团中央联合印发了《关于全面做好扶贫开发金融服务工作的指导意见》	银发〔2014〕65 号
3 月	《关于开办支小再贷款支持扩大小微企业信贷投放的通知》	银发〔2014〕90 号
4 月	银监会和人民银行联合发布《中国银监会　中国人民银行关于加强商业银行与第三方支付机构合作业务管理的通知》	银监发〔2014〕10 号
4 月	中国人民银行、银监会、证监会、保监会、外汇局联合印发《关于规范金融机构同业业务的通知》	银发〔2014〕127 号
6 月	《人民银行关于贯彻落实〈国务院办公厅关于支持外贸稳定增长的若干意见〉的指导意见》	
6 月	《银行办理结售汇业务管理办法》	中国人民银行令〔2014〕第 2 号

---

[1] 执笔：朱小川。

发布时间	文件名	文　号
7 月	《中国人民银行关于银行间外汇市场交易汇价和银行挂牌汇价管理有关事项的通知》	银发〔2014〕188 号
8 月	人民银行、银监会、证监会、保监会联合发布《关于鲁甸地震灾后恢复重建金融服务工作的指导意见》	
9 月	《中国人民银行关于全面推进深化农村支付服务环境建设的指导意见》	银发〔2014〕235 号
9 月	人民银行和银监会联合印发《中国人民银行　中国银行业监督管理委员会关于进一步做好住房金融服务工作的通知》	银发〔2014〕287 号
9 月	《关于开展银行卡领域金融消费权益保护专项检查的通知》	银办发〔2014〕97 号
9 月	银监会、财政部、人民银行联合印发《中国银监会办公厅　财政部办公厅　人民银行办公厅关于加强商业银行存款偏离度管理有关事项的通知》	银监办发〔2014〕236 号
11 月	银监会、财政部、人民银行、证监会、保监会联合发布《金融资产管理公司监管办法》	银监发〔2014〕41 号
11 月	人民银行、证监会联合发布《关于印发〈债券统计制度〉的通知》	银发〔2014〕320 号
11 月	人民银行、证监会联合发布《关于沪港股票市场交易互联互通机制试点有关问题的通知》	银发〔2014〕336 号

资料来源：课题组整理。

（二）2014 年中国人民银行主要监管政策分析

1. 利率汇率市场化改革迈出新步伐

利率是资金要素的价格，利率市场化改革关乎全局。2014 年人民银行推动存款利率市场化改革又迈出新的重大步伐。2014 年 11 月 21 日，在调整人民币贷款和存款基准利率水平的同时，推出利率市场化的重要举措：将人民币存款利率浮动区间上限由基准利率的 1.1 倍扩大至 1.2 倍。同时，还简化了存贷款基准利率的期限档次，扩大了利率市场化定价的空间，健全了上海银行间同业拆放利率和市场利率定价自律机制，稳步扩大同业存单发行交易等。这对于进一步健全市场利率形成机制，提高金融机构自主定价能力具有重要意义。人民银行还鼓励利率衍生品市场发展，利率衍生品交易活跃度明显上升。2014 年，人民币利率互换共交易 4.3 万笔，名义本金总额 4.0 万亿元，同比增加 47.9%；从期限结构来看，1 年及 1 年期以下交易最为活跃，其名义本金总额 2.7 万亿元，占总量的 63.4%。

除利率外，人民币汇率市场化改革也加快推进。2014 年 3 月 17 日，人民银行在充分考虑经济主体适应能力的基础上，把银行间即期外汇市场人民币兑美元交易价浮动幅度由1%扩大至2%，银行柜台汇率报价区间由2%扩大至3%。2014年以来，人民银行大幅减少了外汇干预，自第二季度以来已经基本上退出了常态化的市场干预。此外，人民银行还授权外汇交易中心在银行间市场开展人民币对英镑、欧元、新加坡元、新西兰元等货币的直接交易，以降低经济主体的汇兑成本，提高了市场效率。

2. 扩大直接融资比例

2014年，人民银行继续坚持市场化改革方向，减少行政审批，强化市场约束，加快金融产品和制度创新，稳步扩大银行间债券市场规模，直接融资比例大幅提升。2014年，银行间债券市场累计发行人民币债券10.7万亿元，同比增加24.0%。银行间市场债券托管余额为32.4万亿元，同比增加16.9%。此外，人民银行还采取综合性改革措施恢复和增强股票市场融资功能。2014年直接融资在社会融资规模中的比重提高到17%左右，较上年同期上升了6个百分点。

3. 深化金融市场的对外开放

债券市场对外开放进一步加快，人民银行积极推动境内机构赴香港发行人民币债券，以及境外企业在境内发行人民币债券。截至2014年10月末，共有16家境内金融机构赴境外发行人民币债券1 055亿元，推动境外企业在境内发行人民币债券5亿元。为加快资本市场双向开放，人民银行联合证监会正式启动沪港股票市场交易互联互通，允许人民币合格境内机构投资者（RQDII）以人民币开展境外证券投资，扩大人民币合格境外机构投资者（RQFII）境外试点，允许跨国企业集团开展跨境人民币资金集中运营业务等。特别是沪港通机制的顺利实施，有利于促进内地资本市场与全球资本市场的融合，对内地和香港资本市场的创新发展、资本项目可兑换和人民币国际化进程都将起到积极推动作用。截至2014年末，共有211家包括境外中央银行或货币当局、国际金融机构、主权财富基金、人民币业务清算行、跨境贸易人民币结算境外参加行、境外保险机构、RQFII和QFII等在内的境外机构获准进入银行间债券市场，较2013年末增加73家。此外，人民银行大力推动上海自贸区金融改革先行先试，在自由贸易账户体系、投融资汇兑便利、人民币跨境使用、利率市场化、外汇管理改革等5个方面积累可复制、可推广的改革开放和风险监管经验。

4. 深化人民币国际化程度

2014年人民币使用的国际合作不断深化。截至年末，超过40家的央行和货币当局已将人民币纳入其外汇储备；2014年人民银行与瑞士、斯里兰卡、俄罗斯、卡塔尔、加拿大等5国的中央银行签署了双边本币互换协议，还累计与十几个国家或地区的中央银行签订了人民币清算安排。除在传统的亚洲地区，人民币货币合作已经延伸到欧洲主要经济金融中心，拓展到美洲、大洋洲、中东地区。如前所述，人民银行同时也鼓励开展人民币对部分外币的直接交易，促进人民币与外币在双边贸易和投资中的使用。人民币国际化是我国改革开放不断深化的结果，也是深化改革开放的催化器，涉及的改革有简政放权、汇率利率市场化、金融市场开放、资本项目可兑换、宏观调控方式、金融监管等，意义深远。

5. 多举措缓解企业融资成本高问题

受国际金融危机的后续影响，国内经济下行压力有所加大，部分企业经营效益下降，小微企业融资不易、成本较高的结构性问题依然突出。2014年人民银行按照国务院的要求，多措并举、标本兼治，推动结构性改革和调整，除要求金融机构优化信贷管理、清理不合理的收费、规范影子银行业务、遏制筹资成本不合理上升外，还进一步通过深化金融体制机制改革来缓解企业融资成本高的问题。具体改革措施包括推进利率汇率市场化、发展多层次资本市场、加快发展民营银行等中小金融机构等，这些措施在2014年起到了一定的预期效果，如企业债券融资成本显著走低，年末固定利率企业债券加权平均发行利率为5.52%，较上年末下降148个基点；公司信用类债券收益率曲线大幅下行，年末5年期AAA、AA+企业债收益率较上年末分别下降148个和141个基点。

6. 推动部分地区进行金融改革试点

人民银行积极推动部分区域进行金融改革试点，具体地域范围涵盖东部的沿海发达地区、中部工业化转型地区、西部欠发达地区和民族边疆地区，内容涉及金融对外开放、人民币资本项目可兑换、跨境人民币业务、粤港澳金融合作、农村金融改革、规范发展民间金融和跨境金融合作等。区域金融改革试点以金融服务实体经济发展为出发点，支持条件成熟的地区根据当地经济发展实际和产业结构升级需要，做好金融改革与产业结构升级、金融创新与经济社会发展需求的衔接，引导地方充分利用现有政策，提高金融运行效率，推动符合当地实际、具有地方特色的金融改革创新，取得了初步成效。

7. 保持支付体系持续稳定高效运转

2014年支付业务统计数据显示，支付体系安全、稳定、高效运行，社会资金交易规模持续增大，在支持金融工具创新、改善金融服务水平、提高资源配置效率等方面发挥了积极作用，有力促进了我国社会经济的发展。

8. 鼓励创新发展、分类适度监管互联网金融

人民银行肯定互联网金融在提高金融服务效率，降低交易成本，满足多元化的投融资需求，提升微型金融、农村金融的普惠性水平方面发挥了积极作用；同时认为互联网金融并没有改变金融的风险属性，而且与互联网伴生的技术、信息、安全等风险更为突出。因此，人民银行按照分类适度监管的原则，研究互联网金融的监管框架，充分利用中国支付清算协会，推动支付清算和互联网金融行业自律管理，发挥行业自律在行业治理中的积极作用，形成监管与自律的协同和均衡。

9. 持续推进反洗钱工作

2014年，人民银行重点研究《国家洗钱和恐怖融资风险评估总体规划》，通过反洗

钱部际联席会议完善我国反洗钱的工作机制和制度，深化国际反洗钱和反恐怖融资合作，反洗钱与反恐怖融资监测水平明显提升，执法和监管力度加强。

10. 金融消费者保护工作取得新进展

2014年人民银行金融消费权益保护工作主要包括：强化对社会公众的金融消费权益保护意识，不断完善金融消费权益保护工作体制机制，积极推动制度建设；健全金融消费者咨询投诉受理处理机制，在全国开通"12363金融消费权益保护咨询投诉电话"，初步建立起信息管理平台；积极探索金融消费纠纷非诉解决机制，开展投诉分类标准应用工作；稳步开展银行卡领域金融消费权益保护专项检查，向金融机构通报了检查所发现的六方面十七类问题；探索开展非现场监督管理，试点环境、机构、产品评估。深入宣传和普及金融知识，持续开展"金融知识普及月""金融消费者权益日"活动；开展普惠金融调研和支持移动金融创新试点，积极参与金融消费权益保护和普惠金融领域的国际交流活动，向世界各国展示我国相关成果并分享经验。2014年6月至8月，人民银行上海总部、各分支机构共计对1269家金融机构（含分支机构）进行了专项检查工作（部分地区纳入综合执法检查），共发现了涉及银行卡领域金融消费权益保护方面的六个方面十七类主要问题。

（三）监管政策评价与展望

2014年，面对复杂多变的国际环境和艰巨繁重的国内改革发展稳定任务，在党中央、国务院的领导下，人民银行坚持稳中求进、改革创新，各项工作都取得明显成效。除了继续实施稳健的货币政策外，还在利率汇率市场化改革、债券市场、自贸区等领域取得新突破，政策性金融机构改革迈出新步伐；金融市场创新发展明显加快，金融服务实体经济的功能显著增强；人民币跨境使用进一步扩大；外汇管理体制改革不断深化；金融风险防范切实有效；金融服务和管理水平稳步提升；国际及区域金融合作广泛深入。

2015年是全面深化改革的关键之年，是全面推进依法治国的开局之年，也是全面完成"十二五"规划的收官之年，人民银行将一如既往地坚持稳中求进的工作总基调，准确把握、主动适应经济发展新常态，统筹稳增长、促改革、调结构、惠民生和防风险，继续实施稳健的货币政策，保持监管政策的连续性和稳定性。预计2015年人民银行在利率和汇率的市场化、人民币资本项目可兑换方面将加快改革步伐，可能会适时推进面向企业和个人发行大额存单等方式；同时还将尽快出台和实施政策性金融机构改革方案，建立存款保险制度；按照"适度监管、分类监管、协同监管、创新监管"的原则，建立和完善互联网金融的监管框架，牵头制定促进互联网金融健康发展的指导意见；继续加强对区域金融改革的统筹、引导，积累可复制、可推广经验，落实好已经出台的各地改革试点举措；反洗钱工作在新的形势下已上升到国家战略层面，人民银行牵头的反洗钱工作将在部际联席会议框架下建立起国家层面的洗钱和恐怖融资风险评估机制、进一步完善反洗钱和反恐怖融资法律体系建设、加强信息共享和数据挖掘、深化国际合作、加强人才培养等；2015 年金融消费权益保护工作将继续深入开展监督检查与评估，全面完善金融消费纠纷投诉受理处理机制，持续深化金融消费者教育与宣传工作，积极推进普惠金融发展，继续加强调查研究。

二、中国银监会主要监管政策①

（一）2014 年中国银监会主要监管政策一览

表 6 - 2　　　　　　　　2014 年中国银监会的主要监管政策

时间	文件名	文　　号
1 月	《商业银行流动性风险管理办法（试行）》	银监会令〔2014〕第 2 号
1 月	保监会、银监会联合发布《关于进一步规范商业银行代理保险业务销售行为的通知》	保监发〔2014〕3 号
2 月	银监会、国家发展改革委联合发布《商业银行服务价格管理办法》	银监会令〔2014〕1 号
3 月	《关于 2014 年小微企业金融服务工作的指导意见》	银监发〔2014〕7 号
3 月	《中国银监会办公厅关于支持产业结构调整和化解产能过剩的指导意见》	银监办发〔2014〕55 号
3 月	银监会修订《金融租赁公司管理办法》	银监会令〔2014〕3 号
3 月	银监会修订《农村中小金融机构行政许可事项实施办法》	银监会令〔2014〕4 号
4 月	《中国银监会办公厅关于信托公司风险监管的指导意见》	银监办发〔2014〕99 号
4 月	银监会、人民银行联合发布《中国银监会　中国人民银行关于加强商业银行与第三方支付机构合作业务管理的通知》	银监发〔2014〕10 号
4 月	银监会、证监会联合发布《中国银监会　中国证监会关于商业银行发行优先股补充一级资本的指导意见》	银监发〔2014〕12 号
4 月	人民银行、银监会、证监会、保监会、外汇局联合印发《关于规范金融机构同业业务的通知》	银发〔2014〕127 号
5 月	《中国银监会办公厅关于规范商业银行同业业务治理的通知》	银监办发〔2014〕140 号
6 月	《中国银监会办公厅关于推进简政放权改进市场准入工作有关事项的通知》	银监办发〔2014〕176 号
6 月	《中国银监会关于调整商业银行存贷比计算口径的通知》	银监发〔2014〕34 号
7 月	《中国银监会办公厅关于加强银行业金融机构信息科技非驻场集中式外包风险管理的通知》	银监办发〔2014〕187 号

---

① 执笔：朱小川。

续表

时间	文件名	文　号
7 月	《中国银监会关于完善银行理财业务组织管理体系有关事项的通知》	银监发〔2014〕35 号
7 月	《中国银监会关于完善和创新小微企业贷款服务　提高小微企业金融服务水平的通知》	银监发〔2014〕36 号
7 月	《中国银监会办公厅关于印发金融租赁公司专业子公司管理暂行规定的通知》	银监办发〔2014〕198 号
8 月	《中国银监会办公厅关于推进基础金融服务"村村通"的指导意见》	银监办发〔2014〕222 号
8 月	《中国银监会关于印发银行业金融机构消费者权益保护工作考核评价办法（试行）的通知》	银监发〔2014〕37 号
9 月	人民银行、银监会联合印发《中国人民银行　中国银行业监督管理委员会关于进一步做好住房金融服务工作的通知》	银发〔2014〕287 号
9 月	修订《外资银行行政许可事项实施办法》	银监会令〔2014〕6 号
9 月	银监会和农业部联合发布《中国银监会　农业部金融支持农业规模化生产和集约化经营的指导意见》	银监发〔2014〕38 号
9 月	银监会、财政部、人民银行联合印发《中国银监会办公厅　财政部办公厅　人民银行办公厅关于加强商业银行存款偏离度管理有关事项的通知》	银监办发〔2014〕236 号
9 月	银监会、国家发展改革委、科技部、工信部联合印发《关于应用安全可控信息技术加强银行业网络安全和信息化建设的指导意见》	银监发〔2014〕39 号
9 月	《商业银行内部控制指引》	银监发〔2014〕40 号
9 月	《中国银监会办公厅关于印发银行业金融机构案件风险排查管理办法的通知》	银监办发〔2014〕247 号
11 月	银监会、财政部、人民银行、证监会、保监会联合发布《金融资产管理公司监管办法》	银监发〔2014〕41 号
11 月	《中国银监会关于鼓励和引导民间资本参与农村信用社产权改革工作的通知》	银监发〔2014〕45 号
12 月	《中国银监会关于进一步促进村镇银行健康发展的指导意见》	银监发〔2014〕46 号
12 月	银监会、财政部联合制定《信托业保障基金管理办法》	银监发〔2014〕50 号
12 月	《中国银监会办公厅关于开展银行业金融机构信息科技非驻场集中式外包监管评估工作的通知》	银监办发〔2014〕272 号
12 月	《中国银监会办公厅关于印发加强农村商业银行三农金融服务机制建设监管指引的通知》	银监办发〔2014〕287 号

续表

时间	文件名	文　号
12月	《中国银监会　最高人民检察院　公安部　国家安全部关于印发银行业金融机构协助人民检察院公安机关国家安全机关查询冻结工作规定的通知》	银监发〔2014〕53号
12月	《商业银行并表管理与监管指引》	银监发〔2014〕54号
12月	《中国银监会2014年政府信息公开工作情况》	其他〔2014〕1号

资料来源：课题组整理。

（二）2014年中国银监会主要监管政策分析

2014年银监会系统紧跟党中央、国务院决策部署谋划工作，以"重改革、化风险、惠实体"为主题推动相关监管工作，统筹谋划推进改革开放，多管齐下防范化解金融风险，多策并举服务实体经济，较好地完成了各项任务。银行业各项经营管理和风险监管指标稳步向好，银行业利润增长保持平稳：2014年商业银行当年累计实现净利润1.55万亿元，同比增长9.65%；平均资产利润率为1.23%，同比下降0.04个百分点；平均资本利润率17.59%，同比下降1.58个百分点。针对信用风险计提的减值准备较为充足：2014年12月末，商业银行贷款损失准备余额为1.96万亿元，较年初增加2812亿元；拨备覆盖率为232.06%，较年初下降50.64个百分点；贷款拨备率为2.90%，较年初上升0.07个百分点。资本充足率继续维持在较高水平：2014年12月末，商业银行（不含外国银行分行）加权平均核心一级资本充足率为10.56%，较年初上升0.61个百分点；加权平均一级资本充足率为10.76%，较年初上升0.81个百分点；加权平均资本充足率为13.18%，较年初上升0.99个百分点。流动性水平比较充裕：2014年12月末，商业银行流动性比例为46.44%，较年初上升2.42个百分点；人民币超额备付金率2.65%，较年初上升0.11个百分点。自2014年7月1日起，银监会对商业银行存贷款比例计算口径进行调整，2014年12月末调整后人民币口径存贷款比例（人民币）为65.09%。

除上述各类银行业金融机构运行良好外，各类非银行金融机构运行情况也总体良好，体现出相关监管措施得当到位。截至2014年末，包括信托公司、财务公司、金融资产管理公司、金融租赁公司、汽车金融公司、货币经纪公司、消费金融公司在内的七类非银行金融机构管理的资产总额为22.74万亿元（含信托业务及财务公司委托业务等表外业务），所有者权益为1.21万亿元，实现净利润1659.59亿元。2014年，68家信托公司正常兑付信托产品16016笔，合计金额4.28万亿元，月均兑付3567亿元，信托产品到期兑付态势基本平稳。全年行业化解信托风险项目142笔，涉及金额374亿元。存续风险项目金额由6月末的917亿元下降到12月末的781亿元，占全部信托资产比重由0.73%下降至0.53%。财务公司行业整体资本充足，资产质量良好，拨备充足，经营平稳。2014 年末，行业平均资本充足率为 22.48%，同比上升 1.3 个百分点，不良资产余额为 32.81 亿元，不良资产率为 0.12%。截至 2014 年末，华融、长城、东方、信达四家金融资产管理公司集团口径资产规模总计 17 529.64 亿元，较年初增长 54.10%，所有者权益总计 2 766.05 亿元，合并净利润总计 388.22 亿元，较年初增长 27.50%；母公司法人口径资产规模总计 10 483.52 亿元，较年初增长 52.33%，所有者权益总计 2 048.80 亿元，净利润总计 249.19 亿元，较年初增长 24.99%。2014 年末，全国共有 30 家金融租赁公司（包括一家金融租赁专业子公司），资产总额 12 813.33 亿元，比年初增长 26.55%，负债总额 11 328.99 亿元，所有者权益 1 484.33 亿元，实现净利润 164.20 亿元。2014 年末，金融租赁公司平均资本充足率为 12.43%，平均不良资产率为 0.71%，拨备覆盖率为 269.96%，具备较强的风险抵御能力。汽车金融公司资产质量保持稳定，资本计提充足，抗风险能力较强。2014 年末，平均资本充足率为 16%，不良资产为 13.28 亿元，不良资产率为 0.38%，同比下降 0.03 个百分点。2014 年末，货币经纪公司资产 6.71 亿元，实现净利润 1.42 亿元，全年累计撮合人民币经纪业务 58.04 万亿元，外汇经纪业务 6.09 万亿美元，业务规模持续增长，产品种类日益丰富，市场认知度进一步提升。2014 年末，消费金融公司平均资本充足率为 22.83%，不良资产为 3.54 亿元，不良资产率为 1.56%。

1. 银行业改革开放取得重点突破

2014 年民间资本进入银行业取得新突破，首批 5 家民营银行完成批筹，其中 1 家已批准开业；新设 14 家民营控股的非银行金融机构，新增 162 家民间资本占主导地位的村镇银行；进一步引导民间资本参与农村信用社产权改革。银行业务治理体系改革进展顺利，各主要商业银行均已建立同业业务专营部门，453 家银行建立了理财业务事业部。银行业的对外开放进一步扩大，适当放宽了外资银行准入和经营人民币业务条件，统一中外资银行市场准入标准，首次以"准入前国民待遇加负面清单方式"对港澳银行业扩大开放。

2. 服务实体经济取得成效

银监会通过各类指导性意见，督促银行业金融机构进一步完善差别化信贷政策，支持产业结构调整和化解部分行业的产能过剩，降低企业融资成本高问题，加强对经济社会重点领域的金融服务。小微和涉农贷款继续实现"两个不低于"，即贷款增幅不低于各项贷款增幅，贷款增量不低于上年。全国 49 个金融机构空白乡镇、2308 个城镇社区和 318 个小微企业集中地区增设了银行网点，50 多万个行政村实现了基础金融服务全覆盖。此外，在棚户区改造和居民家庭合理住房消费等住房金融以及云南震区、西藏等地区的金融支持服务方面也做好了相应的政策举措。

3. 重点领域风险得到缓释，较好地守住了不发生系统性、区域性风险的底线

2014 年，我国钢贸、煤贸、铜贸和担保圈、担保链等业务风险逐步缓释，继而影响到银行信贷、信托、理财、影子银行等领域。对此，银监会加强了重点领域的信用风险防控，对过剩产能行业、地方政府融资平台、房地产等贷款实施差别化信贷政策，进一步加强了银行的并表管理；完善分类监管，批准了六家银行实施资本计量高级方法，顺利推出优先股等新型资本补充工具等；同时银监会还积极防范化解非信贷资产和表外业务潜在风险，对于商业银行的流动性风险、科技风险、外部风险和操作风险等也加强了监管。

4. 信息公开、简政放权

2014年，银监会认真贯彻《中华人民共和国政府信息公开条例》和《2014年政府信息公开工作要点》的要求，结合银行业监管工作实际，以银监会官方网站为公开主渠道，不断健全完善政府信息公开工作机制，充实政府信息公开内容，及时、主动、全面地向社会公众公开银行业监管工作情况，提高了银监会监管工作透明度，加深了社会公众对银行业监管的了解，有力地提升了依法监管能力。同时，银监会取消和下放了一批审批事项，印发《中国银监会办公厅关于推进简政放权改进市场准入工作有关事项的通知》，将部分原有审批事项改为报告制管理，要求不得以新的名义、条目变相审批，清减比率达标。

5. 加强消费者保护工作

进一步规范商业银行代理保险业务销售行为和服务价格监管，开展2014年金融知识宣传服务月活动，加强消费者权益保护工作体制机制建设。

6. 深入参与国际金融监管改革，加强国际监管交流与合作

2014年银监会多次参与金融稳定理事会会议、央行行长和监管当局负责人会议和巴塞尔委员会全体会议；分别与加纳中央银行、瑞典金融监管局、蒙古中央银行、秘鲁银行保险基金监管局、卡塔尔中央银行等5家境外监管机构签署了双边监管合作谅解备忘录（MOU），并与法国金融市场管理局签署了《商业银行代客境外理财业务双边监管合作换文》，与英国审慎监管局签署了《中资银行赴英申设分行监管分工协议》；分别与美国、加拿大及中国香港和台湾地区的银行业监管机构举行了双边磋商；此外，银监会还于2014年9月22日至25日在天津承办第18届国际银行监督官大会（ICBS）。

7. 完善非银行金融机构监管体系

信托业在非银行金融机构中占主体地位，其治理体系的"八项机制"建设工作取得突破性进展，并在2014年形成了新的"八项责任"要求。① 2014年，我国经济发展进入"新常态"时期，信托业的竞争和发展格局因此面临深度调整，战略机遇与挑战并存。在银监会的要求和监管下，信托公司适应了新常态，实现发展质量和效益同步提

---

① 八项机制包括完善的公司治理机制、产品登记机制、分类经营机制、资本约束机制、社会责任机制、恢复与处置机制、行业稳定机制和监管评价机制。八项责任指受托责任、经纪责任、维权责任、核算责任、机构责任、股东责任、行业责任和监管责任。

升,切实履行好了"八项责任"。银监会讨论修改《关于调整信托公司净资本计算标准有关事项的通知》《信托公司监管评级与分类监管指引(修订稿)》《信托登记管理办法》《信托公司信托业务尽职指引》等文件,设立了信托业保障基金及管理机构。其他非银行金融机构监管也稳步有效,行业发展健康,未发生重大风险事件。

(三)中国银监会的监管政策评价与展望

2014年中国银监会在从事具体的监管工作方面,首先坚持国际标准与国内实践相结合的道路,牢固树立"管法人、管风险、管内控、提高透明度"的监管理念,严格执行各项国际规则,全面落实资本、杠杆率、流动性等监管指标,并在多个领域采用了更为审慎的标准,包括更高的核心一级资本和杠杆率标准、适用于所有规模银行业金融机构的资本要求、严格"合格优质流动性资产"定义等。同时,针对中国银行业以信贷为主的业务结构,坚定实施了流动性和大额集中度方面的定量监管标准,确立了"准确分类—提足拨备—做实利润—资本充足"的持续监管思路,坚持使用存贷比、拨备覆盖率等简单有效的监管指标。其次,银监会坚持宏观审慎和微观审慎相结合,积极构建宏观与微观相结合的审慎监管体系,形成了涵盖各类机构、业务、高管及公司治理等方面的监管制度体系;并且充分吸取本轮国际金融危机教训,强化动态监管,提高资本充足率和不良贷款拨备率标准,及时增强逆周期监管能力,并加强银行业、证券业、保险业之间的监管协同,推进跨业、跨境监管合作,守住不发生系统性、区域性风险的底线。第三,坚持机构监管与功能监管相结合。在机构监管方面,按照生命周期全覆盖原则,针对不同性质机构,实施了市场准入、非现场监管、现场检查相互依存的监管流程。在功能监管方面,针对金融创新、IT系统、消费者保护等重点领域建立专门机构,推动监管向集约化和专业化发展。第四,坚持风险监管与服务经济相结合。银监会在加强监管和防范风险的同时,始终注重引领银行业和其他金融机构服务实体经济,更好地支持关乎国计民生的重点领域和薄弱环节,不断提升银行业及其他金融机构服务实体经济的效能。

2015年银监会监管工作的总体指导思想是:坚持稳中求进的工作总基调,坚持以提高发展质量和效益为中心,坚持主动适应经济发展新常态,全面推进银行业改革开放,全面推动金融法治建设,全面强化金融风险管理,全面提升服务实体经济能力。具体工作将通过以下四个方面具体展开。

其一,全面提升金融服务质效。牢牢把握国际经济合作深化和国民经济转型升级的战略机遇,为实体经济提供针对性强、附加值高的金融服务。银监会积极支持国家的战略实施、促进产业结构调整、大力推进普惠金融发展,并努力推动降低社会融资成本。

其二,全面落实风险防控责任,加强对客户信用风险、押品价值波动风险、流动性风险、操作风险和社会金融风险的监测和防范。

其三,全面深化银行业和其他非银行金融业的改革开放。支持民间资本多渠道进入各类银行等金融机构，积极推动银行业务和其他非银行金融业的管理架构改革和监管体系改革，完善金融服务设施建设。

其四，全面推进银行业和其他非银行金融业的法治建设，完善法律法规体系，提高监管执法水平，加大违法惩戒力度。

2015年是全面深化改革的关键之年，是全面推进依法治国的开局之年。在深刻认识我国银行业改革发展的新形势、新常态的基础上，银监会将着力增强法治意识，着力完善银行业法律规则体系，着力推进严格执法，着力强化执法监督评价，坚决守住不发生系统性、区域性金融风险的底线，促进提高依法监管和依法经营水平，积极推进银行业治理体系和治理能力现代化，使银行业在法治的轨道上不断提高金融服务水平，促进经济社会持续健康发展。

三、中国证监会主要监管政策[①]

（一）2014年中国证监会主要监管政策一览

表6-3 2014年中国证监会主要监管政策

发布日期	政策名称	发文单位
1月3日	《公开发行证券的公司信息披露编报规则第21号——年度内部控制评价报告的一般规定》	中国证监会、财政部
1月12日	《关于加强新股发行监管的措施》	中国证监会
1月21日	2014年全国证券期货监管工作会议在京召开，中国证券会党委书记、主席肖钢就大力推进监管转型发表讲话	中国证监会
2月25日	《证券公司全面风险管理规范》和《证券公司流动性风险管理指引》	中国证券业协会
3月21日	《关于修改〈证券发行与承销管理办法〉的决定》和《关于修改〈首次公开发行股票时公司股东公开发售股份暂行规定〉的决定》	中国证监会
5月14日	《首次公开发行股票并在创业板上市管理办法》和《创业板上市公司证券发行管理暂行办法》	中国证监会
6月26日	《基金管理公司风险管理指引》	中国证券投资基金业协会
6月23日	《非上市公众公司收购管理办法》	中国证监会
7月4日	《关于改革完善并严格实施上市公司退市制度的若干意见（征求意见稿）》	中国证监会

---

① 执笔：王鑫。

发布日期	政策名称	发文单位
7月18日	《证券期货市场诚信监督管理暂行办法（草案征求意见稿)》	中国证监会
8月21日	《私募投资基金监督管理暂行办法》	中国证监会
8月31日	《关于修改〈中华人民共和国证券法〉〈中华人民共和国保险法〉等五部法律的决定》	全国人大常委会
9月12日	《上市公司独立董事履职指引》	中国上市公司协会
9月19日	发布修改后的《证券期货市场诚信监督管理暂行办法》	中国证监会
10月15日	《关于改革完善并严格实施上市公司退市制度的若干意见》	中国证监会
10月17日	《沪港通项目下中国证监会与香港证监会加强监管执法合作备忘录》	中国证监会
10月31日	《关于沪港股票市场交易互联互通机制试点有关税收政策的通知》《关于QFII和RQFII取得中国境内的股票等权益性投资资产转让所得暂免征收企业所得税问题的通知》	财政部、国家税务总局、中国证监会
11月19日	《证券公司及基金管理公司子公司资产证券化业务管理规定》	中国证监会
12月26日	《证券期货经营机构参与新三板相关业务的有关通知》	中国证监会

资料来源：课题组整理。

（二）2014年中国证监会主要监管政策分析

1. 注册制改革步伐进一步加快

李克强在2014年11月19日主持召开的国务院常务会议中指出，抓紧出台股票发行注册制改革方案，取消股票发行的持续盈利条件，降低小微和创新型企业上市门槛。建立资本市场小额再融资快速机制，开展股权众筹融资试点。2014年11月28日，中国证监会新闻发言人表示，按照中央要求，证监会牵头成立的包括人民银行、法制办、银监会、保监会、人大法工委等在内的股票发行注册制改革工作组，已完成注册制改革方案初稿，将于11月底前上报国务院。

2. 新一轮退市制度改革启动

2014年10月15日，中国证监会正式发布了《关于改革完善并严格实施上市公司退市制度的若干意见》，该意见从健全上市公司主动退市制度、明确实施重大违法公司强制退市制度、严格执行市场交易类财务类强制退市指标、完善与退市相关的配套制度安排、加强退市公司投资者合法权益保护等五个方面改革完善了退市制度。退市制度是资本市场一项基础性制度，只有实施有效的退市机制，才能真正促进证券市场中资源的合理有效配置，推动结构调整和产业升级。进一步改革完善并严格执行退市制度，有利于健全资本市场功能，增强市场主体活力，提高市场竞争能力，有利于实现优胜劣汰，惩戒重大违法行为，引导理性投资，保护投资者特别是中小投资者合法权益。

3. 加强对证券期货市场的诚信监督

2014年9月19日,中国证监会发布了修改后的《证券期货市场诚信监督管理暂行办法》(以下简称《诚信监管办法》)。这次修改《诚信监管办法》,主要是明确规定证监会将专门建立违法失信信息互联网公示平台。这就意味着,今后市场参与主体被行政处罚、市场禁入、纪律处分等重大违法失信信息,通过该平台就可以集中、公开查询到。另外,这次修改还调整完善了违法失信信息在诚信档案中的效力期限,规定一般违法失信信息的效力期限为3年,行政处罚、市场禁入、刑事处罚等重大违法信息的效力期限为5年。① 从2014年12月26日起,证监会正式启动运行证券期货市场失信记录查询平台。社会公众可通过该平台查询到市场参与主体被行政处罚、市场禁入、纪律处分等失信信息。

4. 沪港通监管执法合作开启

2014年10月17日,中国证监会与香港证监会共同签署了《沪港通项目下中国证监会与香港证监会加强监管执法合作备忘录》(以下简称《备忘录》)。至此,内地与香港关于沪港通跨境监管合作的制度安排已完成。《备忘录》由中国证监会主席肖钢与香港证监会主席唐家成共同签署。该备忘录的主要内容有以下七个方面:一是开展监管执法合作的目的、备忘录的效力;二是线索与调查信息通报机制;三是协助调查、联合调查的程序及有关安排;四是信息的使用,包括执法合作中有关信息的使用范围、信息保密有关要求;五是双方互为送达有关文书的安排;六是沪港通下协助执行有关安排;七是其他配套安排,包括投资者权益损害赔偿有关安排、信息发布的协调、磋商及定期联络机制、执法人员的实习、培训和交流等。

5. 发布《私募投资基金监督管理办法》(以下简称《办法》)

《办法》主要明确了以下五项制度安排:一是明确了全口径登记备案制度;二是确立了合格投资者制度;三是明确了私募基金的募资规则;四是提出了规范投资运作行为的有关规则;五是确立了对不同类别私募基金进行差异化行业自律和监管的制度安排。《办法》的推出为建立健全促进各类私募基金特别是创业投资基金发展的政策体系奠定法律基础,以便于下一步推动财税、工商等部门加快完善私募基金财政、税收和工商登记等相关政策,更好地促进私募基金发展,并发挥其促进多层次资本市场平稳运行、优化资源配置和推进经济结构战略性调整等方面的重要作用。

6. 完善新股发行改革相关举措

2014年3月21日,中国证监会发布了《关于修改〈证券发行与承销管理办法〉的决定》和《关于修改〈首次公开发行股票时公司股东公开发售股份暂行规定〉的决

---

① 中国证监会网站:《证监会修改〈诚信监管办法〉 进一步丰富诚信约束手段》,http://www.csrc.gov.cn/pub/newsite/zjhxwfb/xwdd/201409/t20140919_260634.html,2015-03-01。

定》，进一步推进新股发行体制改革。其主要内容包括：一是进一步优化老股转让制度。适当放宽募集资金使用限制，强化募集资金合理性的信息披露。二是规范网下询价和定价行为。规定网下投资者必须持有不少于1 000万元市值的非限售股份。三是进一步满足中小投资者的认购需求。增加网下向网上回拨的档次，对网上有效认购倍数超过150倍的，要求网下保留的数量不超过本次公开发行量的10%，其余全部回拨到网上。四是强化对配售行为的监管。加强规范性要求，增加禁止配售关联方，禁止主承销商向与其有保荐、承销业务合作关系的机构或个人配售。五是进一步加强事中事后监管。对发行承销过程实施后发现涉嫌违法违规或者存在异常情形的，责令发行人和承销商暂停或中止发行，对相关事项进行调查处理。[①]

（三）政策评价与展望

2014年，中国证券市场监管改革的力度空前，推出了许多新政策和新制度。其改革的路径一方面是通过新股发行体制改革和退市制度改革等相关举措来为注册制的改革打下坚实的基础，另一方面则是通过推进证券市场诚信体系的监督力度和加大对市场违法违规行为的处罚力度来促使监管进一步转型。在2015年，我国证券市场的监管政策将会迈开深入改革和创新的步伐，而重点则是加速监管转型，推进股票发行注册制改革；加强多层次股权市场体系建设；积极发展私募市场，健全私募发行制度，推动私募基金规范发展；适时放宽证券期货服务业准入限制；优化沪港通机制；以及加强风险防控，妥善处置违法违约事件。

四、中国保监会主要监管政策[②]

（一）2014年中国保监会主要监管政策一览

表6-4　　　　　　　　　　2014年中国保监会主要监管政策

日期	文件名称	发文单位
1月7日	《中国保监会关于保险资金投资创业板上市公司股票等有关问题的通知》	保监会
1月8日	《中国保监会　中国银监会关于进一步规范商业银行代理保险业务销售行为的通知》	保监会、银监会
1月17日	《中国保监会关于发布〈人身保险伤残评定标准及代码〉行业标准的通知》	保监会
1月23日	《中国保监会关于加强和改进保险资金运用比例监管的通知》	保监会

---

① 中国证监会网站：《中国证监会完善新股发行改革相关措施》，http://www.csrc.gov.cn/pub/newsite/zjhxwfb/xwdd/201403/t20140321_245900.html，2015-03-01。

② 执笔：刘学庆。

续表

日期	文件名称	发文单位
1月23日	《中国保险监督管理委员会关于修改〈保险公司董事、监事和高级管理人员任职资格管理规定〉的决定》	保监会
1月29日	《中国保监会关于规范高现金价值产品有关事项的通知》	保监会
2月14日	《中国保险监督管理委员会关于修改〈中国保险监督管理委员会行政许可实施办法〉的决定》	保监会
2月19日	《保险公司声誉风险管理指引》	保监会
2月27日	《中国保监会关于取消行政审批项目的通知》	保监会
2月28日	《中国保监会关于规范保险资金银行存款业务的通知》	保监会
3月5日	《中国保监会关于外资保险公司与其关联企业从事再保险交易有关问题的通知》	保监会
3月21日	《保险公司收购合并管理办法》	保监会
4月2日	《关于授权北京等保监局开展保险资金运用监管试点工作的通知》	保监会
4月4日	《中国保险监督管理委员会关于修改〈保险资金运用管理暂行办法〉的决定》	保监会
4月4日	《中国保监会关于印发〈保险公司偿付能力报告编报规则——问题解答第21号：次级可转换债券〉的通知》	保监会
4月9日	《中国保监会关于印发〈保险公司偿付能力报告编报规则——问题解答第22号：证券投资基金和资产管理产品〉的通知》	保监会
4月14日	《中国保监会关于印发〈保险公司偿付能力报告编报规则——问题解答第20号：高现金价值产品最低资本〉的通知》	保监会
4月15日	《中国保险监督管理委员会关于修改〈保险公司股权管理办法〉的决定》	保监会
4月24日	《关于规范金融机构同业业务的通知》	中国人民银行、银监会、证监会、保监会、外汇局
5月5日	《关于保险资金投资集合资金信托计划有关事项的通知》	保监会
5月19日	《保险公司资金运用信息披露准则第1号：关联交易》	保监会
5月26日	《关于清理规范保险公司投资性房地产评估增值有关事项的通知》	保监会
6月22日	《保险资金运用内控与合规计分监管规则》	保监会
6月24日	《中国保监会关于规范财产保险公司保险产品开发销售有关问题的紧急通知》	保监会
6月24日	《中国保监会关于印发〈保险公司偿付能力报告编报规则——问题解答第23号：历史存量高利率保单资金投资的蓝筹股〉的通知》	保监会
8月10日	《国务院关于加快发展现代保险服务业的若干意见》	国务院
8月12日	《中国保监会关于废止部分规范性文件的通知》	保监会

日期	文件名称	发文单位
9月16日	《中国保监会关于加强财产保险公司再保险分入业务管理有关事项的通知》	保监会
9月23日	《中国保监会关于印发〈保险公司偿付能力报告编报规则——问题解答第24号：信托计划〉的通知》	保监会
9月28日	《保险公司所属非保险子公司管理暂行办法》	保监会
10月17日	《中国保监会关于保险资金投资优先股有关事项的通知》	保监会
10月17日	《保险资产风险五级分类指引》	保监会
10月24日	《中国保监会 中国银监会关于规范保险资产托管业务的通知》	保监会、银监会
11月14日	《中国保监会关于加强保险消费者权益保护工作的意见》	保监会
11月15日	《中国保监会关于严格规范非保险金融产品销售的通知》	保监会
12月4日	《保险集团并表监管指引》	保监会
12月5日	《中国保监会办公厅关于保险资金运用属地监管试点工作有关事项的通知》	保监会办公厅
12月8日	《中国保监会关于取消和调整行政审批项目的通知》	保监会
12月12日	《中国保监会关于保险资金投资创业投资基金有关事项的通知》	保监会
12月24日	《保险养老社区统计制度》	保监会

资料来源：课题组整理。

（二）2014年中国保监会主要监管政策分析

1. 主干技术标准完成研发，基本建成第二代偿付能力监管体系

为了顺应经济全球化和中国保险业市场化改革的需要，为提高中国保险行业防范和化解风险的能力，促进保险业科学发展，中国保监会积极探索偿付能力监管改革的道路和模式。中国保监会2012年4月正式启动了第二代偿付能力监管制度体系（以下简称偿二代）的建设工作。2013年5月3日，中国保监会发布《中国第二代偿付能力监管制度体系整体框架》，完成了中国偿二代建设的顶层设计，明确了偿二代的总体目标，确立了"三支柱"框架体系，制定了偿二代建设的若干基本技术原则。2014年，中国保监会持续推动偿二代建设。全年，保监会陆续发布全套17个监管规则的征求意见稿，并经过了样本测试、方案测试、参数测试和校准测试等多轮行业测试，偿二代主干技术标准完成研发，基本建成符合中国市场特点的偿付能力监管体系。

偿二代全部主干技术标准共17项监管规则：第一支柱定量监管要求9项，第二支柱定性监管要求3项，第三支柱市场约束机制3项，以及偿付能力报告和保险集团各1项。这些规则相互关联、密切配合，形成一套有机联系的监管标准。

第一支柱定量监管要求的9项监管规则，具体内容包括：1号实际资本规则，规范保险公司认可资产、认可负债和实际资本的评估原则，明确资本分级的标准；2号最低资本规则，规范保险公司最低资本的构成和计量原则；3号寿险合同负债评估规则，规范人身保险公司和再保险公司偿付能力监管目的的寿险合同准备金的评估标准；4 号保险风险最低资本（非寿险业务）、5 号保险风险最低资本（寿险业务）和 6 号保险风险最低资本（再保险公司）规则，分别规范保险公司寿险业务、非寿险业务和再保险公司的最低资本的计量；7 号市场风险最低资本规则，规范保险公司市场风险最低资本的计量；8 号信用风险最低资本规则，规范保险公司信用风险最低资本的计量；9 号压力测试规则，建立了保险公司偿付能力压力测试制度，明确了压力测试的方法和要求。

第二支柱定性监管要求的 3 项监管规则，具体内容包括：10 号风险综合评级（分类监管）规则，通过对保险公司总体的偿付能力风险进行全面评价，建立定量监管与定性监管相结合的监管机制，提高监管的有效性；11 号偿付能力风险管理要求与评估规则，建立了保险公司偿付能力、风险管理能力的监管评估制度，并将风险管理水平与资本要求相挂钩，风险管理能力强的公司，可降低资本要求，反之，则提高资本要求，促使保险公司持续提高风险管理能力；12 号流动性风险规则，建立了财产保险公司和人身保险公司统一的流动性风险监管要求、流动性风险监管指标和现金流压力测试制度，构建了完整的流动性风险防范网。

第三支柱市场约束机制的 3 项监管规则，具体内容包括：13 号偿付能力信息公开披露规则，建立了偿付能力信息公开披露制度，要求保险公司每季度披露有关偿付能力信息，提升偿付能力信息的透明度，增强市场约束力；14 号偿付能力信息交流规则，建立健全了监管部门与保险消费者、投资者、信用评级机构、媒体等市场相关方之间的交流机制，以充分发挥市场相关方对保险公司的监督约束作用；15 号保险公司信用评级规则，规范了保险公司的信用评级制度，以更好地发挥评级机构在风险防范中的作用。

除上述规则外，16 号偿付能力报告和 17 号保险集团两项监管规则，涉及三个支柱的所有内容。16 号偿付能力报告规则将现行以年报为核心的报告体系改为以季报为核心的报告体系，有利于保监会对行业风险早发现、早预警、早处置。17 号保险集团监管规则拓展了集团监管的内涵，将保险（控股）集团以及各种类型的隐性或混合保险集团都纳入到监管范围，对保险集团的定量监管要求、定性监管要求和市场约束机制进行了规范，迈出了保险集团偿付能力监管的实质性步伐。

如上所述，保监会组织全行业开展了多轮定量测试。从测试情况看，偿二代比偿一代的风险识别能力显著增强，风险结构更加合理，能够科学、准确、全面地计量和反映保险业面临的各类风险。

下一步，监管部门将正式发布并试运行偿二代，并在此基础上进一步完善偿二代相关配套制度。第二代偿付能力监管制度体系的基本建成及其后发布实施，将对中国保险业起到积极的作用：首先，通过强化偿付能力监管对保险公司经营的刚性约束，推动保险公司转变粗放的发展方式，促进保险业转型升级、提质增效和可持续发展；其次，偿二代把风险管理能力与资本要求相挂钩，将督促保险公司不断提高风险管理能力，进而提升保险业核心竞争力；第三，偿二代的实施有利于提升保险公司的资本使用效率，增强行业对社会资本的吸引力；第四，偿二代作为我国金融监管领域自主研制的监管规则，有利于扩大我国在国际保险规则制定中的话语权，提升我国保险业的国际影响力。

2. 保险资金运用改革持续推进，简政放权和控制风险并重

2014 年，保监会在资金运用领域持续践行"放开前端，管住后端"的监管思路，推进市场化改革，简政放权，放开投资领域，简化投资比例，支持行业创新，规范投资行为，在激发市场活力的同时，强化风险防范，有效促进保险资金投资效益提升。具体来说，2014 年监管部门发布实施了以下政策：

一是放开投资领域，规范投资行为。2014 年 1 月 7 日，中国保监会发布《中国保监会关于保险资金投资创业板上市公司股票等有关问题的通知》，正式放开保险资金对创业板上市公司股票的投资。2014 年 10 月 17 日，中国保监会发布《中国保监会关于保险资金投资优先股有关事项的通知》，明确保险资金投资优先股的各项内容。2014 年 12 月 12 日，中国保监会发布《中国保监会关于保险资金投资创业投资基金有关事项的通知》，允许保险资金投资创业投资基金，支持创业企业和小微企业健康发展。通过上述规定，保监会在 2014 年进一步放开保险资金投资领域。同时，保监会还加强对各类投资行为的规范，防范投资风险。2014 年 2 月 28 日，中国保监会发布《中国保监会关于规范保险资金银行存款业务的通知》，规范部分保险公司在银行存款业务中存在的操作不透明、约束机制不健全、风险管理薄弱，以及被他人挪用等风险隐患和问题。2014 年 4 月 24 日，保监会会同人民银行、银监会、证监会、外汇局联合发布《关于规范金融机构同业业务的通知》，规范金融机构同业业务经营行为。2014 年 5 月 5 日，中国保监会发布《关于保险资金投资集合资金信托计划有关事项的通知》，完善保险资金投资集合资金信托计划的内控要求，规范投资行为，防范资金运用投资风险。

二是简化比例监管，满足市场需求。2014 年 1 月 23 日，保监会发布实施《中国保监会关于加强和改进保险资金运用比例监管的通知》，建立"以保险资产分类为基础、多层次比例监管为手段、差异化监管为补充、动态调整机制为保障"的比例监管新体系。新制度将资产划分为流动性资产、固定收益类资产、权益类资产、不动产类资产和其他金融资产五个大类资产，并在资产分类基础上，制定了不同大类资产的投资总量及集中度监管比例上限。该制度实现了我国保险资金运用比例监管政策与国际监管惯例的初步接轨。同时，该制度还建立了比例监管政策的动态调整机制。监管部门可根据市场发展情况灵活调整政策，满足市场合理需求。2014 年 4 月 4 日，中国保监会发布《中国保险监督管理委员会关于修改〈保险资金运用管理暂行办法〉的决定》，修改保险资金运用比例的相关规定。

三是成立资管协会，市场改革提速。2014 年 9 月 4 日，中国保险资产管理行业协会

成立。保险资产管理行业协会是保险业市场化改革的重要成果，是保险资产管理监管方式转变的重要体制创新。保险资产管理行业协会的成立、运行并充分发挥服务、创新和自律的功能作用，将有助于进一步推动保险资金运用市场化改革、维护行业利益、服务行业发展、监测市场风险、维护市场秩序，促进行业规范发展。

四是试点授权监管，丰富监管层次。2014年4月2日，中国保监会发布《关于授权北京等保监局开展保险资金运用监管试点工作的通知》；2014年12月5日，中国保监会办公厅发布《中国保监会办公厅关于保险资金运用属地监管试点工作有关事项的通知》。上述制度明确授权北京、上海、江苏、湖北、广东、深圳保监局代行部分资金运用监管职权。授权范围包括：（1）监测辖区内中小保险公司的资金运用风险及辖区内基础设施、股权、不动产等保险资金投资项目的状况及其风险；（2）根据试点保监局监管需求及资源的配备情况，逐步逐项授权对辖区内保险机构有关投资能力评估等监管事项；（3）协调保险资金支持地方经济转型升级和金融创新政策等。同时要求各保险机构在试点区域实施的基础设施、股权、不动产等投资项目接受试点保监局对投资项目的风险监管；要求试点区域经营的保险法人机构的资金运用，接受试点保监局的风险监管。上述制度的发布与实施，有利于增强保险资金运用监管力量，丰富监管层次，强化风险监管工作，建立多层次的保险资金运用监管体系，有效防范系统性、区域性风险。同时，也有利于促进资金运用市场化改革和创新。

五是强化风险控制，守住风险底线。2014年，保监会在进一步推进资金运用市场化的同时，持续强化资金运用风险控制。全年，中国保监会陆续发布《保险公司偿付能力报告编报规则——问题解答第22号：证券投资基金和资产管理产品》《保险公司偿付能力报告编报规则——问题解答第23号：历史存量高利率保单资金投资的蓝筹股》《保险公司偿付能力报告编报规则——问题解答第24号：信托计划》，规范保险公司投资证券投资基金、资产管理产品和信托计划等多类投资产品的偿付能力认可标准，加强投资行为的偿付能力约束，守住风险底线，确保市场稳健运行。2014年6月22日，中国保监会发布《保险资金运用内控与合规计分监管规则》，对保险资金运用内控和合规风险进行量化监管。2014年10月17日，中国保监会发布《保险资产风险五级分类指引》，通过对保险机构投资资产进行风险分类和评估，引导保险机构加强全面资产风险管理工作，及时发现保险资金使用和管理中存在的问题，加强保险机构的资产风险管理水平，改进保险资金使用效率，提升资产质量。

3. 最严银保新规发布，综合治理银保经营秩序

近年来，银邮保险代理渠道业务发展迅速，促进了人身保险业保费规模、资产规模的快速增长。同时，银邮保险代理渠道发展仍处于初级阶段，发展方式较为粗放，业务结构不合理，存在着销售误导、违规经营、退保金大幅上升等问题。社会各方面对银保渠道销售行为中的一系列问题反映较为集中，包括"存单变保单"、产品适销不对路、

产品介绍不全面、客户信息不真实等。鉴于此，中国保监会和中国银监会一直高度重视银保业务的监管。早在 2010 年，银监会即发布《关于进一步加强商业银行代理保险业务合规销售与风险管理的通知》，2011 年保监会、银监会联合发布了《商业银行代理保险业务监管指引》。为进一步规范银保业务销售行为，综合治理银保业务经营秩序，引导行业健康有序发展，中国保监会、中国银监会于 2014 年 1 月 8 日联合发布《中国保监会 中国银监会关于进一步规范商业银行代理保险业务销售行为的通知》（以下简称《规范银保通知》）。

《规范银保通知》要求商业银行建立投保人需求与风险承受能力评估制度，根据评估结果推荐保险产品。加强城乡低收入居民和老年人等特定人群保护措施，要求向其销售的产品应以保单利益确定的普通型产品为主，不得通过系统自动核保现场出单，应由保险公司人工核保，核保中保险公司应对投保产品的适合性、投保信息、签名等情况进行复核。销售的保单利益不确定的产品，在保费较高等情况下，应由投保人在相关风险确认声明书中签名确认后方可承保。

为引导保险公司调整业务结构，充分发挥保险核心功能，转变商业银行代理保险业务发展方式，《规范银保通知》要求保险公司、商业银行应加大力度发展风险保障型和长期储蓄型保险产品，商业银行销售意外伤害保险、健康保险、定期寿险、终身寿险、保险期间不短于 10 年的年金保险、保险期间不短于 10 年的两全保险、财产保险（不包括财产保险公司投资型保险）、保证保险、信用保险的保费收入之和不得低于代理保险业务总保费收入的 20%。

为防止销售误导等违规行为，《规范银保通知》对银邮代理渠道销售行为进一步提出规范性要求。《规范银保通知》将银保渠道保险产品的犹豫期由之前的 10 天延长至 15 天。《规范银保通知》要求保险合同单证与银行单证材料要有明显区别，要求风险提示须明显到位，并对分红险、投连险、万能险等理财型险种详细规定了风险提示语的具体内容。《规范银保通知》延续此前"商业银行不得允许保险公司人员派驻银行网点"及"商业银行网点不得同时与超过 3 家保险公司开展保险业务合作"的限制。《规范银保通知》要求银行加强销售人员管理，不得销售未经授权的保险产品，不得篡改、截留客户信息。《规范银保通知》要求保险公司和商业银行妥善处理投诉、退保事宜。

另外，2014 年 1 月 29 日，保监会进一步发布《中国保监会关于规范高现金价值产品的有关事项的通知》。由于高现金价值产品主要通过银保渠道销售，规范高现金价值产品也将对银保业务带来影响。

这两个监管规则的发布有利于消费者合法权益的保护，有利于引导保险公司和商业银行调整保险业务结构，有利于促进商业银行代理保险业务规范、健康、持续发展，更好地提供相关服务，实现共赢。具体来说，银保新规对有银行股东背景的银邮系保险公司较为有利。传统大型保险公司和以价值为导向的外资公司受银保新规的影响比较有限。高度依赖于银保渠道的中小型保险公司受银保新规的负面影响较大。不同的寿险公司根据自身的特点正在调整产品结构和渠道发展策略。总体来说，银保渠道单一的产品结构正逐步改变，银保渠道的市场份额也逐渐被网销、电销、微信保险等新型的渠道挤占。

4. 开展中介市场清理整顿，保障保险中介行业健康可持续发展

我国保险中介已成为保险市场不可或缺的重要组成部分。截至 2013 年底，全国共有保险专业中介机构 2 500 多家，保险兼业代理机构 20 万余家，保险营销员 300 多万人。保险中介促进完善了保险产业链，提升了保险资源配置效率，改进了保险服务，在消费者与保险机构之间发挥了纽带作用，为保险业改革发展作出了历史性贡献。从整体上看，我国保险中介发展时间短，初级阶段特征明显，市场累积的问题已经日益突出，一些深层次的问题和矛盾未得到有效解决。为深化保险市场改革，促进保险中介市场持续健康发展，中国保监会 2014 年在全国范围内启动并开展了保险中介市场清理整顿工作（以下简称清理整顿工作）。

此次清理整顿工作设定了近期目标和长期目标。近期目标是要通过集中整治，排查化解风险隐患，着力解决当前保险中介市场存在的突出问题，有效净化市场环境，使市场秩序在短期内明显好转；长期目标是要通过深化改革，推进创新，理顺保险中介市场体制机制，推动形成科学合理的市场体系、公开透明的市场规则、规范有序的竞争格局，促进保险中介行业健康可持续发展。

此次清理整顿工作分为五个阶段。第一阶段是摸清底数。组织监管部门、保险公司、保险中介机构、行业组织等各方面力量，全面摸底普查保险中介市场的机构发展、人员队伍、业务经营、制度建设、风险隐患等情况，掌握保险中介市场的整体态势、基本特征及主要问题。第二阶段是整顿秩序。针对保险中介市场秩序和风险等方面存在的突出问题，结合摸底普查进行集中整治，清理、打击、处罚和规范违法违规的机构及人员。第三阶段是深化改革。针对保险中介市场长期积累的深层次矛盾，按体制机制更顺、法律关系更清、运行效率更高、服务能力更强的要求，厘清改革思路，推进市场创新。以市场化为导向，加快完善保险中介市场体系、行业自律体系；从组织架构、激励机制、日常管理等方面，稳妥推进保险营销体制改革；完善保险兼业代理制度，强化保险公司的管控责任；健全保险专业中介机构准入退出管理，强化公司法人治理和内控建设；加强信息化建设，提高监管效率。第四阶段是建章立制。逐步改进完善保险中介制度，及时对经营管理规则和监管法规进行废改立，将清理整顿成果固化为制度，形成长效机制。第五阶段是总结提高。针对前述四个阶段工作的完成情况，组织开展"回头看"，通报情况，总结经验，查漏补缺，研究持续深入推进发展改革的进一步举措。

全年，保险行业按照上述既定的部署，有序推进中介市场清理整顿，有效规范了市场秩序，化解了风险，为保险中介市场可持续发展打下了扎实的基础。

5. 发布收购合并办法，健全市场准入退出机制

兼并重组是企业加强资源整合、实现快速发展的有效措施，也是调整优化产业结构、提高发展质量效益的重要途径。近年来，随着我国保险业加快向国内外资本开放，保险公司数量持续增加，经营管理状况开始分化，不同动机、不同形式、不同规模的保险公司收购合并日益活跃。为促进和规范保险公司的收购合并活动，中国保监会于2014年3月21日发布《保险公司收购合并管理办法》（以下简称《收购合并办法》）。《收购合并办法》于2014年6月1日正式施行。

保险业并购包括保险公司作为目标公司的并购和保险公司作为主导公司的并购两大类。

《收购合并办法》制定了促进保险公司并购的政策，鼓励境内外各类优质资本特别是民间资本投资保险业。一是适度放宽资金来源。即突破《保险公司股权管理办法》中"股东不得用银行贷款及其他形式的非自有资金向保险公司投资"的规定，允许投资人采取并购贷款等融资方式，规模上限为货币对价总额的50%。二是适度放宽股东资质，规定投资人可不适用对保险公司的三年投资年限要求。三是不再禁止同业收购。即突破《保险公司股权管理办法》中"两个以上的保险公司受同一机构控制或者存在控制关系的，不得经营存在利益冲突或者竞争关系的同类保险业务"的规定，允许收购人在收购完成后控制两个经营同类业务的保险公司。

《收购合并办法》在鼓励促进保险公司收购合并的同时，制定了适度的监管措施。包括：一是强化保险公司并购各方的信息披露义务，发挥专业中介服务机构的独立作用；二是设定收购过渡期和股权锁定期，以确保被收购保险公司的持续稳健运营；三是针对虚假陈述、股权代持等违规行为，规定了必要的惩戒机制。

这是保监会贯彻落实十八届三中全会精神、发挥市场机制对保险资源配置决定性作用的又一重要举措，也标志着健全保险市场准入退出机制工作取得了阶段性成果。

6. 发布顶层制度安排，加强保险消费者权益保护

2014年，在持续做好理赔难和销售误导治理、损害消费者合法权益行为查处、投诉处理和纠纷调处、公众保险知识教育和行业诚信建设等工作的同时，中国保监会于2014年11月14日发布《中国保监会关于加强保险消费者权益保护工作的意见》（以下简称《消费者保护意见》），对保险消费者权益保护作出顶层制度安排。

《消费者保护意见》立足于我国保险消费者权益保护工作实际，借鉴国际保险监管组织在消费者保护方面的原则和国际金融消费者权益保护的良好经验，吸收现有法律法规规定，明确了保险消费者保护工作的指导思想、基本原则、工作目标和政策取向，提出了加强保险消费者保护工作的主要任务和具体措施，是我国保险消费者保护工作的顶层制度安排和方向性指导文件。

《消费者保护意见》具有鲜明的特点，强化了保险公司在保险消费者保护中的主体

责任，体现了预防性保护与过程性保护相结合的原则，突出了透明度监管，同时强调发挥相关部门和社会组织的协同作用。

针对保险消费者密切关注的保险产品问题，《消费者保护意见》要求保险公司公平合理设定合同权利义务和厘定产品费率。针对广受社会诟病的保险销售误导问题，明确要求保险公司根据产品特点和消费者风险承受能力建立区分销售制度，将合适的产品销售给有相应需求的消费者，从根源上防范保险销售误导问题。针对"理赔难"问题，要求保险公司及时公允理赔给付。针对客户信息安全等问题，要求保险公司保障消费者信息安全，不得利用非法获取的消费者信息开展经营活动和获取不当利益，不得篡改消费者信息资料。

同时，《消费者保护意见》加大了打击损害消费者合法权益行为的力度，监管机构要加大执法力度，要加强市场跟踪，强化保险公司管理人员的管控责任。保险公司要制定内部责任追究制度，追究违法违规行为人直接责任和管控责任人间接责任。

《消费者保护意见》的发布实施，将对当前和今后一个时期保险消费者保护工作起到积极的作用。

（三）政策评价与展望

中国保监会主席项俊波2015年1月26日在全国保险监管工作会议上明确，2015年的保险监管在持续做好日常监管工作的同时，着重抓好三项重大改革、三项专项工作。

三项重大改革是指：一是稳步推进车险、万能险、分红险等费率改革。商业车险改革方案经国务院批准后，将先启动黑龙江等6个省市试点，条件成熟时在全国范围内推开。正式启动万能险费率改革，随后着手分红险费率改革，力争在2015年底前全面实现人身险费率市场化。研究探索意外险定价机制改革。二是推动实施偿二代。保险业自2015年起进入偿二代过渡期，保险公司在过渡期内同时报送偿一代和偿二代数据，以偿一代作为监管标准。根据过渡期运行情况和行业准备情况，灵活、务实地开展新旧体系的正式切换。三是继续深化保险资金运用市场化改革。更加注重对接实体经济，制定专项支持政策，引导保险资金更好地投资养老健康服务产业，直接投资新型城镇化、棚户区改造、科技型企业、小微企业、战略性新兴产业等领域。依托市场化运作机制，组建全行业的保险资产交易平台和资产托管中心，盘活保险资产存量，做大做强保险资产池，提升行业核心竞争力。

三项专项工作是指：一是按照国务院决策部署，深入开展保险机构"两个加强、两个遏制"专项检查，建立健全遏制违规、防范风险的制度机制。二是推动修订《保险法》。同时，贯彻《关于全面推进依法治国若干重大问题的决定》，出台全面推进保险法治建设的指导性文件。三是建立保险公司经营和保险服务两个评价体系，对推动保险业改进服务、提高消费者满意度、提升监管效率都具有重要意义。

参考文献

［1］中国人民银行：《2014 年金融市场运行情况》。

［2］中国人民银行：《2013 年社会融资规模》《2014 年社会融资规模》。

［3］中国人民银行：《2014 年第四季度货币政策执行报告》，2015 – 02 – 10。

［4］中国银监会：《2014 年度监管统计数据》。

［5］中国银监会：《中国银行业运行报告（2014）》。

［6］薛瑞锋、殷剑峰：《私人银行：机构、产品和监管》，北京，社会科学文献出版社，2015。

［7］王伯英：《2014 年财富管理市场发展报告》，载《建设银行报》，2015 – 03 – 04。

［8］中国信托业协会：《2014 年度中国信托业发展评析》。

［9］陈文辉：《中国偿二代的制度框架和实施路径》，载《中国金融》，2015（5）。

English Version

Part One

Feature Articles and
Thematic Reports

Part One

Feature Articles and
Thematic Reports

CHAPTER 1

"New White Plan" or "New Keynes Plan"?

——Thoughts on Building a Stable and Effective International Monetary System[1]

Wu, Xiaoling

Distinguished Guests, Experts, Ladies and Gentlemen,

Hello everyone! This time we are going to discuss some ideas about the future international monetary system reform, which is a grand topic and has been researched by many experts and scholars very deeply. But as far as I know, no consensus has been reached yet. Today we only do academic discussions. This is an open topic, so everyone can freely speak your mind. As a start, below is my opinion on it.

I. Status Quo & Problems of the Current International Monetary System

It has been almost six years since the outbreak of the international financial crisis in 2008, but the global economy remains in a slow recovery. The academic community generally believes that, this crisis is a total explosion resulted from the continuously accumulated global imbalance over the past decade, and multiple shortcomings existing in the current international monetary system might be one of primary causes for such global imbalance. Unfortunately, this global imbalance issue has not been fundamentally resolved yet, as major countries lack courage and motivation to change the status quo, and the theoretical circle is far from reaching a clear consensus on the future international monetary system arrangement. Problems of the current international monetary system are mainly reflected by:

First, the global liquidity management can easily get out of control. Since the collapse of

---

[1] This article is finished based on the author's speech at the "Rethinking about the International Monetary System—After the 70th Anniversary of Bretton Woods Conference" International Seminar held in Shanghai on June 17, 2014.

the Bretton Woods System, the global liquidity, typically represented by global foreign exchange reserves, has grown rapidly and even at full speed after 2002. According to the World Bank statistics, by the end of 2011, global foreign exchange reserves other than gold reached USD 10.56 trillion, increasing by 52.8 times than those in 1975 and by 3.3 times than those in 2002, while the same-period global GDP only increased by 11.0 times and 1.1 times, and the proportion of foreign exchange reserves in GDP rose from 3.38% in 1975 to 15.08% in 2011, especially on the fast rise after 2000. Therefore, compared with the actual economic growth, the global liquidity appears excessive on a long-term basis.

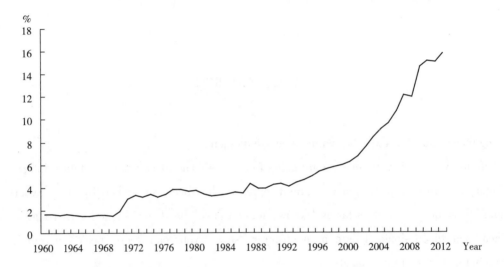

Data Source: IFS, WIND.

Page 1 – 1   Proportion of Global Foreign Exchange Reserves in Global GDP

Second, cross-border capital flows fluctuate wildly. With the growing size of global liquidity and the progress of capital account liberalization, cross-border capital flows become increasingly frequent in an unprecedented size and fluctuate wildly. The proportion of net private capital flows in GDP has fluctuated particularly dramatically over the past two decades, and many regions have experienced large inflows and outflows in a very short term (Darvas, 2014). It has brought huge challenges to financial stability and sustainable development of macro economy.

Third, the development of global imbalance is further intensified. Although the global imbalance might be triggered by multiple factors of non-monetary systems, the current international monetary system has further intensified such imbalance. This is particularly reflected in that the United States can issue U. S. dollars for unlimited financing to cover its current account deficit; and meanwhile, the existing system lacks an effective regulation

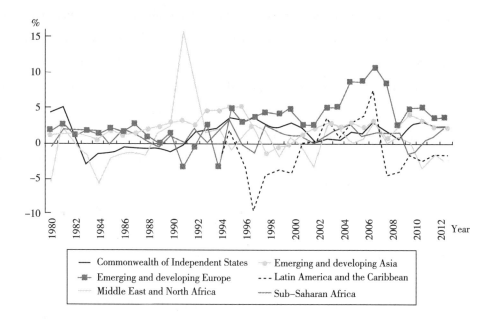

Data Source: IMF WEO April 2014.

Page 1 – 2   Net Private Capital Flows/GDP

mechanism for such imbalance of international balance of payments, which has contributed to the sustained and in-depth development of global imbalance.

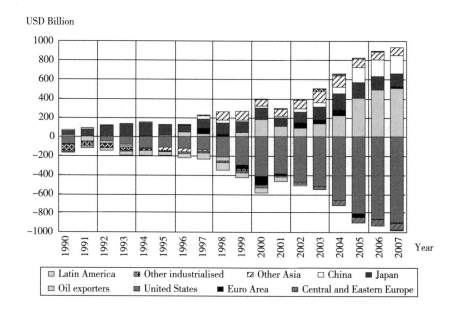

Data Source: IMF (World Economic Outlook and Direction of Trade Statistics) and ECB staff calculations.

Page 1 – 3   Global Current Account Positions (1997 – 2007)

There are profound institutional reasons behind the aforesaid phenomena and problems. First, a constraint mechanism for issuance of reserve currency is absent. After the collapse of the Bretton Woods System, the link between dollar and gold was severed, making currency issuance thoroughly "gold-free" and totally relying on credit issuing. The current international monetary system lacks a subject qualified enough to represent overall interests of the world. Despite the availability of such international organizations as IMF, subject to the well-known institutional design and governance framework, it plays a very limited role in managing global reserve currencies and restraining international currency issuance. As a result, although in practice some reserve currencies have their own domestic "Currency Anchor" (e. g. inflation, employment or other monetary policy targets), their issuance is not based on the world's overall situation, and the institutional framework lacks a constraint on their performance of global reserve currency functions. In this sense, the issuance mechanism of major reserve currencies lacks a "Currency Anchor" based on the global economic and trade development.

Second, two roles are conflicting: sovereign currency and international reserve currency. Under the current system with sovereign currency as main international reserve currency, each reserve currency plays two roles – first a sovereign currency, then a reserve currency. In real life, these two roles are conflicting in many cases, behind which are contradictions between sovereign interests and the world's overall interests. Unfortunately, in realistic choices, the role of sovereign currency often holds an overwhelming advantage; extremely speaking, the reserve currency issuance authority generally will not take into account global interests, unless these interests have an effect on their sovereign interests.

Third, an effective regulation mechanism for imbalance of international payments is lacked. The "Jamaica System", in essence, is a "Non-system" system, which in principle makes no mandatory restrictions on the exchange rate system, exchange control or balance of international payments other than abolishing gold as the basis of currency issuance. If we say under the Bretton Woods System, deficit countries assume the responsibility for the adjustment of balance of international payments, under the Jamaica System, decision makers overly place their hope on the automatic adjustment function of floating exchange rates, and set no mandatory rules for any imbalance adjustment. However, in fact, under the background of financial integration, exchange rates are very likely to get out of line with fundamentals and experience excessive volatility, making its role in the adjustment of balance of international payments become increasingly unstable. Therefore, from the perspective of institutional arrangement, the Jamaica System may be doomed to be an imbalanced system.

To sum up, the current international monetary system, in essence, may contribute to the impulse of reserve currency countries to overissue currency, which probably will distort the global resource allocation mechanism and intensify the imbalance of international payments. The lack of a regulation mechanism further reinforces the existing imbalance, which through continuous accumulation, develops into a global problem.

II. Historical Debate on the International Monetary System Reform: the Keynes and White plans

Taking history as a mirror, you can know the rise and fall. More than 70 years ago, there was a debate on how to design and build the international monetary system, which set the tone for the international monetary system in the subsequent several decades, and even to this day, still plays a significant role. That debate was focused on the "Keynes Plan" and "White Plan". It should be said that, the purposes of these two plans were consistent – trying to build a stable international monetary system. Their divergences were mainly reflected in the following respects:

First is the divergence between the fund system and the banking system. This was the most fundamental divergence between the two plans. White Plan intended to set up just a fund – International Stabilization Fund. Although he also put forward a unita, it was just a unit of account rather than currency, what was in actual use and circulation was still such sovereign currencies as U. S. dollars. Once subscription was completed, fund share would be relatively fixed, leading to its lack of an actual withdrawal channel and the resulting absence of a currency derivation mechanism, so from the date of birth, this plan was doomed to lack flexibility of automatically adapting to the global economic and trade growth. In other words, the gross value of International Stabilization Fund was relatively fixed, and it could be expected that, with the economic and trade growth, its proportion relative to the global economic and trade volume would be bound to fall, and its role in the adjustment for exchange rate stability would also be bound to decline. On the contrary, Keynes Plan intended to build a global central bank – International Clearing Union, which would create and issue a new super-sovereign reserve currency – bancor, and by compulsorily requiring surplus countries to deposit their surplus into the Union account and provide overdraft (loan in nature) for deficit countries, constructed a currency derivation channel, which could provide sufficient payment and clearing mediums required for the global economic and trade development.

Second is the divergence about demonetization of gold. Although White Plan advocated withdrawing gold from currency circulation, its warrant of convertibility between U. S. dollar and gold demonstrated that it essentially was still a deformed gold standard system, in which gold remained as the de facto "Shadow Currency", and the U. S. dollar issuance was still subject to gold reserves. On the contrary, although Keynes Plan stipulated that the value of bancor would be determined by gold, its one-way conversion with gold – gold could be exchanged for bancor, but not the opposite – in fact realized demonetization of gold, and the bancor issuance depended on the global economic and trade scale. Extremely speaking, even if removing gold, the system operation would not be compromised.

Third is the divergence of currency anchor. From the second divergence mentioned above we can reasonably infer that, under the White Plan, gold was still its currency anchor, while under the Keynes Plan, the de facto currency anchor became the global trade volume. In this plan, each member country would be assigned with an initial share, which was calculated by 75% of the average import & export trade of each country in three years before the war, and afterwards, to reflect the global economic and trade development, would be recalculated once every five years.

Fourth is the divergence of adjustment mechanism for imbalance of international payments. First of all, with regard to the adjustment responsibility sharing, White Plan advocated the asymmetric adjustment that, deficit countries assumed almost all of the adjustment responsibility and must maintain their deficit within the range allowed by share, i. e. it could not exceed 150% of their quota in the first year, and could not exceed 200% afterwards; Keynes Plan advocated the symmetrical adjustment that, surplus countries and deficit countries jointly assumed the adjustment responsibility, i. e. when the surplus/deficit in clearing account of a member country exceeded by 25% of their quota, it would be identified as imbalance of payments, and the excess part would be charged with a management fee. Moreover, the member country would be required to take the corresponding expansion or tightening policy, and by the end of the year, the excess capital would be confiscated as public reserve fund. Second, with regard to the adjustment mode, the two plans were different as in mortgages and loans: White Plan took the mode of currency swap, i. e. deficit countries exchanged home currencies for currencies of other countries, which in essence, was mortgaging home currencies to obtain foreign currency loans, while Keynes Plan allowed deficit countries to directly apply for overdraft or drawing.

Table 1 – 1   **Comparison of White Plan and Keynes Plan**

	White Plan	Keynes Plan
Organization Mode	Fund system	Banking system
Reserve Currency	U. S. dollars (unita only used as a unit of account)	Bancor
Issuing Authority	Federal Reserve	International Clearing Union

Continued

	White Plan	Keynes Plan
Distribution Mechanism	Distributed by the bilateral balance of international payments with the United States	Distributed by the relative scale in global trade
Currency Anchor	Gold	Global trade volume
Adjustment Mechanism for Balance of International Payments	Asymmetrical adjustment	Symmetrical adjustment
Triffin Dilemma	Hard to break	Expected to break
Implementation Feasibility	Basically applied	Not applied

In theory, Keynes Plan was more economically rational: Keynes seemed to have truly seen inherent defects of the gold standard system, so he advocated demonetization of gold, and envisaged the global trade volume as an anchor to make currency issuance automatically match with the global economic and trade development. Unfortunately, Keynes Plan was faced a real challenge brought by the "Overwhelming U. S. Dominance" world pattern, as its envisaged International Clearing Union directly compromised America's monetary policy independence and seigniorage, and eventually lost the competition with White Plan. Accordingly, the post-war IMF was also established basically based on White Plan.

III. New Exploration on the International Monetary System: "New White Plan" or "New Keynes Plan"?

This global financial crisis caused us to further reflect on the current international monetary system, explore the structure of an ideal monetary system, and give consideration to the feasibility of future transformation paths. In my opinion, based on the historical debate and in combination with international economic and financial realities at the current stage, we can still carry out exploration along with two thoughts: **first**, drawing on the thought of White Plan (we temporarily call it as "New White Plan"); **second**, drawing on the thought of Keynes Plan (we temporarily call it as "New Keynes Plan"). Their general thoughts and differences are as follows:

(i) International Reserve Currency Choice: Sovereign Currency Standard or Super-sovereign Currency Standard?

Starting from the sterling standard system in the 18th century, the international monetary system has always used sovereign currency to serve as international reserve currency. This arrangement has the advantage of convenient management, as well as such shortcomings as lack of international constraints on currency issuance, which may harm the overall stability of the international monetary system. To address this problem, two directions are available: "New White Plan" advocates imposing international constraints on currency issuance on the basis of continuously using sovereign currency to serve as international reserve currency; "New Keynes Plan" advocates creating super-sovereign currency as international reserve currency.

As to the first option mentioned above (i. e. "New White Plan"), the most recent example is the consideration of using some mutual-evaluation indicators put forward by G20 to restrain currency issuance of major reserve currency issuing countries. The mutual-evaluation program of G20 Seoul Summit 2010 provided a dozen constraining indicators of financial and economic discipline, wherein six core indicators are of great reference value. Once these indicators are satisfied in a compulsory way, they will be expected to form certain financial and economic discipline constraints on major reserve currency issuance. However, as this involves the transfer of a country's economic sovereign and the international policy coordination, there are still an array of realistic difficulties and challenges.

As to the second option mentioned above (i. e. "New Keynes Plan"), many scholars and institutions have done similar research, like Bernstein Plan and Triffin Plan, the SDR establishment is also a beneficial attempt for super-sovereign currency, and of course what's most famous is still Keynes Plan. As a matter of fact, the SDR establishment and distribution by IMF in 1968, to a certain extent, made some reference to the original idea of Keynes. It now appears that, compared with White Plan, Keynes Plan is undoubtedly more rational, in that its design of taking global trade volume as anchor enjoys an added advantage in dealing with the contradiction between currency stability and liquidity supply. However, theoretical rationality and realistic feasibility are not the same thing, as the replacement of sovereign currency with super-sovereign currency will be inevitably faced with numerous obstacles in terms of politics, economy and finance, and will have to address a series of problems, including how to form and distribute, how to expand use, and how to link up with the existing system and how to realize transition. Therefore, from the perspective of feasibility, the practice of "New White Plan" may be more operational.

In short, the main difference behind these two plans is currency issuing authorities. "New Keynes Plan" requires to set up a global central bank for issuing and managing super-sovereign currency to maintain stability of the global monetary system; while under "New White Plan", the responsibility of issuing reserve currency will be assumed by the monetary authority of a sovereign country rather than managed by the global central bank, provided that it requires to impose more international constraints on currency issuance of that country.

(ii) Currency Anchor Choice: "Exogenous Anchor" or "Endogenous Anchor"?

To give full play to the important role of currency, first of all, the stability of currency value should be guaranteed, especially the stability of its role as measure of value, medium of exchange and storage function. As such, the future international monetary system cannot avoid the "Currency Anchor" problem. A suitable "Currency Anchor" must be able to effectively coordinate the contradiction between currency value stability and liquidity supply, which requires to: first, remain fairly constant to restrain currency issuance and ensure relative stability of currency value; second, have a certain correlation with global economic and trade contacts to ensure satisfying the liquidity demand of real economy.

Under the current dollar standard monetary system, the Fed issues international reserve currency (U. S. dollar) taking America's economic condition (inflation and employment) as "Anchor", so from the perspective of the international reserve currency issuance mechanism, this is an "exogenous" currency anchor relative to the global economy, making no reference to the global economic and trade condition. According to "New White Plan", under the premise of continuing dollar standard, to maintain stability of currency value, it is necessary to impose appropriate constraints on the Fed's currency issuance. Such constraints can be realized by seeking a "Commodity Anchor" of its own independent value (e. g. choosing precious metal of more abundance as currency anchor, or creating a commodity basket as currency anchor, or even taking some form of energy as currency anchor), or by creating indicators based on America's macroeconomic condition (e. g. debt ratio, leverage ratio, etc.) to restrain the Fed's currency issuance. Either way, currency anchor in "New White Plan" is always exogenous.

Theoretically, since a currency's main role is a medium of exchange, currency anchor must be commensurate to the global economic and trade development and its exchange, i. e. of endogenous nature in line with the global economic and trade development. Keynes's original idea of taking global trade volume as currency anchor has certain rationality. As per the thought of "New Keynes Plan", considering that the current international capital flows have largely exceeded trade settlement demand, consequently, it is required to choose boarder economic indicators as anchor of currency issuance, such as choosing a certain "Economic Index Basket" which contains representative indicators reflecting global inflation and economic growth, including both quantity indicators and price indicators, all of which are suitable choices. However, the research on what specific indicators to choose and how to determine the weight of each indicator still needs to be deepened. Besides, some scholars also advocate taking SDR as currency anchor. Is it feasible? How to proceed? All these are open topics, on which everyone can freely express your views.

(iii) Adjustment of Balance of International Payments: Symmetrical Adjustment or Asymmetrical Adjustment?

This global crisis has fully demonstrated the importance of an effective imbalance adjustment mechanism to the monetary system. The Bretton Woods System is an asymmetrical adjustment mechanism, while the Jamaica System, despite the existence of such mechanisms as IMF Article IV Consultation, is actually a system lacking adjustment mechanism by reason of its absence of constraining force and execution in practice. With regard to the future monetary system, "New White Plan", in essence, remains asymmetrical adjustment. The reality of dollar standard and strength imbalance among all parties determines that it is by nature impossible to achieve symmetry. "New Keynes Plan" advocates symmetrical adjustment. Of course, as for how to design the adjustment mechanism and how to ensure its effectiveness and enforceability, all these need to be further studied.

(iv) Triffin Dilemma: Continue or Break?

The international monetary system cannot be discussed without mentioning "Triffin Dilemma". Triffin Dilemma originally meant, on the condition of taking sovereign currency (dollar) as international currency, the international trade and investment development needs the United States to constantly export dollars through current account deficit to maintain adequate solvency (i. e. payment instrument); however, long-term deficit will affect confidence in dollar convertibility, which will be bound to cause each country to convert dollars to gold, resulting in the depletion of America's gold reserves and the ultimate damage to the "double-hook" foundation of the Bretton Woods System. After entering the new century, America saw the "Greenspan Puzzle" that, the link of long-end interest rates and short-end interest rates was severed. In the sense of interest rate serving as currency price, this meant that the dollar price got distorted, the long-term and short-term currency values of dollars were no longer constantly consistent, and with the swelling of overseas dollars, such price distortion might become increasingly worse, which could be called the "Price Version" of Triffin Dilemma.

Triffin Dilemma, in essence, referred to the contradiction between currency value stability and liquidity supply. The primary cause of Triffin Dilemma was the disjunction between reserve currency issuance and the global economic and trade development, making it impossible to give equal consideration to currency value stability and liquidity supply. The gold standard system ensured currency value stability, but liquidity supply could not catch up with the global economic and trade development. The Jamaica System ensured liquidity supply, which however, led to long-term global inflation. Therefore, for the sake of truly breaking Triffin Dilemma, it was required to make currency value and supply endogenous; Keynes Plan made a preliminary attempt, but failed to put it into practice. Moreover, under the sovereign currency standard system, as currency issuance depended exclusively on the sovereign country's condition, it was essentially impossible to break this dilemma. Judging from this aspect, as long as "New White Plan" doesn't give up the sovereign currency standard, Triffin Dilemma will be bound to be its hunting nightmare. On the contrary, "New Keynes Plan" inherits Keynes's idea about super-sovereign currency, and therefore will be likely to break this dilemma once and for all.

Table 1 – 2   **Comparison of New White Plan and New Keynes Plan**

	New White Plan	New Keynes Plan
Organization Mode	Fund system	Banking system
Reserve Currency	Sovereign currency	Super-sovereign currency
Issuing Authority	Monetary authority of the sovereign country	Global central bank
Distribution Mechanism	Distributed by the bilateral balance of international payments with the international currency issuing country	Distributed by the relative scale in world economy
Currency Anchor	Exogenous anchor (but impose more constraints including G20 mutual-evaluation on the currency issuing country)	Endogenous anchor (aggregate indicators on world economy, e. g. inflation, growth, etc.)
Adjustment Mechanism for Balance of International Payments	Asymmetrical adjustment	Symmetrical adjustment
Triffin Dilemma	Hard to break	Expected to break
Implementation Difficulty	Relatively small	Relatively large

Taking a general view on "New Keynes Plan" and "New White Plan", in terms of economic rationality, the former undoubtedly has a certain advantage; also, its system structure is more stable and flexible. However, subject to path dependence and institutional change costs, "New White Plan" seems to be more feasible realistically, as the optimization path of the future international monetary system is still very likely to impose certain constraints on its currency issuance on the basis of dollar standard, and make some improvements on the adjustment mechanism for balance of international payments.

(ⅴ) Market Selection or Artificial Design?

In the end, I also would like to talk about an issue seemingly irrelevant, which involves views on market forces and human rationality, i. e. whether the mechanism through artificial design can ensure to be more effective than that through market selection. This puzzle has bothered the theorists for a long time.

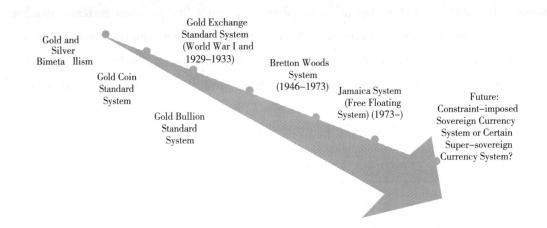

Page 1 – 4　Evolution of the International Monetary System

For example, when discussing currency, Marx said, "Although gold and silver are not by nature money, money is by nature gold and silver." This explained from one side the role of market competition in determining currency materials. In *Denationalization of Money*, Hayek concentrated in expounding the role of market competition in currency issuance. He advocated abolishing government monopoly over currency issuance and allowing private sectors to freely issue different currencies, while forces of market competition were enough to restrain the impulse of currency over-issuance and maintain a stable, effective monetary system.

Compared with the Bretton Woods System, the formation of the Jamaica System seemed to remarkably reflect forces of market competition and selection. After the official collapse of the Bretton Woods System in 1973, many people predicted that U. S. dollar would lose its position as central currency. However, subject to path dependence or network externality, U. S. dollar still keeps its dominance in international economic and trade contacts. Japan, in contrast, "artificially" designed a series of systems in 1980s and 1990s, including pushing forward to establish offshore markets, setting up common-good funds and increase JPY foreign aids, in a bid to vigorously promote internationalization of Japanese Yen. Admittedly, Japanese Yen's proportion in global reserves indeed had some increase for a period of time. However, with ten years of economic stagnation in Japan, that proportion fell back immediately. Therefore, in creating the future international monetary system, how to treat the relationship between market selection and artificial design will be a major issue. How to ensure the monetary system through artificial design better than through market selection? Is this design necessary? Can their relationship be coordinated? All these questions deserve to think deeply.

I believe that crisis drives reform. Rather than design without foundation, artificial design represents a market consensus formed in coping with crisis. By virtue of its advantage of path dependence, New White Plan is expected to be capable of adapting to the new international situation after crisis. If fails to adapt, it will lead to a more profound world economic and financial crisis, on which occasion, artificial design might rely more on a flexible currency supply system. I expect not to see the latter, as the price is heavy, although we should do some research on it.

Above are some of my humble opinions, just for purpose of starting the discussion. Your criticisms and suggestions will be sincerely welcomed.

CHAPTER 2

Thoughts on the Development Space of New Finance from Internet Finance Perspective[①]

Wu, Xiaoling

I. Internet Finance and Third – party Payment

My first point involves internet cross-border finance being an importation direction of the future new finance development. Internet finance represents a new financial service model that uses internet technology and mobile communication technology to provide services for customers, including both financial services performed by traditional financial institutions through the Internet and cross-border financial services performed by internet enterprises through internet technology.

After the explosive growth of internet finance in 2013, the society has gradually reached a consensus that, internet finance actually includes two aspects: on one hand, our traditional financial services make more use of internet technology and new mobile communication technology; on the other hand, our current internet enterprises are engaging in financial services. Recently, we have seen a topic and a term called "internet cross-border finance" frequently appearing in newspapers, which is exactly the other hand of internet finance we are now talking about, i. e. internet finance in a narrow sense.

The traditional financial industry will continue to be the main body of internet finance, although market competition will force it to strengthen the use of internet technology and a variety of communication technology in financial services. 2013 represents the first year of internet finance, in which year however, our traditional finance has experienced great impact and shock. We have seen internet enterprises create many miracles by using internet technology to provide financial services for lots of groups who were unable to enjoy financial services in the past,

---

① This article is finished based on the author's speech at "The 1ˢᵗ Summit of New Finance Union" held on June 29, 2014.

including AliFinance. They sell Tianhong Gain Fund through Alipay, and name it Yu'ebao, bringing such a shock to finance that the traditional financial community begins to think about their own service model and how to better combine with internet technology and mobile communication technology. It should be said that, in the foreseeable future, our traditional financial institutions will make more use of internet technology and mobile communication technology in product sales, risk control and business innovation.

In the face of general internet finance, traditional finance will, under the impact of internet enterprises, catch up vigorously by changing their business model and service mode. In the future, after self-reform of traditional finance, what kind of development space will be left for internet enterprises? In my opinion, direct financing of internet cross-border finance will be the main direction of future development.

First of all, let's take a look at third-party payment, which will return to payment in the professional field. For our internet enterprises of third-party payment, at the very beginning, they carried out business in the professional field, including the booming Alipay who completed its payment function when Taobao enterprises and merchants were doing transactions. However, starting from selling funds, it has broken through commodity transaction services towards trading of financial products. An array of third-party payment enterprises are also starting to develop more services based on third-party payment.

Nevertheless, we should see that, payment is the core of banking business. To ensure the safety of payment and prevent such criminal behaviors as money laundering from payment operations, the regulatory authority will implement strict management on third-party payment.

As we all know, it is the bank that creates credit currency, while the combination of deposits, loans and settlement services constitute a foundation for the creation of credit currency. From internet finance that developed rapidly last year we can see that, among these three services, the core is payment and settlement, because the account of payment and settlement itself is the form of currency existence, and the movement of account balances is the result of completing the medium of exchange function. Besides, the ultimate implementation of our economic activities and the smooth progress of transactions all depend on payment and settlement of currency.

We can also see that, in today's world, when coming to financial competition or currency war, payment and settlement will be the focus. When invoking economic sanctions on a country, the object of such sanctions is actually the payment and settlement network. Therefore, payment and settlement is a very crucial service in the financial industry, as it is not only a bank's core business, but also a lifeline of all financial products and financial transactions. Such a service should be strictly regulated.

In the past, when issuing a third-party payment license, the central bank made it very clear that, third-party payment could only complete micropayments, and capital of third-party payment should reach one tenth of its clients' deposit capital. There was also a restriction on connected banks, which number was limited to five, and if more than five banks, an increase of capital and reserves would be required. All these requirements were put forward to ensure safety of payment and settlement and that no one would use payment and settlement for any criminal behavior or money laundering.

If we now require third-party payment to strictly follow the original purpose of the central bank to issue licenses, third-party payment will gradually all return to payment in the professional field, because it is micropayment, and because it is required to truly realize real-name registration and identity traceability.

Third-party payment's sales of financial products will lose strong momentum in online sales of traditional financial services. Last year, we saw the strong momentum of internet finance reflected by Yu'ebao and various "Baobaos", who was essentially selling financial products and wealth management products on third-party payment platforms. Traditional financial institutions have well-established payment and settlement systems and hundreds of millions of customer accounts; when they come to realize this issue, by virtue of their payment capacity and a large number of accounts, they will enjoy a strong competitive advantage in online sales of financial products, leaving no particularly large development space for online fund sales of third-party payment. Therefore, I hold the opinion that Yu'ebao has basically reached its extreme.

II. Online Loan and Crowd-funding have Broad Prospects

My second point is that the online loan and crowd-funding will have broad prospects. Although its financing amount will be no higher than traditional finance, there will be huge space for expansion of the population it serves.

First of all, I would like to talk about online loan. The lack of a credit investigation system makes it difficult for P2P to realize healthy development. Many companies have gone to the mistake of indirect financing; only those who possess the credit investigation ability can move towards the correct direction. It is said that now there are more than a thousand P2P companies in China; however so far, the number of companies that truly provide peer-to-peer services, if speaking exaggeratedly, is almost zero.

Nevertheless, there do exist several companies that perform relatively well, but they all encounter a bottleneck that, our investors always expect their principal to be guaranteed by someone. Looking from the market, there are two models of guarantee commitment to their principal: first, use third-party guarantee; second, rely on the withdrawal of risk reserves to ensure guarantee for the investor's capital.

Both models have their service limitations. In the case of third-party guarantee, with the increase of P2P operations, the guarantee institution will require a big capital stock, and even if taking 12 times the bank leverage for guarantee, its capital will be 12 times at most. One billion of capital can only realize a business volume of 12 billion. It should be said that, the guarantee institution's capital raising amount determines the business volume developed on your P2P platform.

There is a paradox: for a guarantee company, when its capital is increasing, the volume it can guarantee is also increasing. But how to ensure the safety ofits capital? Put money in the bank to get interest on deposit or buy treasury bonds? These channels are safe, but earn little, making it very difficult to support development of the guarantee company; as a result, many guarantee companies have to walk towards the wrong road of disguised lending and investment on their own. Therefore, it is an unsustainable way to promote development of P2P platform services through third-party guarantee companies.

In the case of ensuring the safety of clients' capital by means of withdrawing risk reserves, with the generation non-performing loans, withdrawal ratio of risk reserves will also rise. What can support an accurate withdrawal of deposit reserves? It is the analysis on the clients' credit, and therefore this way is also subject to the development of credit investigation.

With the lack of a credit investigation system in China, we can hardly conduct adequate analysis on a borrower's credit, and also, our country lacks a property registration system, making it difficult for us to make an accurate judgment on a lender's assets or risk tolerance, so these two elements constitute a big bottleneck on our P2P development. As for online loan based on e-commerce platform, it has a unique credit investigation system that can ensure its healthy development. If an independent credit investigation system can be established on other platforms that enable one to see its clients' behavior, P2P will be able to realize healthy development.

Let us also talk a little about crowd-funding. We know that crowd-funding actually has multiple models. In the original crowd-funding, people raised money together to do some things, on a paid or donated basis. But now, most people in our country are talking about lending-based crowd-funding and equity-based crowd-funding. Lending-based crowd-funding is basically the P2P we just mentioned; currently more people are engaging in equity-based crowd-funding. In the context that our multi-level capital market development is not sound enough, it should be said that equity-based crowd-funding has broad prospects. The amendment to Securities Law this time has also drawn on international experience; and all parties expect to leave space for equity-based crowd-funding.

III. Regulatory Suggestions on and Development Directions of Online Loan and Crowd-funding

My third point involves regulatory suggestions on online loan and crowd-funding. First, a pure information platform should be the bottom line of P2P and crowd-funding supervision. Now for many P2P companies, the biggest risk point lies in that they have a capital pool, and they can use capital from the pool. To realize healthy and robust development, lots of P2P companies have actively proposed to deposit their money at a third party who will be asked to supervise their capital, which I think is very good way to prevent risks. However, it can only guard against the risk of absconding with money but cannot effectively control the lenders' risks. To truly control the lenders' risks, it has to rely on the establishment of a credit investigation system.

Second, small amount and diversification are important ways to protect investors. True disclosure of information is a basic requirement for the financing party. We need to carefully disclose the lenders' information; for equity-based crowd-funding, information disclosure plays a more significant role. At the same time, restricting the investment party's amount is an important precondition of reducing information disclosure costs. If the investing party's investment amount is small, then even some risk appears, it will has less effect on him. In such case, we can properly lower some standards for information disclosure. It is not saying that we subjectively want to lower standards, but saying that our current credit investigation system makes it difficult for us to truly let him make adequate information disclosure. When I cannot truly disclose all information, the best protection for an investor is to let him invest less. If the investment succeeds, he will earn profits; if the investment fails, its damage to him won't be too heavy.

In the context that the property registration system is incomplete, it is more realistic to combine small amount with property ratio. We all know that, P2P and crowd-funding overseas have a restriction for the investor that the investment amount shall not exceed a certain ratio of his disposable property, which means that, the investor will not suffer heavy damage once the investment fails. However, as our country lacks a property registration system, we can hardly know an individual's actual total property. Therefore, on the level of laws and platform rules, one can make provision for a certain property ratio, but in a real sense, it will be safer to determine a relatively small absolute amount.

Property ratio can appropriately be expanded, but there should be a ceiling. In overseas markets, property ratio may represent 5% or a few percent of total property; some people will say, if in this way, my amount will be too small, so they expect to determine a higher property ratio. But I think, from the perspective of effectively controlling risks, an absolute amount ceiling should be available. Therefore, our amendment to Securities Law, although certain legal space for crowd-funding will be left, will also be likely to impose certain control on property ratio and absolute amount. This is our suggestions to the amendment.

Third, encouraging the establishment of private credit investigation companies can help promote the development of direct financing. Now everyone is calling for the credit registration system managed by the central bank to be open to society and to P2P small-loan companies. However, we should also know that, after this system becomes open, as the quantity of borrowers and loans is huge while the amount is very small, the cost of data is actually very high, and searching the loan amount alone cannot fully control an individual's credit risks. Therefore, it is very important to develop private credit investigation companies. In the context of national requirements that government information shall be open in normal cases and not open in special cases, many behaviors that have violated discipline or law can be searched online. Under this circumstance, encouraging the establishment of private credit investigation companies and letting them organize massive negative information and preparing a report on an individual's credit status will be very favorable to the development of various private financial activities.

To this end, I think on one hand, we should call for the central bank's credit registration system to be open to society, but on the other hand, we should focus more on establishment of private credit investigation systems. The central bank has begun to prepare for issuing such licenses. As network companies hold massive information and big data processing capabilities, we should utilize these information and capabilities to establish private credit investigation companies, so as to promote more healthy development of the financial industry.

These are what I think about the development direction of internet finance and new finance. They may appear conservative-in my opinion, the real development space of new finance is P2P and crowd-funding of direct financing. It should be said that, traditional finance is the biggest part of internet finance, but it is not so easy for new finance to get in there. Besides, once traditional financial institutions come to realize this issue and start to make changes, it will bring a huge pressure to other new competitors.

As for some aforementioned small P2P and crowd-funding that ordinary banks fail to do, although in a small amount, the number of people is large; we say that many a little makes mickle, which is vividly expressed by Yu'ebao who starts from one yuan to more than 500 billion in sales. If our private sectors can do some things in 1. 3 billion-population small-amount loan and equity investment, I believe the space will be larger than marching towards traditional finance.

Above are some of my humble opinions. Your criticisms and suggestions will be sincerely welcomed.

CHAPTER 3

Thematic Report: China's Monetary Policy Framework under the New Normal

He, Haifeng[1] Yu, Weiguo[2]

Along with the continuity and deepening of China's economic reform and opening up, as well as new changes in the international economic and financial operation, China's monetary policy framework is being improved constantly. On one hand, it needs to fit in with China's economic and financial system and mechanism; on the other hand, it shall play the main role of macro financial control in China's economic transition. Under the new normal, China is comprehensively deepening reforms of economic system, political system and cultural system, and the monetary policy framework is also having some positive changes.

I. "New Mediocre" of World Economy and "New Normal" of Chinese Economy

Since 2008, each country has put a great deal of effort into coping with the international financial crisis, and the worst days seem to have been in the past; however, the global economic outlook remains unoptimistic. Based on the data, except in 2009 when global economy showed a strong rebound, from 2010 to 2014, the growth of global economy declined all the way down to 3.3%, lower than the average 4.7% during the normal period from 2000 to 2007, and of course lower than the average 5.2% during the boom period from 2004 to 2007.

In 2014, with low growth and high unemployment, world economy was caught in the "New Mediocre", while Chinese economy entered the "New Normal" through new strategies. In 2014, when global economy was still struggling for recovery, which appeared highly unbalanced, American economy outshined others by going upward from low within the year. High-income

---

① He Haifeng, Executive Deputy Director of CEIBS Lujiazui Institute of International Finance, Director of Institute of Financial Policy, Chinese Academy of Social Sciences.

② Yu Weiguo, PhD in Economics, Research Fellow of CEIBS Lujiazui Institute of International Finance, Postdoctor of Tehua Postdoctoral Programme.

economies around the world, especially high-income economies in the Eurozone, still looked weak in their performance; IMF expected that economy of the Eurozone would grow by 0.8% in 2014. Japan's economy recovery was also apparently sluggish; IMF expected that Japanese economy would grow by 0.9% in 2014, and after all three cards of Abenomics were played, it was still hard to take an optimistic attitude towards Japanese economy. In recent two years, emerging economies also gradually slowed down overall. As the largest emerging economy, China has moved from high-speed growth into the "New Normal" of medium and lower speed growth, and economic performance of both Latin America and Russia was unsatisfactory. With economic slowdown and currency volatility, many countries made slow progress in their reforms, and some countries have gone into recession. Lots of emerging economies, including Russia, Brazil, Argentina, Turkey and Indonesia, suffered a currency devaluation crisis of varying degrees, which caused an impact on their financial and economic stability.

Since the outbreak of the international financial crisis, structural contradictions of global economy, such as excessive financial virtualization, high leverage and unbalance development of countries, have not been fundamentally alleviated or improved; faced with the declining economic growth, major economies have successively implemented the "Unconventional Monetary Policy", but economic reform keeps absent. According to the theory of economics, currency in the long term is only a veil over real economy; as such, relying on the "Unconventional Monetary Policy" alone cannot resolve any substantive issues, but on the contrary, will result in a decline of potential growth of global economy. Debt crisis and lack of confidence lead to global demand and investment insufficiency, while demand insufficiency leads to high unemployment, and investment insufficiency leads to productivity impairment; as this cycle repeats, capital, labor and total factor productivity will eventually decline as a whole.

In light of common characteristics that global economy has continuously presented over recent years, including the unbalanced development trend accompanied by low growth and high unemployment, IMF chief Lagarde called this state of global economy as "New Mediocre": job creation and economic inclusivity stay at unacceptable low level, which can exactly describe the current weakness of European (and world) economy, lack of vitality, slow investment, sluggish domestic demand, and government countermeasures that are neither brave nor easy to implement.

The "New Mediocre" of world economy has inevitably affected Chinese economy.

Since the reform and opening up, especially after joining the WTO in 2001, China realized more than 20 years of rapid economic growth through investment expansion and super-currency.

However, in this course, China also accumulated several problems in urgent need to be solved through reform: ecological deterioration, resource exhaustion, excess production capacity and insufficient domestic demand, all of which restricted sustainable economic development. After more than 20 years of high growth, China's economic growth began to slow down.

In May 2014, Xi Jinping said in his visit to Henan, "China's development is still in an important period of strategic opportunities, so we should boost confidence, start from stage characteristics of China's current economic development, adapt to the new normal, and keep a common mentality in strategy." That was the first time that China mentioned the "New Normal". On November 9th, 2014, at the APEC CEO Summit, Xi Jinping systematically elaborated the "New Normal" for the first time. He stated, "The new normal will bring new development opportunities for China." Xi Jinping pointed out that, Chinese economy presented a new normal, which was mainly characterized by the following: first, the growth rate moves from high-speed to medium and high speed; second, the economic structure has been constantly optimized and upgraded, the consumer demand of the tertiary industry has gradually become a main force, the gap between urban and rural areas is narrowing, the resident income share increases, and development fruits benefit more people; third, the driving force moves from factor-driven and investment-driven to innovation-driven. More importantly, he stressed "the obdurability of Chinese economy is the most powerful support for guarding against risks".

The new normal of Chinese economy will bring new development opportunities for China in four respects. First, under the new normal, although China's economic growth slows down, the actual increment remains considerable. The increment of Chinese economy in 2013 equaled the year-round economic aggregate in 1994, and could be ranked 17th in the world. Second, under the new normal, China's economic growth becomes more stable and driven by more diversified forces. China is in a concerted effort to push forward the new industrialization, urbanization, informatization and agricultural modernization, which can help resolve various growing pains. Chinese economy relies more on domestic consumer demand, and avoids reliance on external risks of export. Third, under the new normal, China's economic structure is optimized and upgraded, and the development prospect becomes more stable. In the first three quarters of 2014, China's final consumption contributed 48.5% to economic growth, exceeding the investment. The added value of the service industry accounted for 46.7%, continuing to exceed the secondary industry. The high-tech industry and equipment manufacturing industry grew by 12.3% and 11.1% respectively, apparently higher than the average industrial growth. The energy consumption per unit of GDP fell by 4.6%. Fourth, under the new normal, Chinese government vigorously streamlines administration and institutes decentralization, and market vitality is further released.

The "New Normal" of Chinese economy is likely to profoundly change the relationship between China and the world. In 2010, China replaced Japan and became the world's second largest economy. In 2014, China's GDP exceeded USD 10 trillion and became the second country (only next to the United States) with its GDP more than USD 10 trillion. In the meantime, China's contribution to global economic growth remained ranked 1st; according to IMF's estimation, in 2014, China's economic growth contributed 27.8% to world economy, while the United States only contributed 15.3%. Presently, consumption replaces investment and becomes the largest engine of China's economic growth; "Chinese demand" and "Chinese market" gradually replace "Made in China". In full 2014, China's total retail sales of consumer goods had a nominal growth of 12%, with the market size ranked 2nd in the world. According to the statistics of the Ministry of Commerce and the State Administration of Foreign Exchange, in 2014, China's total outward investment exceeded the actual use of foreign capital, making China a net exporter of capital for the first time in history, which indicates that China has entered a new era of resource allocation on a global scale. Under the "New Normal", China accelerates the construction of an open economy to provide such public products as long-term infrastructure for the world through capital-industry combination; from New Development Bank to Asian Infrastructure Investment Bank and Silk Road Fund, from vigorously pushing forward the construction of "One Belt and One Road" to enhancing trade facilitation, China is continuously increasing "Adhesion" with world economy.

II. China's Monetary Policy Framework from the Traditional Perspective

The new normal of Chinese economy can be simply understood as "Three-period Superimposed" —economic growth shifting period, structural adjustment pain period and early-stage policy digestion period. After entering the new normal, it is required to observe and analyze China's economic operation from the law of economic development and the new normal perspective. At present, China's economic growth is generally consistent with expectations, employment and price situations are stable, and the pace of structural adjustment is somewhat accelerated, but the endogenous economic growth momentum remains to be enhanced, such structural contradictions as growth overly relying on debts and investments are still prominent, the economic downturn pressure and risk exposure in the process of structural adjustment increase to some extent, and the excessive load and constraints of the resource environment are more highlighted. Subject to complex factors, including the high debt ratio, risk premium rising and structural distortion, such issues as difficult and expensive financing for business have aroused wide attention from all sectors of society.

In recent years, affected by the rapid expansion of currency and credit, problems such as the excessive expansion of China's financial assets, overhigh corporate leverage ratio and real estate bubble have become apparent, and the endogenous vulnerability of economic and financial system have been enhanced. Under this circumstance, once the asset price bubble bursts, the "Balance Sheet Recession" might appear, which is an important factor with an effect on monetary policy regulation.

In this context, it is of great significance to actively adapt to the new normal of economic development, build a new monetary policy framework and establish an effective macro financial control mechanism.

(i) Target of China's Monetary Policy

Except the Fed implements a dual target of low inflation and full employment, developed countries and many emerging market countries of a high degree of marketization, especially in over twenty years before the financial crisis, most set a single target for their monetary policy, i. e. inflation targeting. For twenty years before the financial crisis in 2008, major economies implementing inflation targeting were successful in controlling inflation, and meanwhile, maintained a certain economic growth. European Central Bank, Bank of Japan and Bank of England all implemented the single target of price stability.

The target of China's monetary policy has always been diversified. Article 3 of the *Law of the PRC on the People's Bank of China* clearly states that, "The target of monetary policy is to maintain stability of currency value, and thereby promote economic growth." Stability of currency value consists of two connotations: on one hand, domestic price stability, and on the other hand, foreign exchange rate stability. Thus it can be seen that, the target diversification of China's monetary policy is derived from the *Law of PRC on the People's Bank of China*. Since the reform and opening up, China has moved from the planned economic system to the market-oriented economic system, faced with double surplus of balance of payments and excessively passive injection of domestic liquidity for a long time, which has forced the central bank to pay attention to such issues as balance of payments and give overall consideration the relationship among targets like price, employment, growth and balance of payments in monetary policy making. Therefore, specifically, the ultimate target of China's monetary policy consists of: maintaining a moderate economic growth, price stability, full employment and maintaining equilibrium in balance of payments. Besides, due to certain coordination between financial stability and monetary policy, financial stability is also an important aspect under the management of China's central bank.

(ii) Conduction Mechanism of Monetary Policy

The conduction mechanism of monetary policy refers to the process from using monetary policy to reaching the target of monetary policy; whether the conduction mechanism of monetary policy is improved or not directly affects the implementation effect of monetary policy and its contribution to economy.

For economies of a high degree of marketization, their conduction mechanism of monetary policy mainly uses price (interest rate) channels, generally with three basic steps in the following order: (1) short-term market interest rates are adjusted through open operation in the financial market; (2) short-term interest rates affect long-term interest rates, asset prices and exchange rates through the financial market; (3) financial market conduction to real economy produces an effect on economic activities of enterprises and individuals, including investments, savings and consumptions, which further affects inflation, output and employment.

In the past, China's conduction mechanism of monetary policy mainly used quantity (base money, reserve rate and credit supply) channels, wherein the credit channel played a major role in China's conduction mechanism of monetary policy, mainly because: local governments and state-owned enterprises, subject to soft budget constraints, were insensitive to capital prices, as a result price (interest rate) instruments could hardly play a role, while bank credit could directly affect investment behaviors of local governments and state-owned enterprises; as RMB exchange rates were not in free floating, the central bank's intervention through the foreign exchange market would affect the issue of base money.

The conduction mechanism of monetary policy determines the intermediary target of monetary policy. The intermediary target of China's monetary policy consists of: money supply, interest rate level and credit volume. In 1996, the People's Bank of China used money supply M_1 and M_2 as the control target of monetary policy, marking that China began to introduce the intermediary target of monetary policy. In 1998, as the credit scale control was abandoned, money supply as the intermediary target became indisputable. Currently, China's money supply indicator to a great extent is still regarded as a weather vane of monetary policy orientation.

(iii) Monetary Policy Instruments

China's monetary policy instruments mainly include: quantity instruments, price instruments, open market operation and window guidance. Quantity instruments include required deposit reserve and excess deposit reserve rates; price instruments include loan-deposit benchmark rates and refinance (rediscount) rates. The open market operation functions as an important tool of daily liquidity management. It should be stressed that, the role of window guidance in our country cannot be ignored. The People's Bank of China holds window guidance meetings from time to time; as our financial system still keeps a certain degree of administrative color, in some cases, window guidance undoubtedly plays a more direct and effective role.

III. Unconventional Monetary Policy: Theory and Practice

(i) Theory of Unconventional Monetary Policy

The conventional monetary policy means, during economic downturn, the central bank releases liquidity through price control by adjusting benchmark rates or through quantity control by open market operation or adjusting required deposit reserve rates, so as to reach the intended targets. However, under the impact of global financial crisis in 2008, banks suffered heavy attacks, bank system functions declined, the conduction mechanism of monetary policy was severely hindered, the money supply dramatically shrank, and meanwhile, the central bank's operating target—short-term interest rates approached zero, and interest rate cuts alone were not enough to restore market confidence; in this case, the conventional monetary policy fell into trouble, and the unconventional monetary policy became a major tool for the central bank to cope with the crisis.

The unconventional monetary policy means, in the context that there is no room for interest rate cuts or the market transmission mechanism of interest rates is severely hindered, for example, the lower limit of short-term nominal interest rates approaches zero or interest rate cuts alone are not enough to restore market confidence, the central bank directly injects liquidity into the market by adjusting the structure of balance sheet or expanding the size of balance sheet, so as to ensure continued market liquidity when interest rates are extremely low.

The unconventional monetary policy mainly has three types: commitment effect, credit easing and quantitative easing.

The commitment effect means, the central bank, through communication with the public, provides a clear commitment to maintain short-term rates at zero or a low level for quite a long time, so as to change market interest rate expectations. The commitment effect generally represents a conditional commitment, i. e. the central bank undertakes not to step away from easy monetary policy before reaching a certain target of economic recovery. The commitment effect enables the public to make an accurate judgment on the future monetary policy to be promulgated by the monetary authority, and under the commitment effect, the public firmly believes that the long-term existence of short-term interest rates will be bound to result in the decline of long-term market interest rates. Therefore, the commitment effect is able to change market interest rate expectations, avoid delay in consumption or expenditure and stimulate demand increase.

The credit easing means, under the premise that the overall size of balance sheet of the central bank basically remains unchanged, the central bank purchases assets of poor liquidity or high risks from private sectors, so as to change the asset-side structure of balance sheet of the central bank; in this course, proportions and relative prices of various assets held by private sectors have also changed, which will further produce an effect on the real economy.

The quantitative easing policy means, the central bank, by buying securities, increases commercial banks' excess reserve deposits at the central bank, so as to expand its balance sheet, making it exceed the level required for maintaining interest rates at zero, and thus affecting asset prices and economic outputs in the financial market. By buying long-term treasury bonds held by the government or financial institutions, the central bank realizes a rise in prices of treasury bonds, which will reduce the yield of long-term treasury bonds. The yield of treasury bonds represents the benchmark interest rate of various financial assets; with the reduction of the yield of long-term treasury bonds, long-term market interest rates will come down accordingly. The central bank's purchase of securities from a financial institution is equivalent to depositing the same amount of money into the deposit reserve account of that financial institution, which means an expansion of base money.

(ii) Practice of Unconventional Monetary Policy

After the outbreak of the financial crisis in 2008, in the context that the conventional monetary policy became ineffective, major economies around the world have successively implemented the unconventional monetary policy.

1. Unconventional Monetary Policy Implemented by the Fed

In terms of commitment effect, the Fed made an unconditional commitment to maintain interest rates at the boundary of zero, continued to maintain the Federal fund target rate unchanged at $0 \sim 0.25\%$, and in a policy statement published after seven regular meetings held in March-December 2009, undertook to maintain that rate unchanged for quite some time. In terms of credit easing and quantitative easing, from November 2008, the Fed successively carried out several rounds of large-scale asset purchase, and in November 2008, announced to implement the asset purchase program of USD 500 billion mortgage-backed securities and USD 100 billion federal agency bonds; on March 18, 2009, the Fed announced to implement three unconventional monetary policy measures: first, purchase of a maximum of USD 300 billion long-term treasury bonds in the next six months; second, purchase of USD 750 billion federal agency mortgage-backed securities, making the total purchase of these securities reach USD 1.25 trillion within the year; third, purchase of USD 100 billion bonds issued or guaranteed by Fannie Mae and Freddie Mac, making the total scale reach USD 200 billion within the year. In

November 2010, the Fed announced the USD 600 billion long-term treasury bond purchase program, and in September 2011, implemented a typical balance sheet structure change initiative, announced to buy USD 400 billion 6-30-year long-term treasury bonds, and meanwhile, sold the same amount of three-year and shorter-term treasury bonds, so as to lower long-term interest rates, which was called an "Operation Twist"; in September 2012, the Fed announced to buy USD 40 billion mortgaged-backed securities on a monthly basis until the economic situation became satisfactory.

2. Unconventional Monetary Policy Implemented by the Bank of Japan

Taking advantage of the stability of the new government in power, through Japan-style quantitative easing policy, by form of reversing deflation with inflation, Japan has not only freed itself from the current crisis, but also hopes to pull Japanese economy out of more than ten years of stagflation. In October 2010, the Bank of Japan began to implement a broad easing policy by buying a wide range of assets, including government bonds, as well as credit products (e. g. commercial papers and corporate bonds), equity products (e. g. exchange-traded funds) and Japanese real estate investment trusts, with the aim of directly lowering part of yield curves within the 3 year period, and meanwhile, compressing various risk premiums. In February 2012, the Bank of Japan introduced the "Medium- and Long-term Price Stability Target", and announced to set a current target, that is to achieve a YoY growth of 1% on CPI. Although these policies supported economic development by providing an easy financial environment, they failed to change deflation expectations deep-rooted in families and enterprises. In April 2013, the Bank of China introduced the quantitative & qualitative easing policy, i. e. QQE Policy, which covered two elements: quantitative and qualitative. To reinforce the price stability commitment, the policy clearly and firmly undertook to realize 2% of the price stability target within two years, and to directly act on inflation expectations of private entities. To consolidate this commitment, the Bank of Japan decided to implement a new round of bold easing monetary policy, including both qualitative easing and quantitative easing. Through this policy, the Bank of Japan will double base money (directly provided by the Bank of Japan), and buy a large number of Japanese government bonds, including bonds of longer residual maturity. This policy is different from previous policies in that, it tries to actively affect the expectation formation of private entities (Haruhiko Kuroda, 2014).

3. The European Central Bank "Strengthens Credit Support" and Securities Purchase

On June 24, 2009, the European Central Bank announced to provide unlimited mortgage loans to commercial banks at the current policy interest rate of 1%, with a term up to a year. In 2010, the government bond market in the Eurozone deteriorated sharply, and on May 10, the

European Central Bank announced to implement the "Securities Market Program" to purchase government bonds from the secondary market. On October 6, 2011, the European Central Bank implemented the second round of EUR 40 billion secured bond purchase program. At the end of 2011, the European debt crisis spread to core countries in the Eurozone, and on December 21, 2011 and February 29, 2012, the European Central Bank carried out two three-year refinancing operations respectively, and offered a total of EUR 1.0187 trillion loans to banks.

4. China's Unconventional Monetary Policy

Faced with the financial crisis in 2008, China's unconventional monetary policy mainly included that from September 2008, the People's Bank of China started moving to the moderately easy monetary policy, specifically, cut loan-deposit benchmark rates five times, cut deposit reserve rates four times, loosened constraints against credit planning of financial institutions, and intensified financial support to economic development.

(iii) Effect of Unconventional Monetary Policy

From early 2009, the effect of unconventional monetary policy has begun to appear. Looking from major economic indicators reflecting the real economy, such as the industrial output index, retail index, world GDP growth rate, PMI (manufacturing purchasing managers index), and world trade indicators, etc., the unconventional monetary policy, to a great extent, has played a positive role: save some financial institutions and enterprises on the verge of bankruptcy in a timely manner, and effectively prevent the occurrence of systematic financial risks; inject a great deal of liquidity and capital into the financial market, and gradually restore market confidence.

Of course, the implementation of unconventional monetary policy also has an array of negative effects. First, the central bank's independence is weakened. In the financial crisis, the central bank bought long-term treasury bonds and securities issued by private sectors, resulting in fiscal monetization and weakening its independence of formulating and implementing the monetary policy. Second, the unconventional monetary policy leads to the rapid expansion of the central bank's balance sheet and a surge in risks, increasing vulnerability of the whole economic and financial system. Third, the global liquidity grows sharply, bringing some hidden troubles to the future inflation.

IV. New Requirements of Reform and Development

As world economy enters the new mediocre, especially as Chinese economy enters the new normal, China's macro financial control dominated by monetary policy is faced with new challenges, and China's monetary policy framework also has positive changes.

(ⅰ) New Challenges Faced by China's Macro Financial Control

First, with the rapid development of shadow banking and financial innovation, the monetary operation law has changed, reflected by more complex structural characteristics and reduced effectiveness of financial supervision. In China's financial industry, from 2009, financial innovation services represented by bank financing, trust schemes and folk finance reached a development climax, and under this impact, the share of new loans in total social financing fell quickly from 75.7% in 2009 to 57.9% in 2012.

Second, long-term reliance on the high-investment growth model results in a big volume of monetary credit, a high leverage ratio and limited space for further expansion. By the end of 2014, the local and foreign currency loan balance of financial institutions reached RMB 86.8 trillion, accounting for 136.5% of GDP of the year. By the end of 2014, M_2 reached RMB 122.8 trillion, quite high compared with history or with other countries. By the end of 2013, China's corporate debts was approximately RMB 68 trillion, accounting for 120% of GDP (less than 80% in America's case), and the A-share non-financial corporate asset-liability ratio rose from 40% in 2000 to more than 60% in 2013. Compared with international, China's non-financial corporate sector debt ratio in 2013 (equivalent to 120% of GDP) was in the highest level range among OECD countries. As far as mature economies are concerned, corporate debts generally reach 50% ~70% of GDP; while China's corporate debts double this number.

Third, with the accelerated development of financial market and financial innovation, quantity control is faced with growing challenges, the task of improving the price control mechanism remains heavy, the difficulty of keeping "Quantity" and "Price" balanced in monetary policy during the transition period increases, and the requirements for guiding and stabilizing expectations become more demanding.

Last, as China's economic and financial system has been integrated into globalization, US dollar's going strong and macro policy differentiation of major economies will further increase complexity and uncertainty of the external environment.

(ⅱ) The Target, Mechanism and Instruments of China's Monetary Policy are Changing

From the perspective of the target of monetary policy, in addition to four traditional targets, the dynamic target in close relation to the new normal receives attention. First, under the new normal, the creation of a neutral moderate financial environment for structural adjustment and upgrading perhaps will become a focus of the target of monetary policy. Presently, China's economic development enters the new normal, the core of which is the change of economic development mode and economic structure, so it is necessary to properly handle the relationship between economic structural adjustment and macro gross policy. Second, the weight of stabilizing growth in multiple targets of monetary policy is falling. China's GDP grew by 7. 4% in 2014, 7. 7% in 2013, 7. 8% in 2012 and 9. 2% in 2011. From 2011, GDP growth has declined year by year, although the employment situation suffers no obvious deterioration. In the meantime, governments at all levels are lowering the GDP growth goal and downplaying the GDP assessment. The 2015 Government Work Report delivered by Premier Li Keqiang sets the GDP growth goal at around 7%, which will be bound to reduce the weight of stabilizing growth in multiple targets of monetary policy. Third, the real estate bubble and corporate leverage remain high, making it more important to maintain financial stability. The weight of financial stability in the conventional monetary policy framework was not large; however after the outbreak of the financial crisis in 2008, the central bank of each country has realized that, the asset bubble is of great significance to financial stability. In addition to the real estate bubble, China's corporate leverage remains high and keeps rising; the rapidly rising share of corporate debts in GDP is also an important potential factor with an effect on financial stability. Fourth, the problem of difficult and expensive financing becomes increasingly pressing, which must be addressed by monetary policy. In recent years, China's population structure and saving rate have changed profoundly, while constrained by the financial system and structural defects, effective interest rates and financing costs of enterprises remain high. In 2014, the financing issue was mentioned in eight consecutive executive meetings of the State Council (March 25, May 21, July 2, July 16, July 23, September 17, January 24, November 19), which formed a consensus to reduce corporate financing costs as a bounden duty of monetary policy.

From the perspective of the conduction mechanism of monetary policy, Chinese economy enters the "New Normal", creating conditions for the conduction mechanism of monetary policy to move form quantity channels to price channels. First, the contribution of money supply and debt growth to economic growth is declining; looking from the relevance of M_2 and GDP & CPI, in 2000 – 2007, the relevance of M_2 growth and CPI reached 0. 67, while in 2008 – 2013, this ratio was reduced to 0. 19; the relevance of M_2 growth and GDP growth was also reduced from 0. 32 to 0. 24. [1] Second, the proportion of current account surplus in GDP falls back, and new funds outstanding for foreign exchange show a downward trend. In the past, the issuance of base money mainly came from changes in funds outstanding for foreign exchange. However, with the market-oriented exchange rate reform, from 2014, exchange rates have changed from unilateral appreciation to bilateral floating, and the proportion of current account balance in GDP has

---

[1]　Curtain Opening of Monetary Policy Framework Transformation by China's Central Bank, *Wuhan Finance*, Issue 11, 2014.

fallen from 10% in 2006 to the present 2% or so. [1] Third, the risk preference of commercial banks becomes lower, and the desire to expand assets declines. Economic growth moves from high speed to medium & high speed, and the unemployment rate remains low, which objectively has created conditions for the conduction mechanism of monetary policy to move from quantity channels to price channels.

From the perspective of the intermediary target of monetary policy, in the past, credit channels were the most important conduction mechanism of China's monetary policy, so the intermediary target of monetary policy consisted of such quantity indicators as the line of credit and M_2 growth, and the monetary policy operation could not be done without such quantity operations as window guidance and reserve rate adjustment. Under the "New Normal", the central bank tries to give more play to the role of interest rates in monetary policy conduction and realize monetary policy transition from quantity control to price control, which requires the central bank to treat inter-bank market interest rates as the intermediary target of monetary target and concentrate the monetary policy operations in the inter-bank market.

From the perspective of the instruments of monetary policy, in 2013 – 2014, the People's Bank of China began to stress that, monetary policy should move from quantity instruments to price instruments more apparently. In fact, the transition was not apparent, mainly because the central bank once made large purchases of foreign currency for the purpose of realizing the gradualness, persistence and continuity of exchange rate reform. In May 2014, People's Bank of China? President Zhou Xiaochuan clearly pointed out in Tsinghua PBCSF Global Finance Forum that, "China's future monetary policy should adopt the 'Interest Rate Corridor' model, with a range of short-term interest rates. When reaching the lower limit, financial institutions may apply for financing from the central bank; when reaching the upper limit, the central bank will reduce such financing. The median is the central bank's short-term policy interest rate, which will be the direction of our development." In fact, the central bank has already begun to use the "Interest Rate Corridor" system for reference, specifically reflected by the establishment of SLO (Short-term Liquidity Operations) and SLF (Standing Lending Facility). The central bank started to use SLF in 2013 and PSL (Pledged Supplementary Lending) in 2014. On January 20, 2014, the central bank carried out pilot SLF operations with part of local corporate financial structures, which was regarded by the market as a small-scale experiment for the Chinese version of interest rate corridor. Afterwards, the central bank introduced within-seven-day short-term liquidity operations.

---

① Curtain Opening of Monetary Policy Framework Transformation by China's Central Bank, *Wuhan Finance*, Issue 11, 2014.

(iii) Actively Explore the Role of Monetary Policy in the Structural Adjustment of Macro Economy

Generally, monetary policy mainly plays the role of gross control. For the current Chinese economy, it probably needs to actively explore the role of structural adjustment. The People's Bank of China adheres to the overall thought of stable macro policy and dynamic micro policy, coordinates stabilizing growth, promoting reform, adjusting structure, benefiting people's livelihood and guarding against risks, continuously implements a prudent monetary policy, maintains policy continuity and stability, sticks to the orientation of "Gross Stability, Structure Optimization", and makes active measures and fine tuning in due time, so as to realize healthy and sustainable economic development. In the meantime, monetary policy control will be combined closely with deepening reform, and the decisive role of market will be given full play in resource allocation. The control pattern will be further improved, the conduction mechanism will be smoothed, and by increasing supply and competition, financial services will be improved and financial operation efficiency and ability to serve the real economy will be enhanced. According to previous relevant practices of the People's Bank of China, the differential reserve dynamic-adjustment measure and credit policy guidance have played the role of structural adjustment.

(iv) Establish an Effective Cooperation Mechanism for Prudent Management Policy and Monetary Policy

The monetary policy mainly plays the role of counter-cyclical adjustment and structural guidance in gross control, while the prudent management policy pays more attention to the stability of financial system. After entering the new normal, China's economic operation law and structure will change, China's financial system and operation mechanism will lay more emphasis on the principle of market-oriented reform, and the sound operation of financial system will be further required for giving better play to the control role of monetary policy. The prudent management policy includes both macro prudent management policy and micro prudent management policy. In particular, with the deepening of China's market-oriented interest rate reform and the further opening of financial industry both at home and abroad, individual financial institutions and increasingly diversified financial systems will be faced with more complex potential financial risks. Therefore, it is necessary to establish an effective cooperation mechanism between control policy such as monetary policy and prudent management policy in respects of organization framework, operation mechanism, instruments and means.

The international financial crisis has provided a new case for the theory and practice of monetary policy, put forward new problems, and meanwhile, promoted the new development of theory and practice of monetary policy. China's monetary policy needs to draw on sophisticated theories and international experiences, and also needs to start from the practice of China's reform and opening up as well as the new stage of China's economic development to broaden horizons, make continuous innovations, and establish a framework system and operation mechanism under the new normal.

References

[1] Zhou Xiaochuan, Evolution of the Monetary Policy Framework since the Financial Crisis in 2008, May 2014, Speech in the Tsinghua PBCSF Global Finance Forum.

[2] Zhang Xiaohui, Monetary Policy under the New Normal, *China Finance*, January 2015.

[3] Zhao Yang, Bian Quanshui, Liu Liu, Wu Jieyun, Global Interest: Monetary Policy Framework Transformation, CICC Macro Economy Analysis Report, September 21, 2014.

[4] He Dexu, New Framework of Monetary Policy, *China Economic Report*, Issue 1, 2015.

[5] Curtain Opening of Monetary Policy Framework Transformation by China's Central Bank, *Wuhan Finance*, Issue 11, 2014.

[6] Li Daye, Zhang Haiyang, New Thought of Monetary Policy Framework, *China Finance*, Issue 20, 2014.

[7] Chen Minqiang, Unconventional Monetary Policies of America, Europe, Britain and Japan and Comparative Analysis on Their Effects, *Studies of International Finance*, July 2010.

[8] Li Liang, Theory and Practice of Unconventional Monetary Policy, *Financial Development Review*, Issue 6, 2013.

[9] Wang Liangliang, Li Mingxing, Miao Yongwang, Unconventional Monetary Policy: Theory, Practice, Performance and Withdrawal, *Shanghai Journal of Economics*, Issue 5, 2010.

[10] PBC Monetary Policy Analysis Group, Report on the Implementation of China's Monetary Policy—2014 Q3, November 6, 2014.

[11] Zhang Monan, Possible Orientation of Unconventional Monetary Policy under the Current Environment, *Shanghai Securities News*, April 15, 2014.

[12] Haruhiko Kuroda, Theory and Practice of Unconventional Monetary Policy, June 7, 2014, Speech of Haruhiko Kuroda (President of the Bank of Japan) in The 17 World Congress Held by the International Economic Association, *Financial Development Review*, Issue 9, 2014.

Part Two

China's Financial Policies in 2014

CHAPTER 4

Macro Financial Policies

I. Monetary Policy[1]

(i) Highlights of Monetary Policy in 2014

Major monetary policies formulated and promulgated by the PBC in 2014 are outlined in the table below.

Table 4 – 1   Summary of Monetary Policy Operations by the PBC in 2014

Date	Policy
Jan. 17	The PBC released the *Notice on Launching the Pilot Standing Lending Facility (SLF) Program* (PBC [2014] No. 19), introducing SLF operations in branch offices in Beijing, Jiangsu, Shandong, Guangdong, Hebei, Shanxi, Zhejiang, Jilin, Henan and Shenzhen in a bid to address the liquidity needs of local corporate financial institutions in compliance with the macro-prudential requirement, maintain stability of market expectation and boost sound performance of the money market
Jan. 30	The PBC released the *Notice on Reclassification of Re-lendings* (PBC [2014] No. 36), to reclassify re-lendings into four categories instead of three previously. The liquidity re-lending category was subdivided into liquidity re-lending and credit policy support re-lending, while financial stability re-lending and special policy re-lending remained unchanged
Mar. 1	The PBC decided to lift interest rate caps on small-amount foreign currency deposits in China (Shanghai) Pilot Free Trade Zone. The FTZ will act as a spearhead and accumulate practicable and reproducible experience in the liberalization of small-amount foreign currency deposit rates countrywide and set the stage for deepening the reform of interest rate liberalization
Mar. 5	The PBC allocated an additional re-lending quota of 20 billion yuan for the agricultural sector to support financial institutions in financial services for the upcoming spring ploughing season
Apr. 22	The PBC decided to cut the RMB deposit required reserve ratio of county-level rural commercial banks by 2 percentage points, and that of county-level rural cooperative banks by 0.5 percentage point, effective from April 25

---

[1] Written by Yu Weiguo.

Continued

Date	Policy
Apr. 25	To act on the resolutions made on the 43rd executive meeting of the State Council, the PBC introduced Pledged Supplementary Lending (PSL) to provide long-term, stable and cost-effective sources of funds to support slum redevelopment with developmental finance
Jun. 9	The PBC decided to cut, effective from June 16, the RMB deposit required reserve ratio by 0.5 percentage point for commercial banks (excluding those that benefit from the deposit reserve ratio reduction on April 25) that comply with the prudence requirement and have lendings to the agricultural sector, rural areas and farmers, and to small and micro enterprises accounting for a certain percentage of total lendings. In addition, the RMB deposit required reserve ratio applicable to finance companies, financial lease companies and auto finance companies was lowered by 0.5 percentage point as well
Sep.	The PBC introduced Medium-termLendingFacility (MLF) to provide medium-term base money to financial institutions in compliance with the requirement for macro-prudential regulation. MLF is designed to make the most of medium-term policy rates to lower the financing costs of the society
Nov. 22	The PBC applied asymmetricalbenchmark deposit and lending rate cuts to financial institutions. The one-year benchmark lending rate was lowered by 0.4 percentage point to 5.6 percent, and the one-year benchmark deposit rate was lowered by 0.25 percentage point to 2.75 percent. At the same time, the upper limit to the floating band of deposit rates was raised from 1.1 to 1.2 times the benchmark level in support of market-oriented interest rate reform. Adjustments were made to benchmark interest rates on deposits and loans of other maturity ladders accordingly. Moreover, the benchmark rate maturity ladder was consolidated and simplified as appropriate
Dec. 23	The PBC issued the *Notice on Matters Concerning Deposit Reserve Policy and Interest Rate Management Policy after Adjustment of Deposit Base* (PBC [2014] No. 387). The PBC is going to change the statistical base of deposits from 2015, to include in the summation of all deposits securities and transaction settlement deposits taken in by deposit-taking financial institutions and previously counted in interbank deposits, non-deposit dues from banks, SPV deposits, and dues from other financial institutions and overseas financial institutions. These newly included deposits are counted in required deposit reserve. The applicable RRR is zero for the time being. The interest rate management policy applicable to these deposit categories remains unchanged and the interest rate is decided by both parties through negotiations under the principle of market

Source: The People's Bank of China.

(ii) Review of Monetary Policy in 2014

1. Background for Monetary Policy-Making in 2014

The New Normal of the Chinese economy is characterized by an overlap of gear shifting of economic growth, restructuring and digestion of previously implemented policies. Generally speaking, the Chinese economy continued to run within a healthy range, added value of the tertiary industry claimed a bigger share of the GDP and consumption made greater contribution to economic growth. Consumer price advanced moderately, employment appeared stable and imports and exports delivered steady growth. In 2014, China's GDP posted a 7.4 percent growth year on year and CPI gained 2.0 percent year on year. Meanwhile, some structural contradictions, such as overdependence of economic growth on indebtedness and investment, remain unabated. Downside pressure and risk exposure intensify during economic restructuring. The environment and resources are further strained and business entities are burdened with costly financing.

Since the outbreak of international financial crisis, the world economy has slid into a spell of rebalancing and readjusting. The economies differ in macro policies. The US monetary policy might undergo material adjustments. Significant uncertainty hangs over economic recovery in Europe and Japan. The fluctuation range of exchange rates between main currencies and cross-border capital flow hold the potential to enlarge further. All of these pose challenges and obstacles to macro policy-making.

2. Review of Monetary Policy Operations in 2014

The PBC held on to a robust monetary policy, by continually enriching and optimizing a mix of monetary policy tools, and making fine-tuned and proactive adjustments with good timing and moderate intensity through restructuring. In the context of slackening injection of the funds outstanding for foreign exchange into base money, the PBC flexibly conducted open market operations, short-term liquidity operations and SLF, among a wide range of monetary policy tools, to assure adequate liquidity, and introduced MLF and PSL to encourage financial institutions to pump low-cost funds into the real sectors towards which government policies are biased. In the year, asymmetrical benchmark deposit and lending rate cuts and two targeted deposit reserve reductions were implemented, the upper limit to the floating band of deposit rates was raised to 1.2 times the benchmark rate and the benchmark rate maturity ladder was consolidated and simplified. *Draft Rules for Deposit Insurance* was unveiled to canvass public opinions.

Open market operations were carried out skillfully. In the first half of 2014, repo operations played the lead, supported by reverse repo operations and SLO in the open market flexibly, to address first quick and then slow growth of the funds outstanding for foreign exchange and the significant impact of seasonal factors, such as the Spring Festival, on liquidity. In the second half, in view of relatively sufficient liquidity as a whole, yet further slackening growth of the funds outstanding for foreign exchange and increasing uncertainties affecting liquidity supply and demand, the PBC tempered the intensity and frequency of open market repo operations gradually, and injected liquidity in a timely and controlled manner by means of repo, maturity of central bank bills and SLO. In the year, repo operations in the open market were worth RMB 3021 billion and reverse repo operations RMB 525 billion cumulatively; liquidity injection through SLO totaled RMB 1021 billion and RMB 100 billion of liquidity was soaked up. By the end of the year, the balance of open market repo and reverse repo operations was 0; the balance of liquidity injection by SLO was RMB 100 billion and that of liquidity soak-up was 0; and outstanding central bank bills were worth RMB 422.2 billion.

SLF was conducted at the right moment and MLF was introduced. The PBC asked its branch offices in 10 provinces and cities to try out SLF in January, 2014 and provided short-term liquidity support to local corporate financial institutions compliant with the requirement for macro-prudential regulation, with a view to reinforce and perfect liquidity management of the banking system, keep liquidity at a reasonable and moderate level and boost sound performance of the money market. The PBC launched MLF in September, 2014 to provide medium-term base money to commercial banks and policy banks in accordance with the requirement for macro-prudential regulation. In 2014, the PBC conducted MLF operations worth RMB 1.14 trillion on a cumulative basis, with the ending balance at RMB 644.5 billion. The maturity was three months and the interest rate was 3.5 percent. Generally speaking, in the context of slackening injection of the funds outstanding for foreign exchange into base money, MLF replenished base money proactively.

Targeted deposit reserve reductions were implemented. In April and June, 2014, the PBC cut the RMB deposit required reserve ratio of county-level rural commercial banks by 2 percentage points, and that of county-level rural cooperative banks by 0.5 percentage point. A 0.5 percentage point cut was applied to the RMB deposit required reserve ratio for commercial banks that comply with the prudence requirement and have lendings to the agricultural sector, rural areas and farmers, and to small and micro enterprises accounting for a certain percentage of total lendings. In addition, the RMB deposit required reserve ratio applicable to finance companies, financial lease companies and auto finance companies was lowered by 0.5 percentage point as well.

The benchmark deposit and lending rates of financial institutions were lowered. In response to the problem of difficult and costly financing and the ongoing price trends, the PBC applied asymmetricalbenchmark deposit and lending rate cuts to financial institutions on Nov. 22, 2014. The one-year benchmark lending rate was lowered by 0.4 percentage point to 5.6 percent, and the one-year benchmark deposit rate was lowered by 0.25 percentage point to 2.75 percent.

The reform of interest rate liberalization was pushed ahead. The control over interest rates of financial institutions was lifted in a well-organized manner. On Mar. 1, 2014, the interest rate caps on small-amount foreign currency deposits were lifted in China (Shanghai) Pilot Free Trade Zone. On Nov. 22, in tandem with benchmark deposit and lending rate cuts, the upper limit to the floating band of RMB deposit rates was raised from 1.1 to 1.2 times the benchmark level. Moreover, the benchmark rate maturity ladder was consolidated and simplified as appropriate, to make more room for financial institutions to decide on prices at their discretion. The self-regulatory pricing mechanism for market interest rates was further better. The membership of the self-regulatory pricing mechanism grew with the addition of 93 new members and the incentive and restraint function of the mechanism was brought into play further.

Thanks to the implementation of a robust monetary policy, the economy and society made strides ahead in a sound financial environment, both monetary & credit and all-system financing aggregates achieved steady growth, the loan structure was further optimized and the problem of high financing costs weighing on business entities was eased to some extent. At end – 2014, outstanding M_2 posted a 12.2 percent increase year on year and outstanding RMB loans expanded by 13.6 percent year on year. All-system financing aggregates came in at 16.46 trillion yuan. In December, the weighted average lending rate offered to non-financial institutions and other sectors was 6.77 percent, down 0.42 percentage point from that at the beginning of the year.

(iii) Policy Outlook

In the New Normal era of the Chinese economy, the key is to change the economic growth pattern and economic structure. Against this backdrop, we must address the relationship between economic restructuring and macroeconomic policy properly. In terms of macroeconomic policy, it is important to have a good command of the direction and intensity and to make timely and due adjustments whenever significant changes happen to the basic conditions, to prevent the economy from being dragged down by inertia. In the meantime, excessive liquidity injection should be avoided as it may cement the structural distortion and heighten indebtedness and financial leverage. While keeping money aggregates at a stable level, we should further optimize the structure and adopt well-targeted restructuring measures to solve some acute problems in the economy, so as to activate existing money supply, optimize the use of incremental money, and support economic restructuring and upgrade.

The PBC will continue to follow the guiding rule of robust macro policy and flexible micro policy, coordinate the missions of preserving stable economic growth, driving reform, adjusting the economic structure, improving people's livelihood and preventing risks, uphold a robust monetary policy, stick to the stance of keeping money aggregates at a stable level and optimizing the structure, conduct fine-tuned and proactive adjustments with good timing and proper intensity against changes in the basic conditions of the economy, make macro control more flexible, targeted and effective, create a neutral and opportune monetary and financial environment for economic restructuring and upgrade and foster scientific and sustainable economic growth. Meanwhile, reform will be integrated into macro control, monetary policy control will be combined with deepening of the reform closely, and the market will fully play a decisive role in resource allocation.

First, quantitative and price tools will be combined to perfect the macro-prudential policy framework, and realize reasonable growth of monetary & credit and all-system financing aggregates. Based on the impact of changes in the economic and financial situation and financial innovations on liquidity of the banking system, a wide range of monetary policy tools such as open market operations will be utilized flexibly to optimize the central bank's collateral management framework, fine-tune liquidity level and prop up stability of the money market.

Second, it is important to activate existing money supply, optimize the use of incremental money, and support economic restructuring and upgrade. Targeted deposit reserve reductions will be put into practice and the support of credit policy given to re-lending and rediscount policy will be brought into play to encourage financial institutions to optimize their credit structure. Continued efforts will be made to assure moderate growth of monetary & credit aggregates, perfect the multi-level capital market, increase financial supply, step up efforts on reform and restructuring, address both the symptoms and root causes, and press down social financing costs.

Third, the form of interest rate liberalization will be pushed forward. The self-regulatory pricing mechanism for market interest rates will be optimized and financial institutions will sharpen their discretionary pricing ability. Continued efforts will be made to foster Shibor and LPR and to build a nearly flawless market interest rate system. The central bank interest rate regulation framework will be improved and a price regulation and conduction mechanism will be strengthened.

Fourth, the financial market system will be brought to perfection to allow the financial market to buoy up economic growth, drive economic restructuring and upgrade, deepen the reform and open-up and prevent financial risk. Market infrastructure will be beefed up, to provide an efficient investment and financing market and set the stage for economic restructuring and upgrade. Direct financing will be encouraged and the multi-level capital market will be promoted.

Fifth, precautions will be taken against systematic financial risk to protect stability of the financial system. Macro-prudential regulation will be strengthened. Robust operations will be recommended to financial institutions and financial institutions will be urged to tighten liquidity management, internal control and risk management. Detection and prevention of hidden risks in interbank operations and wealth management business must be reinforced. Monitoring of local government indebtedness and solvency must be strengthened to prevent debt risk. The deposit insurance system must be put in place as early as possible and the exit mechanism of financial institutions must be improved. An organic combination of measures should be employed to preserve financial stability and defend the bottom-line of non-occurrence of systematic or regional financial risk.

II. Exchange Rate and Balance of Payments Policy[1]

(i) Highlights of Exchange Rate and Balance of Payments Policy in 2014

Table 4 – 2   **Highlights of Exchange Rate and BOP Policy in 2014**

Date	Policy
Mar. 15	The PBC announced the floating band of the RMB trading price against the US dollar on the interbank spot foreign exchange market is enlarged from 1 percent to 2 percent, effective from 17 March 2014. On a given trading day, the spread between RMB/USD cash buying and selling rates offered by designated exchange banks to their clients shall be no more than 3 percent, raised from 2 percent previously, above the published central parity rate of the US dollar on that day
Mar. 18	Authorized by the PBC, China Foreign Exchange Trade System (CFETS) announced the launch of direct trading between the RMB and the New Zealand dollar (NZD) on the interbank foreign exchange market
Apr. 25	The PBC and the Reserve Bank of New Zealand renewed the bilateral local currency swap agreement. The size of the renewed swap facility is RMB 25 billion, or NZD 5 billion. The agreement will be valid for three years and can be extended upon mutual consent
May 30	The PBC used 400 million won (or about RMB 2.4 million) under the China-ROK bilateral currency swap arrangement to support trade financing for the corporate sector. This was the first time that the PBC used foreign currency fund under the bilateral currency swap agreements
Jun. 18	Authorized by the PBC, CFETS announced the launch of direct trading between the RMB and the Pound Sterling (GBP) on the interbank foreign exchange market. This marked an important step to boost bilateral trade and investment between China and the United Kingdom, facilitate the use of RMB and Pound Sterling in bilateral trade and investment settlement, and lower currency conversion cost for economic entities
Jul. 1	To further improve the market-based RMB exchange rate regime, the PBC issued the *Notice on Management of Trading Prices of the Interbank Foreign Exchange Market and the Margin of Bank Quotations* (PBC [2014] No. 188) to lift all controlsover the spread of bank quotations of RMB/foreign currency buying and selling prices to clients

---

[1] Written by Yu Weiguo.

Continued

Date	Policy
Jul. 18	The PBC and the Central Bank of Argentina renewed the bilateral local currency swap agreement. The size of the swap facility is RMB 70 billion/90 billion Argentina pesos. The agreement is valid for three years and can be extended upon mutual consent
Jul. 21	The PBC and the Swiss National Bank signed a bilateral local currency swap agreement. The size of the swap facility is RMB 150 billion/21 billion Swiss francs. The agreement is valid for three years and can be extended upon mutual consent
Aug. 21	The PBC and the Bank of Mongolia renewed a bilateral local currency swap agreement. The size of the renewed swap facility is RMB 15 billion/4.5 trillion Mongolian tugriks. The agreement is valid for three years and can be extended upon mutual consent
Sep. 16	The PBC and the Central Bank of Sri Lanka signed a bilateral local currency swap agreement. The size of the swap facility is RMB 10 billion/LKR 225 billion. The agreement is valid for three years and can be extended upon mutual consent
Sep. 29	Authorized by the PBC, CFETS announced the launch of direct trading between the RMB and the euro on the interbank foreign exchange market. This marked an important step to boost bilateral trade and investment between China and the euro zone member states, facilitate the use of the RMB and the euro in bilateral trade and investment settlement, and lower currency conversion costs for economic entities
Oct. 11	The PBC and the Bank of Korea renewed their bilateral local currency swap agreement. The size of the renewed swap facility is RMB 360 billion/64 trillion won. The agreement is valid for three years and can be extended upon mutual consent
Oct. 13	The PBC and the Central Bank of the Russian Federation signed a bilateral local currency swap agreement. The size of the swap facility is RMB 150 billion /815 billion rubles. The agreement is valid for three years and can be extended upon mutual consent
Oct. 27	Authorized by the PBC, CFETS announced the launch of direct trading between the RMB and the Singapore Dollar (SGD) on the interbank foreign exchange market, effective as of October 28. This marked an important step to boost bilateral trade and investment between China and Singapore, facilitate the use of RMB and SGD in bilateral trade and investment settlement, and lower currency conversion cost for economic entities
Nov. 2	The PBC issued the *Notice on Centralized Operations of Cross-border RMB Funds by Multinational Corporate Groups* (PBC [2014] No. 324)
Nov. 3	The PBC and the Qatar Central Bank signed a bilateral local currency swap agreement. The size of the swap facility is RMB 35 billion/20.8 billion Qatari riyals. On the same day, the two parties signed an MOU on establishing RMB clearing arrangements in Doha

Continued

Date	Policy
Nov. 8	The PBC and the Bank of Canada signed a bilateral local currency swap agreement. The size of the swap facility is RMB 200 billion/C $ 30 billion. The agreement is valid for three years and can be extended upon mutual consent. On the same day, the two parties signed an MOU on establishing RMB clearing arrangements in Canada
Nov. 22	The PBC and the Hong Kong Monetary Authority renewed the bilateral local currency swap agreement. The size of the renewed swap facility is RMB 400 billion/HK$505 billion. The agreement is valid for three years and can be extended upon mutual consent
Dec. 14	The PBC and the National Bank of Kazakhstan renewed the bilateral local currency swap agreement. The size of the renewed swap facility is RMB 7 billion/200 billion KZT. The agreement is valid for three years and can be extended upon mutual consent
Dec. 22	The PBC and the Bank of Thailand renewed the bilateral local currency swap agreement. The size of the renewedswap facility is RMB 70 billion/370 billion Thai baht. The agreement is valid for three years and can be extended upon mutual consent. On the same day, the two parties signed an MOU on establishing RMB clearing arrangements in Thailand
Dec. 23	The PBC and the State Bank of Pakistan renewed the local currency swap agreement. The size of the renewed swap facility is RMB 10 billion/165 billion Pakistan rupees. The agreement is valid for three years and can be extended upon mutual consent

Source: State Administration of Foreign Exchange.

(ii) Review of Exchange Rate and BOP Policy Operations in 2014

On March 15, 2014, the PBC announced the floating band of the RMB trading price against the US dollar on the interbank spot foreign exchange market is enlarged from 1 percent to 2 percent. On July 2, the PBC lifted the control over the spread between RMB/USD quoted buying and selling prices offered by banks to their clients. Thereby, the central bank has almost withdrawn from regular interventions in foreign exchange and built a regulated floating exchange rate regime, to allow market demand and supply to exert more influence on the formation of exchange rates, enhance the resilience of RMB exchange rates and divide exchange rate expectations.

In order to boost bilateral trade and investment, the PBC took more actions to drive direct trading of the RMB. The year of 2014 witnessed the initiation of direct trading between the RMB and NZD, GBP, EUR and SGD on the interbank foreign exchange market, as well as the launch of regional interbank market trading of the RMB against KZT. Active direct trading of the RMB on the interbank foreign exchange market increased liquidity of the currency immensely and lowered currency conversion cost for economic entities.

In 2014, the overseas monetary authorities conducted trade worth RMB 1130. 55 billion under bilateral local currency swap agreements concluded by the PBC with them and employed RMB 38. 007 billion in total, with the balance at RMB 15. 801 billion. This gave a fresh impetus to bilateral trade and investment.

Five required administrative approvals were abolished and eighty-eight regulations on foreign exchange were annulled in 2014. The reform of trade and foreign exchange administration was deepened to further facilitate frontier trade and personal trade. Administrative license requirement for frontier trade accounts was cancelled and documentation requirement for personal trade was simplified to boost diversified development of foreign trade. Cross-border receipts and payments by 22 pilot enterprises across the country exceeded one billion US dollar. Forceful support was given to innovative services, including e-Commerce.

Permission for centralization of domestic and overseas foreign exchange funds was given to 200-odd state-owned, private-owned and foreign-invested multinational corporations to effect concrete reduction in the financial costs of large companies and multinational corporations.

In line with the negative list policy, voluntary settlement of foreign exchange capital is being tried out in 17 state-level economic and financial reform pilot zones, including the Shanghai FTZ and Tianjin Binhai New District. Business entities may exercise their discretion and have options in the settlement of foreign exchange capital.

Foreign exchange administration over round-trip investment is much simplified. Purchasing or paying foreign exchange used to open or run overseas SPV is permitted and the restraint on overseas lending by SPV is lifted. Two-way open-up of the capital market is broadened further. The RMB quota management of QFII is simplified and some regions are encouraged to try out QDLP.

All required prior approvals of cross-border guarantee are abolished. A consistent policy for domestic loan under overseas guarantee is enforced on Chinese and foreign enterprises. Clearance to convert foreign debts into lendings is no longer necessary. A self-regulatory system governing the percentage of foreign debts in foreign-invested enterprises is being tried out in some regions, to lower financing costs.

In 2014, the central parity rate of the RMB against the US dollar peaked at 6. 0930 yuan per dollar and hit a trough at 6. 1710 yuan per dollar. It appreciated on 107 out of 245 trading days and depreciated on the remaining 138 days, with the largest intraday appreciation at 0. 37 percent (or 225 points) and the sharpest one-day depreciation at 0. 18 percent (or 111 points).

The RMB appreciated against the euro, the Japanese yen and other major international currencies. At the end of 2014, the central parity rate of the RMB against the euro and the

Japanese yen stood at 7. 4556 yuan per euro and 5. 1371 yuan per 100 yen, representing an appreciation of 12. 92 percent and 12. 46 percent, respectively, from a year ago. The RMB appreciated 34. 32 percent against the euro and 42. 22 percent against the Japanese yen on a cumulative basis by the end of 2014 since the reform of the RMB exchange-rate regime in 2005.

In 2014, China posted a current account surplus worth 1, 314. 8 billion yuan and a capital and financial account deficit worth RMB 593. 9 billion and added RMB 720. 9 billion to its international reserve assets. The current account surplus in 2014 was equivalent to USD213. 8 billion, comprised of a cargo trade surplus of USD471. 9 billion, a service trade deficit of USD198. 1 billion, an income deficit of USD29. 8 billion and a current transfer deficit of USD30. 2 billion. The capital and financial account deficit was equivalent to USD96 billion, including net inflow of direct investments to the tune of USD198. 5 billion. International reserve assets added USD117. 8 billion, resulting from an increase of USD118. 8 billion in foreign exchange reserve assets and a reduction of USD1. 1 billion in the positions with special drawing right and held in funds.

The PBC has almost withdrawn from regular interventions in foreign exchange. RMB exchange rates have stabilized at a reasonable and balanced level with increased floating resilience in both ways. By the end of 2014, the central parity rate of the RMB against the US dollar came in at 6. 1190 yuan per dollar, representing the depreciation by 0. 36 percent from the end of last year.

(iii) Policy Outlook

Numerous uncertainties and variables are present at home and abroad. The BOP of China might take on volatility both ways, in the context of a sustained sizable surplus arising from trade and direct investments. Interest rate raise by the Federal Reserve, if it happens, may trigger violent fluctuations of capital flow worldwide and then de-dollarization of debts may weigh heavily on business entities in China. The prospect for the European and Japanese economy is hard to tell. Emerging economies are under significant stress from downside potential. The external environment is still very complicated. Moreover, emergencies such as geopolitical conflicts also compound the uncertainty over cross-border capital flow in China.

Given the new tasks and requirements coming with comprehensively deepening reform and the extreme complexity of domestic and international situations, the foreign exchange administration will further put into practice the decisions and policies made on the 18th CPC National Congress and the Third Plenum of the 18th CPC Central Committee, stick to the strategic goal of BOP breakeven, drive trade and investment facilitation forcefully and sharpen its ability to prevent foreign exchange risk and serve the real economy. First, the authority will press ahead with the reform and innovation of foreign exchange administration, streamline administration and delegate powers, shift the role of the government, drive ongoing and afterwards management, develop the foreign exchange market and manage and use foreign exchange reserves properly. Second, the authority will solidify the base of statistics and monitoring, perfect the statistical system consistently, improve statistical methods, optimize data gathering and comprehensive utilization, quicken the development and integration of the monitoring and analytical system and heighten monitoring and analytical capacity and quality. Third, the authority will defend the bottom line of non-occurrence of systematic or regional financial risk, consummate the cross-border capital flow monitoring, alarm and risk response mechanism explore a cross-border capital flow management system under the macro-prudential framework and reinforce the pertinence and effectiveness of foreign exchange inspection.

CHAPTER 5

Highlights of Financial Market Development Policy

I. Banking Market Development Policy[①]

(i) Overview of Banking Market Development Policy

In 2014, the global economy presented a mild recovery. The Chinese economy continued growing at a steady pace. The Chinese government held on to a proactive fiscal policy and a robust monetary policy. Commercial banks experienced steadily expanding assets and liabilities, and consistently improving profit margin, provision coverage and capital adequacy. Economic slowdown, interest rate liberalization and the rise of Internet finance, among other factors, dragged down the banking sector to some extent, but on the whole, the banking sector managed to stay in good shape.

According to CBRC statistics, as of the end of December, 2014, total assets of banking institutions in China denominated in RMB and foreign currencies and held at home and abroad combined were reported at 172. 3 trillion yuan; total liabilities amounted to 160. 0 trillion yuan; net profit came in at 1. 56 trillion yuan; the capital adequacy ratio and NPL ratio stood at 13. 18 percent and 1. 25 percent.

Table 5 – 1   **Performance of Banking Institutions in 2014**   Unit: 100 million yuan, %

Key Indicator	2010	2011	2012	2013	2014
Total assets	942, 600	1, 115, 000	1, 336, 000	151. 3	1, 723, 000
Total liabilities	884, 300	1, 043, 000	1, 250, 000	141. 1	1, 600, 000
Net profit	7, 637	10, 412	12, 386	14, 180	15, 548
ROA	1. 10	1. 30	1. 28	1. 27	1. 23
ROE	19. 20	20. 40	19. 85	19. 17	17. 59

---

①   Written by Wang Min.

Continued

Key Indicator	2010	2011	2012	2013	2014
Net interest margin	2.50	2.70	2.75	2.68	2.70
Proportion of non-interest income	17.50	19.30	19.83	21.15	21.47
Cost-to-income ratio	35.30	33.40	33.10	32.90	31.62
Core tier-1 capital	42,985	53,367	64,340	75,793	90,739
Capital adequacy ratio	12.20	12.70	13.25	12.19	13.18
Core tier-1 capital adequacy ratio	10.10	10.20	10.62	9.95	10.56
Liquidity ratio	42.20	43.20	45.83	44.03	46.44
Loan-deposit ratio	64.50	64.90	65.31	66.08	65.09
RMB excess reserve ratio	3.20	3.10	3.51	2.54	2.65
Outstanding NPLs	4,336	4,279	4,929	5,921	8,426
NPL ratio	1.10	1.00	0.95	1.00	1.25
Loan loss provision	9,438	11,898	14,564	16,740	19,552
Provision coverage ratio	217.70	278.10	295.51	282.70	232.06

Source: CBRC.

Table 5 – 2   **Major Policies Having Impact on Development of the Banking Sector in 2014**

Policy and Content	Issued by
Regulations on Foreign-funded Banks	State Council
Guiding Opinions on Taking Various Measures Simultaneously to Focus on Alleviating the Problem of High Cost of Corporate Financing	State Council
Notice on Regulating Interbank Business of Financial Institutions	PBC
Notice on Matters Concerning Strengthening the Administration of Deposit Deviation Degree of Commercial Banks	PBC
Notice on Launching the Pilot Standing Lending Facility (SLF) Program	PBC
Opinions of General Office of the PBC on Doing Well in Credit Policy Related Jobs in 2014	PBC
Notice on Doing Better in Housing Financial Service	PBC
Deposit Insurance Regulations (Draft for Comments)	PBC
Notice on Matters Concerning Deposit Reserve Policy and Interest Rate Management Policy after Adjustment of Deposit Base	PBC
Guiding Opinions on Fostering Healthy Development of Rural Banks	CBRC
Guiding Opinions on Commercial Banks Offering Preferred Shares to Replenish Tier 1 Capital	CBRC
Measures for the Administration of Leverage Ratio of Commercial Banks	CBRC
Measures for the Liquidity Risk Management of Commercial Banks (for Trial Implementation)	CBRC
Notice on Adjusting the Base for Calculating Loan-to-Deposit Ratio of Commercial Banks	CBRC

Source: PBC, CBRC.

(ii) Review of Banking Market Development Policy

1. Bank Asset Expansion Continued, but Bank Lending Growth Decelerated

As of the end of 2014, total assets of commercial banks added 21 trillion yuan to count 172.3 trillion yuan, representing a slightly accelerating year-on-year growth of 13.87 percent. But bank lending growth decelerated further. As of the end of December, outstanding loans of all commercial banks totaled 67.47 trillion yuan, an increase of 8.24 trillion yuan, or 13.9 percent, year on year, underperforming the 14.62 percent growth registered in 2013.

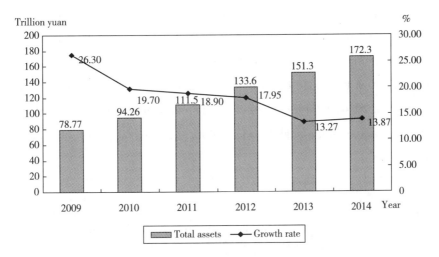

Source: CBRC.

Page 5 – 1   Total Assets and Growth Rate of Commercial Banks (2009 – 2014)

In response to downside pressure weighing against the Chinese economy, the PBC applied targeted deposit reserve reductions on two occasions in 2014. In April, the PBC cut the RMB deposit required reserve ratio of county-level rural commercial banks by 2 percentage points, and that of county-level rural cooperative banks by 0.5 percentage point. In June, the PBC cut the RMB deposit required reserve ratio by 0.5 percentage point for commercial banks that comply with the prudence requirement and have lendings to the agricultural sector, rural areas and farmers, and to small and micro enterprises accounting for a certain percentage of total lendings. In addition, the RMB deposit required reserve ratio applicable to finance companies, financial lease companies and auto finance companies was lowered by 0.5 percentage point as well. The targeted deposit reserve reduction policy is designed to encourage commercial banks to beef up their support selectively to the agricultural sector, rural areas and farmers, and to small and micro enterprises, and expand credit support to the real economy. Given the enormous monetary & credit supply and high-speed growth, it is inadvisable to try to uproot structural problems with aggressive monetary & credit expansion.

In the meantime, the PBC kept liquidity of the banking system at a moderate and appropriate level by rolling out the trial of SLF and launching MLF. In January, branch offices of the PBC in 10 provinces and cities, including Beijing, Jiangsu and Shandong, extended SLF support to qualified small-/medium-sized financial institutions. The roll-out of SLF trial can help improve the liquidity of small-/medium-sized banks, preserve stability of the financial market and polish the liquidity management skills of small-/medium-sized banks. In September and October, the PBC injected base money to the tune of 500 billion yuan and 269. 5 billion yuan, respectively, into the banking system through MLF. The launch of MLF can help keep market liquidity at a moderate and appropriate level and motivate commercial banks to lower lending rates and social financing cost, in support of growth of the real economy.

2. Bank Liabilities Expanded Consistently and the Pressure of Deposit Outflows Intensified

As of the end of 2014, total liabilities of commercial banks added 19. 82 trillion yuan to hit 160 trillion yuan, representing a slightly accelerating year-on-year growth of 13. 35 percent.

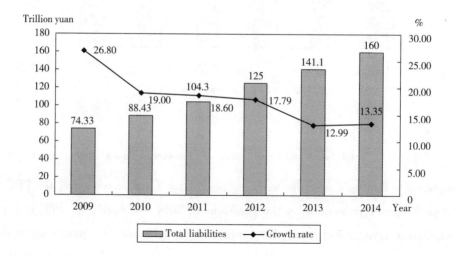

Source: CBRC.

Page 5 – 2   Total Liabilities and Growth Rate of Commercial Banks (2009 – 2014)

What deserves our attention is that commercial banks are under increasing stress from an outflow of deposits. The gap between loan and deposit growth rates has widened further. Bank deposit growth decelerated noticeably, owing to interest rate liberalization, the rise of Internet finance, revival of the stock market, shrinkage in improper interbank dealings and reduced derivative deposits as a result of contained behaviour of Deposit Inflation. According to CBRC statistics, in 2014, commercial banks recorded a balance of deposits of all kinds at 98. 34 trillion yuan, representing an 8. 61 trillion yuan, or 9. 6 percent, increase year on year. This underperformed the 10. 52 trillion yuan, or 13. 29 percent, increase registered in 2013, by 1. 91

trillion yuan, or 3. 69 percentage points. In the meantime, the growth of deposits fell behind that of loans and the deposit-loan growth rate gap widened further in the second half. The deposit growth rate stood at 14. 3 percent at the end of June, but slid to 9. 6 percent by the end of December in 2014. Over the same time frames, a loan growth rate of 14. 2 percent and 13. 1 percent was registered, respectively, indicating widening gap.

Two policies were introduced during the year to boost healthy growth of deposits. First, the CBRC issued *Notice on Adjusting the Base for Calculating Loan-to-Deposit Ratio of Commercial Banks*. According to the Notice, six types of agriculture-related loans, including relending in support of the agriculture, relending in support of small businesses and bank debentures designated for the agriculture, rural areas and farmers are no longer parts of the numerator (loans) in the calculation formula of loan-to-deposit ratio, while high-value negotiable certificate of deposits issued by banks to corporate or individual clients and net dues from overseas parent banks with more than one-year maturity taken in by foreign corporate banks are included in the denominator (deposits). The adjusted base for calculating loan-to-deposit ratio helps defuse the pressure of meeting the required loan-to-deposit ratio on banks and allows them to devote more credit resources to the real economy, particularly to the agriculture, rural areas, farmers and small and micro enterprises. The control over loan-to-deposit ratio did its part to control liquidity risk, check overly quick credit expansion and preserve stability of the banking system, but also gave rise to distorted behaviour of commercial banks and bred a series of money brokers buying and selling deposits, thus, undermining liquidity management and financial stability. Hence, future development necessitates revisions to the *Law on Commercial Banks* without delay. The loan-to-deposit ratio should be freed from restriction and replaced by Liquidity Coverage Ratio (LCR) and Net Stable Funding Ratio (NSFR), to better adapt to the ongoing diversification of assets and liabilities of the banking sector.

Second, the CBRC, the MOF and the PBC jointly released the *Notice on Matters Concerning Strengthening the Administration of Deposit Deviation Degree of Commercial Banks*. The Notice demands commercial banks to tighten deposit stability management, stop using any performance indicator based on deposit size at a given point of time, and refrain from taking in or fraudulently inflating deposits by means of high interest rates, illegal kickbacks or conversion of loans into deposits. Any commercial bank having a month-end deposit deviation degree beyond 3 percent shall be subject to corrective or punitive measures, including access control, downgrading, operation restrictions and higher NSFR. The deviation degree approach can put a lid on the impulse of commercial banks to inflate deposits at certain points of time, temper deposit volatility of commercial banks, stabilize deposit cost and curb quarter-end violent interest rate fluctuations of the money market. Nevertheless, in the context of loan-to-deposit ratio control, a period of adaptation and transition is needed before a fundamental change to the transient deposit expansion model of commercial banks takes place.

3. Bank Profit Achieved Consistent Growth, but Profitability Weakened

In 2014, the banking sector of China was faced with multi-faceted challenges, increasing operational pressure and deceleration of profit growth when compared with prior years. According to CBRC statistics, in 2014, commercial banks in China yielded net profit of 1.55 trillion yuan on a cumulative basis, an increase of 136.9 billion yuan, or 9.7 percent, year on year. This underperformed the growth rate registered in 2013 by 4.8 percentage points. ROA and ROE averaged 1.23 percent and 17.59 percent, down 0.04 percentage point and 1.58 percentage points year on year, respectively.

A combination of factors contributed to the change in net profit of commercial banks. First, as the reform of interest rate liberalization goes further, the cost of debt of the banking sector has climbed up. In November, the PBC raised the upper limit to the floating band of deposit rates from 1.1 to 1.2 times the benchmark level. The five leading state-owned banks in China applied a conditional mark-up to deposit rates, while almost all joint-stock banks raised deposit rates to the ceiling. Thus, banks have to take in deposits at a higher cost now. Second, intermediary business growth slowed down. The income from financial consulting business that experienced rapid growth in previous years declined in 2014, owing to the policy to alleviate the burden on business entities. As a result, the income from intermediary business of commercial banks registered a much slower growth than in 2013. According to CBRC statistics, commercial banks earned non-interest income to the tune of 902.2 billion yuan, an increase of 145.5 billion yuan, or 19.2 percent, year on year. The growth speed decelerated by 1.5 percentage points. Third, the increase in provisions is the most important reason for slower profit growth. In 2014, commercial banks were exposed to increasing credit risk and a substantial increase in provisions offset significant before-provision profit of commercial banks, due to a combination of factors, like economic slowdown and continued growth of NPLs to small and micro enterprises and some sectors with excess capacity. As of the end of 2014, commercial banks reported outstanding NPLs at 842.6 billion yuan, adding 250.6 billion yuan to that at the end of last year; and the NPL ratio gained 0.25 percentage point from a year ago to reach 1.25 percent.

4. Interbank Business Grew within the Bounds of the New Rules

Interbank business of commercial banks has thrived in recent years. Some banks try to circumvent the regulator's control over loan-to-deposit ratio, capital, and destination of credit injection through interbank operations and provide financing to their corporate clients. As lucrative for banks as it is, this kind of business entails hidden financial risk and gives rise to a streak of problems, such as higher financing cost, improper development, inadequate information disclosure, evasion of financial regulation and macro control. In May, 2014, the PBC, CBRC, CSRC, CIRC and SAFE jointly released the *Notice on Regulating the Interbank Business of Financial Institutions*, in a bid to instruct commercial banks to develop interbank business properly and preserve robust performance of the banking system. Under the influence of the new policy, the consistent uptrend of interbank assets and liabilities of commercial banks slackened off, the business model of dealing in non-standard assets by means of interbank operations and taking advantage of regulatory arbitrage was stifled effectively and interbank business was put on the right track in 2014.

5. The Offering of Preferred Shares and the Application of Advanced Capital Management Approach Replenished Capital Adequacy of the Banking Sector

In 2014, the offering of preferred shares and the application of advanced capital management approach, among other actions, beefed up capital adequacy of the banking sector. As of the end of 2014, the weighted average tier-1 capital adequacy ratio of commercial banks was reported at 10. 76 percent, up 0. 81 percentage point from the end of last year, and the weighted average capital adequacy ratio was 13. 18 percent, up 0. 99 percentage points from the end of last year.

In March, the CSRC and CBRC released *Measures for the Administration of the Pilot Program of Preferred Shares and Guiding Opinions on Commercial Banks Offering Preferred Shares to Replenish Tier 1 Capital*, respectively. According to the new rules, funds raised by offering preferred shares can be included in core capital and used to replenish tier-1 capital. The offering of preferred shares widens the financing channels of commercial banks and may help alleviate the capital strain on banks, improve capital quality and mitigate the procyclicality of banking capital. As of the end of December, 2014, Agricultural Bank of China and Bank of China were the first two banks to complete the offering of domestic preferred shares worth 40 billion yuan and overseas preferred shares worth USD7 billion, respectively. Then, more than 10 banks, including Ping An Bank, China Everbright Bank, China Minsheng Bank and Bank of Ningbo, unveiled their preferred share offering plans in succession.

In April, the CBRC approved the application of advanced capital management approach by six banks, namely, Industrial and Commercial Bank of China, Agricultural Bank of China, Bank of China, China Construction Bank, Bank of Communications and China Merchants Bank. The advanced approach, when compared with the weighting approach currently in use, can effectively lessen risk weighted assets, especially the risk weight of mortgage loans, and thereby heighten banks' capital adequacy ratios regardless of the calculation base. As for the result, all of the aforesaid six banks saw their capital adequacy ratios enhanced more or less with other variables kept unchanged. More importantly, the application of the advanced approach has far-reaching influence on the ongoing change of commercial banks, because it propels the risk management of banks towards a quantitative and qualitative combined model, helps banks optimize their risk management framework and internal capital adequacy evaluation procedures and urges banks to progressively form an endogenous capital accumulation model supplemented by extraneous sources of capital.

6. The New Reform and Open-up Policy for the Banking Sector was Unveiled to Effectively Boost Private-invested and Foreign-invested Banks

At the end of September, the first five projected private-invested banks, namely, Webank, KinCheng Bank of Tianjin, Minshang Bank of Wenzhou, Zhejiang Internet Commerce Bank and Shanghai HuaRui Bank, all got approval from the CBRC. The successful launch of the first pilot program of private-invested banks not only proves that private capital should be able to compete in the market economy on equal footing, but also motivates private-invested banks to provide better financial services by means of differentiation, unleashes the inner energy of finance and makes the allocation of financial resources more efficient.

In December, the State Council issued the *Decision of the State Council to Revise Regulations of the PRC on Foreign-funded Banks*. The revised regulations have loosened the admittance and RMB business control over foreign-funded banks. Where a wholly foreign-funded bank or Sino-foreign joint venture bank decides to open a branch in the PRC, the head office is no longer required to appropriate a minimum of 100 million yuan for free as working capital. The wholly foreign-funded bank or Sino-foreign joint venture bank may allocate working capital among its branches effectively based on actual needs. The presence of a representative office in the PRC is no longer a prerequisite for the start-up of a foreign bank's branch. Meanwhile, in the case of application for RMB business, a foreign-funded bank is required to have business outlet (s) operating in the PRC for no less than one year, instead of three years required previously. And the requirement for making profit for two consecutive years prior to the application is struck off. The regulations on foreign-funded banks are revised to get rid of double standards, quicken the pace of marketization and globalization of the banking sector, enable foreign-funded banks to play their role better, foster the fusion between the domestic and international finance sector in terms of capital, technologies, products and management and bring service and management of China's banking sector to the next level.

(iii) Policy Outlook

Looking ahead to 2015, commercial banks will still face moderation of economic growth, progress in interest rate liberalization, and the overwhelming impact from Internet finance. Nevertheless, commercial banks will enjoy a better business environment, thanks to the stable growth policy, an active fiscal policy, a neutral to expansionary monetary policy and readjustment to the bank regulatory policy.

1. An Active Fiscal Policy and a Neutral to Expansionary Monetary Policy Administer to Bank Asset Growth

The top priority on the economy-related agenda of China in 2015 is still to keep the economy growing at a steady pace. An active fiscal policy will be revved up. The fiscal deficit will expand to 1620 billion yuan, adding 270 billion yuan to that of 2014. Infrastructure investment will continue with undiminished strength. The One Belt and One Road strategy will bring along a boom in outbound direct investment. A package of key strategies, like coordinated development of Beijing, Tianjin and Hebei and the Yangtze River economic belt, will unfold. All of these factors will stimulate loan demand. In the meantime, the housing market holds the potential to bottom out in the first half of 2015 and the demand for mortgage loans and development loans will pick up, owing to the combined effect of some stimuli, like credit policy, tax policy, cancellation of home purchase restrictions and interest rate cuts. Moreover, in the context of a neutral to expansionary monetary policy, the M_2 growth rate target is set at 12 percent and loan additions in the year are estimated at 11 trillion yuan approximately, driving steady growth of commercial banks' assets.

2. The Growth of Liabilities will Slow Down with Pros Offset by Cons

The market-wide trend of outflow and slower growth of deposits happening to commercial banks will continue unabated in 2015, given the influence of slowdown of money creation, financial disintermediation and the rise of Internet finance. Still, deposits are propped up by three policies. First, the control over loan-to-deposit ratio might be loosened further, which will create some derivative deposits for banks from credit injection. Second, there is a good chance of a moderate cut in RRR, which may help banks increase deposits. After the unilateral expectation of RMB appreciation came to the end, the growth of funds outstanding for foreign exchange has decelerated. The RRR might be lowered further in 2015 and this is conducive to the growth of bank deposits. Third, in the context of liquidity easing, money market funds like Yu'. e Bao are expected to deliver a lower ROR. This can defuse the pressure of continued deposit outflow on banks.

Interbank liabilities, however, are expected to keep soaring in 2015. The new rules on interbank business introduced by the PBC in 2014 include some interbank deposits in total deposits and exempt interbank deposits from the reserve requirement. This will motivate commercial banks to develop interbank liability business. In the long run, those deposits flowing out of banks will return to the banking system in the form of interbank liabilities after entering the capital market, along with roll-out of asset backed securitization, deepening of the capital market and the resulting growth of direct financing and aggravation of financial disintermediation. It is a long-term trend that interbank liabilities will carry ever more weight in total liabilities of commercial banks. Interbank liabilities of commercial banks are expected to keep soaring in 2015.

3. Profit Growth of Commercial Banks will Level off and Net Interest Margin will Still be a Strain

Commercial banks are expected to witness slower growth of operating revenue and net profit in 2015 when compared with 2014, owing to flat growth of assets, deepening interest rate liberalization, increasing asset impairment or loss provisions and intensifying interbank and cross-industry competition. In particular, net interest margin will come as a structural strain on banks in 2015. First, the repricing process triggered by asymmetrical interest rate cuts at the end of 2014 will have a vital bearing on the spread between existing deposits and loans of banks in 2015. In November, 2014, the PBC applied asymmetrical benchmark deposit and lending rate cuts to financial institutions. The one-year benchmark lending rate was lowered by 0.4 percentage point to 5.6 percent, and the one-year benchmark deposit rate was lowered by 0.25 percentage point to 2.75 percent. Asymmetrical interest rate cuts will pose negative impact on net interest margin of banks. Second, as interest rate liberalization goes further, low-cost deposits are growing slowly and banks are under the stress of consistently climbing cost of debt. Third, it is possible that the floating band of deposit rates will be relaxed further and benchmark deposit and lending rates will be lowered further in 2015. This is adverse to net interest margin of commercial banks. Fourth, the business model and development speed of private-invested banks cast uncertainty over the degree to which net interest margin of banks will narrow in 2015. Immoderate competition aiming at a bigger market share will undermine net interest margin of the banking sector. To sum up, net interest margin of the banking sector is expected to narrow by a wider range in 2015 than in 2014, possibly by 15～30 base points.

4. The Introduction of Deposit Insurance will Benefit Sustainable Growth of the Banking Sector

In 2014, the State Council considered and approved the *Implementation Plan for Deposit Insurance scheme and Deposit Insurance Regulations (Draft for Comments)* and canvassed public comments widely. The deposit insurance scheme is expected to come into force in 2015. According to the Draft, the deposit insurance scheme will cover commercial banks, rural cooperative banks, rural credit cooperatives, and other deposit-taking banking institutions based in the PRC, and rates will be differentiated for different types of institutions. A coverage ceiling of 500, 000 yuan per depositor has been proposed. The deposit insurance scheme can protect the legitimate rights and interests of depositors, guard against and mitigate financial risk in a timely manner, reduce implicit government guarantee, foster sound development of financial institutions, preserve financial stability, and facilitate healthy, steady and sustainable development of China's financial system.

II. Stock Market Development Policy[①]

(i) Highlights of Stock Market Development Policy in 2014

Table 5 – 3   Highlights of China's Stock Market Development Policy in 2014

Date	Title of Policy	Issued by
Jan. 7	*Notice on Matters Concerning Investment of Insurance Funds in Shares of GEM Listed Companies*	CIRC
Feb. 10	*Data Exchange Protocol for Securities Trading*, *Data Exchange Coding and Decoding Protocol for Securities Trading*, and *Private Equity Product Coding and Management Specifications for the Securities and Futures Sector*	CSRC
Mar. 21	*Administrative Measures for the Pilot Program of Preferred Shares*	CSRC
Mar. 24	*Opinions on Further Optimizing the Business Merger and Reorganization Market Environment*	State Council
Mar. 25	It was resolved on an executive meeting of the State Council to push forward the stock issuance registration system reform in a safe manner, build a multi-level equity market and encourage market-based M&A and reorganization.	State Council
Mar. 25	*Notice on Matters Concerning Private Equity Investment Fund Open Account and Settlement*	CSDC
Apr. 4	The CSRC unveiled information disclosure rules for issuance of preferred shares by listed companies, including *Application Documentation for Issuance of Preferred Shares*, *Plan and Report for Issuance of Preferred Shares*, and *Prospectus for Issuance of Preferred Shares*.	CSRC

① Written by Wang Xin.

Continued

Date	Title of Policy	Issued by
Apr. 10	The CSRC and SFC of Hong Kong jointly announced that Shanghai Stock Exchange, The Stock Exchange of Hong Kong, CSDC and Hong Kong Securities Clearing Company are permitted to pilot the Shanghai-Hong Kong Stock Connect Program.	CSRC, SFC of Hong Kong
Apr. 22	*Several Opinions on Financial Services for the Agriculture, Rural Areas and Farmers*	State Council
May 9	*Several Opinions on Further Promoting the Healthy Development of the Capital Market*	State Council
May 9	*Administrative Measures for the Pilot Program of Preferred Shares of Shanghai Stock Exchange*	Shanghai Stock Exchange
May 15	*Opinions on Driving Innovation and Development of Securities Brokers*	CSRC
Jun. 12	*Implementation Rules for the Pilot Program of Preferred Shares of Shenzhen Stock Exchange*	Shenzhen Stock Exchange
Jun. 13	*Rules on the Shanghai-Hong Kong Stock Connect Pilot Program*	CSRC
Jun. 20	*Guiding Opinions on the Trial Implementation of Employee Share Scheme by Listed Companies*	CSRC
Aug. 15	*Guiding Opinions on Taking Various Measures Simultaneously to Focus on Alleviating the Problem of High Cost of Corporate Financing*	State Council
Sep. 19	*Notice on Arrangement for Going Live of the Unified Account Platform*	CSDC
Sep. 26	*Shanghai Stock Exchange Measures for the Shanghai-Hong Kong Stock Connect Pilot Program*	Shanghai Stock Exchange
Oct. 17	*Notice on Matters Concerning Participation of Securities Brokers in the Shanghai-Hong Kong Stock Connect Pilot Program*	CSRC
Nov. 26	*Guiding Opinions on Innovating the Investment and Financing Mechanism in Key Sectors and Encouraging Private Investment*	State Council
Dec. 16	*Operational Guidelines for Public Offering of Securities Investment Funds No. 1—Guidelines for Commodity Futures Trading Open-Ended Funds*	CSRC

Source: collected by the research group.

(ii) Review of Stock Market Development Policy in 2014

1. The New Nine State Regulations Depict the Superstructure Design of the Capital Market

On May 9, 2014, the State Council released *Several Opinions on Further Promoting the Healthy Development of the Capital Market*, called the New Nine State Regulations widely. The Opinions unfold a panoramic blueprint for the capital market, encompassing the stock market, the bond market, and the futures market, and define the hierarchy, essential requirements of the equity market, and the policies and measures for the development of the bond market and the futures market. It proposes to build an equity market characterized by multiple channels, extensive coverage, strict supervision and high efficiency, develop the bond market in a regulated manner, expand the futures market, put forth effort to optimize the market system and structure, running mechanism, infrastructure and external environment and realize diversity of offering and trading modes, a great variety of investment and financing instruments, complete risk management functions and coordinated development of exchange trading and OTC trading, public offering and private placement. By the year of 2020, a well-structured, fully functional, disciplined and transparent, robust and efficient, open-ended and all-inclusive multi-level capital market system will shape up.

2. The Shanghai-Hong Kong Stock Connect Pilot Program was Kicked Start

On Apr. 10, 2014, the CSRC and SFC of Hong Kong jointly announced that Shanghai Stock Exchange, the Stock Exchange of Hong Kong, CSDC and Hong Kong Securities Clearing Company are permitted to pilot the Shanghai-Hong Kong Stock Connect Program. On Jun. 13, 2014, the CSRC unveiled *Rules on the Shanghai-Hong Kong Stock Connect Pilot Program*. There are 19 articles in the Rules, wherein the duties of Shanghai Stock Exchange, the Stock Exchange of Hong Kong, securities trading service providers, CSDC and Hong Kong Securities Clearing Company in the program are defined, essential requirements for domestic securities brokers in the conduct of Shanghai-Hong Kong Stock Connect business are set out, and the scope of the program, shareholding by foreign enterprises, clearing and delivery methods, currencies, and requirements for investor protection, supervision and management, and file preservation are made clear.[1] On Sep. 26, 2014, Shanghai Stock Exchange released *Shanghai Stock Exchange Measures for the Shanghai-Hong Kong Stock Connect Pilot Program*. The program, as a key component of open-up of China's capital market, may help strengthen the tie between the capital market of mainland and Hong Kong, propel two-way open-up of the capital market, build up China's capital market, confirm the position of Shanghai and Hong Kong as financial center and add fuel to globalization of the RMB.

3. IPO Restarted During this Year

Jan. 17, 2014 witnessed the listing of Neway Valve in Shanghai Stock Exchange, marking the first new stock since IPO was called off over one year ago. On Jan. 21, eight companies got listed in Shenzhen Stock Exchange, three on SME and five on GEM. This is the first group of new stocks listed in Shenzhen Stock Exchange since the reform of the issuance system was launched. After that, Shanghai Stock Exchange and Shenzhen Stock Exchange revised the

---

[1] Xinhuanet: CSRC unveiled *Rules on the Shanghai-Hong Kong Stock Connect Pilot Program*, http://news. xinhuanet. com/fortune/2014-06/13/c_1111139985. htm, visited on Feb. 1, 2015.

method of online subscription based on market capitalization of IPO. The Securities Association of China amended and released *Specifications for Underwriting of IPO Stocks*. On Jun. 9, 2014, the CSRC approved 10 companies' IPO applications, five in Shanghai and five in Shenzhen. The aforesaid companies and their underwriters are expected to fix an IPO date with Shanghai Stock Exchange and Shenzhen Stock Exchange and publish their prospectuses. This marks the long-awaited restart of IPO. Along with the progress in the reform of the new stock issuance mechanism, the restart of IPO this time has restored the financing function of the stock market and suggests that the IPO registration system reform is around the corner.

4. Listed Companies Started Trial Implementation of Employee Share Scheme

On Jun. 20, 2014, the CSRC unveiled *Guiding Opinions on the Trial Implementation of Employee Share Scheme by Listed Companies*. Listed companies may allow their employees to acquire and hold shares of the companies in a lawful way by implementing employee share scheme, according to the Guiding Opinions. Shareholders' equity will be attributed to employees as previously agreed upon. Under an employee share scheme, funds can come from employees' salaries or be raised by other lawful means, while the sources of shares can be repo by listed companies, direct purchase from the secondary market, subscription to privately offering shares and voluntary donation by shareholders. The Guiding Opinions have also specified the implementation procedure, management model, information disclosure and prevention and control of insider trading relating to employee share scheme. The trial implementation of employee share scheme among listed companies can help build and perfect a profit sharing mechanism between employees and employers, improve corporate governance and heighten group cohesion and company competitiveness, the CSRC spokesman said. [1]

5. The CSRC Unveiled the *Administrative Measures for the Pilot Program of Preferred Shares*

On Mar. 21, 2014, the CSRC released the *Administrative Measures for the Pilot Program of Preferred Shares*, which is comprised of 70 articles in nine sections, including General Provisions, Exercise of Preferred Shareholders' Rights, Issuance of Preferred Shares by Listed Companies, Private Offering of Preferred Shares by Non-listed Public Companies, Transfer, Registration and Settlement, Information Disclosure, Repo, M&A and Reorganization, Regulatory Measures and Legal Responsibilities and Supplementary Provisions. According to the *Administrative Measures*, listed companies may offer preferred shares, while non-listed public companies may place preferred shares privately. A listed company may apply for issuance of

---

[1]　CSRC official site: The CSRC drafted and promulgated *Guiding Opinions on the Trial Implementation of Employee Share Scheme by Listed Companies*, http://www.csrc.gov.cn/pub/newsite/zjhxwfb/xwdd/201406/t20140620_256427.html, visited on Feb. 4, 2015.

preferred shares once, but conduct offerings several times. One private offering of preferred shares is limited to a maximum of 200 qualified investors as specified in the *Administrative Measures*. The pilot program of preferred shares marks a revolutionary innovation in the capital market of China and involves a wide and complicated range of stakeholders, the CSRC spokesman said. The CSRC will draw upon the experience learned from the pilot program and fine-tune and perfect the preferred share system unremittingly.

6. An Expanded New Third Board Pilot Program was Introduced

On Jan. 24, 2014, National Equities Exchange and Quotations (NEEQ) held the first group listing ceremony in Beijing following countrywide expansion of the New Third Board. 285 companies were present at the ceremony and 266 of them got listed officially on the same day. This is the first group listing ceremony held by NEEQ since the State Council released *Decisions on Some Matters Concerning National Equities Exchange and Quotations*. The pilot program of NEEQ is rolled out countrywide, the service coverage and channels of the capital market are broadened and exchange listing is no longer the only way out, the CSRC spokesman said on the same day. Companies have the option to get listed in a stock exchange or NEEQ as necessary. This may defuse the pressure of offering and listing on the A-shares market and play down the expectation for expansion of the A-shares market. Generally speaking, the listing of a large number of companies in NEEQ is unlikely to trigger an outflow of money from the A-shares market. [1]

(iii) Policy Review and Outlook

The stock market reform in China took big strides in 2014. A lot of important reform measures and development policies were introduced, such as the New Nine State Regulations, the Shanghai-Hong Kong Stock Connect pilot program and the restart of IPO. All of these are crucial to the capital market reform oriented towards marketization, legalization and globalization. Many moves can claim to be milestones in the history of direct connection and open-up of China's securities market. In 2015, first priority will be given to carry out all guiding opinions and quicken the pace of globalization and institutionalization of the capital market. Meanwhile, efforts on institutional innovation, business innovation and product innovation of the capital market will be redoubled. By taking the lead in innovation, the capital market will act as a spearhead of financial reform.

---

[1] finance. ifeng. com: Press Conference of the CSRC on Jan. 24, 2014, http://finance. ifeng. com/a/20140124/11549144_0. shtml, visited on Feb. 21, 2015.

III. Insurance Market Development Policy[①]

(i) Highlights of Insurance Market Development Policy in 2014

Table 5 – 4　Highlights of China's Insurance Market Development Policy in 2014

Date	File Name	Issued by
Mar. 3	*Opinions of the CIRC and Beijing Municipal Government on Accelerating Innovation and Development of BeijingInsuranceIndustrial Park*	CIRC, Beijing municipal government
Mar. 21	*Guiding Opinions of the CIRC on the Insurance Industry's Supporting Revitalization and Development of Such Former Soviet Regions of the CPC as Dingnan County of Ganzhou City in Jiangxi Province*	CIRC
Mar. 25	*Guiding Opinions on the Insurance Industry's Serving New-Type Urbanization*	CIRC
May 15	*Notice of the General Office of the CIRC on Further Streamlining of Administration and Delegation of Powers in Support of Development of China (Shanghai) Pilot Free Trade Zone*	General Office of CIRC
Jun. 17	*Guiding Opinions of the CIRC on Piloting Reverse Mortgage Pension Scheme*	CIRC
Jul. 28	*Notice of the CIRC and Zhejiang Provincial Government on Launching Insurance Innovation Demo Zone in Ningbo of Zhejiang Province*	CIRC, Zhejiang provincial government
Aug. 10	*Opinions of the State Council on Accelerating Development of Modern Insurance Service Industry*	State Council
Oct. 27	*Opinions of the General Office of State Council on Accelerating Development of Commercial Health Insurance*	General Office of State Council

Source: Collected by the research group.

(ii) Review of Insurance Market Development Policy in 2014

Xiang Junbo, Chairman of the CIRC, commented in his address to 2015 National Insurance Regulation Work Conference that the insurance industry managed to reverse the trend of weakening performance in the context of economic downslide and embarked on a fast track in 2014, by giving play to the reform driver, demand driver and policy driver simultaneously. Firstly, business growth picked up speed consistently. Total premium income in the year exceeded the 2 trillion yuan mark. Total assets of the insurancesectorexceeded the ten trillion yuan mark. The insurance sector registered the quickest annual growth, at 17. 5 percent, since the international financial crisis. Property insurance yielded premium income of 720. 3 billion

---

① Written by Liu Xueqing.

yuan, up 16 percent year on year. Life insurance gained premium income of 1. 3 trillion yuan, up 18. 2 percent year on year. Secondly, restructuring went into more depth. Surety insurance, which is closely tied to the real economy, grew 66. 1 percent year on year. Annuity insurance, which has a bearing on people's livelihood, posted a 77. 2 percent year-on-year growth, and health insurance obtained 41. 3 percent year-on-year growth. Regular premium as a percentage of new policies with a longer than decadal maturity gained 5. 9 percentage points year on year. Thirdly, profitability of the industry was much heightened. Insurance firms posted a total profit of 204. 66 billion yuan, a 106. 4 percent jump year on year, the best ever. The insurance funds employed yielded proceeds to the tune of 535. 88 billion yuan, up 46. 5 percent year on year, also the best ever. The ROI of insurance funds was 6. 3 percent and the overall ROR was 9. 2 percent, gaining 1. 3 and 5. 1 percentage points from last year, respectively, and both marking five-year highs. Fourthly, capital adequacy of the industry was beefed up significantly. As of the end of 2014, net assets of the industry increased 56. 4 percent from the beginning of the year to count 1. 3 trillion yuan. Meanwhile, the insurance sector improved its ability to serve the economy and the society. In 2014, the insurance sector provided the whole society with risk cover worth 1, 114 trillion yuan in total, up 25. 5 percent year on year. Claims settled and benefits paid out totaled 721. 62 billion yuan, up 16. 2 percent year on year. The insurance sector is in a better place to consummate social security, participate in social management, serve the agriculture, rural areas and farmers and bolster up the economy.

The achievements in the insurance sector in 2014 were owing to a set of important policies instituted or enforced by the central government and the CIRC. These reform policies and innovative measures catalyzed indigenous momentum in the insurance sector, were of significance for the insurance sector to serve the economy and the society and laid a solid foundation for future development.

1. The New Ten National Rules Unfold a Blueprint for Reform, Development and Supervision of the Insurance Sector in the New Era

On Aug. 10, 2014, the State Council released *Opinions on Accelerating Development of Modern Insurance Service Industry* (referred to as the New Ten National Rules hereinafter). The New Ten National Rules aim at modernization of the country governance system and capability, define the guidelines, basic rules and goal of the modern insurance service industry and map out a blueprint for reform, development and supervision of the insurance sector in the new era.

First, the goal of the insurance sector is defined. The New Ten National Rules propose that a modern insurance service industry that offers universal coverage, complete functions, the highest level of safety and reliability, observes rules with good faith, has strong service, innovation capabilities and international competitive strength and caters to the needs for economic and social development of China will take shape by 2020 and the insurance sector of China will become powerful rather than be big only. Insurance will become an essential means of risk management and wealth management to the government, business entities and residents, an important channel to take security coverage and quality to the next level and an effective tool that may be utilized by the government to improve public services and strengthen social management. By then, the insurance penetration rate (premium income/GDP) will reach 5 percent and the insurance density (premium income/total population) will hit 3500 yuan per person. Insurance will better play its role as stabilizer of the society and booster of the economy.

Second, the service fields and functions of insurance are broadened. Pursuant to the New Ten National Rules, an insurance network for the wellbeing of the people will be constructed and the multi-level social security system will be perfected by developing commercial insurance as a pillar of the social security system, innovating pension insurance products and services and diversifying health insurance services. The insurance mechanism can be employed to innovate the way public services are delivered. Liability insurance can be of avail to the settlement of contradictions and disputes. The risk management function of insurance should be brought into play. The social governance system can thereby become better. Insurance should be embedded into the disaster and accident prevention and relief system. A catastrophe insurance system should be deployed. The insurance compensation mechanism should be improved to raise the degree of involvement in disaster relief. Insurance intended for the agriculture, rural areas and farmers is encouraged, and support and benefit to the agriculture, rural areas and farmers should be provided in an innovative way. The unique advantage of insurance funds in long-term investment should be brought into play. Coordinated development of the insurance market, the money market and the capital market should be fostered. The insurance sector should better serve economic restructuring and step up support to globalization of Chinese companies. The service functions of insurance should be broadened to help upgrade the quality and efficiency of the economy.

Third, the policies in support of the insurance sector are refined. The New Ten National Rules have proposed a set of much-needed new policies and measures in support of the insurance sector. To be more specific, an insurance regulatory coordination mechanism will be built. The government is encouraged to purchase insurance services by varied means. Tax policies that may boost the insurance sector will be worked out and perfected. The supply of land for the elderly service industry and health service industry will be assured. Government subsidies for agricultural insurance will be improved.

Fourth, reform and openup of the insurance sector are deepened. The aims of deepening the reform are clarified, for example, to establish a modern insurance corporation system, deepen the reform of market-based life insurance and commercial vehicle insurance rates, press ahead with the reform of the admittance control and exit mechanism of the insurance market, consummate the insurance market system, and support domestic and overseas listing of insurance firms. Main tasks relating to openup are outlined, for example, encouraging globalization of Chinese-funded insurance firms, providing risk protection to overseas Chinese companies, raising funds through the international capital market, expanding export insurance service, and motivating foreign insurance firms to bring advanced practice and technologies to China. Meanwhile, innovation in insurance products and services is encouraged. Development of the reinsurance market must quicken and the insurance intermediary market will play a better role.

Fifth, the main content of industrial infrastructure construction is specified, inclusive of, building the insurance sector credit system, creating a risk database, and developing asset custody center, asset trading platform, reinsurance exchange and disaster and loss prevention center, among other basic platforms; strengthening publicity and education and enhancing insurance awareness of the whole society.

Sixth, it is required to further tighten and improve insurance regulation. A risk-oriented insurance regulatory system must be put in place as early as possible. It is necessary to develop the second-generation solvency regulatory system, refine the insurance laws and regulations, propel regulatory information system development, give play to the role of self-regulatory organizations like the Insurance Association, strengthen grassroots insurance regulation, and modernize the regulatory system and regulatory skills. It is required to protect the legitimate rights and interests of insurance consumers, refine the laws, regulations and provisions on the protection of legitimate rights and interests of insurance consumers, explore a diversified insurance consumer dispute settlement mechanism, and make sure insurance organizations perform all obligations to insurance consumers properly. It is required to intensify risk management of the insurance sector, pursue accountability strictly, strengthen financial regulation and coordination, prevent cross-industry risk transmission, perfect the insurance and security fund management system and running mechanism and defend the bottom line of non-occurrence of systematic or regional financial risk.

The New Ten National Rules elevate growth of the insurance sector from a vision of the industry to a state will. The insurance sector will become a vital component of the economy and the society. After all of the New Ten National Rules are put into practice, the insurance sector is set to embark on a fast track at a higher level.

2. The State Council Unveiled *Opinions on Accelerating Development of Commercial Health Insurance*, Bringing Policy Benefit to Commercial Health Insurance Again

Commercial health insurance has made enormous strides in China over the past more than 30 years. Compared with some developed countries and regions in the world, however, commercial health insurance is still backward in China and health insurance premium still represents a small percentage of total health expenses and the industry features small size and deficiency in supply. In 2009, the CPC Central Committee and the State Council released *Opinions on Deepening the Reform of the Medical and Health Care System* and proposed to boost commercial health insurance. In September, 2013, the State Council released *Several Opinions on Promoting the Development of the Health Service Industry*, further clarifying the direction for the commercial health insurance sector. In August, 2014, the State Council again proposed to develop diversified health insurance services in *Several Opinions on Accelerating Development of Modern Insurance Service Industry*.

On Oct. 27, 2014, *Several Opinions of the General Office of State Council on Accelerating Development of Commercial Health Insurance* (hereinafter referred to as *Opinions on Commercial Health Insurance*) were released to further put into action the aforesaid policies made by the CPC Central Committee and the State Council and continually develop commercial health insurance. This is the first time the government identifies the function and role of commercial health insurance from the perspective of deepening the health care reform, developing the health service industry and upgrading the quality and efficiency of the economy. It is the first document outlining the master plan for commercial health insurance. Main content of the *Opinions on Commercial Health Insurance* are described as follows:

The definition of commercial health insurance is clarified. The *Opinions on Commercial Health Insurance* define commercial health insurance as an insurance cover where in a commercial insurance organization indemnifies the insured for a loss incurred by some health problem or medical treatment. It includes medical insurance, disease insurance, disability income loss insurance, nursing insurance and related medical accident insurance, and medical liability insurance, etc.

Ideal commercial health insurance is envisaged. According to the *Opinions on Commercial Health Insurance*, by 2020, a modern commercial health insurance service industry providing a full-fledged market system and a great variety of products in good faith will come into existence. The commercial health insurance running mechanism will be better, the service capabilities will be heightened noticeably, the service fields will be broadened, the number of insured will grow largely and commercial health insurance payout as a percentage of total health expenses will be enlarged considerably.

An incentive is given to expand commercial health insurance supply. Commercialinsurance organizations are encouraged to enrich commercial health insurance products, extend the industrial chain, and move from reimbursement and indemnification to comprehensive health insurance management, before, in the middle of and after illness. Commercial insurance covering rehabilitation, care and nursing of the disabled and family property trust for the mentally retarded is encouraged. The coverage of medical practice insurance should be expanded. Support should be given to scientific and technical innovation in the health industry.

A better medical insurance service system is desired. The provision of major disease insurance by commercialinsuranceorganizations to urban and rural residents will be promoted and regulated properly. One-stop service, higher level of social pooling, independent accounting, and medical expense control are required. The government is required to beef up procurement of services and involve commercial insurance organizations in all sorts of medical insurance services. The cooperation mechanism between commercial insurance organizations and healthcare organizations should be optimized and cooperation in these fields is proposed: contract healthcare organizations of commercial health insurance, mitigation of information asymmetry and contradiction between doctors and patients, reduction of unnecessary medical expenses through a commercial health insurance premium regulation mechanism, supervision, control and evaluation of medical expenses at contract medical organizations for major disease insurance for urban and rural residents by commercial insurance organizations.

It is required to sharpen the skills in commercial health insurance. The *Opinions on Commercial Health Insurance* require commercial insurance organizations to strengthen management, sharpen service skills, provide quality services, enhance information technology and improve management and service. It is also required to tighten and optimize regulation and management and keep the commercial health insurance market in order.

The policies in support of commercial health insurance are refined. The *Opinions on Commercial Health Insurance* require strengthening leadership and cross-department synergy, driving sustainable growth of the commercial health insurance service industry, encouraging insurance organizations to invest in the health service industry, assuring availability of land for the use of non-profit commercial health insurance, fine-tuning supportive fiscal and tax policies, and fostering a sound social environment conducive to the development of commercial health insurance by means of awareness and publicity activities.

The promulgation of *Opinions on Commercial Health Insurance* marks a solid move taken by the State Council with a view to innovate the reform strategy, deepen the healthcare reform by making use of the market mechanism, overcome the challenges in economic and social development, and support and improve people's livelihood. It is bound to create great policy opportunities and reform dividends for the development of commercial health insurance and is vital to develop the insurance sector and serve the economy and society.

3. The Pilot Program is Pushed Ahead with Double Efforts and the Catastrophe Insurance System has Made Strides

China is one of the nations with the most serious natural disasters in the world. Earthquake, flood, drought and typhoon, among other natural calamities, occur frequently. A catastrophe insurance system is badly needed for catastrophic risk diversification. The catastrophe insurance system has made strides in 2014 since *Decision of the CPC Central Committee on Some Major Issues Concerning Comprehensively Deepening the Reform* voted through on the 3rd Plenary Session of the 18th CPC Central Committee proposed to "perfect the insurance compensation mechanism and erect a catastrophe insurance system" and the CIRC launched catastrophe insurance in Shenzhen, among other regions.

First, superstructure design of the catastrophe insurance system has started and the roadmap and timetable have been made. In August, 2014, the State Council unveiled the New Ten National Rules for the insurance sector. For the first time, the framework of the catastrophe insurance system is clearly illustrated, the superstructure design is disclosed and "a multi-level catastrophic risk diversification mechanism supported by public finance" is envisaged. Zhou Yanli, Vice Chairman of the CIRC, disclosed the three-step roadmap and timetable for the catastrophe insurance system in Beijing in October. Step 1, research on the proposed catastrophe insurance system will be completed before the end of 2014 and the framework of the catastrophe insurance system will be mapped out. Step 2, catastrophe insurance legislation will be completed, the *Earthquake Catastrophe Insurance Regulations* will be promulgated and a catastrophe insurance fund will be initiated before the end of 2017. Step 3, in the phase of full operation between 2017 and 2020, the catastrophe insurance system will be fit into the nationwide comprehensive disaster prevention and alleviation system progressively.

Second, progress is made in institutional framework and legislation. In 2014, the CIRC wrapped up the research on the catastrophe insurance system and mapped out the framework. The draft *Earthquake Catastrophe Insurance Regulations* was completed. The trial run plan for earthquake catastrophe insurance was drawn up. Progress is also made in the development of urban and rural residence earthquake insurance products and earthquake co-insurance.

Third, the pilot program of catastrophe insurance is pushed ahead with double efforts. Shenzhen Bureau of Civil Affairs inked *Shenzhen Catastrophe Insurance Agreement* with an insurance company and put the agreement into effect officially as of Jun. 1, 2014, after *Shenzhen Catastrophe Insurance Plan* was voted through and the catastrophe insurance system was put into operation in 2013. Thereby, the first catastrophe insurance contract in China came into effect. The launch of catastrophe insurance undoubtedly marks a significant innovation in the insurance sector in Shenzhen. It may set an example of catastrophe insurance for other cities. On Nov. 11, 2014, catastrophe insurance was put into practice in Ningbo, and Ningbo became the second city following Shenzhen to pilot catastrophe insurance. Loss suffered by residents and disaster relief are covered. Shanghai, Zhejiang and Sichuan are also working on their regional catastrophe insurance mechanism in full swing.

Catastrophe insurance is a global challenge. The CIRC's vigorous efforts on project research, superstructure design, policymaking and legislation and pilot program in 2014 are bound to help bring into being a catastrophe insurance system well suited to the reality of China.

4. New Approaches to Deepen the Reform of the Insurance Sector Comprehensively are Explored through Pilot Programs

In accord with the tenet of the Third Plenum of the 18th CPC Central Committee, the CIRC launched a package of experimental policies and measures for streamlining of administration and delegation of powers in Shanghai Free Trade Zone, Qianhai Shenzhen-Hong Kong Modern Service Industry Cooperation Zone, Beijing Insurance Industrial Park and Ningbo Insurance Innovation Comprehensive Demo Zone, in a bid to explore new approaches to deepen the reform of the insurance sector comprehensively, expedite reform and innovation in the insurance sector and further heighten the capacity of the insurance sector to serve the real economy and contribute to harmony and stability of the society.

Three measures are adopted to streamline insurance regulation in Shanghai Free Trade Zone. On the basis of eight policies in support of China (Shanghai) Free Trade Zone launched in 2013, the CIRC circulated the *Notice of the General Office of the CIRC on Further Streamlining of Administration and Delegation of Powers in Support of Development of China (Shanghai) Pilot Free Trade Zone* on May 15, 2014. These three measures are closely tied to development of the insurance market in China (Shanghai) Free Trade Zone, have long-term significance, and are immediately operational. Shanghai Institute of Marine Insurance (SIMI) is permitted to prepare insurance terms and clauses of SIMI, which will then be adopted by members at their discretion after filing. Prior approval is no longer required for opening branches of Shanghai-based marine insurance operating centers and reinsurance companies in the Free Trade Zone, replaced by filing with the CIRC Shanghai branch. Prior approval is no longer required for appointment of senior management of insurance branches in the Free Trade Zone, replaced by filing with the CIRC Shanghai branch. This is a move taken by the CIRC to support the construction of China (Shanghai) Free Trade Zone and simplify prior admittance control, but strengthen ongoing and afterwards supervision as proposed in the master plan made by the State Council, as well as an important step to further innovate the system, streamline administration and delegate powers.

Eight policies in support of insurance innovation and development in Shenzhen are unveiled. The CIRC introduced eight policies with a view to quicken the development of the insurance innovation and development pilot zone in Shenzhen and support experiments and pilot programs of finance and insurance in Qianhai in August, 2014. (1) Supporting the development and openup of Qianhai and deepening Shenzhen-Hong Kong economic ties are key components of Shenzhen Insurance Innovation and Development Pilot Zone. (2) New-type insurance organizations, such as self-insurance firms and mutual insurance firms, as well as insurance firms specialized in marine insurance, liability insurance, health insurance and pension insurance, are encouraged in Qianhai. A reinsurance center is to be built in Qianhai. (3) Fusion and synergy between the insurance sectors in Shenzhen and Hong Kong are desired. The ways and forms of partnership between Shenzhen and Hong Kong in terms of insurance products, services, capital, and human resources will be explored. (4) The qualifications for opening branches or conducting business in Qianhai applicable to Hong Kong-based insurance firms will be loosened as appropriate under the framework of *Mainland and Hong Kong Closer Economic Partnership Arrangement (CEPA)*. Vigorous support will be given to qualified Hong Kong-based insurance brokers to open insurance agencies in Qianhai. Insurance firms are encouraged to expand their capital sources by taking advantage of the Hong Kong market and to conduct RMB insurance business by setting up overseas branches. (5) Shenzhen-based Insurance firms are encouraged to innovate the use of insurance funds and pilot overseas investment with insurance funds, so as to further broaden the channels and scope of insurance fund use. (6) Innovative Internet insurance is supported in Qianhai. Innovations in insurance products, marketing, services and trading mode that cater to the characteristics of Internet finance are encouraged. New forms of Internet insurance and innovative element trading platforms shall be fostered. (7) Trial run of short-term export credit insurance is supported, so as to provide financing facility and risk protection for development of the real economy and imports&exports. (8) Exploration into insurance regulatory innovation in Qianhai is supported.

Innovation and development of BeijingInsuranceIndustrial Park is pushed forward. On Mar. 3, 2014, the CIRC and Beijing municipal government released *Opinions on Accelerating Innovation and Development of Beijing Insurance Industrial Park* and proposed to develop Core

Zone, Radial Zone and Extended Zone of the insurance sector at Shijingshan State Pilot Zone for Comprehensive Reform of the Service Industry, create a state financial innovation demo zone led by the insurance sector, and build the Insurance Industrial Park as an insurance innovation test field, insurance industry cluster and the forefront of insurance culture in the country in a well-organized, scientific and progressive manner. The industrial orientation should be fitted to the development phase and functional positioning of the capital city, focus on reform and innovation of the insurance sector and attraction of more resources, and highlight the importance of business headquarters and regional headquarters. Innovative forms of insurance are encouraged. The main sector and entire industrial chain of insurance should be consummated. Pilot insurance exchanges should be built to form a modern market system. Regulators, industrial organizations and R&D institutes are encouraged to envisage the industrial architecture and create an insurance policy think tank. Insurance digital zones will be launched across the country. The market admittance control and exit mechanism will be put in place. At the same time, a series of supportive measures are laid out.

Construction of Ningbo Insurance Innovation Comprehensive Demo Zone proceeds. On Jul. 28, 2014, the CIRC and Zhejiang provincial government issued the *Notice of the CIRC and Zhejiang Provincial Government on Launching Insurance Innovation Demo Zone in Ningbo of Zhejiang Province*. In Sep., 2014, Ningbo Insurance Innovation Comprehensive Demo Zone broke ground, marking the first project of this kind in China. The CIRC is going to try out some reform and innovation projects in Ningbo that may set examples for the whole country. To build the demo zone, Ningbo has six things on its to-do list. First, stick to the creed of institutional innovation and construct an innovation self-fertile platform. Second, propel innovation in insurance organization and cluster elements of the insurance industry. Third, innovate insurance products, heighten the quality and efficiency of the economy, develop signature insurance products tailored to the insurance demand of the marine and export-oriented economy of Ningbo and small and micro enterprises and support development of the local real economy. Fourth, innovate public services provided by the government and consummate the social governance system. Fifth, develop health and pension insurance and optimize the social security system. Sixth, innovate the use of insurance funds and support transformation and upgrade of the industries. Ningbo Insurance Innovation Comprehensive Demo Zone is conducive to boosting innovations in insurance organization, products and technologies in Ningbo, enriching the insurance market system, strengthening and improving insurance services in some disadvantaged fields of the economy and society and reinforcing supportive insurance policies and other experimental moves.

5. Insurance Service for New-type Urbanization is Explored and Insurance Service for the Real Economy is Promoted

To fulfil the requirements outlined in *National New-type Urbanization Plan* (2014 – 2020), the CIRC issued *Guiding Opinions on the Insurance Industry's Serving New-Type Urbanization* on Mar. 25, 2014.

Guiding Opinions on the Insurance Industry's Serving New-Type Urbanization uphold the rules of human orientation, reform and innovation, dominant role of the market and steering by the government and propose six important moves. First, take a holistic approach to develop commercial pension and health insurance, improve the multi-level social security system covering both cities and rural areas, and alleviate the burden on social security arising from floating population during new-type urbanization. Second, deepen the reform of fund use, innovate the way funds are used, and support infrastructure construction and operation in cities and towns, as well as the development of projects concerning people's livelihood, like elderly healthcare and affordable housing. Third, optimize and upgrade the industrial mix of cities by administering to the open-ended economy, improving the financing environment of small and micro enterprises, providing insurance for technical innovations and serving the low-carbon economy. Fourth, enhance the efficiency of public service resource allocation by means of government procurement of insurance products and services. Boost liability insurance closely concerning public interests and help the government innovate the way of public administration. Build a catastrophe insurance system supported by policies and enhance response to disasters. Fifth, consummate the agricultural insurance service system, and foster coordinated development of new-type urbanization and modernization of the agriculture. Sixth, deepen reform and innovation, create an insurance innovation mechanism dominated by insurance firms, oriented towards the demand arising from new-type urbanization, and driven by moderate policy stimuli, to activate indigenous momentum and vitality in the insurance sector to serve new-type urbanization.

The effective mechanism and mode of insurance service for new-type urbanization are explored. The insurance sector is envisaged as a key pillar to prop up the multi-level social security system covering cities and rural areas, an important source of funding for new-type urbanization, an important tool to perfect social governance and improve public services and a crucial means to cope with potential disasters and accidents in the course of new-type urbanization.

6. Reverse Mortgage Pension Scheme is Piloted to Expand the Variety of Pension Schemes

On Sep. 6, 2013, the State Council released *Several Opinions on Accelerating the*

Development of the Elderly Service Industry, depicting the blueprint for the elderly service industry of China and proposing to pilot reverse mortgage pension scheme to expand the variety of pension schemes. To carry out the aforesaid requirements, the CIRC released *Guiding Opinions on Piloting Reverse Mortgage Pension Scheme* on Jun. 17, 2014.

Reverse mortgage pension scheme is a new type of commercial pension insurance that combines mortgage with lifelong pension insurance. An elderly person who enjoys full ownership of a house may mortgage the house with an insurance firm, but continues to have the right to occupy, use, earn proceeds from and dispose of the said house with the prior permission of the mortgagee, and at the same time receives pension subject to previously agreed-upon terms until his or her death. After his or her death, the said insurance firm will have the right to dispose of the collateralized house and any proceeds from such disposal shall be first used to cover the costs related to pension payment. Reverse mortgage pension scheme is claimed to be an important supplement to the pension insurance regime and of significance to the development of a multi-level pension insurance system in China and to healthy growth of the pension insurance market. It may enable the insurance sector to contribute in risk management and money management and play a part in the elderly service industry.

Guiding Opinions on Piloting Reverse Mortgage Pension Scheme have laid down a 2-year trial period and chosen four pilot cities, namely, Beijing, Shanghai, Guangzhou and Wuhan. The qualifications of insurance firms taking part in the pilot program are also specified therein. An eligible insurance firm must have been in business for five whole years, with a minimum registered capital of RMB 2 billion yuan; satisfy the solvency requirement and have posted a solvency margin ratio of no lower than 120 percent as of the end of last year and the end of the last quarter prior to the application; have the technologies, management capabilities and professionals needed to conduct reverse mortgage pension scheme.

In order to protect the legitimate rights and interests of the elderly, *Guiding Opinions on Piloting Reverse Mortgage Pension Scheme* has set out strict rules on publicity, sales team management, sales process management and information disclosure. First, publicity of insurance firms must be objective and unbiased, and all brochures and flyers must be prepared and managed by the head offices strictly. Second, the CIRC will instruct the Insurance Association of China to launch a reverse mortgage pension insurance salesman qualification examination in good time. Before that, insurance firms are expected to develop a salesman management system on their own, define qualifications, establish training and exam framework and post the information of qualified salesmen on the website. Third, insurance firms are required to specify the profile of and criteria for target clients and forbid sales to any client who doesn't meet the requirements.

Property valuation agencies with a Class A rating shall be engaged for property valuation and the resulting costs shall be shared by insurance firms and consumers. Insurance firms are required to coach consumers before contracts are signed, and assure fairness and justice of the whole process by making records or videos thereof, or in the presence of a third-party witness. Fourth, a cooling-off period of 30 calendar days is applied to reverse mortgage pension scheme. Insurance firms should refresh the insured's memory of the reverse mortgage pension scheme during the cooling-off period and confirm the insured's true will to buy. Fifth, insurance firms are required to disclose information concerning the reverse mortgage pension scheme to their clients in a regular manner. Sixth, insurance firms are encouraged to extend the service fields, diversify the service content and creat new service tools, to perfect the elderly service chain tied to reverse mortgage pension insurance. Seventh, insurance firms are required to place a premium on client complaints and do well in explanation, communication and aftersale services.

(iii) Policy Review and Outlook

In 2014, in the face of adversity and complexity, the insurance sector still managed to make solid progress in all aspects, embark on a fast track, and take big strides in reform and development by improving services, tightening regulation, preventing risks and driving development. The insurance sector is now standing at a new starting line. Looking ahead to 2015, CIRC Chairman Xiang Junbo, in addressing National Insurance Regulation Work Conference held in January, 2015, called for understanding of and adaptation to the New Normal, and jumping at the golden opportunity for the insurance sector, by pressing ahead with reform and innovation boldly and changing the way and drivers of development, to successfully turn China into a nation with a powerful insurance sector from a nation with a big insurance sector, and realize the goal set under the New Ten National Rules. Jobs to be done to drive development of the insurance sector in 2015 are detailed as follows:

First of all, three major policies must be enforced. First, catastrophe insurance will be promoted. On the basis of the breakthrough made in trial implementation of catastrophe insurance and institutional construction in the recent two years, step 2 of the three-step plan for catastrophe insurance will begin. Catastrophe insurance legislation will be pushed ahead, the core mechanism will be put in place, the *Earthquake Catastrophe Insurance Regulations* and other catastrophe insurance legislation jobs will be pushed ahead, a catastrophe insurance fund will be initiated, residence earthquake insurance will be implemented, catastrophe co-insurance will be put into operation and the pilot program of catastrophe insurance will be rolled out. Second, the tax incentive for pension insurance and health insurance will be put into effect. The pilot program of commercial pension insurance based on deferred personal income tax will be kicked start. The tax incentive for health insurance will be unveiled as early as possible. The regulatory framework, standard products, workflow and information platform in support of health insurance and pension insurance will be developed without delay, so that the tax incentive will be implemented immediately once it is promulgated. Third, major disease insurance will be rolled out countrywide. *Several Opinions on Accelerating Development of Commercial Health Insurance* issued by the General Office of the State Council and *Guiding Opinions on Major Disease Insurance for Urban and Rural Residents* jointly released by six ministries and commissions must be complied with, and the coverage of major disease insurance shall be enlarged consistently to cover all provinces and cities. The rules on major disease insurance need revising, and financial accounting, open bid and market admittance control and exit shall be managed in a proper manner to guarantee lawful operation of major disease insurance.

Next, the insurance sector should sharpen its capability to serve the economy and the society and focus on national key strategies and those fields concerning people's livelihood. First, innovate the mechanism and means of serving national key strategies and support the One Belt and One Road, and other strategies. Second, refine and develop the agricultural insurance system and agricultural insurance products, promote the agricultural reinsurance union running mechanism and agricultural catastrophic risk diversification mechanism and facilitate modernization of the agriculture. Third, unveil the policies and proposals for quickening the development of commercial pension insurance, allow insurance firms to take part in the operation and management of basic pension insurance funds, expand corporate annuity business, push forward trial implementation of the reverse mortgage pension scheme step by step, carry out *Several Opinions on Accelerating Development of Commercial Health Insurance*, encourage insurance firms to undertake all sorts of medical insurance services, including New Rural Cooperative Medical Service, revise *Administrative Measures for Health Insurance*, tighten supervision over health insurance and optimize the social security service system. Fourth, develop liability insurance and contribute to optimization of the social governance system. Fifth, draw upon the experience of the insurance sector in serving small and micro enterprises and allow small and micro enterprises to enjoy equal access to financial resources.

In addition, the CIRC promised to deepen the reform of administrative approval system, optimize the insurance market system and beef up infrastructure development of the industry in 2015.

IV. Bond Market Development Policy[①]

All policies, concerning institutional construction, infrastructure development, product innovation, and diversity of investors, for example, were implemented steadily in 2014. The bond market showed sustained growth and increasing expansion. The circulation of corporate credit bonds swelled and openup of the market was taken to the next level. The Chinese bond market has gained importance in the economy.

(i) Bond Market Policy

On Jan. 28, the PBC issued the *Notice on the Establishment of Central Clearing Mechanism for OTC Derivatives and the Launch of Central Clearing for RMB Interest Rate Swaps*, with a view to boost sound development of China's OTC derivatives market and create a central clearing mechanism for OTC derivatives. The Notice requires mandatory central clearing to be applied to all OTC derivative contracts, including RMB interest rate swaps, concluded among participants in the interbank bond market across the country. Shanghai Clearing House is the central clearing service provider.

In March, the PBC issued [2014] No. 3 Announcement, wherein the variety of bonds offered to the public via commercial bank counters is expanded to include, in addition to book-entry treasury bonds, bank debentures issued by China Development Bank, policy debentures, and bonds issued by government-sponsored entities such as China Railway Corporation. This is the first time new bond types are added to the portfolio traded via commercial bank counters since trading of book-entry treasury bonds was launched in 2002. Meanwhile, the Announcement has called off the administrative approval required for commercial banks who conduct over-the-counter trading of book-entry treasury bonds. The PBC imposes no admittance control or material restriction over the entities involved in the OTC business. Moreover, the Announcement permits banks to distribute bonds to investors via their network and e-Banking platform, buy and sell bonds from and to investors and handle bonds depository and clearing.

On Apr. 9, the PBC released on the *Notice on Open Bid for Bond Offering on the Interbank Bond Market (NAFMII [2014] No. 16)*, wherein the minimum requirements for non-financial entities using the bid system to issue bonds are revised to encourage and support non-financial entities to organize open bid for bond offering. The Notice has loosened the requirements for credit rating of issuer, size of offering, and the number of bidders, and specified the requirements for information disclosure to the public and filing with the PBC to be done by

---

① Written by Rong Yihua.

issuers and agencies after the bid is over.

On Apr. 24, National Development and Reform Commission (NDRC) released *Guidelines for Book Building in Issuance of Corporate Bonds (Provisional)* and *Guidelines for Bidding in Issuance of Corporate Bonds (Provisional)*, in an attempt to enhance the corporate bond issuance system, assure proper conduct of book building and bidding in issuance of corporate bonds and protect the legitimate rights and interests of all stakeholders.

In May, the MOF unveiled *Measures for the Pilot Program of Discretionary Issuance and Repayment of Municipal Bonds in 2014* and decided to pilot discretionary issuance and repayment of municipal bonds in ten provinces and cities, namely, Shanghai, Zhejiang, Guangdong, Shenzhen, Jiangsu, Shandong, Beijing, Jiangxi, Ningxia and Qingdao. For the sake of effective risk prevention and mitigation, the Measures have proposed a bond rating mechanism and required local governments to disclose basic facts of bonds, financial and economic performance, and local debts to the public. This marks another move aiming at tightened control over local government debts since the pilot program of discretionary issuance of municipal bonds was launched at the end of 2011.

On May 8, the PBC and the CBRC jointly released [2014] No. 8 Announcement, with a view to encourage qualified financial lease firms, auto finance firms and consumer finance firms to issue debentures. Consumer finance firms are incorporated in the interbank bond market as a debenture issuer. At the same time, the threshold for financial lease firms and auto finance firms to qualify as a debenture issuer is lowered. Rules on filing and use of funds raised are specified.

In June, China Foreign Exchange Trade System & National Interbank Funding Center (CFETS) issued *Rules on Trial Market Makers of the Interbank Bond Market*, with a view to refine the market maker rules of the interbank bond market and give full play to the role of trial market makers.

On Sep. 26, NDRC unveiled *Opinions on Strengthening Precautions against Risks in Corporate Bonds*. An organic set of policies will be shaped to prevent risks associated with corporate bonds by imposing strict admittance control over bond offering, tightening ongoing supervision throughout the life cycle of bonds, assuring adequate solvency margin and regulating and disciplining the conduct of underwriters and credit rating agencies.

On Oct. 15, NDRC released *Additional Tips for the Examination and Approval of Corporate Bonds*, which contains rules specified in support of *Opinions on Strengthening Precautions against Risks in Corporate Bonds*. Additional documents and data required to be made available along with the application for offering corporate bonds are specified, to raise the threshold and assure proper conduct of corporate bond issuance.

On Oct. 17, the PBC released the *Notice on Matters Concerning Qualified Non-financial Institutional Investors' Access to the Interbank Bond Market* (*PBC* [2014] *No.* 35), wherein permission is given for qualified non-financial institutional investors to trade bonds through the qualified non-financial institutional investors trading platform, the role of the regulator, self-regulatory organization and market platform is defined and the requirements for settlement process, continuous quotation by lead underwriter and conditional swap of bonds are specified.

On Nov. 28, the PBC issued the *Notice of the Financial Market Department of the PBC on Selected Qualified Institutional Investors' Access to the Interbank Bond Market* (*PBC* [2014] *No.* 43), wherein access to the interbank bond market is given to qualified rural commercial banks, rural cooperative banks, rural credit cooperatives and village banks and to non-corporate investors such as trust products, asset management schemes of securities firms, asset management schemes for specified clients of fund management companies and their subsidiaries, and asset management products of insurance asset management companies.

On Dec. 18, the PBC introduced *Administrative Measures for When-Issued Trading of Bonds on the Interbank Bond Market* (*PBC* [2014] *No.* 29), to heighten transparency and degree of competition in the pricing of bonds, perfect the bond yield curve and vitalize trade in the secondary market. The *Administrative Measures* have specified the requirements for the bond variety, trading and settlement methods of When-Issued Trading and proposed risk controls accordingly.

(ii) Policy Review

More policies concerning the bond market were introduced in China in 2014 when compared with prior years. Multi-level and multi-faceted reform and development measures regarding issuance, trading, investor team building, product innovation and infrastructure construction, among others, were launched and attached equal importance to regulation and innovation, effectively unleashing the vitality and boosting sound growth of the bond market.

NDRC launched a set of rules and measures to further intensify administration over corporate bond issuance. *Opinions on Strengthening Precautions against Risks in Corporate Bonds and Additional Tips for the Examination and Approval of Corporate Bonds* released by NDRC have raised the threshold and assured proper conduct of corporate bond issuance.

For the purpose of more transparent pricing during bond issuance, the PBC released *Notice on Open Bid for Bond Offering on the Interbank Bond Market*, to loosen the requirements for credit rating of issuer, size of offering, and the number of bidders, and to specify the requirements for information disclosure to the public and filing with the PBC to be done by issuers and agencies after the bid is over, and thus to encourage non-financial entities to organize open bid for bond offering. After that, *Administrative Measures for When-Issued Trading of Bonds on the Interbank Bond Market* was introduced to further heighten transparency and degree of competition in the pricing of bonds. Moreover, NDRC drafted and published, following negotiations with all stakeholders, *Guidelines for Book Building in Issuance of Corporate Bonds* (*Provisional*) and *Guidelines for Bidding in Issuance of Corporate Bonds* (*Provisional*), in an attempt to enhance the corporate bond issuance system, assure proper conduct of book building and bidding in issuance of corporate bonds and protect the legitimate rights and interests of all stakeholders.

The practice of trial market making can help pick out competent market makers and has become a key component of the market maker system, thanks to the large number and great variety of institutions and consistent expansion of market making turnover. *Rules on Trial Market Makers of the Interbank Bond Market* have been released to refine the market maker rules of the interbank bond market, give full play to the role of trial market makers and heighten activity of the secondary market.

Bank debentures offered via commercial bank counters feature low investment threshold, low risk, high yield and strong flexibility and provide more asset management options to ordinary investors. After the PBC [2014] No. 3 Announcement came out, at the end of 2014, China Development Bank and the Export-Import Bank of China distributed bonds worth 6.7 billion yuan and 3 billion yuan via commercial banks counters, respectively. The expanded variety of bonds traded through commercial bank counters not only widens the public's access to bank debentures for investment purpose, but also helps improve market liquidity and the efficiency of fund use, optimize the investor mix of bonds, and further expand the possibilities and penetration of the bond market.

In 2014, the PBC adopted a wide range of measures to improve the diversity of investors in the interbank bond market and enrich the mix of market players. Pursuant to the *Notice on Matters Concerning Qualified Non-financial Institutional Investors' Access to the Interbank Bond Market*, qualified non-financial institutional investors are allowed to access the interbank bond market via the qualified non-financial institutional investors trading platform. Thus, the multi-level bond market is fully-fledged and the investor base of the interbank bond market is fortified. According to the *Notice of the Financial Market Department of the PBC on Selected Qualified Institutional Investors' Access to the Interbank Bond Market*, access to the interbank bond market is given to qualified rural commercial banks, rural cooperative banks, rural credit cooperatives and village banks and to non-corporate investors such as trust products, asset management schemes of securities firms, asset management schemes for specified clients of fund management companies and their subsidiaries, and asset management products of insurance asset management companies. This move satisfies the investment needs of rural financial institutions and varied asset management products and further expands the diversity of investors.

No product-specific innovation policy was introduced in 2014, but the regulator gave market innovation full endorsement, adapted to economic growth needs and catered to the necessity of countrywide restructuring and transformation, on the basis of an issuance system brought to perfection over the past years. A series of important innovative bond types were introduced to the interbank bond market, such as carbon revenue notes, M&A notes, negotiable directional instruments and project revenue notes. The product mix of the bond market is enriched and more options are made available to issuers and investors. In May, CGN Wind Energy Limited successfully issued the first green bond related to energy saving and emission reduction in the interbank bond market, a carbon revenue note that effectively connects the domestic carbon trading market to the capital market. In June, the first debt financing instrument intended to pay M&A consideration exclusively, an M&A note worth one billion yuan, was successfully offered by Guizhou Kailin (Group) Co., Ltd. As of the end of 2014, a total of nine companies offered nine M&A notes valued 15.638 billion yuan cumulatively. July saw the successful offering of the first negotiable directional instrument, 2014 Phase I of negotiable directional instrument by Besum Group based in Yangling. The instrument not only caters to the risk-return preferences of different types of investors, but also satisfies the financing needs of companies to the utmost, while minimizing financing cost. Also in July, 14 Zhengzhou Dikun PRN001, the first project revenue note in China, was officially launched. It demonstrates the important role played by the bond market in support of new-type urbanization, helps detach the government financing function from local government financing platforms progressively and explores a transparent and proper urban construction investment and financing system.

It is the mission and fundamental goal of the finance sector to support growth of the real economy. In 2014, the bond market continued to prop up growth of the real economy effectively, and meanwhile, the competent ministries and commissions introduced more policies to step up concrete support to local governments, small and micro enterprises and consumption.

To support the development of local governments, the MOF unveiled *Measures for the Pilot Program of Discretionary Issuance and Repayment of Municipal Bondsin 2014* and decided to pilot discretionary issuance and repayment of municipal bonds in ten provinces and cities, namely, Shanghai, Zhejiang, Guangdong, Shenzhen, Jiangsu, Shandong, Beijing, Jiangxi,

Ningxia and Qingdao. The governments of these pilot provinces and cities are allowed to offer municipal bonds, and pay interest and principal at their discretion, subject to the bond issuance quota assigned by the State Council. After the Measures came into effect, Guangdong province issued the first municipal bond at its discretion on Jun. 23. The rest pilot provinces and cities are proceeding with their bond issuance work smoothly. Discretionary municipal bonds offered in this pilot round are worth 109.2 billion yuan in total. The pilot program of discretionary issuance and repayment of municipal bonds marks an important step to explore a proper local government debt financing mechanism and is good to defuse the pressure of debt service on local governments, mitigate debt risks and improve transparency of local finance. After the revised *Budget Law of the PRC* was voted by the standing committee of the NPC on Aug. 31, expansion of discretionary issuance and repayment of municipal bonds and the municipal bond market is foreseeable.

The PBC released the *Notice of the PBC on Issues Concerning Follow-up Supervision and Administration of Bank Debentures Earmarked for Loans to Small and Micro Businesses*, in support of bank debentures issued by commercial banks for the purpose of loans to small and micro businesses. This move can make sure all funds raised thereby are used for lendings to small and micro businesses and provide better financial services to small and micro businesses.

In [2014] No. 8 Announcement jointly released by the PBC and the CBRC, consumer finance firms are incorporated into the interbank bond market as a debenture issuer for the first time. At the same time, the threshold for financial lease firms and auto finance firms to qualify as a debenture issuer is lowered. Thus, consumption gets more financial backing.

In order for the treasury bond yield curve to better reflect market supply and demand dynamics, on Nov. 2, the MOF published China's treasury bond yield curve of key terms on its website for the first time. Charts of treasury bonds of five maturities, i. e. 1 year, 3 years, 5 years, 7 years, and 10 years, and their yield rates are compiled and provided by China Central Depository & Clearing Co., Ltd (CCDC). By making public the treasury bond yield curve, the MOF seeks to drive information disclosure relating to public finance, heighten the transparency of treasury bond policies, bring into play the role of treasury bonds as pricing benchmark for market-based interest rates, refine the treasury bond yield curve and boost sustainable and sound growth of the treasury bond market.

In order to construct highly efficient and transparent financial market infrastructures, in 2014, the PBC and the CSRC started an evaluation of China's financial market infrastructures jointly based on the *Principles for Financial Market Infrastructures* and cooperated in the management and supervision of financial market infrastructures. Now, a series of concrete and effective evaluations are going on, including infrastructure self-evaluation, cross evaluation and external evaluation by the regulator.

To keep abreast with international self-regulatory organizations and international infrastructures, Shanghai Clearing House and Euroclear Bank SA signed a Memorandum of Understanding in August, to explore commercial and technical cooperation possibilities. In September, Shanghai Clearing House signed a Memorandum of Understanding with the Chicago Mercantile Exchange (CME), to start all-around cooperation in product development, platform technologies, and exchange of views between the staff. Also in September, National Association of Financial Market Institutional Investors (NAFMII) attended the Sino-British Financial Roundtable, an event on the agenda of the sixth Sino-British economic and financial dialogue, and the two parties reached an agreement on strengthening cooperation between self-regulatory organizations of the financial market in both countries. In October, CCDC hosted the 18th Asia-Pacific Central Securities Depository Group (ACG) annual general meeting and released *Xi'an Initiative*. As proposed in *Xi'an Initiative*, all ACG members shall be committed to unblocked communication and central depositories, among other core financial infrastructures, shall work together to foster a robust, highly efficient, all-inclusive and systematic Asia financial infrastructure partnership circle to drive growth of the Asia-Pacific securities market; central depositories shall give play to the economy of scale, improve market order and efficiency and develop cross-border interconnection; shall adhere to the rules of equality, mutual help, openup and win-win, adapt to market diversity effectively and seek to involve stakeholders at home and abroad widely.

(iii) Bond Market Outlook

The year of 2015 is crucial to comprehensively deepening the reform and to the reform, openup and takeoff of the bond market in the era of New Normal. In the New Normal context of stable growth, restructuring and reform, market vitality will be further unleashed, innovations in all fields will be flourishing, the bond market will embrace a New Normal mode of growth, the market will further expand, product innovations will pick up speed, the investor base will be broadened, the infrastructures will be enhanced, and openup will be taken to the next level.

V. Money Market Development Policy[①]

Against the backdrop of deepening the reform and upholding a robust monetary policy, the

---

① Written by Rong Yihua.

regulator took varied moves to foster healthy and orderly development of the money market in 2014. The number of market players increased and the variety was expanded. The market size was enlarged further. The median interest rate moved downwards and the floating band narrowed. The money market functioned properly in terms of transmitting monetary policy, driving interest rate liberalization and managing liquidity.

(i) Interbank Borrowing Market

No new policy of consequence came out in the interbank borrowing market in 2014. Under the framework of *Measures for the Administration of Interbank Lending* brought into effect in 2007, market management became more flexible and the focus was shifted from prior management to ongoing and afterwards management, the importance of information disclosure management was highlighted and market transparency was heightened. In this context, the number of players in the interbank borrowing market surged and the trade turnover expanded steadily in 2014. The median interest rate declined and the floating band narrowed gradually. Openup and liquidity management were taken to the next level.

The PBC redoubled its efforts to boost the interbank borrowing market. In 2014, 97 new financial institutions joined in the interbank borrowing market. A total of 1,219 members are classified into nine categories, including 902 banking institutions, 129 financial firms, 87 securities brokers, 54 trust companies, 10 insurance firms, 4 asset management firms, 18 financial lease firms, 13 auto finance firms and 2 other institutions.

The interbank borrowing market continued growing steadily after reaping a nearly 400 percent jump in 2007, but experienced a 24.00 percent slump to 35.52 trillion yuan in 2013 from 46.74 trillion yuan in the prior year. In 2014, the interbank borrowing market revived with a yearly cumulative turnover of 37.66 trillion yuan, and an average daily turnover of 150.651 billion yuan, representing a 6.04 percent growth year on year.

A U-shaped interbank offered rate curve was seen in the year. The weighted average interest rate of interbank borrowings was posted at 2.96 percent, down 71 basis points from 2013. The interest rate of 7-day interbank borrowings, for example, soared from mid-January around the Spring Festival and hit the peak of the year at 6.64 percent on Jan. 20, but retreated all the way to 2.34 percent by Mar. 12, the nadir in the year; from Apr., the market interest rate started minor fluctuations within the range of 3 to 4 percent and the floating band narrowed gradually; towards the year-end, a strong rebound occurred, buoying up the market interest rate to the second highest in the year at 6.26 percent on Dec. 22; the market interest rate then declined mildly, closing at 4.89 percent on Dec. 31. The floating band of interest rates was narrower this year when compared with last year. The extreme interest rate spread in the year came in at 430 basis points, 540 basis points narrower than a year ago.

In terms of maturity, short-term borrowings still dominated the interbank borrowing market. In 2014, transactions within seven days took up 94.53 percent of total turnover.

In terms of trading structure, transactions of banking institutions continued to take up a share of more than 80 percent. In 2014, banking institutions claimed an 82.58 percent share of all interbank borrowing transactions, while non-banking institutions concluded the rest 17.42 percent of transactions. To be more specific, joint-stock banks took up the biggest share, 36.33 percent of total turnover of the entire market. Next, city commercial banks and policy banks accounted for 13.58 percent and 8.89 percent, respectively. The annual turnover of non-banking institutions totaled 13.12 trillion yuan, a 53.27 percent increase year on year. Securities brokers and financial firms performed the most actively, with a 10.84 percent and 4.88 percent market share, respectively.

Net lending by banking institutions and net borrowing by non-banking institutions continued to define the financing structure of the money market. Top net fund providers were policy banks, with a cumulative net lending of 47.40 trillion yuan, up 53.40 percent year on year, followed by the four leading stated-owned banks with a cumulative net lending of 37.02 trillion yuan (net borrowing worth nearly 200 billion yuan was recorded in 2013). Joint-stock commercial banks also posted a net lending of 14.43 trillion yuan, a 232.49 percent jump year on year. These three types of financial institutions totally provided a net lending of 13.67 trillion yuan, which represented 83.51 percent of gross net lendings in the interbank borrowing market. In the money market, top net fund borrowers were city commercial banks, securities companies and rural financial institutions in descending order, with an annual net borrowing of 33.97 trillion yuan, 27.52 trillion yuan and 21.49 trillion yuan, representing 31.35%, 25.41% and 19.84% of the gross amount of all net fund borrowers, respectively. These three types of financial institutions totally received a net borrowing of 13.09 trillion yuan, which represented 79.95 percent of gross net borrowings in the interbank borrowing market. Non-banking institutions were net fund borrowers on the whole. Except that asset management companies, trust companies and financial lease companies reported a small net lending, all of the rest non-banking institutions were net fund borrowers. Among them, securities companies received the largest net borrowing of 27.52 trillion yuan, up 75.29 percent year on year.

In 2014, Singapore branch of Industrial and Commercial Bank of China (ICBC) and Taipei branch of Bank of China (BOC) became new members of the interbank borrowing market. They are another two overseas RMB clearing banks after Bank of China (Hong Kong) Limited and Macau branch joined in the mainland interbank borrowing market in 2009 and 2010.

Accordingly, the trade turnover of overseas RMB clearing banks in the mainland interbank borrowing market exploded to 478. 86 billion yuan in 2014, 27 times the amount registered in 2009, that is, 17. 74 billion yuan. This gives a strong stimulus to cross-border use of RMB.

In 2015, the regulator of the interbank borrowing market will pay more attention to ongoing and afterwards management, attach more importance to information disclosure management, and heighten market transparency. Against the backdrop of reform and openup in China, interest rate liberalization will be pushed ahead, the exchange rate formation mechanism will be optimized, capital account convertibility and openup of the financial sector will progress in an orderly manner, regional financial reform including free trade zone will be deepened, the globalization of the RMB will proceed faster, and innovations in the financial market will be a great draw. Ongoing reform and openup of the financial sector will help unleash the vitality in the interbank borrowing market, enrich the variety and increase the number of members, enlarge the market size and upgrade openup and strengthen liquidity management of the market.

(ii) Bond Repo Market

The bond repo market, the bulk of which is the interbank bond repo market, thrived with consistently expanding breadth and depth over the last more than one decade, since the interbank bond market came into being in 1997. The turnover of bond repos in the interbank market exceeded the 200 trillion yuan mark in 2014 after reaching 100 trillion yuan for the first time in 2011. The repo market plays an increasingly important role in balance sheet management and liquidity management of financial institutions, and has become a crucial platform of open market operations for the PBC, as well as benchmarks for short-term interest rates of the money market.

No policy concerning the repo market was launched in 2014. After the Master Agreement for Bond Repurchase Transactions in the Interbank Market of China (2013) came into effect, the market has boomed. The trade turnover has exploded, the maturity mix is more skewed towards short-term, the repo rates have declined on the whole, policy bank debentures form the greatest part of underlying assets and large commercial banks and policy banks are net fund providers.

In 2014, the turnover of bond repos in the interbank market totaled 224. 42 trillion yuan, with an average daily turnover of 897. 69 billion yuan, an increase of 41. 89 percent year on year. The cumulative turnover of pledge-style repos came in at 212. 42 trillion yuan, with an average daily turnover of 849. 676 billion yuan, up 39. 77 percent year on year. The cumulative turnover of buyout repos was reported at 12. 00 trillion yuan, with an average daily turnover of 48. 014 billion yuan, up 93. 97 percent year on year.

A U-shaped repo rate curve appeared, but repo rates and the floating band both moderated when compared with 2013. The weighted average interest rate of pledge-style repos was posted at 2.98 percent, a decrease of 56 basis points year on year. The intraday peak value of pledge-style repo rate in 2014, 5.90 percent, occurred on Jan. 29, and the nadir, 1.93 percent, occurred on Mar. 11; the extreme interest rate spread in the year was 397 basis points, a retreat of 570 basis points from 2013. The weighted average interest rate of buyout repos was reported at 3.44 percent, a retreat of 52 basis points year on year; the extreme interest rate spread in the year was 399 basis points.

In terms of maturity, pledge-style repo transactions within seven days took up 92.72 percent of total turnover. Overnight transactions aggregated 166.91 trillion yuan, representing 78.57 percent of total turnover of pledge-style repos. Repo transactions with maturity longer than 14 days took up a smaller share. 14-day repo transactions represented 4.52 percent of total turnover, and that of 21 days and longer 2.76 percent. The maturity of buyout repo transactions shortened again, with the turnover of transactions within seven days accounting for 87.31 percent of total turnover, up 4.29 percentage points from 2013.

With respect to the mix of underlying bonds of repos, underlying assets of pledge-style repos were mainly comprised of treasury bonds, central bank bills and policy bank debentures, which totally represented a market share of 79.09 percent, up 1.13 percentage points from 2013. The proportion of repo transactions with central bank bills as underlying in total turnover nosedived to 0.76 percent from 4.11 percent in 2013, but that of policy bank debentures gained 4.55 percentage points to reach 40.70 percent. Meanwhile, pledge-style repos with short-term financing bills, super-short-term financing bills, medium-term notes, collective notes and enterprise bonds as underlying assets accounted for 15.86 percent, down 0.79 percentage point from 2013. The proportion of repo transactions with treasury bonds, central bank bills and policy bank debentures as underlying in total turnover of buyout repos gained 0.28 percentage point from 2013 to 45.44 percent, while that with short-term financing bills, super-short-term financing bills, medium-term notes, collective notes and enterprise bonds as underlying ascended to 51.30 percent from 49.28 percent in 2013.

In terms of financing structure, top three net fund borrowers were city commercial banks, rural commercial banks and cooperative banks, and joint-stock commercial banks, representing 30.13 percent, 14.89 percent and 14.40 percent of total value of repos, respectively. Top three net fund providers were large commercial banks, policy banks and city commercial banks, accounting for 21.56 percent, 19.08 percent and 17.03 percent of total value of reverse repos, respectively.

Along with progress in interest rate liberalization and expansion of reform and openup of the financial market in China, the interbank bond repo market will also continue growing steadily. The product variety will be further expanded, and all systems and infrastructures will be enhanced. The interbank bond repo market, as a key platform of open market operations for the PBC, will set the stage for steering the interest rate trends and modulating the liquidity of the money market.

(iii) Bill Market

In 2014, the bill market presented steady performance. Banker's acceptance bills continued growing. The total value of bill financing declined first but rebounded then, and registered a rapid year-on-year growth. Institutions continued to perform with a high level of activity. In Q1, the balance of bill financing declined mildly, owing to strong ordinary credit demand at the year beginning. From Q2 onwards, the balances of both bill acceptance and financing advanced, thanks to ample money supply. After interest rate cuts and deposit reserve reductions were implemented, interest rates of the bill market moved downwards and rebounded by quarter-end, in pace with the movements of open market, rediscount and relending rates. The downward curve of interest rates eased up quarter by quarter and ticked up by the year-end.

In February, NDRC and the CBRC jointly released the *Notice on Issuing the Catalogue of Government-Guided Pricing and Government-Fixed Pricing for Services Provided by Commercial Banks* (*NDRC* [2014] *No.* 268). Pursuant to the Notice, basic financial services provided by commercial banks to bank clients shall be subject to government-guided pricing and government-fixed pricing, including some remittance transfers, cash remittances, cash withdrawal, bills and other services of commercial banks. Compared with *Interim Measures Governing Service Prices of Commercial Banks* released in 2003, banker's acceptance bills are no longer subject to government-guided pricing.

In April, the PBC, CBRC, CSRC, CIRC and SAFE jointly released the *Notice on Regulating Interbank Business of Financial Institutions* (*PBC* [2014] *No.* 127), wherein 18 pieces of regulatory advice are proposed, to specify interbank business variety and accounting standards, strengthen and improve internal and external management of interbank business, and encourage innovations in balance sheet activities. It is made clear in the Notice that financial assets purchased under resale agreements (sold under repo agreements) should be banker's acceptance bills, bonds and central bank bills, among other types of financial assets that are highly liquid and traded at fair values in the interbank market and securities exchanges, but should exclude commercial acceptance bills. Financial assets under interbank investments include bank debentures and subordinated debts that are purchased by or on behalf of financial institutions, among other interbank financial assets traded in the interbank market or securities exchanges, and wealth management products of commercial banks, trust investment schemes, securities investment funds, asset management plans of securities companies, asset management plans of fund management companies and their subsidiaries, and asset management products of asset management entities in the insurance sector, among other SPVs, but banker's acceptance bills and commercial acceptance bills are excluded.

In May, the General Office of the CBRC released the *Notice on Proper Governance of Interbank Business of Commercial Banks* (*CBRC* [2014] *No.* 140). As provided for in the Notice, commercial banks shall have an interbank business governance system commensurate with the scale and complexity of interbank activities they are involved in. Corporate headquarters shall manage interbank business in a consistent manner, and incorporate interbank business into comprehensive risk management. Commercial banks shall have a department take charge of interbank business exclusively. Corporate headquarters shall establish or designate a department in charge of interbank business. The designated department must not delegate any interbank transaction that it may conduct by electronic means in the financial market to any other department or branch. An interbank business authorization system, credit management policy and counterparty access control mechanism shall be put in place.

In May, the Shanghai head office of the PBC unveiled *China (Shanghai) Pilot Free Trade Zone Implementation Rules for Free Trade Accounting (For Trial Implementation)* and *China (Shanghai) Pilot Free Trade Zone Prudential Risk Management Rules for Free Trade Accounting (For Trial Implementation)* (see PBC HO [2014] No. 46). Electronical commercial bills may be used for Free Trade Accounts of institutions. Banking institutions shall examine all electronic commercial bills drawn or transferred under Free Trade Accounts.

In August, the PBC assigned an additional rediscount quota worth 12 billion yuan to some branches and sub-branches and required the quota to be used entirely to support financial institutions to increase lendings to small and micro businesses and to the agricultural sector, rural areas and farmers, in order to fulfil the requirement for beefing up relending and rediscount to the agriculture and small businesses put forward on an executive meeting of the State Council, and step up financial service to the such weak parts of national economy as agricultural sector, rural areas and farmers, and small and micro businesses. Meanwhile, effective measures are warranted to refine rediscount management, encourage financial institutions to expand credit facilities to the agricultural sector, rural areas and farmers, and small and micro businesses and lower financing cost of the society.

In 2014, the PBC adopted a robust monetary policy and effectively modulated market liquidity and instructed the financial sector to support the real economy, by wielding a wide range of monetary policy tools and combining quantitative and structural regulation flexibly. Relending and rediscount support to the agricultural sector, rural areas and farmers, and small and micro businesses was intensified to motivate financial institutions to expand credit facilities to these fields and lower financing cost of the society.

Fine-tunings and proactive adjustments to all directional monetary easing policies helped create abundant market liquidity and provide a positive market environment for the growth of bill business of commercial banks. The balances of bill acceptance and financing posted by financial institutions demonstrated consistent growth. Bill rediscount trade appeared buoyant. The function of bills in support of the real economy, restructuring and credit upgrade and financing of small- and medium-sized enterprises is brought into full play. Moreover, guided by benchmark lending and deposit rates, rediscount rates and open market operation rates of the PBC, interest rates of the bill market have waved downwards on the whole, which can help bring down marketwide financing cost.

In recent years, interbank business, rather than as a means of position swap, has become an effective tool to circumvent on-balance-sheet credit control, defuse capital constraint, lower the loan-to-deposit ratio and expand the balance sheet. Financial institutions have actually evolved interbank business into a credit equivalent. Bill rediscount and repo form an important component of interbank business. In April, 2014, five ministries and commissions, the PBC included, issued the *Notice on Regulating Interbank Business of Financial Institutions*, with a view to assure proper conduct of interbank business by commercial banks, minimize intermediate links along the money market chain, and boost capital flow into the real economy. The CBRC released the *Notice on Proper Governance of Interbank Business of Commercial Banks* soon afterwards. These two notices have specified interbank business variety and accounting standards, and internal and external management of interbank business. As reflected in the bill market, the aforesaid rules not only make impossible the use of commercial acceptance bills as underlying of repos and narrow the manoeuvrability of bill assets available to commercial banks, but also urge commercial banks to withdraw bill business to the head office and chill down trade of the bill repo market. After the notices were released, the activity and turnover of bill repos both slackened off obviously.

In October and December, the CBRC released *Notice on Special Inspection of Banking Institutions' Compliance with New Rules on Interbank Business* and *Notice on Special Inspection of Tightening Internal Control of Banking Institutions and Combating Malpractices and Crimes*. The former notice contains 14 provisions on bills, capital charge, wealth management, transfer of credit assets and governance of interbank businesses. The latter is more concentrated on screening of credit, deposit, bill, interbank, wealth management, and financial management activities of banks with a high incidence of malpractices and crimes. These two inspections pay special attention to bill repos, bill management system reform and compliance in commercial banks and are positive to specialized management and sound growth of bills, though the growth of all bill activities has decelerated in the short run.

The release of the *Catalogue of Government-Guided Pricing and Government-Fixed Pricing for Services Provided by Commercial Banks* puts an end to the fixed fee rate at 0.5‰ for banker's acceptance bills that has existed for twenty years and marks the beginning of market-based pricing. When a market-based pricing mechanism applies to banker's acceptance bills, banks can derive income from more intermediary sources, and the substantial risk associated with bill acceptance can prompt banks to develop a discretionary pricing ability and thus contribute to healthy development of the bill market.

China (Shanghai) Pilot Free Trade Zone Prudential Risk Management Rules for Free Trade Accounting (For Trial Implementation), as a supplement to *China (Shanghai) Pilot Free Trade Zone Implementation Rules for Free Trade Accounting (For Trial Implementation)*, gives permission to the use of electronical commercial bills for Free Trade Accounts of institutions, and thus makes available a convenient and effective means of payment settlement and trade finance to entities in the Free Trade Zone and boosts the use of electronic bills. Moreover, the experiments and explorations going on in the Free Trade Zone can fuel innovations in the bill market and cross-market development.

The New Normal features of the Chinese economy will become more and more evident in the coming years. Against the backdrop of industrial upgrade and restructuring, the bill market will continue to enjoy promising growth opportunities, but face more intense and extensive competition in terms of price, channel and asset use. Electronic bills, Internet-based trading, capitalization of bills and cross-market innovations might emerge as the highlights of the future market.

VI. Wealth Management Market Development Policy[1]

China's per-capita disposable income reached 20,167 yuan in 2014, up 10.1 percent in nominal terms, or 8 percent in real terms after deducting the price factor from the prior year,

---

① Written by Wang Qi.

and the per-capita disposable income of rural residents reached 10, 489 yuan, up 11. 2 percent in nominal terms, or 9. 2 percent in real terms after deducting the price factor, outpacing the GDP growth in the same year, the National Bureau of Statistics (NBS) reported on Jan. 20, 2015.

The growth of residents' income is the cornerstone of the wealth management market. In 2014, China's wealth management market continued expanding, but the competition among institutions intensified and different wealth management products showed divergent yields. Wealth management products offered by commercial banks were still in the lead, followed by trust products, while collective wealth management products offered by securities brokers, albeit small in size, presented good performance thanks to a strong stock market.

(ⅰ) Commercial Banks' Wealth Management Product Market

According to statistics released by the Wealth Management Research Center, Institute of Finance and Banking, Chinese Academy of Social Sciences, the bank wealth management market continued growing steadily all through 2014, and 291 commercial banks issued a total of 68, 500 wealth management products and raised about 43. 0 trillion yuan. The number of products launched and the amount of funds raised increased 57. 1 percent and 49. 7 percent year on year, respectively (see the chart below). The bank wealth management segment was still in the lead of the Chinese wealth management market. The continued expansion of banks' wealth management products is driven not only by proactive innovations made by commercial banks seeking changes, but also by the society's objective financing demand.

The bank wealth management market continued becoming bigger, but not more profitable. In 2013, against the backdrop of restructuring and de-leveraging, there was a strained

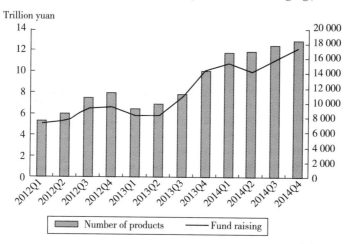

Data source: WealthManagementResearchCenter, Institute of Finance and Banking, CASS.

Page 5 – 3 Number of Banks' Wealth Management Products and Fund Raising (2012 – 2014)

atmosphere in the financing sector and market interest rates stood at a high level. From the second half onwards, the yield curve of banks' wealth management products headed north consistently, giving rise to a cash crunch. With the arrival of 2014, the yield curve reversed the uptrend and took a downturn, mainly because of monetary easing and tightening of interbank business. The risk preference of financial institutions declined noticeably and the control over offering design and risk of banks' wealth management products was tightened, after a payment crisis happened to Evergrowing Bank, among others. Given the downside pressure on the Chinese economy, the central bank adopted varied measures to guide interest rates to the downward course and set the tone for lower expected ROR of banks' wealth management products.

In November, 2014, the ROR of banks' wealth management products hit one-year low. The average ROR of one-month products and three-month products was reported at 4. 40 percent and 4. 92 percent, respectively. Contrary to expectation, the ROR of banks' wealth management products climbed up after the central bank announced interest rate cuts on Nov. 22. In December, a rally in the ROR of wealth management products occurred. This is the result of year-end effect combined with the pressure of deposit outflow imposed by the strengthening stock market on commercial banks, who then wanted to retain clients' funds by raising the ROR of their products.

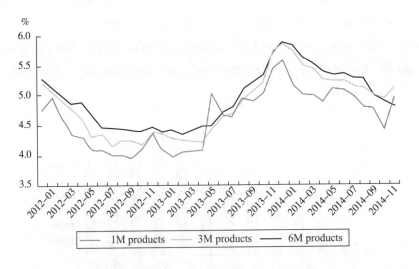

Data source: Wealth Management Research Center, Institute of Finance and Banking, CASS.

Page 5 – 4　Monthly Yield Curve of Banks' Wealth Management Products

The theme of wealth management business governance in 2014 is defined by exploration into new products and new modes of bank wealth management in support of the real economy, incentive to direct investment, removal of risks hidden in wealth management and the transition from wealth management to asset management.

In tune with this theme, the CBRC released *Guiding Opinions of the General Office of the CBRC on Governance of Bank Wealth Management Business in 2014* (Document No. 39) in February, 2014, wherein eight key points about regulatory work in the year are outlined. To echo Document No. 107, Document No. 39 also addresses some crucial topics such as information disclosure, rigid payment and risk transmission, and is intended to explore new modes of wealth management in support of the real economy. In terms of information disclosure, off-site supervision over wealth management business shall be strengthened and the rules on the wealth management information registration system shall be put into practice. In terms of risk control, a wealth management risk segregation mechanism based on regulatory restructuring, and encompassing use of capital, risk control, accounting and information disclosure shall be established. The wealth management business division of banks will be reformed to unify product design, cost accounting and risk control. In terms of business innovation, banks are encouraged to explore new wealth management products and modes and make concrete investments, so as to better serve the real economy directly.

In July, 2014, the CBRC released the *Notice on Optimizing the Organization and Management Framework of Bank Wealth Management Business* (Document No. 35), with a view to press ahead with the wealth management business division reform. In the Notice, banking institutions are ordered to carry out the reform as per the requirements for separate accounting, risk segregation, proper conduct and accountability, form a wealth management business unit to take charge of bankwide wealth management activities in a centralized and consistent manner, bring risks in wealth management under the bankwide risk management system and implement risk mitigations. In addition, Document No. 35 clearly puts a ban on the presence of any expression referring to explicitly or suggesting implicitly the nature of rigid payment in any brochure or flyer of wealth management products offered by banks. The regulator is determined to drive changes in wealth management business, as reflected in the launch of direct financing instruments and bank wealth management schemes, as well as the ban on any reference to or hint of rigid payment. Nevertheless, it is not easy to change investors' understanding of wealth management products as something born with rigid payment.

With respect to deposit deviation degree management, the CBRC, the MOF and the PBC jointly released the *Notice on Matters Concerning Strengthening the Administration of Deposit Deviation Degree of Commercial Banks* (Document No. 236) in September, 2014, to rein in the impulse of commercial banks to inflate deposits at month end or quarter end. The month-end deposit deviation degree of commercial banks must not go beyond 3 percent. An explicit ban is put on any act of feeding funds under wealth management into deposits at month end or quarter end, or any other critical point of time, by means of backflow of wealth management products into deposits, improper maturity design of wealth management products, and offering and maturity deliberately scheduled on the latter part of each month. Thanks to Document No. 236, the maturity of wealth management products might be more evenly distributed, and changes may also happen to the maturity mix and yield mix of banks' wealth management products. Products of longer maturity and principal protection may be offered to raise the daily average balance of deposits.

The Administrative Measures have been revised. In December, 2014, the CBRC unveiled *Administrative Measures for the Supervision of Wealth Management Business of Commercial Banks* (*Consultative Document*), to canvass comments widely from commercial banks. The goal of defusing risks hidden in bank wealth management business effectively and driving the return of wealth management to the essence of asset management is defined therein. The main content of the document is described as follows:

First, defuse risks and drive the change of wealth management. It is important to break away from implicit guarantee and rigid payment and clarify the risk taker. The Substance over Form Principle shall be applied to the measurement of risk-weighted assets and risk provisioning. The part of non-standard assets in principal-protected products and expected-return products shall be included in on-balance sheet accounting. It is unnecessary to restate non-standard assets invested by NAV-based open-ended products and project financing products without maturity mismatch in the balance sheet. The policy partially supportive and partially inhibitory aims at driving the transition of expected-return wealth management products of commercial banks to NAV-based open-ended products and project financing products without maturity mismatch.

Second, cater to the financing needs of enterprises and directly serve the real economy. The independence of wealth management products and the legal consequence of bankruptcy remoteness are made clear. Separate capital accounts and securities accounts can be opened for wealth management products, to encourage direct investment with wealth management products and aim at de-leveraging, de-chaining and de-channelling. Thus, funds under wealth management can be directly paired with real projects that need funding, and the financing cost of enterprises can be lowered.

Third, intensify risk matching and better protect the interests of investors. It is important to refine risk rating standards and realize sales segmentation. Project financing, equity investment and alternative investment categories are intended for high net worth clients, private banking clients and institutional clients only.

Fourth, adapt proactively and apply unified regulatory standards. Regulatory standards consistent with those applicable to other financial products in other asset management sectors will be put in place.

Fifth, be market-oriented and achieve a high level of specialization. Banks' wealth management products are definitely classified into the following categories, namely, structured products, NAV-based open-ended and closed-ended products, expected-return products, project financing products, equity investment products, alternative investment and other innovative products.

All regulatory moves over the past two years, in retrospect, from the definition of non-standard assets in Document No. 8 in 2013, to the pilot program of bank wealth management schemes and direct financing instruments, to the reform of independent wealth management business division, and finally to the revision of the *Law of the PRC on Commercial Banks* kicked start lately, point to a direction crucial to the future development of bank wealth management business, that is, the return to the essence of asset management. As more banks get involved in bank wealth management schemes, the issuance and trading turnover of direct financing instruments are expected to keep growing steadily, giving a push to de-channelling of non-standard investment and open-ended, pro-fund change of wealth management products.

In 2015, NAV-based open-ended wealth management products might enjoy a dominant position in the market. This is also an important tool to be used by the regulator who is attempting to put an end to rigid payment. The most important upside of NAV-based wealth management products is their highly flexible redemption terms. Traditional rollover-based wealth management products are only available for subscription and redemption on open days, while NAV-based wealth management products have made a significant breakthrough in the flexibility of funds. Any client may apply for subscription or redemption of a product anytime, and the application will be accepted on the open day every month. Since banks post NAV of each product on a daily basis, NAV-based wealth management products also provide ideal transparency and keep clients posted on the latest NAV trends anywhere and anytime.

The ROR of a wealth management product is undoubtedly an indicator that investors are most interested in. As NAV-based wealth management products are non-principal-protected, the market is widely concerned about the volatility of expected return before asset management schemes are launched. As a matter of fact, NAV-based wealth management products not only deliver an annualized ROR higher than that of most comparable wealth management products available in the market place, but also post highly stable ROR for any period. This is mainly owing to the fact that NAV-based wealth management products mostly target claims and are mostly invested in highly liquid assets and creditor's assets, such as bonds and bond funds, money market funds, and due to banks, and the asset portfolios provide a high level of safety and stable yield.

According to statistics, in 2014H1, NAV-based open-ended wealth management products achieved the quickest growth and raised a total of 1. 17 trillion yuan, a 174. 53 percent jump year on year, and the said amount as a percentage of total funds raised by all wealth management products gained 1. 27 percentage points from 2013H1 to reach 2. 37 percent. In the future, the number and market share of NAV-based wealth management products hold the potential to grow further.

(ii) Brokers' Collective Wealth Management Product Market

As of the end of 2014, total assets under the management of securities brokers were worth 7. 95 trillion yuan, an increase of 2. 74 trillion yuan, or 53 percent, from the end of 2013, according to statistics released by the Asset Management Association of China (AMAC) on Mar. 6, 2015. As for the product mix, actively managed products of securities brokers accounted for 17 percent only, while passively managed products took up the rest 83 percent.

Thanks to a bull A-shares market and bond market at the same time, in 2014, collective wealth management products of securities brokers presented stunning performance. The ROR of 1631 collective wealth management products offered by securities brokers with performance data available (excluding those already wound up or initiated less than one year ago) averaged 13. 22 percent, indicating a sweeping uptrend. More than 90 percent of these collective wealth management products, or 1534, posted a positive profit, and 25 of them delivered a higher than 100 percent ROR. These 25 products, almost all being of Class B, include 13 bond funds, 9 hybrid funds and 3 stock funds.

In 2014, asset management institutions under the jurisdiction of the CSRC embraced a new round of institutional dividends. On May 9, 2014, the New Nine State Regulations shed light on the direction for the reform of the capital market. The CSRC introduced *Opinions on Promoting Innovation and Development of Securities Brokers* on May 13 and *Opinions on Promoting Innovation and Development of the Securities Investment Fund Sector* on June 12 (referred to as two Opinions on Innovation and Development hereinafter), wherein three goals are set, namely, developing modern asset management institutions, supporting product innovations and driving regulatory reform. In September, 2014, the regulator unveiled *Administrative Measures for Asset Management Business of Securities and Futures Brokers (Consultative Document)* (referred to as the Consultative Document hereinafter) and *Notice on Regulating Asset Management Schemes For*

Specified Clients of Securities Brokers, Fund Management Companies and Their Subsidiaries (*Consultative Document*) (referred to as the Notice hereinafter), which reshaped the regulatory framework and business boundary of asset management institutions under the jurisdiction of the CSRC.

The adjusted regulatory framework suggests the transition from regulation by institution classification to regulation by business classification when it comes to asset management business. To reshape the regulatory framework, first of all it is necessary to have only one regulator and a consistent set of code of governance. In April, 2014, the CSRC carried out a partial organization reshuffle and merged the former Institutions unit and Funds unit, in charge of asset management and fund subsidiaries of securities brokers, respectively, into the Department of Securities and Funds Institutions, to bring asset management business under supervision. The Consultative Document sets out consistent rules governing securities brokers, fund management firms, futures brokers and their asset management subsidiaries, and authorizes the AMAC to register securities brokers, fund management firms and their subsidiaries and to handle filing of their asset management schemes, and China Futures Association to take charge of registration and filing relating to asset management business of futures brokers. The said two Opinions on Innovation and Development highlight the reform of regulatory mode and loosened industrial access as part of innovation and development. The reform of regulatory mode is intended to create a regulatory mode well adapted to innovation and development, stake out the boundary of regulation consistently, shift the focus from prior approval to ongoing and afterwards supervision, streamline the administrative formalities, and explore a Negative List approach. For the purpose of loosened industrial access, license management is preferred and functional supervision is worth a try.

The adjusted business boundary is first of all manifested in the widened scope of investment, which can sharpen the competitive strength of asset management business of securities brokers, futures brokers and funds and reshape the industry. The Consultative Document differentiates two forms of asset management, that is, one to one and one to many. "Equity, claims and other property rights that are not transferred through stock or futures exchanges, or NEEQ or the interbank market, and other properties recognized by the CSRC" are included in the scope of investment officially and named "alternative asset management scheme", but investment of collective asset management schemes of securities brokers therein is forbidden. Fund firms are required to launch specified asset management schemes through subsidiaries formed for that purpose only before making investment. Moreover, the Notice released as an accompaniment to the Consultative Document specifies a wide range of rules on asset management business for the purpose of rigorous risk control. It talks about consummating the investor suitability system and distributor selection mechanism, encouraging the development of actively managed products, banning the access of channels to multiple specified clients, matching leverage design with risk-return profile of split asset management schemes, prohibiting maturity mismatch among multiple products, cash pool and related party transactions, among other improper dealings, and requiring asset management institutions to set up a Compliance and Risk Control unit.

The aforesaid new policies concerning asset management bring direct dividends to asset management business of institutions under the jurisdiction of the CSRC. Meanwhile, innovation and development of other fields in the securities sector bring indirect dividends to asset management business. Among them, the Shanghai-Hong Kong Stock Connect program and asset securitization are the most influential. In accordance with the *Notice on Matters Concerning Participation of Securities Brokers in the Shanghai-Hong Kong Stock Connect Pilot Program* released by the CSRC, asset management business of securities brokers may be involved in trading under the Shanghai-Hong Kong Stock Connect, and an asset management scheme can be launched for the purpose of investment in Hong Kong-listed shares only or in both mainland-listed and Hong Kong-listed shares. This can help broaden the investment scope and drive upgrade of asset management business of securities brokers. The first Shanghai-Hong Kong Stock Connect fund, China Southern Asset Management Hang Seng Index ETF, is in the pipeline. The launch of Shanghai-Hong Kong Stock Connect funds will lower the threshold for investors to take part in the Shanghai-Hong Kong Stock Connect program. On Nov. 19, 2014, the CSRC unveiled *Rules on Asset Securitization of Subsidiaries of Securities Brokers and Fund Management Firms*, and a handbook attached thereto. After that, prior approval requirement is abolished. Instead, the AMAC will manage filing afterwards and a negative list of underlying assets. The change of asset-backed securities from a non-standard asset to a standard asset is an established fact. Securities brokers are experienced in running asset-backed securities—specified asset management schemes and corporate asset securitization. Against the backdrop of activation of resources in stock, the enormous assets accumulated in the financial system and companies will buoy up asset securitization as a great draw standing out from the asset management business of securities brokers.

The boom seen in the collective wealth management market of securities brokers is likely to extend into 2015, and the market turnover might exceed the 8 trillion yuan mark in Q1. The performance of the A-shares market as a whole decides the yield of collective wealth management products of securities brokers. Following margin trading and short selling and stock-pledged loans, asset management of securities brokers may become another business to experience a burst of trading.

(iii) **Trust Product Market**

Given the challenge posed by economic slowdown and heated competition, the consistent high-speed growth of the trust sector since 2008 came to the end and a phase of change-driven growth began in 2014.

According to data released by China Trustee Association, as of the end of 2014, the industry-wide trust assets under management were worth 13.98 trillion yuan (205.588 billion yuan per trust company), an increase of 10.91 trillion yuan, or 28.14 percent, year on year, but the growth decelerated obviously; as of the end of 2014, the trust sector delivered total operating revenue of 95.495 billion yuan (1.404 billion yuan per trust company), a growth of 83.26 billion yuan, or 14.69 percent, year on year, but the growth slowed down by 15.73 percentage points compared with the 30.42 percent year-on-year growth registered at the end of 2013.

In contrary to the slowdown of operating revenue growth of trust companies, the trust proceeds brought by the trust sector to beneficiaries were on the increase in 2014. According to statistics provided by the CBRC, in 2014, all trust programs that finished clearing delivered total proceeds to the tune of 450.6 billion yuan for beneficiaries, an increase of 156.2 billion yuan, or 53.06 percent, compared with 294.4 billion yuan recorded in 2013. This dwarfs the growth of trustees' own profit.

In terms of risk control, a primary mission of the trust sector in 2014 was to control trust risk transmission strictly and maintain sound growth of the trust sector. From the payment crisis of Credit Equals Gold No. 1 at the year beginning, to the promulgation of *Administrative Measures for Trust Security Fund*, the trust sector stuck to the theme of Risk throughout the year of 2014.

On Apr. 8, 2014, the General Office of the CBRC unveiled *Guiding Opinions on Risk Control over Trust Companies* (*CBRC* [2014] *No.99*). In summary, the Guiding Opinions address the topic of supervision from three aspects, due diligence, clarification and change.

1. **Due Diligence**

(1) Project manager exercises duediligence. Document No. 99 states explicitly that all trust programs, especially high-risk ones, must be tracked by a designated person and any duty must be assigned to a known person. (2) Shareholders exercise duediligence. Shareholders of trust companies shall promise or agree in the Articles of Association, to provide necessary liquidity support in case of liquidity risk. Where the capital of a trustee is undermined by

operating loss, the full amount shall be reduced from net capital, and the business shall be downsized accordingly, or shareholders may replenish the capital without delay. (3) Trustees exercise duediligence. Trustees are expected to perform all-around, whole-process, and dynamic management in terms of product design, due diligence, risk control, product marketing, ongoing management, information disclosure and risk mitigations. Constant follow-up and risk monitoring are especially important during post-investment management of projects. Stress test must be performed in a regular manner on some key sectors exposed to risks, like the housing sector. Risk mitigations must be market-based. (4) Salesmen exercise duediligence. Compliance with the qualified investor standards and private placement standards is required. The investor population shall be segmented accurately. The rule of selling the right products to the right clients must be adhered to. Sales must be done in a responsible manner. (5) The regulator exercises duediligence. Strict admittance control and approval requirement must be imposed on the business activities of trustees. A reporting system applies to all products within the specified business scope. Any product coming into the market must be reported to the regulator on a case-by-case basis ten days in advance according to the specified procedures and requirements.

2. Clarification

(1) Clarify the cash pool in trust. "Trustees are banned from dealing in non-standard cash pool and other activities bearing the hallmarks of shadow banking". In the meantime, detailed explanations on non-standard cash pool activities already started, along with a correction plan, must be prepared and submitted to the regulator no later than Jun. 30, 2014. (2) Clarify the rights and obligations, and remunerations, incentive and punishment mechanism of all functions and roles, clarify the duties and power of Annual General Meeting, Board of Directors, Board of Supervisors and the management of trustees, to assure proper performance of duties, and develop a well-thought-out restoration and response mechanism. (3) Clarify the regulatory mechanism. Stake out the boundary of regulatory responsibilities, and keep a close eye on risk exposures in financing platforms, the housing market, the mining industry, all industries with overcapacity and shadow banking.

3. Change

A very important topic in Document No. 99 is where the trust sector is heading for. The asset management products of funds have been accepted and recognized by the market gradually since 2013. Thus, trust products are not as competitive as before. In Document No. 99, the CBRC encourages trustees to differentiate themselves from others, and proposes equity investment, M&A, fee-bearing services, trust asset-backed securities, family wealth management and charitable trusts in the real sense.

In August, 2014, the CBRC introduced the strictest ever trust rating standards, *Guidelines for the Regulatory Rating and Classification of Trust Companies (Consultative Document)*, in view of the explosion of trust assets and the rising risks in trust products. Pursuant to the Guidelines, rating elements include risk management, asset management and compliance. Risk management is further divided into four parts, corporate governance, internal control, trust business risk management and net capital. Asset management is comprised of five parts, comprehensive management capabilities, trust business management capabilities and profitability, R&D and innovative capabilities, marketing capabilities, and reputation. Compliance is broken down into seven parts, compliance system, compliance of regular business, compliance of trust business, compliance of information disclosure, compliance of related party transactions, evaluation of operating performance, and restrictive clauses.

At the end of 2014, the regulator put forward eight duties of the trust sector in its annual review delivered on 2014 Annual Conference of the trust sector, with a view to enhance governance and boost robust growth and change. First, fiduciary duties are defined and the boundary of buyer's and seller's duties is drawn up. Next, the CBRC is going to draft guidelines for the performance of fiduciary duties, to urge trustees to perform their duties better and realize effective accountability. Second, broking duties are defined. Broking duties are internal duties that must be made clear after trustees accept a commission and set up a trust, and can be billed as a Tripartite system designed to realize checks and balances. The management of every trust program must be a Tripartite team, made up of project sponsor, project manager and project reporter. The due diligence, project initiation and product design duties of project sponsor, the first person who discovers or proposes a trust, must be clarified. Project manager is responsible for product sales organization, cash sweep, transfer, payment and use of cash and whole-process management. Project reporter is supposed to follow up throughout the project life cycle and report reliable facts based on the preset information disclosure rules. Third, claim duties are clarified. A unitary property right system is in force currently in China. As provided for in the *Trust Law*, a fiduciary property is merely something put in trust by the principal with the trustee, thus confusing fiduciary properties. Hence, a fiduciary property registration system is recommended to resolve the problem of inadequate transfer of fiduciary properties. Fourth, accounting duties are defined. Trustees are expected to conduct separate accounting and management and notify all trust stakeholders. Accounting records of fiduciary properties and proceeds derived therefrom preserved by trustees must be original and reliable. Fifth, institutional duties are defined. A quantitative gauge of institutional duties is institutional rating. Trustees are rated based on a set of performance indicators. For this purpose, the CBRC plans to introduce an institutional rating framework. Rating will be done on an annual basis, and the rating result will be tied up to the business scope and to the dismissal or retention of directors and senior management. The rating covers competency indicator, compliance indicator, risk indicator and social responsibility indicator. Sixth, shareholder duties are defined. Shareholder duties are broken down into four tasks, i. e. defending independence of the company, assuring good conduct of the Board of Directors and Board of Supervisors, undertaking risk and loss, and drawing up restoration and response plans. Seventh, duties of the industry are defined. A trust security fund shall be set up to give mutual help, make investment, provide paid service and impose punishment. A trust security mechanism represents a novel institutional arrangement and an effective attempt at a market-based safeguarding mechanism. Eighth, regulatory duties are defined, to defuse potential risks. Risk prevention shall start with access control. Then, it is important to identify, measure and mitigate risks.

In 2015, the trust market of China is expected to expand in size further but see a slump in growth speed. Meanwhile, risk buildup and exposure in trust assets will continue unabated. There is a good chance that the disposal of projects at risk will become a focal topic of the industry. We don't rule out the possibility of some trustees heading for financial trouble because of drained cash. Risk prevention will still be a regulatory job of first priority in 2015.

VII. Financial Derivatives Market Development Policy[①]

(i) List of New Policies or Policy Adjustments in 2014

On Jan. 28, 2014, the PBC issued the *Notice on the Establishment of Central Clearing Mechanism for OTC Derivatives and the Launch of Central Clearing for RMB Interest Rate Swaps*, (*PBC* [2014] *No.* 29).

On Jan. 28, 2014, the Self-Disciplinary Mechanism for the Pricing of Market-Oriented Interest Rates unveiled *Implementation Measures for Qualification and Prudence Assessment of Financial Institutions* (Self-Disciplinary Mechanism [2014] No. 1).

On Mar. 18, 2014, CFETS released the *Announcement on the Launch of Direct Trading Between the RMB and the New Zealand Dollar (NZD)* (CFETS [2014] No. 20).

On Jun. 23, 2014, SAFE released the *Notice on Issuing Regulations on Banks' RMB and Foreign Exchange Derivatives Client Services* (SAFE [2014] No. 34).

On Oct. 27, 2014, CFETS released the *Notice on the Launch of Standard Interest Rate Derivatives*.

---

① Written by Chu Youyang.

On Oct. 30, 2014, CFETS released the *Notice on Issuing Bond Trading Rules for CFETS Market Makers and Qualified Non-financial Institutional Investors* (CFETS [2014] No. 255).

On Oct. 31, 2014, CFETS released the *Notice on Issuing CFETS Standard Interest Rate Derivatives Trading Rules* (*CFETS* [2014] *No.* 260).

On Dec. 26, 2014, CFETS released the *Notice on Issuing CFETS Administrative Measures for Data Interface Services for the Local Currency Market* (*CFETS* [2014] *No.* 328).

(ii) Highlights of Financial Derivatives Market Development Policy in 2014

1. Boost and Govern Development of the Foreign Exchange Derivatives Market

On Jun. 23, 2014, SAFE unveiled *Regulations on Banks' RMB and Foreign Exchange Derivatives Client Services* (the Regulations) and released the *Notice on Issuing Regulations on Banks' RMB and Foreign Exchange Derivatives Client Services* (*SAFE* [2014] *No.* 34), with a view to govern the foreign exchange derivatives market, improve the transparency and accessibility of policies and better satisfy market players' needs for exchange rate risk management. For the purpose of the Notice, RMB and Foreign Exchange Derivatives (derivatives in short hereinafter) include RMB and foreign exchange forwards, swaps and options. The Regulations govern banks' OTC RMB and foreign exchange derivatives trading in the following respects and have far-reaching influence on sound development of China's bank OTC market. The Regulations came into effect as of Aug. 1, 2014.

First, basic rules on banks' trading of RMB and foreign exchange derivatives are specified. Banks shall only conduct derivatives trading for clients with actual needs. By actual needs, it means that clients have a real background to justify derivatives trading as a hedge against foreign exchange risk exposure, and spot sale or settlement of foreign exchange assets or liabilities held as underlying and estimated future foreign exchange receipts or expenses in compliance with the regulations on foreign exchange is supported. Before closing a derivatives deal with a client, banks are expected to follow the rules of Know Your Client, Know Your Business and Due Diligence, confirm that the client actually needs derivatives trading and receive from the client a Statement, Letter of Acknowledgement, or any other written document that may prove the presence of actual needs.

Second, SAFE is empowered to supervise banks' conduct of derivatives client services. Depending on balance of payments and dynamics of the foreign exchange market, SAFE may adopt contingency measures as necessary against banks' conduct of derivatives trading, to make sure sound running of the foreign exchange market. SAFE requires centralized filing by the HO of banks involved in derivatives client services. Wherein a national commercial bank or policy bank plans to start derivatives business, it may file an application with SAFE and then SAFE shall complete filing. Other banks shall file an application with local SAFE branch, which will then complete filing and make a copy of the result for SAFE. SAFE or its branches (Foreign Exchange Department) shall complete filing within 20 working days from the day a complete set of application documents as required are received. Banks are expected to submit reports and documents relating to derivatives required by SAFE. Rules on statistical reporting shall be specified otherwise. SAFE may check banks' documents and reports, risk management system, internal control system and business processing system relating to derivatives either regularly or irregularly for compliance with the rules of Know Your Client, Know Your Business and Due Diligence, and give risk hints or warnings to those banks found to have vulnerabilities in management. SAFE shall organize banks and other foreign exchange market players to establish a self-disciplinary mechanism, refine code of conduct concerning derivatives client management, risk control and etc., and uphold a foreign exchange market that always allows competition on equal footing.

Third, eligibility criteria for banks providing derivatives client services are specified. A bank is considered eligible for derivatives client services, where it is licensed to deal in spot foreign exchange settlement or sale, has a robust derivatives trading risk management system and internal control system, as well as an appropriate risk identification, measurement, management and trading system, is equipped with all professionals needed to deal in derivatives and satisfies the eligibility criteria for financial derivatives trading defined by the CBRC.

Fourth, the variety of derivatives banks that are allowed to trade on behalf of clients and operational requirements are detailed. First, banks are allowed to deal in four types of derivatives, that is, forwards, options, foreign exchange swaps and currency swaps. Second, banks and their clients may negotiate and reach agreement on the currency, maturity and price, among other elements of derivatives trading, based on actual needs and in compliance with common business practice. Banks may lawfully discontinue any ongoing deal with any client who is found to make up a background of actual needs for derivatives trading or be involved in repeated hedging, and restrict this kind of clients' access to derivatives trading in the future by means of credit rating or other internal controls. Third, where netting is applied to options transactions, the indicative price used to determine the net amount must be a real and effective exchange rate available in the domestic market. Fourth, derivatives clients of banks are limited to domestic institutions, and individually-owned businesses are considered equivalent to domestic institutions. In the event of foreign exchange risk exposure arising from outbound investments made by domestic individuals, as long as the regulations on foreign exchange are complied with, banks may provide derivatives services thereto based on actual needs. Fifth, banks should place a high premium on derivatives client management, and perform continued and thorough client suitability evaluation and risk disclosure on the basis of well-thought-out derivatives classification and client classification. Sixth, banks should confirm that clients are effectively authorized internally and have received all prior permissions needed from the competent authority to trade derivatives and have sufficient risk tolerance. Seventh, banks should properly preserve all documents generated from derivatives client services for a minimum of five years and make available such documents on demand. Eighth, banks dealing in derivatives shall observe the rules on synthetic positions in settlement and sale of foreign exchange and measure and manage derivatives positions in an accurate and proper manner. Where branches trade derivatives on behalf of clients, the HO shall square off open positions, manage exposures and control risks in a centralized manner.

2. Establish a Central Clearing Mechanism for OTC Derivatives and Launch Central Clearing for RMB Interest Rate Swaps

On Jan. 28, 2014, the PBC issued the *Notice on the Establishment of Central Clearing Mechanism for OTC Derivatives and the Launch of Central Clearing for RMB Interest Rate Swaps*, with a view to boost sound development of China's OTC derivatives market and create a central clearing mechanism for OTC derivatives. By central clearing for RMB interest rate swaps mentioned in the Notice, it means that a member submits a RMB interest rate swap transaction that it has concluded to Shanghai Clearing House (SCH) for central clearing. SCH, as a Central Counterparty (CCP), will then inherit all rights and obligations of both parties, compute net interest of each party on the same clearing day by applyingthemultilateral netting approach, and set up a risk control mechanism accordingly, to assure the performance of contracts and completion of interest netting. The Notice has laid down the following rules.

First, central clearing is mandatory for all OTC derivative contracts, including RMB interest rate swaps, concluded among participants in the interbank bond market across the country. SCH is the central clearing service provider. The Notice requires RMB interest rate swaps to be confirmed via CFETS, SCH to provide members with central clearing service for RMB interest rate swaps, and central clearing members for RMB interest rate swaps to sign a RMB Interest Rate Swap Central Clearing Agreement with SCH. SCH shall process central clearing for RMB interest rate swaps, subject to the RMB Interest Rate Swap Central Clearing Agreement inked with members. Moreover, starting from Jul. 1, 2014, all RMB interest rate swaps newly concluded between financial institutions, maturing in or within five years and benchmarked against FR007, Shibor_ON and Shibor_3M rates, shall be submitted to SCH for central clearing, provided that the parties and contract elements comply with the rules of SCH.

Where central clearing is impossible, explanations must be given to the PBC.

Second, SCH is expected to put in place a central clearing system as required in the Notice. The Notice demands SCH to formulate the criteria for central clearing member and create a member credit risk monitoring and evaluation system; set up margin, clearing fund and risk provision, among other risk management systems, measure the mark-to-market value and risk exposure of open positions of members properly and conduct regression test and stress test regularly; establish a central clearing member default treatment mechanism, assure presence of bank credit and other liquidity supports, and guarantee safe and reliable clearing. SCH is supposed to segregate margins and clearing funds received from RMB interest rate swap central clearing members from its own assets and forbid embezzlement in any way or by any means. Margins and clearing funds put in SCH by members for central clearing purpose are properties of members, and are supposed to be used for claims, debts and defaults arising from central clearing exclusively. Members are required to keep an amount of money on their capital accounts that is enough for capital delivery and margin delivery anytime. The capital or margin in transit can only be used for settlement of a given deal. Any deal settled is irrevocable.

Third, the function and power of the PBC in central clearing are defined. As provided for in the Notice, the PBC shall perform continued and effective supervision and administration over SCH according to the qualified CCP standards set out in the *Principles for Financial Market Infrastructures*. Members shall calculate risk-weighted assets as per the qualified CCP standards for RMB interest rate swaps subject to central clearing by SCH, in accordance with relevant regulatory requirements. SCH shall make available regular updates on central clearing of RMB interest rate swaps conducted by institutions under its jurisdiction to the PBC Shanghai head office, all branches, business administration departments, and central sub-branches in the capital city, provincial capital cities, and sub-provincial cities. All branches and divisions of the PBC shall strengthen daily management of institutions involved in central clearing of RMB interest rate swaps under their jurisdiction. The PBC shall identify other OTC derivatives categories to be included in central clearing and applicable central clearing types as appropriate, based on risk exposure, trade activity, pricing mechanism, and degree of standardization of OTC derivatives and preparedness of designated central clearing agencies.

Fourth, duties of CFETS and SCH in central clearing are specified. CFETS and SCH shall reinforce cooperation and coordination, do well in daily monitoring of RMB interest rate swap trading and clearing, and submit a written report on central clearing of RMB interest rate swaps in the previous month to the PBC within the first ten working days of each month, making a copy for NAFMII. Any exception shall be ironed out and reported in a timely manner. CFETS and

SCH shall detail trading and clearing business rules as per the Notice and put these rules into force once the PBC gives sanction.

3. Refine and Broaden the Self-disciplinary Mechanism for Market Interest Rates

On Jan. 28, 2014, following proper filing with the PBC, *Implementation Measures for Qualification and Prudence Assessment of Financial Institutions* (Self-Disciplinary Mechanism [2014] No. 1) were prepared and promulgated to drive the reform of interest rate liberalization in an well-organized manner, pick out members of the Self-Disciplinary Mechanismfor the Pricing of Market-Oriented Interest Rates (referred to as the Self-Disciplinary Mechanism hereinafter) and vest more market-based pricing power in members. This can prompt financial institutions to exercise stricter financial constraints, sharpen their discretionary pricing capability and thus optimize the interest rate formation mechanism decided by supply and demand. The Self-Disciplinary Mechanism is a self-disciplinary and coordination mechanism for market-based pricing comprised of financial institutions. Subject to compliance with the state regulations on interest rates, the Self-Disciplinary Mechanism manages interest rates of the money market or the credit market, or other financial segments decided by financial institutions at their discretion, keep market competition in order and boost healthy development of the market. Members include general members and core members. General members are financial institutions that are assessed for qualification and prudence and found to satisfy the financial constraints and the macro-prudential policy framework and run soundly. Core members are financial institutions that stand out among general members and are recognized through comprehensive competency assessment as highly important to the system, extensively influential in the market and fully capable of discretionary pricing.

The Self-Disciplinary Mechanism, as an infrastructure of interest rate liberalization, was broadened for the first time in July, 2014. 93 banks have become general members voluntarily, following qualification and prudence assessment by the Self-Disciplinary Mechanism in accordance with *Implementation Measures for Qualification and Prudence Assessment of Financial Institutions*, a CFETS Notice shows. These 93 banks are comprised of joint-stock banks, like China Minsheng Bank, Ping An Bank, China Everbright Bank, and Huaxia Bank, and city commercial banks such as Bank of Beijing, Bank of Nanjing, and Bank of Chongqing. Some rural commercial banks, rural cooperative banks, credit cooperatives, and foreign banks are also on the lengthened list. These 93 banks are general members, that is, financial institutions that are assessed for qualification and prudence and found to satisfy the financial constraints and the macro-prudential policy framework and run soundly. Core members are general members recognized as highly important to the system, extensively influential in the market and fully capable of discretionary pricing. There are ten core members for the time being, namely, ICBC, ABC, BOC, CCB, Bank of Communications, CDB, China CITIC Bank, China Merchants Bank, Industrial Bank and SPD Bank.

As introduced in the said Notice, members may apply for participating in Shibor and LPR off-floor quotation, issuance of interbank certificate of deposit, and other financial products contributing to benchmark interest rates, are entitled to take part in other activities as appropriate, and are required to abide by all rules and provisions formulated by, carry out the resolutions made by and finish the tasks assigned by the Self-Disciplinary Mechanism.

To perfect the Self-Disciplinary Mechanism is one of the most pressing targets leading to interest rate liberalization, which will be carried out in three steps. The target of step 1 is to optimize the Self-Disciplinary Mechanism, and enhance the discretionary pricing capability of financial institutions; and do well in LPR quotation to provide reference for the pricing of credit products. The target of step 2 is to develop a full-fledged market-based interest rate system and refine the central bank interest rate modulation framework and interest rate transmission mechanism. The target of step 3 is to fully liberalize interest rates and perfect the market-based interest rate macro control mechanism.

4. Develop Standard Interest Rate Derivatives Trading Rules and Start Trading

On Oct. 27, 2014, CFETS released the *Notice on the Launch of Standard Interest Rate Derivatives*, which disclosed CFETS's decision to launch standard interest rate derivatives on Nov. 3, 2014, and the *Glossary of Standard Interest Rate Derivatives* was unveiled on the same day. On Oct. 31, CFETS released *CFETS Standard Interest Rate Derivatives Trading Rules* (*CFETS* [2014] *No.* 260). Then, CFETS officially launched standard interest rate derivatives on Nov. 3, to meet members' demand. Standard interest rate derivatives are interest rate derivatives, such as interest rate swaps and forward interest rate agreements, the elements of which, like maturity date and term, are standardized. The first four derivatives launched this time are 1-month standard overnight index swaps, 3-month standard Shibor1W interest rate swaps, 3-month standard seven-day repo interest rate swaps, and 3-month standard Shibor3M forward interest rate agreements. The trading system of standard interest rate derivatives includes the following elements:

(1) Trade party: all members of the interbank interest rate derivatives market may trade standard interest rate derivatives.

(2) Trade mode: standard interest rate derivatives are traded via the X-Swap system in the form of bilateral credit authorization and anonymous click. At present, credit line is shared with interest rate swaps on the X-Swap system.

(3) Transaction confirmation: after a deal is sealed, both parties shall confirm it on the post-trade service platform of CFETS. The process of transaction confirmation is the same as that of interest rate swaps. Any transaction closed within four working days prior to the last trading day must be confirmed no later than 12: 00 O'clock at the noon of the last trading day.

(4) Clearing and delivery: members may choose bilateral clearing or clearing with CCP. On the delivery date of a contract, both parties complete cash delivery according to the delivery order generated by the post-trade service platform of CFETS.

(5) Holidays: CFETS will release an announcement on changes to maturity date and value date of relevant contracts according to the calendar released by the State Council. Members may adjust transaction data in their internal system accordingly and confirmation of closed deals is unnecessary.

Standard interest rate derivatives differ from the existing interbank Interest Rate Swaps (IRS) mainly in fixed maturity and definite delivery date. Under the rollover maturity mechanism of IRS, existing net positions of hedgers can be squared off by means of reverse operations. If the positions are not closed on the same day, it will be impossible to eliminate existing risk exposure completely through reverse operations. Since standardized swap contracts mature on the same day, no risk exposure is left after the positions are offset. In this way, investors may manage market risk by applying trade strategies flexibly, such as repo yielding + swap and swap portfolio.

The standardized product mix launched this time covers major benchmarks of existing interest rate swaps, i. e., FR007, Shibor_0/N and Shibor_3M. The maturity ladder doesn't match up exactly, but a desired maturity can be achieved by working out a combination of contracts with each derivative maturing in a different month. This can attract more attention to and heighten the trading activity of existing swaps and forwards.

At the beginning, trade of standard interest rate derivatives might be slack and an outflow of capital from existing products might even occur, but in the long run, a positive effect will be produced.

5. Optimize the Multi-level Bond Market and Expand the Variety of Products Traded

To act on the PBC's call for optimizing the multi-level bond market and heighten liquidity of the interbank bond market, on Oct. 30, 2014, CFETS released *Bond Trading Rules for CFETS Market Makers and Qualified Non-financial Institutional Investors*, giving permission for qualified non-financial institutional investors to access quotation, trade, and quotations and information inquiry functions of the interbank bond market.

Authorized by the PBC, direct trading between the RMB and the NZD in the interbank foreign exchange market is enabled from Mar. 19, 2014, with a view to boost bilateral trade and investment between China and New Zealand, facilitate the use of RMB and NZD in bilateral trade and investment settlement, and lower currency conversion cost for economic entities.

(iii) Policy Outlook

Policy developments in 2015 will possibly be focused on these aspects:

As OTC RMB derivatives continue to thrive, floor-traded standard RMB interest rate derivatives, such as 10-year treasury bond futures, 30-year treasury bond futures and 1-year treasury bond futures, might be launched one after another. These products can make up the situation with only 5-year treasury bond futures currently, contribute to a complete treasury bonds yield curve and provide more financial hedging instruments to institutional investors.

Along with the progress in interest rate liberalization, more and more entities will start using RMB interest rate derivatives as a hedge, the investor base of the interbank market will be expanded further, and relevant policies will come out.

As the Chinese cabinet quickens the tempo of market-oriented reform and deepens streamlining of administration and delegation of power, the role of the government in the financial sector will shift from regulation to macro control gradually. The transition from direct government policy-making to market-driven spontaneous rule development will take place. Future policy-making will possibly put more weight on promoting self-discipline, and developing and perfecting a market-based pricing mechanism and competitive mechanism for interest rates.

VIII. Commodity Futures Market Development Policy[①]

(i) Highlights of Commodity Futures Market Policy in 2014

Table 5 – 5　　　　　　　Highlights of Commodity Futures Market Policy

Date	Policy	Issued by
Jan. 2	*Notification on Adjustment to the Rate of Offsite Discount for Natural Rubber of Certified Delivery Warehouses in Yunnan* (SQBF [2014] No. 1)	Shanghai Futures Exchange
Feb. 19	*Notice on Publishing and Implementing "Polypropylene Futures Contract of Dalian Commodity Exchange" and Amendments to Related Detailed Rules for Implementation* (DCE [2014] No. 33)	Dalian Commodity Exchange
Feb. 26	*Notice on Adding Designated Futures Margin Depository Banks* (DCE [2014] No. 40)	Dalian Commodity Exchange

---

① Written by Gan Zhengzai.

Continued

Date	Policy	Issued by
Mar. 10	*Notice on Adjusting Designated LLDPE and PVC Delivery Warehouses* (DCE [2014] No. 47)	Dalian Commodity Exchange
Mar. 17	*Announcement on the Issuance of Hot-rolled Coil Contract Specifications and Related Rules of Shanghai Futures Exchange* (SHFE [2014] No. 2)	Shanghai Futures Exchange
Mar. 17	*Notification on Supplemental Provisions on Hot-rolled Coil Products for Futures Delivery* (SHFE [2014] No. 26)	Shanghai Futures Exchange
Mar. 17	*Notification on Premium and Discount and Storage Fee for Hot-Rolled Coil Futures* (SHFE [2014] No. 27)	Shanghai Futures Exchange
Mar. 17	*Announcement on the Issuance of Steel Deliverable Registration Rules of Shanghai Futures Exchange* (Revised) ([2014] No. 3)	Shanghai Futures Exchange
Mar. 20	*Notification on Adjusting Transaction Fee Standards of Some Products* (SHFE [2014] NO. 32)	Shanghai Futures Exchange
Apr. 2	*Notice on Announcing the Ceiling Price of Designated Delivery Warehouse in/out Charges for the Bulk Grain of No. 1 Soybeans* (DCE [2014] No. 65)	Dalian Commodity Exchange
Apr. 10	*Notification on Adjusting Transaction Fee Standards of Some Products* (DCE [2014] No. 71)	Dalian Commodity Exchange
Apr. 18	*Notice on Announcing and Implementing Dalian Commodity Exchange Detailed Rules for Implementation of Bonded Delivery* (for Trial Implementation) (DCE [2014] No. 81)	Dalian Commodity Exchange
Apr. 18	*Notice on Piloting Futures Bonded Delivery Business* (DCE [2014] No. 82)	Dalian Commodity Exchange
Apr. 18	*Notice on Adjusting Designated Delivery Warehouses of No. 2 Soybeans* (DCE [2014] No. 84)	Dalian Commodity Exchange
May. 4	*Notice on Getting Well Prepared for White Sugar Options* (ZCE [2014] No. 90)	Zhengzhou Commodity Exchange
May. 9	*Several Opinions on Further Promoting Sound Development of the Capital Market* (State Council [2014] No. 17)	State Council
Jun. 13	*Notice on Revising Relevant Rules in Measures for Management of Members* (DCE [2014] No. 130)	Dalian Commodity Exchange
Jun. 13	*Notice on Revising Deliverable Quality Standards of Linear Low Density Polyethylene* (DCE [2014] No. 131)	Dalian Commodity Exchange
Jun. 13	*Notice on Revising Methanol Futures Contract and Trading Rules for Some Products* (ZCE [2014] No. 115)	Zhengzhou Commodity Exchange

Continued

Date	Policy	Issued by
Jun. 20	*Notice on Releasing Amendment to Rules for Futures Trading Risk Management of Zhengzhou Commodity Exchange* (ZCE [2014] No. 116)	Zhengzhou Commodity Exchange
Jun. 26	*Notice on Publishing and Implementing Relevant Contracts and Detailed Rules for Implementation of Night Trading* (DCE [2014] No. 142)	Dalian Commodity Exchange
Jul. 4	*Notice on Releasing Late Indica Rice Futures Contract and Trading Rules of Zhengzhou Commodity Exchange* (ZCE [2014] No. 135)	Zhengzhou Commodity Exchange
Jul. 11	*Notice on Adjusting Delivery Process and Related Contract Rules* (DCE [2014] No. 153)	Dalian Commodity Exchange
Jul. 15	*Notice on Adding Designated Futures Margin Depository Banks* (DCE [2014] No. 154)	Dalian Commodity Exchange
Jul. 30	*Notice on Implementing Pilots in Factory Warehouse Receipts Swap within Soybean Meal Groups* (DCE [2014] No. 171)	Dalian Commodity Exchange
Aug. 1	*Notice on Releasing Ferroalloy Futures Contract and Trading Rules of Zhengzhou Commodity Exchange* (ZCE [2014] No. 155)	Zhengzhou Commodity Exchange
Aug. 19	*Notification on Reducing the Transaction Fees for Hot-rolled Coil* (SHFE [2014] No. 91)	Shanghai Futures Exchange
Aug. 20	*Notice on Adding the Factory Warehouse Delivery System for the Product of Blockboard* (DCE [2014] No. 190)	Dalian Commodity Exchange
Aug. 22	*Notice on Releasing Chinese Securities and Futures Markets OTC Derivatives Master Agreement (2014 Edition) and Chinese Securities and Futures Markets OTC Equity Derivatives Trading Derivatives Definition File (2014 Edition)* (CFA [2014] No. 68)	China Futures Association
Aug. 26	*Notice on Releasing Guidelines for the Pilot Program of Futures Firms Setting Up Subsidiaries Primarily Engaged in Risk Management Services (Revised) and Associated Documents* (CFA [2014] No. 73)	China Futures Association
Aug. 27	*Notice on Releasing Revised Editions of Guidelines for Information Technology Management of Futures Firms and Examination Rules* (CFA [2014] No. 75)	China Futures Association
Sep. 10	*Notice on Amending the Risk Management Measures and Other Business Rules* (DCE [2014] No. 211)	Dalian Commodity Exchange
Sep. 16	*Opinions on Promoting Innovation and Development of Futures Brokers*	CSRC
Sep. 26	*Notification on Adjusting the Handling Fee for Delivery of Silver Futures* (SHFE [2014] No. 103)	Shanghai Futures Exchange
Sep. 26	*Notification on Adjusting the Fee Schedule for Certified Depositories for Silver Futures* (SHFE [2014] No. 104)	Shanghai Futures Exchange
Sep. 26	*Notification on Adjusting the Fee Schedule for Certified Delivery Warehouses for Natural Rubber Futures* (SHFE [2014] No. 105)	Shanghai Futures Exchange

Continued

Date	Policy	Issued by
Sep. 29	*Notification on Adjusting the Regional Premium and Discount Rate for Delivery of Lead Futures in Guangdong Province* (SHFE〔2014〕No. 106)	Shanghai Futures Exchange
Oct. 20	*Notice on Adjusting the Storage Capacity of Certified Delivery Warehouses for Lead Futures in Guangdong Province* (SHFE〔2014〕No. 117)	Shanghai Futures Exchange
Oct. 22	*Notice on Adjusting the Rules for the Quality Dispute Re-inspection Institutions for Some Products* (DCE〔2014〕No. 243)	Dalian Commodity Exchange
Oct. 22	*Notice on Revising the Process of Repaying the Delivery Forecast Deposits for No. 2 Soybeans* (DCE〔2014〕No. 245)	Dalian Commodity Exchange
Oct. 29	*Measures for the Supervision of Futures Firms* (Order No. 110)	CSRC
Nov. 4	*Notice on Carrying out Pilot for Intra-group Warehouse Receipts Swap for Soybean and Palm Oil* (DCE〔2014〕No. 255)	Dalian Commodity Exchange
Nov. 21	*Notice on Releasing Amendments to Night Shift Trading Rules and Detailed Implementation Rules* (ZCE〔2014〕No. 229)	Zhengzhou Commodity Exchange
Nov. 24	*Notification on Reducing the Transaction Fees for Copper Contracts* (SHFE〔2014〕No. 135)	Shanghai Futures Exchange
Dec. 3	*Notice on Amendments to Cotton Futures Trading Rules* (ZCE〔2014〕No. 229)	Zhengzhou Commodity Exchange
Dec. 4	*Notice on Amendments to Strong Gluten Wheat and Common Wheat Futures Trading Rules* (ZCE〔2014〕No. 240)	Zhengzhou Commodity Exchange
Dec. 4	*Notice on Amendments to Early Indica Rice and Japonica Rice Futures Trading Rules* (ZCE〔2014〕No. 241)	Zhengzhou Commodity Exchange
Dec. 4	*Notice on Adjusting Standard Storage Charges for High-quality Strong Gluten Wheat and Early Rice* (〔2014〕No. 40)	Zhengzhou Commodity Exchange
Dec. 4	*Notice Issuing Rules for the Management of Asset Management Business of Futures Companies (for Trial Implementation)* (CFA〔2014〕No. 100)	China Futures Association
Dec. 5	*Notice on Amendments to Some Contracts* (ZCE〔2014〕No. 243)	Zhengzhou Commodity Exchange
Dec. 8	*Notice on Promulgating and Implementing Corn Starch Futures Contract of Dalian Commodity Exchange and Amendments to Detailed Rules for Implementation* (DCE〔2014〕No. 276)	Dalian Commodity Exchange
Dec. 10	*Notice on Amendments to Delivery Rules* (ZCE〔2014〕No. 254)	Zhengzhou Commodity Exchange
Dec. 11	*Notice on Strengthening Self-discipline of Futures Brokers and Professionals* (CFA〔2014〕No. 102)	China Futures Association

Continued

Date	Policy	Issued by
Dec. 15	*Notice on Releasing Application Documentation Specifications for Asset Management Business of Futures Companies* (CFA [2014] No. 107)	China Futures Association
Dec. 16	*Operational Guidelines for Public Offering of Securities Investment Funds No. 1— Guidelines for Commodity Futures Trading Open-Ended Funds* (CSRC [2014] No. 51)	CSRC
Dec. 18	*Notice on Adjusting Load-in and Load-out Fee Rates of Certified Delivery Warehouses of Early Indica Rice* ([2014] No. 46)	Zhengzhou Commodity Exchange
Dec. 22	*Announcement on Distribution of Amendments to Steel Rebar and Natural Rubber Contract Specifications* (SHFE [2014] No. 8)	Shanghai Futures Exchange
Dec. 22	*Notice on the Launch of Continuous Trading Program for Steel Rebar, Hot-rolled Coil, Natural Rubber and Bitumen Futures* (SHFE [2014] No. 173)	Shanghai Futures Exchange
Dec. 24	*Notice on Adjusting Trade Margin Requirements for Wire Rod and Fuel Oil Futures* (SHFE [2014] No. 182)	Shanghai Futures Exchange
Dec. 26	*Futures Trading Data Exchange Protocol* (CSRC [2014]) No. 55)	CSRC

(ii) Content and Review of Commodity Futures Market Policy in 2014

1. Enforcement and Fine-tunings of Regulatory Policies for Futures Trading

The CSRC, China Futures Association (CFA), Shanghai Futures Exchange (SHFE), Zhengzhou Commodity Exchange (ZCE) and Dalian Commodity Exchange (DCE) made continued efforts on explorations and innovations and introduced a series of policies to stimulate revival of the futures sector in 2014, while refining the existing policies and rules and abiding by the New Nine State Regulations and *Opinions on Promoting Innovation and Development of Futures Brokers*, in a bid to address the downturn of the futures market in 2013.

(1) Adapt contract design and raise market recognition. In order to carry out *Several Opinions of the State Council on Further Promoting Sound Development of the Capital Market*, better adapt to market demand and facilitate delivery, all commodity exchanges in China have added new products, revised the contracts and settlement and delivery rules of methanol, plastics, cotton, wheat, early indica rice, japonica rice, steel rebar, rubber and silver, and adjusted the delivery warehouses and brands of most products, to raise market recognition, attract more corporate clients and better serve the real economy.

(2) Tighten risk control and polish trading rules. To polish the trading rules and tighten risk control is the cornerstone to sustainable growth of the futures market. The futures market

performed soundly in 2014, with no occurrence of major risk event. This is impossible without the perfected trading rules of the futures market. On Apr. 18, 2014, *Dalian Commodity Exchange Detailed Rules for Implementation of Bonded Delivery* (*For Trial Implementation*) came into effect officially. On Jun. 20, 2014, ZCE revised the *Rules for Futures Trading Risk Management of Zhengzhou Commodity Exchange*. On Oct. 22, 2014, DCE revised the process of repaying the delivery forecast deposits for No. 2 Soybeans.

(3) Lower the futures transaction fees and fuel revival of the futures sector. Transaction fee exemptions and reductions were carried on and more diversified in 2014, as mainly reflected in SHFE. From Apr. 1, 2014, no transaction fee will be charged for closing positions of aluminum, zinc, lead and steel rebar of SHFE opened on the same day. From Aug. 25, 2014, the transaction fee rate of hot-rolled coil futures contracts will be lowered to 0.04‰ from 0.08‰ of contract value. Between Nov. 26, 2014 and Mar. 31, 2015, the transaction fee of copper contracts will be halved.

(4) Perfect the variety of products traded in night shift and launch continuous trading of commodity futures. Since SHFE successfully launched night shift continuous trading of gold, silver, copper, aluminium, lead and zinc in 2013, DCE and ZCE also started night shift trading of some products in 2014. The variety of products traded in night shift is completed bit by bit, making important contribution to the continuity and activity of trade. As of the end of 2014, the number of products continuously traded increased to 23 from 6 in 2013. SHFE added four products, namely, steel rebar, hot-rolled coil, natural rubber and bitumen, DCE added eight products in two batches, including palm oil, coke, soybean collection, coking coal and iron ore, and ZCE started night shift trading of five products, namely, white sugar, cotton, rapeseed meal, methanol and PTA. Henceforth, night shift trading has gone live at all three commodity exchanges in China and the commodity futures market of China ushers in an era of continuous trading.

(5) Loosen control and encourage innovation. To echo the New Nine State Regulations, CFA released *Rules for the Management of Asset Management Business of Futures Companies* (*for Trial Implementation*), which is brought into effect officially as of Dec. 15, 2014. Permission is given to One-to-Many business, that is, futures firms and their subsidiaries engaged in asset management for specified single client or specified multiple clients. The One-to-Many business model broadens the wealth management possibilities of the futures sector and supports the transition of futures firms towards asset management and risk management. Other rules involve lowering the threshold for futures firms to take part in asset management, lowering net capital and classified rating requirements, adopting the registration filing approach, requiring filing with

CFA and the private placement registration filing system, and forbidding appointment of third-party individuals as investments advisors.

While relaxing control, the CSRC encourages business innovation. In September, 2014, the CSRC unveiled *Opinions on Promoting Innovation and Development of Futures Brokers*, which specified guiding rules and concrete measures for promoting innovation and development of futures brokers in the near future, and set out eight pivotal policies.

2. Rollout of More Innovations in Product Variety and Business Model of Futures Trading

(1) Innovate product variety. In 2014, futures contracts of polypropylene, hot-rolled coil, late indica rice and ferroalloy made their debut in China; the preparation of consultative documents on and simulated trading of commodity options and frozen pork, among other new products, were going on in full swing; crude oil futures got clearance officially and relevant policies and administrative measures were implemented step by step; and guidelines for commodity futures ETF were released officially, injecting new life into the futures market. The rollout of these new products not only enriches the collection of futures and expands the market growth potential, but also provides more hedging instruments to business entities and enables the futures market to serve the real economy better. In particular, *Operational Guidelines for Public Offering of Securities Investment Funds No. 1—Guidelines for Commodity Futures Trading Open-Ended Funds* promulgated by the CSRC in December specified the definition, investment scope, risk control, duties of stakeholders and regulatory requirements relating to commodity futures ETF. The launch of commodity futures funds can connect the securities market and the commodities market, and involve institutional investors in commodity futures, so as to heighten the liquidity of commodity futures.

(2) Innovate business model. DCE innovatively piloted intra-group warehouse receipts swap for soybean meal, soybean oil and palm oil following in-depth fieldwork and achieved positive results, in order to bring into full play the function of the soybean meal, soybean oil and palm oil futures market, enable the futures market to serve the industries better, lower delivery costs and drive integration between futures and spots.

(3) Encourage OTC derivatives. The CSRC, CFA and AMAC prepared *Chinese Securities and Futures Markets OTC Derivatives Master Agreement* (*2014 Edition*) and supplemental agreement, and *Chinese Securities and Futures Markets OTC Equity Derivatives Trading Derivatives Definition File* (*2014 Edition*) in August, 2014, on the basis of *China Securities Market Financial Derivatives Master Agreement* (*2013 Edition*), with a view to refine the securities and futures markets derivatives master agreement and associated documents, boost securities and futures markets OTC derivatives trading, and explore OTC derivatives.

3. System Perfection and Solid Foundation of the Futures Market

The CSRC introduced *Measures for the Supervision of Futures Firms* (*the Measures*) in October, 2014, to act on the advice for sharpening the competitive strength of the securities and futures service industries in *Opinions of the State Council on Promoting the Healthy Development of the Capital Market* (*the New Nine State Regulations*) and relevant provisions in *Decision of the State Council on the Sixth Group of Administrative Examination and Approval Items to Be Cancelled and Adjusted and Decision of the State Council on Amending the Regulations on Futures Trading*. It embodies the philosophy of functional regulation and moderate regulation and can help enhance the service capability and international competitiveness of futures firms.

Key points in the *Measures* are summarized as follows. First, fulfil the requirement for streamlining of administration and delegation of power and stick to regulatory transition; second, lower the threshold and optimize the qualifications for shareholders of futures firms; third, fine-tune the business scope of futures firms; fourth, clarify requirements for diversification of futures firms; fifth, perfect the regulatory system and endeavour to protect the legitimate rights and interests of investors; sixth, reinforce the information disclosure obligation of futures firms; seventh, consummate the regulatory measures and legal responsibilities of futures firms; and eighth, lay out institutional arrangements for offshore traders to participate in futures trading of specified products.

(iii) Review of Futures Market Policy Enforcement in 2014 and Outlook for 2015

1. Review of Futures Market Policy Enforcement in 2014

(1) A massive uplift in the activity of products traded. In 2014, DCE posted a contract volume of 769, 637, 100 lots, up 9. 87 percent year on year; SHFE recorded a contract volume of 837, 452, 000 lots, up 30. 35 percent year on year, and ZCE delivered a contract volume of 676, 343, 300 lots, up 22. 97 percent year on year, according to statistics released by the CSRC.

The aggregate turnover of China's futures market achieved a significant growth in 2014 compared with that of 2013, but the activity of products traded didn't show up well until January, 2015, as continuous trading of most products went live in December, 2014. As of closing on Jan. 26, 2015, the aggregate turnover of continuous trading of steel rebar, hot-rolled coil, natural rubber and bitumen reached 1. 01 trillion yuan, with a total contract volume of 28, 755, 700 lots, according to data provided by SHFE. To be more specific, 26, 044, 400 steel rebar contracts were concluded, with a turnover of 662. 334 billion yuan, representing 31. 35 percent and 31. 34 percent of all-day trading of this species; 47, 000 hot-rolled coil contracts were concluded, with a turnover of 1. 29 billion yuan, representing 29. 46 percent and 29. 41 percent of all-day trading of this species; 2, 628, 400 natural rubber contracts were concluded, with a turnover of 342. 28 billion yuan, representing 19. 93 percent and 19. 96 percent of all-day trading of this species; and 36, 100 bitumen contracts were concluded, with a turnover of 1. 049 billion yuan, representing 57. 52 percent and 57. 06 percent of all-day trading of this species, respectively. During the same time frame, steel rebar was the second most traded commodity, behind only silver, with an average daily continuous trading volume of 1, 446, 900 lots. In terms of open interest, the open interest in hot-rolled coil futures declined, while that in all of the rest products newly included in continuous trading climbed up.

(2) Institutions plunged into trading with immense zeal. In the first month continuous trading of the said products went live, the price gaps narrowed obviously and the price curves flattened considerably. The average daily price gaps of steel rebar, hot-rolled coil, natural rubber and bitumen narrowed by 3. 83 percent, 21. 81 percent, 26. 67 percent and 37. 47 percent on a month-on-month basis, respectively. Narrower price gaps have improved the price continuity and strengthened the price discovery function of these products.

Flatter price curves have aroused the enthusiasm of clients for trading. The breadth and depth of market participation in the said products have expanded. For example, the average daily client participation count of steel rebar and hot-rolled coil grew 7. 41 and 56. 12 percent month on month, respectively. The number of steel rebar, hot-rolled coil, natural rubber and bitumen transactions per client increased by 161. 44 percent, 10. 93 percent, 19. 51 percent and 28. 29 percent month on month, respectively.

2. Outlook for Commodity Futures Market Policy

In May, 2014, *Several Opinions of the State Council on Further Promoting the Healthy Development of the Capital Market* was released. As proposed in the New Nine State Regulations, futures contracts of more resource commodities will be launched, commodity options, commodity index and carbon credit, among other trading instruments, will be developed, the access restrictions on institutional investors and the corporate market will be loosened, the securities and futures service industries will become more competitive, openup of the securities and futures industries will be taken to the next level, the change in regulation of securities and futures will be pushed ahead, and the legitimate rights and interests of investors, especially small-/medium-sized ones, will be well protected, to optimize the external environment and add fuel to innovation and development of the market. In September, the CSRC released *Opinions on Promoting Innovation and Development of Futures Brokers*, which specified guiding rules and concrete measures for promoting innovation and development of futures brokers in the near future.

First, more ETF options and commodity options will be launched. From the end of 2013, all exchanges started marketwide simulated trading of options. Feb. 9, 2015 witnessed the debut of SSE 50ETF options. The launch of options has far-reaching and profound influence on the commodity futures market of China.

Second, what's next after the listing of crude oil futures The first international commodity futures species in China, crude oil futures, was approved for listing on Dec. 15, 2014. That means global trading of crude oil futures will start in Shanghai Free Trade Zone in the first half of 2015 at the earliest, after necessary procedures are completed. China will then join in the competition for crude oil pricing benchmark in Asia Pacific officially. Next, SHFE will give all support needed to Shanghai International Energy Exchange, its subsidiary, to liaison with all stakeholders and do well in market organization, rules making, technical system and investor education, after relevant policies are unveiled, to assure successful roll-out and smooth running of crude oil futures, an executive of SHFE said.

Third, continuous trading will be further fine-tuned and optimized. By drawing upon the successful experience in continuous trading accumulated last year, the three exchanges will further enrich the variety of products in continuous trading, optimize continuous trading hours, strengthen ties with the international market, and enable the futures market to serve the real economy better. In the meantime, investor education will be carried on and extensive trainings for futures firms, industrial clients, and SPVs, among other investors, will be organized. Trainings will be well-targeted and technical.

Fourth, regulatory restrictions will be loosened step by step. To be more specific, it is proposed to support futures brokers to provide risk management services, expand the pilot program of risk management companies and broaden the business scope of subsidiaries; make clear the basic positioning of futures brokers, encourage futures brokers to grow better and stronger and propel future brokers to change and upgrade the business model; accelerate the growth of asset management business of futures brokers; encourage foreign investors to hold shares of domestic futures brokers; support futures brokers to provide trade settlement service to overseas institutions involved in trading in the domestic futures market; and support futures brokers to set up or acquire companies abroad.

Fifth, a trader system will be explored and a trader team of high caliber will be developed. A trader system aiming at hedging and risk management will be built. Securities and futures brokers are encouraged to grow into professional traders and to get involved in floor-based market making lawfully, or in OTC derivatives trading as counterparty by designing non-standard products, so as to meet entity-specific risk management needs.

Sixth, the degree of concentration of the industry will be raised by encouraging M&A and reorganization of futures firms. The number of futures firms has decreased to 154 now from 183 in 2006. Even so, the futures industry is still characterized by small size, low competitiveness and low concentration to some extent. The degree of concentration of the futures industry is lower than that of other financial sectors in China, and much lower than that of the futures industry in those mature foreign markets. This restricts service capacity of the futures industry. In 2015, market-oriented policies will be reinforced, the approval process will be simplified and the supportive measures will be perfected, to motivate futures firms to conduct M&A and reorganization at home and abroad and support qualified overseas institutions to get involved in merger of domestic futures firms in a lawful manner, so as to heighten the degree of concentration of the industry.

Seventh, online account opening will come true and exploration into Internet finance will be made. With the end of the event of China Eastern Airlines and the rise of Internet finance, as proposed in the *Opinions on Promoting Innovation and Development of Futures Brokers*, futures firms may expand their market presence by enabling onlineaccount opening and exploring into Internet finance. Internet finance, however, is a newborn thing to the futures sector and entails numerous unknown opportunities, as well as risks. Tightened risk control and sharpened service skills are prerequisites for futures firms to have a try at Internet finance. Futures firms are recognized for good services, but clients have individualized demand. This is a challenge that Internet-based futures firms must overcome. Hence, a high level of expertise is a prerequisite to integrating Internet into the futures industry.

Eighth, policies and rules will be polished to set the stage for innovation and development. Futures brokers are advised to put in place a risk accountability mechanism commensurate with innovation and development, make innovations in a responsible manner, assign the primary responsibility for risk prevention to futures brokers strictly and attain a dynamic tradeoff between innovation and development and risk prevention.

IX. Foreign Exchange Market Development Policy[①]

(i) New Policies or Policy Adjustments in 2014

On Jan. 10, CFETS released the *Notice on Adding New Modes of Principal Exchange in Currency Swaps to the Foreign Exchange Trade System* (CFETS [2014] No. 5).

On Mar. 14, the PBC decided to enlarge the floating band of the RMB against the US dollar in the foreign exchange market (PBC [2014] No. 5).

---

① Written by Chu Youyang.

On Jun. 11, the PBC issued *Guiding Opinions on Implementing Opinions of the General Office of State Council on Supporting Steady Growth of Foreign Trade.*

On Jun. 22, the PBC unveiled *Administrative Measures for Settlement and Sales of Foreign Exchange by Banks* (PBC [2014] No. 2).

On Jul. 1, the PBC issued the *Notice on Management of Trading Prices of the Interbank Foreign Exchange Market and the Margin of Bank Quotations* (PBC [2014] No. 188).

On Jul. 10, CFETS issued the *Notice on Releasing Guidelines for Professional Ethics and Market Practices of the Interbank Foreign Exchange Market* (CFETS [2014] No. 173).

On Oct. 17, NAFMII released the *Notice of the Financial Market Department of the PBC on Qualified Non-financial Institutional Investors' Access to the Interbank Bond Market* (NAFMII [2014] No. 35).

On Dec. 5, SAFE released the *Notice on Adjusting Policies Related to the Administration of Financial Institutions' Access to the Interbank Foreign Exchange Market* (SAFE [2014] No. 48).

On Dec. 22, CFETS issued the *Notice on Adjusting the Fee Schedule of Spot Auction Trading in the Interbank RMB and Foreign Exchange Market* (CFETS [2014] No. 308)

On Dec. 25, SAFE issued the *Notice of SAFE on Releasing Rules for the Implementation of Administrative Measures for Settlement and Sales of Foreign Exchange by Banks* (SAFE [2014] No. 53).

On Dec. 25, CFETS issued the *Notice on the Launch of Forwards and Swaps between the Yuan and Ringgit, Russian Ruble and New Zealand Dollar* (CFETS [2014] No. 321).

On Dec. 26, CFETS issued the *Notice on Adjusting Guidelines for Access to the Interbank RMB and Foreign Exchange Market* (CFETS [2014] No. 327).

(ii) Policy Implications

1. The Central Bank Gives Access to the Interbank Bond Market to Qualified Non-financial Institutional Investors

On Oct. 17, 2014, NAFMII released the *Notice of the Financial Market Department of the PBC on Qualified Non-financial Institutional Investors' Access to the Interbank Bond Market* (NAFMII [2014] No. 35), wherein qualified non-financial institutional investors are allowed to invest in and trade bonds via the qualified non-financial institutional investors trading platform, which has gone live officially.

The qualified non-financial institutional investors trading platform is designed to serve the real economy, perfect the multi-level debt capital market, cater to the needs of institutional investors, including non-financial institutions, create a direct finance and investment platform for the real economy in short of cash and affluent investors, and thus lower the financing cost of the real economy. The platform is intended for non-financial institutional investors who have real trading needs and other institutional investors permitted by the PBC. The platform has made clear arrangements for investor eligibility, pre-trade bond and capital examination, and settlement method, as precautions against market risk.

2. The Floating Band of the RMB Against the US Dollar in the Foreign Exchange Market is Enlarged

The foreign exchange market of China is running soundly and trade entities are gaining a higher level of competence in discretionary pricing and risk management. To conform to the market development needs, heighten the degree to which exchange rates are decided by the market, and build a regulated floating exchange rate system on market supply and demand, the PBC decided to enlarge the floating band of the RMB against the US dollar in the foreign exchange market (PBC [2014] No. 5).

The floating band of the RMB against the US dollar in the interbank spot foreign exchange market is enlarged from 1 percent to 2 percent, effective from Mar. 17, 2014. In other words, the traded price of the RMB against the USD in the interbank spot foreign exchange market on any day may move within a range of 2 percent above and below the RMB's central parity rate against the US dollar released by CFETS on that day. On a given trading day, the spread between RMB/USD buying and selling prices offered by designated exchange banks to their clients shall be no more than 3 percent, raised from 2 percent previously, above the published central parity of the US dollar on that day. As for other rules, the *Notice of the PBC on Management of Trading Prices of the Interbank Foreign Exchange Market and the Margin of Designated Exchange Bank Quotations* (PBC [2010] No. 325) shall still apply. The PBC will make continued efforts to improve the market-based RMB exchange rate regime, bring into better play the role of the market in RMB exchange rate formation, strengthen two-way floating resilience of RMB exchange rates and keep RMB exchange rates at an appropriate and balanced level.

3. Support to Steady Growth of Foreign Trade is Sustained

In response to *Opinions of the General Office of State Council on Supporting Steady Growth of Foreign Trade* (State Council [2014] No. 19), the PBC issued *Guiding Opinions on Implementing Opinions of the General Office of State Council on Supporting Steady Growth of Foreign Trade.*

(1) Optimize the corporate financing environment and step up credit support. It is advisable to further diversify the financing sources of enterprises, encourage banking institutions to innovate financial products and services, broaden financing with export credit insurance

policies, step up credit support to importers and exporters and foreign trade comprehensive service providers that have orders and are trading profitably by flexibly using working capital lendings, imports&exports credits, factoring, bill discount, bill advance and external guarantee, and boost exports of small and micro businesses. Qualified enterprises are encouraged to issue non-financial corporate debt financing instruments, so as to diversify the financing sources of importers and exporters, including SMEs, through innovative combinations of SME collective notes, SME regional collective notes and credit enhancement.

Policy-based finance should give the greatest possible support to foreign trade. The Export-Import Bank of China is encouraged to enlarge special export buyer credits and lendings, simplify the formalities for special lendings and export buyer credits and capital approval, and step up support to enterprises going global, especially to imports&exports credits to SMEs. Policy financial institutions are encouraged to beef up support to service trade and fund key service trade programs.

It is necessary to boost financial lease. Financial lease with tangible movable properties as underlying can be developed to facilitate imports and exports of large machinery. Qualified financial lease firms and other non-bank financial institutions are encouraged to expand financing channels by offering bank debentures and taking part in the pilot of credit asset-backed securities.

(2) Boost cross-border trade settlement and implement centralized cross-border RMB fund operation. It is necessary to simplify the cross-border trade and investment RMB settlement workflow. Banking institutions may complete cross-border RMB settlement under current accounts and direct investment accounts directly upon receiving payment or collection orders from domestic enterprises, while following the rules of Know Your Client, Know Your Business and Due Diligence.

Centralized cross-border RMB fund operation shall be implemented. Multi-national corporate groups may conduct centralized cross-border RMB fund operations, including cross-border two-way RMB cash pool and centralized cross-border RMB payment and collection under current accounts, subject to relevant rules of the PBC. The headquarters of multi-national corporate groups may appoint a member (including finance firm) that is an independent corporate entity legally registered and actually engaged in business or investment activities in the PRC as a national or regional lead entity responsible for centralized cross-border RMB fund operations. The lead entity may apply netting to centralized cross-border RMB collection and payment under current accounts, a settlement procedure whereby total payables are offset against total receivables under current accounts on a group-wide or member by member basis to arrive at the net amount payable or receivable. Centralized cross-border RMB fund operation obligates a return of international balance of payment to be submitted in accordance with the rules on international balance of payment.

⁘ RMB settlement in cross-border trade is made accessible to individuals. Banking institutions may provide RMB settlement service to individuals for cross-border cargo and service trade. Banking institutions may complete RMB settlement in cross-border trade directly for individual clients who present valid personal identity document or business license, subject to the rules of Know Your Client, Know Your Business and Due Diligence, as well as trade proofs where necessary.

Banking institutions are encouraged to align with payment agencies on the provision of cross-border RMB settlement. Banking institutions may enter into partnership with payment agencies that have lawfully received an Internet Payment business license, to make RMB settlement in cross-border cargo and service trade accessible to both corporate and individual clients. Banking institutions are required to ink a cross-border e-Commerce RMB settlement agreement with payment agencies and complete filing with the local branch of the PBC.

(3) Further improve the market-based RMB exchange rate regime and diversify exchange rate hedging instruments. It is important to further improve the market-based RMB exchange rate regime, heighten the degree to which exchange rates are decided by the market, and thus help achieve international balance of payment. Depending on the degree of maturity of the foreign exchange market and economic and financial situations, it is advisable to strengthen two-way floating resilience of RMB exchange rates and keep RMB exchange rates at an appropriate and balanced level. The decisive role of the market in the formation of exchange rates shall be brought into full play and a regulated floating exchange rate system built on market supply and demand shall be perfected. Continued efforts will be made to drive direct trading between the RMB and other currencies.

It is necessary to redouble efforts on innovations in foreign exchange products, expand the variety of instruments in the foreign exchange market and explore foreign exchange options portfolio and innovative futures, to form an ideal combination of spots, forwards, futures and options and a mix of exchange rate products and interest rate products. Diversity in foreign exchange market players shall be enriched, the threshold for commercial banks to deal in foreign exchange derivatives shall be lowered and the eligibility criteria for forward settlement and sales of foreign exchange applicable to small-/medium-sized banks shall be loosened as appropriate. Trading, clearing and information infrastructures shall be enhanced to better satisfy the actual needs of corporate and individual clients for hedging against exchange rate risk.

4. Optimize Regulation of Settlement and Sales of Foreign Exchange by Banks

To optimize regulation of settlement and sales of foreign exchange by banks and preserve stability of the foreign exchange market, the PBC revised *Interim Measures for the Administration of Foreign Exchange Settlement and Sales Operations by Designated Foreign Exchange Banks* (*PBC* [2002] *Order No. 4*) (*Interim Measures*) and unveiled *Administrative Measures for Settlement and Sales of Foreign Exchange by Banks* (*Administrative Measures*) (*PBC* [2014] *Order No. 2*) on Jun. 22, 2014, effective as of Aug. 1, 2014. The said *Interim Measures* were repealed on the same day.

The promulgation of the *Administrative Measures* marks an important move to cater to the development of settlement and sales of foreign exchange and the realistic demand for a shift in the role of foreign exchange regulator, as well as an advertisement for the reform aiming at streamlining of administration and delegation of power and construction of an appropriate regulatory framework. The *Administrative Measures* contain the following revisions. First, settlement and sales of foreign exchange are divided into spot foreign exchange transactions, and RMB and foreign exchange derivatives. Rules are mapped out therefore separately. Second, the threshold for banks to provide settlement and sales of foreign exchange is lowered and market access control is minimized. Third, positions in settlement and sales of foreign exchange are managed in a different way, to vest a high level of autonomy in banks and give full play to the initiative of foreign exchange market players. Fourth, some administrative license and qualification requirements are abolished and the focus is shifted to supervision afterwards from prior approval. Fifth, some penalty provisions are amended based on the practice and latest developments of the foreign exchange market.

The *Administrative Measures* are promulgated without prejudice to the existing license for settlement and sales of foreign exchange held by banks.

On Dec. 25, SAFE issued the *Notice of SAFE on Releasing Rules for the Implementation of Administrative Measures for Settlement and Sales of Foreign Exchange by Banks* (SAFE [2014] No. 53) (hereinafter referred to as the *Rules*), with a view to facilitate settlement and sales of foreign exchange by banks.

To carry out the reform aiming at streamlining of administration and delegation of power, the *Rules* contain provisions for access to settlement and sales of foreign exchange by banks, administration of spot settlement and sales of foreign exchange, administration of RMB and foreign exchange derivatives and synthetic positions in settlement and sales of foreign exchange, along with some amendments. Main content is described as follows:

Access control over spot settlement and sales of foreign exchange and RMB and foreign exchange derivatives is merged to simplify banks' information update filing procedures relating to settlement and sales of foreign exchange.

The requirement for consistent personal currency exchange signage is abolished and banks are required to put up visible personal currency exchange signage at places where private settlement and sales of foreign exchange are provided.

Synthetic positions of banks in settlement and sales of foreign exchange are checked on a weekly basis instead of on a daily basis. The link between foreign exchange synthetic positions and foreign exchange loan-to-deposit ratio is severed.

The power to approve conversion of banks' capital in cash (working capital) between local currency and foreign currencies is delegated and the approval requirement for settlement and sales of foreign exchange by banks on behalf of debtors is abolished.

The essential requirements for Know Your Client, Know Your Business and Due Diligence must be complied with by banks in settlement and sales of foreign exchange.

The *Rules* come into effect as of Jan. 1, 2015.

5. Further Improve the Market-based RMB Exchange Rate Regime

To further improve the market-based RMB exchange rate regime, the PBC issued the *Notice on Management of Trading Prices of the Interbank Foreign Exchange Market and the Margin of Bank Quotations (PBC [2014] No. 188)* on Jul. 1, 2014, to set out rules on the management of trading prices of the interbank foreign exchange market and the margin of bank quotations.

The PBC authorizes CFETS to publicize at 9:15am of each working day the current central parity rates of the Renminbi against the US Dollar, euro, Japanese Yen, Hong Kong Dollar, Great Britain Pound, Malaysian Ringgit, Russian Ruble, Australian Dollar, Canadian Dollar and New Zealand Dollar, which serve as the central parity rates for exchange rates in interbank spot foreign exchange transactions (including transactions in an over-the-counter or open-outcry form). The current central parity rates publicized by CFETS under the authorization of the PBC are effective during the period from when such rates are publicized till the next central parity rates are publicized.

How the central parity rate of the Renminbi against the US Dollar is formulated: CFETS makes inquiries of market makers before opening of the interbank foreign exchange market every day and uses quotes received from market makers as the samples to calculate the current central parity rate of the Renminbi against the US Dollar, by excluding the highest and lowest offers and arriving at the weighted average of the rest quotes. The weight applied thereto is determined by CFETS after taking into account the trading volume and quotes of dealers in the interbank foreign exchange market, among other indicators.

The central parity rates of the Renminbi against the euro, HKD and CAD are arrived at by CFETS via the cross rates of these currencies against the US Dollar, at the 9:00am prices on major international currency markets. CFETS gets the central parity rates of the Renminbi against the JPY, GBP, AUD, NZD, Malaysian Ringgit and Russian Ruble by averaging market makers' pre-session quotes in the interbank foreign exchange market directly every day.

The bands for permissible fluctuations of the daily trading price of the RMB against the US Dollar in the interbank spot foreign exchange market around the central parity announced by CFETS are 2 percent, while the bands for permissible fluctuations of the daily trading prices of the RMB against the EUR, JPY, HKD, GBP, AUD, CAD and NZD around the central parity rates are 3 percent. The trading prices of the RMB against Malaysian Ringgit and Russian Ruble are allowed to move within a fluctuation band of 5 percent below and above the central parity rates. The allowable range for daily variation around the central parity of the RMB against any other currency other than US dollar shall be specified otherwise.

Banks may exercise discretion to quote RMB exchange rates, or buying and selling rates in spot cash settlement against other currencies to clients based on market demand and their pricing power, subject to no restriction. Banks should put in place an internal management system governing the margin of quotations to prevent risks effectively and avoid improper competition.

The Notice shall enter into force as of the date of promulgation. *Notice of the PBC on Management of Trading Prices of the Interbank Foreign Exchange Market and the Margin of Designated Exchange Bank Quotations (PBC [2005] No. 183), Notice of the PBC on Improving Management of Trading Prices of the Interbank Foreign Exchange Market and the Margin of Designated Exchange Bank Quotations (PBC [2005] No. 250)* and *Notice of the PBC on Management of Trading Prices of the Interbank Foreign Exchange Market and the Margin of Designated Exchange Bank Quotations (PBC [2010] No. 325)* shall lapse on the same day. Regarding other matters concerning management of trading prices of the interbank foreign exchange market and the margin of bank quotations addressed in other documents of the PBC and SAFE, the Notice shall prevail.

6. Fine-tune the Control over Financial Institutions' Access to the Interbank Foreign Exchange Bank

To further streamline administration and delegate power, diversify market players and boost the foreign exchange market, on Dec. 5, 2014, SAFE released the *Notice on Adjusting Policies Related to the Administration of Financial Institutions' Access to the Interbank Foreign Exchange Market (SAFE [2014] No. 48)*, to fine-tune the policies related to domestic financial institutions' access to the interbank foreign exchange market, in accordance with *Regulations of the PRC on Foreign Exchange Administration.*

After qualifying for spot foreign exchange settlement and sales upon the approval of SAFE and qualifying for derivatives trading upon the approval of competent monetary authorities, domestic financial institutions can, provided that the commercial and technical specifications for the interbank foreign exchange market are complied with, become members of the interbank foreign exchange market and conduct spot trading and derivatives trading of RMB against foreign exchange. SAFE imposes no ex-ante control over access to the interbank foreign exchange market.

Financial institutions are required to submit to CFETS for the record their internal operational procedures and risk management system designed for interbank spot trading and derivatives trading of RMB against foreign exchange.

The trading of RMB against foreign exchange conducted by financial institutions in the interbank foreign exchange market shall be conducted for the purpose of hedging risks arising from the exchange settlement and sale business on behalf of clients and for themselves, conducting market-making and proprietary transactions within the limit to synthetic positions in foreign exchange settlements and sales, as well as engaging in lawful hedging activities for themselves. Financial institutions shall observe the laws and regulations on interbank foreign exchange trading, clearing, and information, as well as the stipulations of competent monetary authorities.

Currency brokerage companies (including branches) incorporated with the approval of the banking regulatory authority can, as specified by the foreign exchange administration, conduct foreign exchange brokerage business, such as derivatives trading of RMB against foreign exchange and trading of foreign exchange against foreign exchange and foreign exchange lending, in the interbank foreign exchange market. SAFE requires no ex-ante qualification approval. In their conduct of foreign exchange brokerage business, currency brokerage companies shall observe the laws and regulations governing the interbank foreign exchange market.

CFETS and the Interbank Market Clearing House Co. , Ltd (hereinafter referred to as Shanghai Clearing House) shall, in line with the requirements in the Notice, adjust relevant business rules and systems accordingly, and provide effective technical support and services. CFETS and Shanghai Clearing House shall be responsible for daily monitoring of interbank trading and clearing of RMB against foreign exchange and report to SAFE any exceptional trading or clearing event without delay.

Financial institutions shall observe professional ethics and follow market practices so as to promote self-disciplined management and proper development of the foreign exchange market.

The Notice comes into force as of January 1, 2015. At the same time, the *Reply of SAFE on Relevant Issues Concerning the Conduct of RMB and Foreign Currency Swap Transactions by the Bank of China in the Interbank Foreign Exchange Market* (*SAFE Reply* [2006] *No. 61*), *Circular of SAFE on Relevant Issues Concerning the Introduction of Renminbi-Against-Foreign Exchange Options Trading* (*SAFE* [2011] *No. 8*), *Circular of SAFE on Adjustments to the Administration of Some Businesses in the Interbank Foreign Exchange Market* (*SAFE* [2012] *No. 30*), and *Circular of SAFE on Adjustments to the Administration of the Renminbi-against-Foreign Exchange Derivatives Business* (*SAFE* [2013] *No. 46*) are repealed. Regarding other matters concerning access to the interbank foreign exchange market discussed in other documents, the Notice shall apply.

On Dec. 26, 2014, CFETS issued the *Notice on Adjusting Guidelines for Access to the Interbank RMB and Foreign Exchange Market* (*CFETS* [2014] *No. 327*), to adjust the rules governing access to the interbank RMB and foreign exchange market, effective as of Jan. 1, 2015.

7. Expand the Variety of Foreign Exchange Products, Adjust the Fee Schedule and Promote Professional Ethics in the Foreign Exchange Market

On Jan. 10, 2014, CFETS released the *Notice on Adding New Modes of Principal Exchange in Currency Swaps to the Foreign Exchange Trade System* (*CFETS* [2014] *No. 5*). As resolved in the Notice, CFETS will add "No physical exchange of principal on effective date and Physical exchange of principal on maturity date" to RMB and foreign exchange swaps in the foreign exchange trade system, effective as of Jan. 13, 2014.

On Dec. 25, 2014, CFETS issued the *Notice on the Launch of Forwards and Swaps between the Yuan and Ringgit, Russian Ruble and New Zealand Dollar* (*CFETS* [2014] *No. 321*), announcing the decision to launch forwards and swaps between the Yuan and Ringgit, Russian Ruble and New Zealand Dollar on Dec. 29, 2014.

On Dec. 22, 2014, CFETS issued the *Notice on Adjusting the Fee Schedule of Spot Auction Trading in the Interbank RMB and Foreign Exchange Market* (*CFETS* [2014] *No. 308*). It is decided in the Notice to adjust the fee schedule of spot auction trading in the interbank RMB and foreign exchange market as follows: to lower the fee rate for RMB and foreign exchange spot auction trading (excluding clearing fee) to 0. 03‰ and to cancel the progressive discount from the fee rate for RMB and foreign exchange spot auction trading, effective as of Jan. 1, 2015.

To preserve a fair, trustworthy and orderly market environment, under the leadership of SAFE, on Jul. 10, 2014, CFETS issued the *Notice on Releasing Guidelines for Professional Ethics and Market Practices of the Interbank Foreign Exchange Market* (*CFETS* [2014]

No. 173). All interbank foreign exchange market makers have endorsed the *Guidelines*, demonstrating their commitment to compliance with the provisions therein and trading with good faith. The *Guidelines* represent a self-regulatory handbook for the interbank foreign exchange market and come into force as of the date of promulgation. CFETS will, under the leadership of SAFE, unite all members to take self-regulatory organization of the interbank foreign exchange market to the next level.

(iii) Policy Outlook

The year of 2015 is crucial to deepening the reform comprehensively and the year to witness the completion of the 12th Five-Year Plan. Foreign exchange administrations are expected to adapt themselves to the New Normal of the economy, crack the hard nuts in the reform, enhance convertibility of cross-border capital and financial transactions in a well-organized manner, and boost the foreign exchange market with tightened risk control.

Volatility of the international financial market is compounded by the complex and changeful international environment, the strengthening US Dollar and the world economy that is in the midst of in-depth adjustment. Against this backdrop, foreign exchange administrations are faced with some grave challenges in the era of New Normal of the economy in 2015, for example, how to cope with the impact from cross-border capital flow following two-way openup, and how to keep the value of foreign exchange reserves intact and appreciable when the return on investment with foreign exchange reserves becomes more volatile.

Equal importance should be attached to reform and innovation and risk prevention. A job of first priority to foreign exchange administrations in 2015 is still to build up the ability to serve the real economy. Two-way openup of the capital market is an irresistible trend, because the Chinese government has declared that RMB capital account convertibility will be accelerated. Then, quick cross-border capital inflow and outflow will probably become commonplace after openup. SAFE needs to raise its tolerance of cross-border capital flow and build up its inner power. Meanwhile, it is important to put in place a macro-prudential cross-border capital flow management system and mechanism, under the condition that the reform is pressed ahead with smoothly and the distorted prices are put to rights. Therefore, some highlights of policymaking in 2015 will be streamlining of administration and delegation of power, trade and investment facilitation, capital account convertibility and enhanced cross-border capital flow detection, alert and risk control.

X. Chinese Gold Market Development Policy[①]

(ⅰ) New Policies or Policy Adjustments in 2014

On Jan. 2, the Shanghai Gold Exchange launched Mini gold deferred contract [mAu (T + D)].

On Jun. 10, the Shanghai Gold Exchange started partnership with Shanghai Futures Exchange.

On Jun. 18, the PBC Shanghai head office held the Free Trade Account launch ceremony. Shanghai Gold Exchange and the PBC Shanghai head office inked a Memorandum of Understanding (MOU).

On Jul. 25, the Ping An Bank and Bank of Shanghai completed the first interbank gold leasing deal via the Price Asking System of Shanghai Gold Exchange.

In August, the Bank of Communications and Bank of Shanghai completed the first deal cash and net settled under Gold Price Asking via the Price Asking System of Shanghai Gold Exchange.

On Sep. 18, the launch ceremony of Shanghai Gold Exchange International Board was held.

On Sep. 19, the Shanghai Gold Exchange signed a MOU with the Chinese Gold and Silver Exchange Society in Shanghai.

On Nov. 10, the Shanghai Gold Exchange and the Chicago Mercantile Exchange Group (CME Group) signed a MOU in Shanghai.

(ⅱ) Review of Gold Market Policy in 2014

1. Improve the Gold Market Trading and Running Mechanism

(1) Introduce new types of spot gold trading. On Jan. 2, 2014, Shanghai Gold Exchange (SGE) launched Mini gold deferred contract (mAu (T + D)), with the minimum trading volume of 100g as one lot. At the same time, the minimum trading volume of Au99. 99 was reduced to 10g from 100g as one lot. These two products have been actively traded by investors and widely applauded by the market since going live.

(2) Close the first deal via the interbank gold leasing platform of SGE. On Jul. 25, 2014, Ping An Bank and Bank of Shanghai completed the first interbank gold leasing deal via the SGE Price Asking System. This marks the kick-start of the interbank gold leasing market officially. The interbank gold leasing market is a new channel of financing with physical gold that SGE

---

① Written by Chu Youyang.

provides to financial institutions in accordance with the master plan mapped out by the PBC, as well as one of the infrastructures laid to develop the OTC gold trading platform and cultivate the interbank gold lease rate curve. The market is envisaged as a wholesale market for physical gold finance that mainly involves all sorts of financial institutions and provides wholesale finance, price formation, market making and interest arbitrage, among other market services and transactional functions.

By interbank gold leasing, it means that members certified by SGE borrow or lease gold in the form of bilateral price asking via the SGE Price Asking System. The trading hours of interbank gold leasing are 9:00am-11:30am, and 13:30pm-17:00pm, Mondays through Fridays (except for days on which SGE is closed as notified otherwise); trading activities are suspended from 11:30am to 13:30pm. SGE may adjust the trading hours as warranted by market developments and shall publish the trading hours so adjusted. Products listed in the SGE Price Asking System covered by the Transactions include LAU99.95 and LAU99.99, the underlying assets of which are gold with a fineness of no lower than 99.95% and 99.99%, respectively. Where any new interbank leasing product underlied by gold, silver or any other precious metal is listed, SGE shall give a notification accordingly.

SGE will make continued improvement in the interbank gold leasing platform based on market demand and subsequent feedback, to better satisfy the demand for interbank physical gold finance, diversify the Price Asking product lines, develop the gold benchmark rate system and better serve the entire lease market.

(3) Close the first deal cash and net settled under Gold Price Asking via SGE. In August, 2014, Bank of Communications and Bank of Shanghai completed the first deal cash and net settled under Gold Price Asking via the SGE Price Asking System. In this deal, SGE benchmark of gold prices was referenced for the first time in net settlement in cash and clearing, and delivery were completed without a hitch. The launch of net settlement in cash suggests that product lines of the gold price asking market are expanded and improved further. By gold price asking, it means that members certified by SGE strike a deal in the form of bilateral price asking via the SGE Price Asking System or the foreign exchange trade system of CFETS, wherein the products traded must be products designated by SGE for listing in the foreign exchange trade system of CFETS. Net settlement in cash is one of the common clearing and delivery practices in the international financial market, wherein the parties to a price asking transaction don't need to deliver physical gold and pay the full consideration upon maturity of the transaction, but settle the transaction in cash instead against the difference between the indicative price agreed upon in the contract and the traded price. SGE has launched net settlement in cash for gold price asking

transactions in line with the master plan mapped out by the PBC and the prevailing market demand. It is an important move to standardize and normalize the gold OTC market, diversify the price asking product lines denominated in RMB and bring registration and clearing services of the gold OTC market to the next level. SGE will make continued improvement in the gold price asking system based on market demand and subsequent feedback, develop the gold OTC market and better serve the entire gold market.

2. Build Shanghai as an International Financial Center and Globalize the Chinese Gold Market

(1) Include international gold settlement of SGE in the FTA system officially. On Jun. 18, 2014, the PBC Shanghai head office held the Free Trade Account (FTA) launch ceremony. Xu Luode, Chairman of SGE, inked a Memorandum of Understanding (MOU) with the PBC Shanghai head office, a signal that SGE is officially connected to the system of the PBC Shanghai head office and may facilitate gold trading of international investors through the FTA system henceforth. SGE also signed a Cooperation Agreement of Settlement Banks with ICBC, CCB, BOC (Shanghai Branch) and SPDB (Shanghai Branch), respectively. According to the Agreement, qualified customers from overseas and in the FTZ are allowed to open Free Trade Accounts in the Free Trade Accounting Unit at the said banks and start trading gold.

Free Trade Account (FTA) is a pivotal component of the financial openup framework designed for Shanghai FTZ. Residents in the FTZ are allowed to open FTAs in local currency and foreign currencies to realize separate accounting and start innovative financing and investment activities. Non-residents are allowed to open FTAs for Non-residents in local currency and foreign currencies at banks based in the FTZ and to enjoy financial services according to pre-establishment national treatment principles. The PBC proposed in *Opinions of the PBC to Support China (Shanghai) Pilot Free Trade Zone in Financial Sector* released on Dec. 2, 2013 that residents and financial institutions in the FTZ will be allowed to open FTAs in local currency and foreign currencies and full RMB convertibility will be allowed when conditions are right. The so-called FTA system is characterized by separate accounting, off-shore liberalization, two-way connectivity and limited penetration. Pursuant to *Opinions of the PBC to Support China (Shanghai) Pilot Free Trade Zone in Financial Sector*, residents in the FTZ are allowed to open FTAs in local currency and foreign currencies to realize separate accounting and start some innovative financing and investment activities. Non-residents are allowed to open FTAs for Non-residents (hereinafter referred to as FTN) in local currency and foreign currencies at banks based in the FTZ and to enjoy financial services according to pre-establishment national treatment principles. To be more specific, money can be freely transferred between FTAs and offshore accounts, domestic non-free-trade non-resident accounts, FTNs and FTAs of other residents. Fund transfer between FTAs and settlement accounts in other banks held by the same non-financial institution for the purpose of transactions under current accounts, loan repayment, industrial investment and other cross-border transactions compliant with the rules is allowed as well. Capital flow between FTAs and domestic non-free-trade bank settlement accounts is managed as equivalent to cross-border transactions. In the cross-border capital monitoring system, FTAs are treated as Offshore Accounts to a large extent. The FTA system has been structured to form a financial environment in the FTZ that is segregated from other domestic markets to some extent and is highly pegged to the international financial market, so as to cater to a wide range of international economic activities. Financial institutions based in Shanghai may open FTAs for qualified FTZ residents by initiating a Free Trade Accounting Unit and provide financial services accordingly as per the rules of the PBC.

SGE will open FTAs in the Free Trade Accounting Unit at the designated banks to provide settlement and clearing services for international transactions to FTZ-based and international investors.

(2) Launch Shanghai Gold Exchange International Board. The launch ceremony of SGE International Board was held in the evening of September 18. Zhou Xiaochuan, Vice Chairman of the National Committee of the Chinese People's Political Consultative Conference and President of the PBC, and Yang Xiong, Deputy Party Chief and Mayor of Shanghai, co-launched the International Board and delivered a speech respectively. Liu Shiyu, Vice President of the PBC, and Ai Baojun, member of the Municipal Standing Committee of the CPC and Vice Mayor of Shanghai, jointly unveiled the plaque of Shanghai Gold Exchange. The launch ceremony was presided over by Xu Luode, Chairman of SGE, and witnessed by the officials of the PBC and the Shanghai municipal government, as well as representatives of SGE members and other institutions. On the spot, the first transaction of the International Board was concluded by MKS (Switzerland), HSBC, BOC, ICBC and BOCOM. This marks a substantial step forward in China's openup of the gold market, where Shanghai Gold has officially gone global. The launch of the International Board is a strategic choice of SGE to embrace the global market and go with the global trends. After the International Board went live, SGE will make four breakthroughs:

First, the member base is globalized. SGE enrolled 40 international members this time, including some of the best known commercial banks and institutional investors in the world and some top-notch gold refineries. More international members will join in SGE in the future. International members are allowed to deal in all contracts in SGE at their discretion or handle transactions in SGE as the agents of international investors. International investors include those registered in Shanghai FTZ and offshore investors.

Second, the capital source is globalized. The International Board may involve offshore capital in trading. Offshore capital can be offshore capital in the FTZ or in other countries or regions and includes offshore RMB and other convertible currencies. These types of capital can all be involved in the trading of gold and other precious metals quoted in RMB under the FTA framework.

Third, pricing is globalized. All products traded in SGE are denominated in RMB. As the diversity of participants grows and the trading volume expands, the profound fusion between onshore investors, onshore capital and offshore investors, offshore capital will help the traded prices in SGE gain international recognition and form RMB gold pricing benchmarks of international influence. We call this pricing mechanism, along with the product and physical delivery standards, "Shanghai Gold". The launch of Shanghai Gold will enable the gold market to discover the RMB price effectively, strengthen synergy between the Chinese market and the international market, bring into play the role of China as the largest physical gold consumer, producer and importer in the international market, heighten the international influence of RMB and propel globalization of RMB.

Fourth, storage and delivery are globalized. After the International Board is launched, clients may choose to deliver physical gold at the vault of SGE in the FTZ. Since the FTZ upholds the "deregulated frontier" policy, the physical gold can either be imported into China by qualified agencies engaged by SGE or transported to other countries freely. This can provide more convenient and efficient entrepot services to investors in Asia Pacific and help Shanghai grow into a gold entrepot center in Asia Pacific. For this purpose, SGE has launched three gold spot contracts designed for delivery in the FTZ, that is, iAu100 and iAu99. 99, with the minimum trading volume of 100g and 1000g as one lot and a fineness of 99. 99, and iAu99. 5, with the minimum trading volume of 1250g as one lot and a fineness of 99. 5. In addition, a Kiloton modernized vault has been built in the FTZ, to provide delivery, storage and logistics services in support of gold imports and entrepot trade.

3. Forge Ties with the International Gold Market

In 2014, SGE entered into partnership with the Chinese Gold and Silver Exchange Society and CME Group.

(1) SGE enters into partnership with the Chinese Gold and Silver Exchange Society. In the afternoon of Sep. 19, 2014, SGE signed a MOU with the Chinese Gold & Silver Exchange Society (CGSE) in Shanghai. Xu Luode, Chairman of SGE, Haywood Cheung, President of

CGSE, Shen Gang, Deputy General Manager of SGE and Steven Chan, Vice President of CGSE attended the signing ceremony. Both parties agree to strengthen cooperation and work closely with each other to push forward the sound development and openup of China's gold market by taking advantage of the SGE International Board in the future.

(2) SGE enters into partnership with CME Group. SGE signed a Memorandum of Understanding (MOU) with the Chicago Mercantile Exchange Group (CME Group) in Shanghai on Nov. 10, 2014. Xu Luode, Chairman of SGE, and Leo Melamed, Chairman Emeritus of CME Group, attended the signing ceremony and signed the MOU on behalf of each party. The partnership with CME Group is one of the most important approaches for SGE to implement its openup policy and internationalization strategy. In the future, under the framework of the MOU, both parties will explore possibilities of cooperation in the domestic and international markets, vigorously expand the ways to serve investors at home and abroad and mutually promote the sound, healthy and orderly development of the global gold market in line with the principle of reciprocal benefit, cooperation and win-win.

(iii) Policy Outlook

Economic pictures are divergent worldwide. The US economy is showing a clear sign of revival, economic growth is set to continue losing momentum in Europe, while emerging economies are facing grave difficulties. The New Normal of the Chinese economy is shaping up and reform and openup of the domestic financial market is going into more depth. Hence, both the international market and the domestic market are fostering new growth opportunities for China's gold market. Looking ahead to 2015, we expect all policies for the gold market to stay focused on driving reform of the domestic gold trade mechanism, accelerating openup and international cooperation of the gold market and beefing up the International Board.

1. Forge ahead with the Reform of the Gold Market Regime

For the purpose of developing Shanghai as an international financial center, a basket of policies will be introduced to boost synergy between the gold market, and the foreign exchange market and the capital market and to construct the multi-level financial market architecture.

For the purpose of expansion of Shanghai FTZ and accelerated openup of capital accounts in China, a basket of policies will be introduced to involve the gold market more in the development of the FTZ regime and globalization of RMB and realize full convertibility of capital accounts in gold investment and trade.

In 2015, SGE will broaden the investor base, attract more non-bank financial institutions and qualified foreign investors to the gold market and promote "Shanghai Gold". The arrival of non-bank financial institutions will create another strategic opportunity for the development of

China's gold market. It is foreseeable that more innovations in and openup of precious metal trade will come forth in the future.

2. Quicken the Tempo of Openup and Global Cooperation of the Gold Market

In 2015, exchanges in China will step up cooperation with the World Gold Council and all major gold exchanges around the world, provide a whole set of market services of higher quality to global investors and boost prosperity of the Chinese gold market and the world gold market.

3. Beef up the Gold International Board

In 2015, the SGE International Board will take large strides on top of the achievements made in 2014.

The International Board deserves strategic importance as a booster for China's gold market to gain a foothold in the international arena. Policies will be introduced to integrate resources at home and abroad with the SGE International Board as a platform and take the International Board to the next level.

Innovations in institutional design of the SGE International Board are important. Successful experience of other countries can be drawn upon to introduce specific trading rules and incentives. New progress will be made in the trade turnover, client base, products traded, market services and international cooperation and communication of the International Board by improving the investor mix, product mix, system development, risk control and compliance system, market awareness and services, OTC market development, human resources management and internal management. Driven by innovations and reform, the International Board will become a more mature market.

In the context of competition among exchanges at home and abroad, Internet-based gold products and services will be launched by drawing support from the mobile Internet boom. The marriage of the Internet and finance has given birth to loads of Internet-based wealth management products. Most of these products are money market funds, and cannot meet the needs for diversification of investments and risks and for long-term investments. Internet-based physical gold investment provides a possibility of diversified and long-term investment to investors and an ideal complement to the present limited investment portfolio. In the future, the Chinese government is likely to introduce incentives for Internet-based gold wealth management products. Physical gold products that are accessible via mobile App will change the present situation of the gold market dominated by commercial banks, raw material providers and manufacturers of jewelry, enhance the efficiency of resource allocation of the physical gold market and connect China's gold market to the international market closely.

CHAPTER 6

Highlights of Financial Regulatory Policy

I. Highlights of Regulatory Policy of the PBC[①]

(i) Highlights of Regulatory Policy of the PBC in 2014

Table 6 – 1　　　　　　**Regulatory Policy of the PBC in 2014**

Date	File Name	File No.
Jan.	The PBC jointly with the Ministry of Science and Technology, the CBRC, the CSRC, the CIRC, and the State Intellectual Property Office issued *Opinions on Vigorously Promoting Institutional Innovations and Improving Financial Services for Science and Technology Development*	PBC〔2014〕No. 9
Jan.	*Administrative Measures for the Freezing of Assets Relating to Terrorist Activities*	PBC, MPS, MSS Order〔2014〕No. 1
Feb.	*Notice on the Establishment of Central Clearing Mechanism for OTC Derivatives and the Launch of Central Clearing for RMB Interest Rate Swaps*	PBC〔2014〕No. 29
Feb.	*Guidelines on Improving Financial Services to Family Farms and Other New Types of Agricultural Entities*	PBC〔2014〕No. 42
Mar.	*Opinions on Accelerating the Development of Small and Micro Enterprises and Rural Credit System*	PBC〔2014〕No. 37
Mar.	The PBC, jointly with the MOF, the CBRC, the CSRC, the CIRC, the State Council Leading Group Office of Poverty Alleviation and Development, and the Central Committee of the Communist Youth League, issued *Guidelines on Improving Financial Services for Poverty Alleviation and Development*	PBC〔2014〕No. 65
Mar.	*Notice on Launching Central Bank Loans Earmarked for Small and Micro Enterprises to support Credit Extensions to Small and Micro Enterprises*	PBC〔2014〕No. 90

---

① Written by Zhu Xiaochuan.

Continued

Date	File Name	File No.
Apr.	The CBRC and the PBC jointly released the *Notice on Strengthening the Administration of Cooperative Business between Commercial Banks and Third-party Payment Institutions*	CBRC [2014] No. 10
Apr.	The PBC, CBRC, CSRC, CIRC and SAFE jointly released the *Notice on Regulating Interbank Business of Financial Institutions*	PBC [2014] No. 127
Jun.	*Guiding Opinions of the PBC on Implementing Opinions of the General Office of State Council on Supporting Steady Growth of Foreign Trade*	
Jun.	*Administrative Measures for Settlement and Sales of Foreign Exchange by Banks*	PBC Order [2014] No. 2
Jul.	*Notice on Management of Trading Prices of the Interbank Foreign Exchange Market and the Margin of Bank Quotations*	PBC [2014] No. 188
Aug.	The PBC, CBRC, CSRC and CIRC jointly released Guiding *Opinions on Financial Services in Support of Post-quake Restoration and Reconstruction in Ludian*	
Sep.	*Guidelines on Comprehensively Deepening the Construction of Rural Payments Services*	PBC [2014] No. 235
Sep.	The PBC and the CBRC jointly released the *Notice on Further Improving Housing Financial Services*	PBC [2014] No. 287
Sep.	*Notice on the Launch of Inspection on Financial Consumer Protection in the Bank Card Sector*	PBC [2014] No. 97
Sep.	The CBRC, MOF and PBC jointly released the *Notice on Matters Concerning Strengthening the Administration of Deposit Deviation Degree of Commercial Banks*	CBRC [2014] No. 236
Nov.	The CBRC, MOF, PBC, CSRC and CIRC jointly released *Administrative Measures for Financial Asset Management Companies*	CBRC [2014] No. 41
Nov.	The PBC and the CSRC jointly released the *Notice on Issuing Statistical System for Bonds*	PBC [2014] No. 320
Nov.	The PBC and the CSRC jointly issued the *Notice on Issues Relating to the Pilot Shanghai-Hong Kong Stock Connect Scheme*	PBC [2014] No. 336

Source: Collected by the research group.

(ii) Review of Regulatory Policy of the PBC in 2014

1. The Reform of Interest Rate and Exchange Rate Liberalization Took Big Strides

Interest rates are the price of capital and interest rates liberalization is a matter of overall importance. The PBC took big strides in deposit rates liberalization in 2014. On Nov. 21, 2014, the upper limit to the floating band of RMB deposit rates was raised from 1. 1 to 1. 2 times the benchmark level, while adjustments were made to RMB benchmark deposit and lending rates. Moreover, the benchmark rate maturity ladder was consolidated and simplified as appropriate, to make more room for market-based pricing of interest rates, perfect the Shibor and the self-regulatory pricing mechanism for market interest rates and expand both issuance and trade of interbank certificates of deposit progressively. These moves were of significance to consummate the market-based interest rate regime, and increase the discretionary pricing powers of financial institutions. The PBC also encouraged the development of interest rate derivatives, giving a powerful spur to the trade activity of interest rate derivatives. In 2014, 43,000 RMB interest rate swap transactions were concluded and the notional principal totaled 4.0 trillion yuan, a 47.9 percent surge year on year. In terms of the maturity mix, contracts maturing in or within one year were the most actively traded, with a total notional principal value of 2.7 trillion yuan, representing 63.4 percent of the total volume.

RMB exchange rate liberalization was also progressing in full blast. Taking into the considertation of the adaptability of economic entities, the PBC announced on Mar. 17, 2014 that the floating band of the RMB against the US dollar in the interbank spot foreign exchange market was enlarged from 1 percent to 2 percent and the band of bank quotations at counters was widened from 2 percent to 3 percent. The PBC has slashed interventions in foreign exchange since 2014 and has almost withdrawn from regular interventions in the market since the second quarter. Moreover, the PBC has authorized the CFETS to provide direct trading between the RMB and the GBP, EUR, SGD and NZD in the interbank market, with a view to lower currency conversion cost for economic entities and enhance market efficiency.

2. Expanded the Share of Direct Financing

In 2014, the PBC persisted in the market-oriented reform, by slashing administrative approvals, enforcing market discipline, accelerating innovations in financial products and systems, enlarging the interbank bond market steadily and expanding the share of direct financing immensely. RMB bonds issued in the interbank bond market in 2014 were worth 10.7 trillion yuan on a cumulative basis, representing a year-on-year growth of 24 percent. The balance of bonds under custody in the interbank market was reported 32.4 trillion yuan, up 16.9 percent year on year. In addition, the PBC launched comprehensive reforms to restore and reinforce the financing function of the stock market. Direct finance grew 6 percentage points year on year, representing 17 percent of all social financing scale in 2014.

3. Deepened Opening-up of the Financial Market

Opening-up of the bond market was accelerated. The PBC encouraged domestic institutions to issue RMB bonds in Hong Kong and overseas enterprises to issue RMB bonds in mainland China. As of the end of October, 2014, 16 domestic financial institutions issued RMB bonds overseas worth 105.5 billion yuan in total, and RMB bonds issued by overseas enterprises in mainland China amounted to 500 million yuan. To accelerate the opening-up of the capital market in both directions, the PBC worked with the CSRC to launch the Shanghai-Hong Kong Stock Connect program, giving permission to the RQDIIs to invest in overseas securities with the RMB, expanding the overseas pilot program of RQFIIs and allowing multi-national corporate groups to centralize cross-border RMB fund operations. The successful implementation of the Shanghai-Hong Kong Stock Connect, in particular, boosted fusion between the mainland capital market and the global capital markets and spurred innovation and development of the mainland and Hong Kong capital markets, convertibility of capital accounts and internalization of the RMB. As of the end of 2014, total 211 overseas entities, 73 more than the number in 2013, were admitted into the interbank bond market, including central banks or monetary authorities of other countries and regions, international financial institutions, sovereign wealth funds, RMB clearing banks, overseas participating banks in cross-border RMB trade settlement, overseas insurance firms, RQFIIs and QFIIs. Moreover, the PBC encourages China (Shanghai) Pilot Free Trade Zone (FTZ) to pioneer and experiment with financial reforms boldly, in an effort to accumulate practicable and copyable experience in reforming, opening-up and risk management, namely, in such five areas as the FTA system, ease of currency exchange for investment and financing, cross-border use of RMB, interest rate liberalization, and the reform of foreign exchange administration.

4. Went Further with Internationalization of the RMB

Internationalization of the RMB was taken further in 2014. As of the end of 2014, more than 40 central banks and monetary authorities included the RMB to their foreign exchange reserves. In 2014, the PBC signed bilateral currency swap agreements with the central banks of Switzerland, Sri Lanka, Russia, Qatar and Canada, and established official RMB clearing arrangements with the central banks of more than a dozen of countries or regions. Besides Asia, the traditional arena, curreny cooperation in RMB extended to main economic and financial centers in Europe, and also to the Americas, the Oceania and the Middle East. As discussed in the foregoing paragraphs, the PBC also encouraged direct trading between the RMB and some foreign currencies, so as to boost the use of the RMB and those foreign currencies in bilateral trade and investment. Internationalization of the RMB was a result of advancement in the reform and opening-up of China, as well as a catalyst for deepening reforms and opening-up. It involved streamlining of administration and delegation of power, exchange rate and interest rate liberalization, opening-up of the financial market, convertibility of capital accounts, macro fine-tuning approach and financial supervision, and had far-reaching consequence.

5. Took a Combination of Steps to Bring down the Financing Cost of Enterprises

As an aftermath of the international financial crisis, downside pressure weighed on the Chinese economy, some enterprises profited less, and small-and-micro enterprises found financing either inaccessible or unaffordable. In 2014, in conformity with the requirements of the State Council, the PBC continued to drive structural reforms and adjustments by taking a combination of steps and addressing both the symptoms and root causes. While asking financial institutions to optimize loan management, clear up improper charges, rein in shadow banking and put a brake on overly quick growth of financing cost, the PBC tried to tackle the problem of high financing cost on enterprises by deepening financial reforms. Some steps taken were: pressing ahead with interest rate and exchange rate liberalization, developing multi-layer capital markets, and boosting private-banks and other smalland-medium-sized financial institutions. These steps achieved the expected results in 2014. For example, the cost of corporate bonds declined noticeably. As of the end of 2014, the weighted average rate of fixed-rate corporate bonds was 5.52 percent, down 148 basis points from a year ago. The yield curve of corporate credit bonds nosedived. By the end of 2014, the ROR of five-year AAA and AA + rated corporate bonds shed 148 and 141 basis points, respectively, from a year ago.

6. Piloted the Financial Reform in Some Regions

The PBC pushed pilot programs of financial reforms in some regions, including the developed eastern coastal regions, central regions in the midst of industrialization and transition, the underdeveloped western regions and frontier regions inhabited by minority groups. These pilot programs covered areas such as the opening-up of the financial sector, the convertibility of RMB capital accounts, cross-border RMB transactions, financial cooperation among Guangdong, Hong Kong and Macau, financial reforms in rural areas, regulated development of private finance and cross-border financial cooperation. These regional pilot programs of the financial reform aimed at serving the real economy, and supporting well-placed regions to combine financial reforms with the upgrade of the industrial mix, financial innovation and economic and social developments, based on local economic performance and the needs for upgrade of the industrial mix. Local governments were advised to make the most of existing policies, to improve the efficiency of the financial sector, and drove financial reform and innovations that conformed to the local reality and had local characteristics. These programs have achieved initial success.

7. Kept the Payment System Running Safely and Efficiently

Payment statistics showed that the payment system was running safely, reliably and efficiently, and fund trading turnover of the whole society swelled further in 2014. The payment system has made contribution to driving innovations in financial instruments, improving financial services and making resource allocation more efficient and added fuel to the development of the Chinese society and economy.

8. Encouraged Innovation and Development, and Practice Moderate and Classified Supervision on Internet Finance

The PBC acknowledged the positive contributions by Internet Finance as it made financial services more efficient, lowered transaction costs, satisfied diversified investment and financing needs, and promoted inclusive micro finance and rural finance. At the same time, the PBC believed that Internet finance didn't change the risk nature of finance and entailed greater risks concomitant with technologies, information and safety. Hence, the PBC applied the rule of moderate and classified supervision to the design of the supervisory framework for Internet Finance, brought into full play the role of the Payment and Clearing Association of China, promoted self-regulatory management of payment and clearing and Internet Finance, allowed the self-regulatory mechanism to do its part in the governance of the industry and achieved synergy and balance between regulatory and self-regulatory forces.

9. Combatted Money Laundering with Unremitting Effort

In 2014, the PBC studied *National Risk Assessment on Money Laundering and Terrorist Financing* carefully, and perfected China's AML working mechanism and system, deepened international AML and ATF cooperation, and enhanced AML and ATF monitoring, law enforcement and supervision through the Inter-Ministerial Anti-Money Laundering Joint Conference.

10. Made New Progress in Financial Consumer Protection

Jobs done by the PBC in 2014 to protect financial consumer rights include: heightening the public's awareness of financial consumer rights protection, perfecting the working mechanism and system of financial consumer rights protection and laying out the institutional framework; optimizing the financial consumer information and complaint service, putting into service the nation-wide Financial Consumer Information and Complaint Hotline "12363", serving as an information management platform; exploring alternative financial consumer dispute resolutions, and starting the application of complaint classification standards; phasing in an inspection on financial consumer rights protection in the bank card sector and disclosing to financial institutions 17 findings covering six aspects; exploring off-site supervision and finishing the assessment of pilot environment, institutions and products; imparting and spreading financial knowledge and staging Financial Knowledge Month, Financial Consumer Rights Day and other events; conducting a survey on inclusive finance and supporting innovations in and experiments with mobile finance, taking an active part in international events relating to financial consumer rights protection and inclusive finance, and sharing the achievements and experience of China with other nations. Between June and August, 2014, the PBC Shanghai head office and all branches checked up on 1269 financial institutions (including branches) (incorporated into comprehensive law enforcement inspection in some regions) and found 17 main problems in six aspects involving financial consumer rights protection in the bank card sector.

(iii) Policy Review and Outlook

Under the leadership of the CPC Central Committee and the State Council, the PBC did its best to seek growth amid stability and drive reform and innovation in 2014 and made great achievements in all respects, in spite of the complex and changeful international environment and the heavy mission of keeping domestic reform, development and stability. While holding firmly to a robust monetary policy, the PBC made new breakthroughs in interest rate and exchange rate liberalization, the bond market and the FTZ. It advanced reforms on policy financial institutions. As a result, innovation and development of the financial market obviously picked up speed and the financial sector was able to serve the real economy better. Cross-border use of the RMB was expanded further. The reform of foreign exchange administration was deepened. Precautions against financial risk were effective. Financial service and management were improved. The breadth and depth of international and regional financial cooperation were both taken to the next level.

The year of 2015 is crucial to deepening the reform comprehensively and the year to witness the beginning of full implementation of the rule of law and the completion of the 12th Five-Year Plan. The PBC will pursue stable growth as diligently as ever, make an accurate understanding of and adapt to the New Normal Situation of the economy. It will plan for stable growth, keep reforms and restructuring, benefit the people and prevent risks, hold on to stable monetary policy and keep continuity and stability of regulatory policies. The PBC is expected to quicken the tempo of interest rate and exchange rate liberalization, and convertibility of RMB capital accounts, and is likely to stage high-value certificates of deposit intended for corporate and individual clients when the timing is right in 2015. Meanwhile, the PBC will unveil and put into practice the reform plan for policy financial institutions as early as possible and promulgate the deposit insurance rules. The PBC will structure and fine-tune the Internet Finance supervisory framework and lead the guidelines preparation for boosting healthy growth of Internet finance pursuant to the rules of Moderate Supervision, Classified Supervision, Coordinated Supervision and Innovative Supervision. The PBC will strengthen coordination and guidance in regional financial reforms, accumulate practicable and reproducible experience and implement the existing regional pilot programs. Anti-money laundery has been escalated to a national strategy in new circumstances. The PBC will head up AML-related jobs. Under the Inter-Ministerial Anti-Money Laundery Joint Conference framework, the PBC is going to put in place a national risk assessment mechanism for money laundery and terrorist financing, refine the AML and ATF legal system, enhance information sharing and data mining, go further with international cooperation and strengthen talents development. In 2015, in terms of financial consumer rights protection, the PBC will proceed with supervision, inspection and evaluation more deeply, optimize the financial consumer dispute and complaint settlement mechanism, go further with financial consumer education and publicity, boost inclusive finance and conduct survey and research with continued and redoubled efforts.

II. Highlights of Regulatory Policy of the CBRC[1]

(i) Highlights of Regulatory Policy of the CBRC in 2014

Table 6 – 2   **Regulatory Policy of the CBRC in 2014**

Date	File Name	File No.
Jan.	*Measures for the Liquidity Risk Management of Commercial Banks (for Trial Implementation)*	CBRC Order [2014] No. 2
Jan.	The CIRC and the CBRC jointly released the *Notice on Regulating the Conduct of Bancassurance by Commercial Banks*	CIRC [2014] No. 3
Feb.	The CBRC and NDRC jointly released *Interim Measures Governing Service Prices of Commercial Banks*	CBRC Order [2014] No. 1
Mar.	*Guiding Opinions on Financial Services to Small and Micro Enterprises in 2014*	CBRC [2014] No. 7
Mar.	*Guiding Opinions of the General Office of the CBRC on Supporting Industrial Restructuring and Relieving Overcapacity*	CBRC [2014] No. 55
Mar.	The CBRC revised *Measures for the Administration of Financial Lease Companies*	CBRC Order [2014] No. 3
Mar.	The CBRC revised *Implementation Measures for Administrative Licensing Items Concerning Small- and Medium-Sized Rural Financial Institutions*	CBRC Order [2014] No. 4
Apr.	*Guiding Opinions on Risk Control over Trust Companies*	CBRC [2014] No. 99
Apr.	The CBRC and the PBC jointly released the *Notice on Strengthening the Administration of Cooperative Business between Commercial Banks and Third-party Payment Institutions*	CBRC [2014] No. 10
Apr.	The CBRC and the CSRC released *Guiding Opinions on Commercial Banks Offering Preferred Shares to Replenish Tier 1 Capital*	CBRC [2014] No. 12

---

① Written by Zhu Xiaochuan.

Continued

Date	File Name	File No.
Apr.	The PBC, CBRC, CSRC, CIRC and SAFE jointly released the *Notice on Regulating Interbank Business of Financial Institutions*	PBC [2014] No. 127
May	*The General Office of the CBRC released the Notice on Proper Governance of Interbank Business of Commercial Banks*	CBRC [2014] No. 140
Jun.	*Notice on Matters Concerning Streamlining of Administration, Delegation of Power and Improvement in Market Access*	CBRC [2014] No. 176
Jun.	*Notice on Adjusting the Base for Calculating Loan-to-Deposit Ratio of Commercial Banks*	CBRC [2014] No. 34
Jul.	*Notice on Strengthening the Management of Risks Involved in the Offsite and Centralized Information Technology Outsourcing of Banking Financial Institutions*	CBRC [2014] No. 187
Jul.	*Notice on Improving the Organization and Management System of Wealth Management Business of Banks*	CBRC [2014] No. 35
Jul.	*Notice on Perfecting and Innovating Lendings to Small and Micro Enterprises and Improving Financial Services to Small and Micro Enterprises*	CBRC [2014] No. 36
Jul.	*Interim Regulations on Subsidiaries of Financial Lease Companies*	CBRC [2014] No. 198
Aug.	*Guiding Opinions on Accessibility of Grassroots Financial Services to All Villages*	CBRC [2014] No. 222
Aug.	*Assessment of Consumer Rights Protection by Banking Financial Institutions (for Trial Implementation)*	CBRC [2014] No. 37
Sep.	The PBC and the CBRC jointly released the *Notice on Further Improving Housing Financial Services*	PBC [2014] No. 287
Sep.	Revised *Measures for the Implementation of Administrative Licensing Items Concerning Foreign Banks*	CBRC Order [2014] No. 6
Sep.	The CBRC and the Ministry of Agriculture jointly released *Guiding Opinions on Financial Support to Mass Production and Intensive Management of Agriculture*	CBRC [2014] No. 38
Sep.	The CBRC, the MOF and the PBC jointly released the *Notice on Matters Concerning Strengthening the Administration of Deposit Deviation Degree of Commercial Banks*	CBRC [2014] No. 236
Sep.	The CBRC, NDRC, the Ministry of Science and Technology and the Ministry of Industry and Information Technology jointly released *Guiding Opinions on Strengthening the Banking Network Security and Information Technology Construction through the Application of Safe and Controllable Information Technologies*	CBRC [2014] No. 39
Sep.	*Guidelines for Internal Control of Commercial Banks*	CBRC [2014] No. 40
Sep.	*Administrative Measures for Crime Risk Screening Involving Banking Financial Institutions*	CBRC [2014] No. 247

Continued

Date	File Name	File No.
Nov.	The CBRC, the MOF, the PBC, the CSRC and the CIRC jointly released *Administrative Measures for Financial Asset Management Companies*	CBRC [2014] No. 41
Nov.	*Notice on Encouraging and Instructing Private Capital to Participate in the Property Right Reform of Rural Credit Cooperatives*	CBRC [2014] No. 45
Dec.	*Guiding Opinions on Further Promoting Healthy Development of Rural Banks*	CBRC [2014] No. 46
Dec.	The CBRC and the MOF jointly promulgated *Administrative Measures for Trust Security Fund*	CBRC [2014] No. 50
Dec.	*Notice on Assessment of Banking Financial Institutions' Supervision over Off-site Centralized Outsourcing*	CBRC [2014] No. 272
Dec.	*Guidelines for Tightening Supervision over the Mechanism of Financial Services to Agriculture, Rural Areas and Farmers by Rural Commercial Banks*	CBRC [2014] No. 287
Dec.	*The CBRC, the Supreme People's Procuratorate, the Ministry of Public Security, and the Ministry of State Security jointly released Provisions on Banking Financial Institutions' Assistance in Inquiry and Freezing by the People's Procuratorates, the Public Security and the State Security*	CBRC [2014] No. 53
Dec.	*Guidelines for Consolidated Management and Supervision of Commercial Banks*	CBRC [2014] No. 54
Dec.	*Report on Government Information Disclosure of the CBRC, 2014*	Others [2014] No. 1

Source: Collected by the research group.

(ii) Review of Regulatory Policy of the CBRC in 2014

In 2014, the CBRC followed closely after the decisions, arrangements and plans made by the CPC Central Committee and the State Council, upheld the tenet of *Focus on Reforms, Mitigate Risks and Benefit the Real Economy* in discharging its supervisory duties, pushed forward reforms and opening-up in the context of overall interests, took a synthesis of measures to prevent and defuse financial risks, introduced a set of policies to serve the real economy and fulfilled all tasks satisfactorily. All performance and risk indicators of the banking sector turned out better and the industry-wide profit kept growing steadily. In 2014, commercial banks delivered cumulative net profit of 1.55 trillion yuan, up 9.65 percent year on year; the average ROA was 1.23 percent, down 0.04 percentage points year on year; and the average ROE was 17.59 percent, down 1.58 percentage points year on year. Sufficient impairment provision was made against credit risks. As of the end of December, 2014, the balance of loan loss provisions at commercial banks totaled 1.96 trillion yuan, an increase of 281.2 billion yuan from the beginning of the year. The provision coverage ratio was 232.06 percent, down 50.64 percentage points from the beginning of the year. The loan provision ratio edged up 0.07 percentage points from the year beginning to reach 2.90 percent. The capital adequacy ratio continued to stay at high levels. As of the end of December, 2014, commercial banks (excluding branches of foreign banks) posted a weighted average core tier-1 capital adequacy ratio at 10.56 percent, adding 0.61 percentage points to that at the beginning of the year; the weighted average tier-1 capital adequacy ratio was 10.76 percent, up 0.81 percentage points from the beginning of the year; and the weighted average capital adequacy ratio gained 0.99 percentage points from the year beginning to 13.18 percent. The market showed ample liquidity. As of the end of December, 2014, the liquidity ratio of commercial banks was reported at 46.44 percent, up 2.42 percentage points from the year beginning; and the RMB excess reserve ratio inched up 0.11 percentage points from the year beginning to 2.65 percent. From Jul. 1, 2014, the CBRC adjusted the base for calculating loan-to-deposit ratio of commercial banks. The RMB loan-to-deposit ratio calculated with the adjusted base was 65.09 percent as of the end of December, 2014.

Banking financial institutions were not the only ones that achieved good performance, so did non-bank financial institutions of all kinds, suggesting proper and effective work of the regulator. As of the end of 2014, seven categories of non-bank financial institutions, including trust companies, finance companies, asset management companies, financial lease companies, auto finance companies, currency brokers and consumer finance companies, had a total of 22.74 trillion yuan of assets under management (including off-balance sheet activities like trusts and agency business of finance companies), with owners' equity of 1.21 trillion yuan and net profit of 165.959 billion yuan. In 2014, 68 trust companies completed 16,016 trusts schemes, distributing trust assets of 4.28 trillion yuan and a monthly average of 356.7 billion yuan. Distribution of trusts schemes upon maturity appeared stable. In the year, the trusts industry wound up 142 risk projects, involving a total value of 37.4 billion yuan. The value of remaining projects at risk were reduced to 78.1 billion yuan by the end of December, from 91.7 billion yuan at the end of June, and the amount as a percentage of total trust assets declined to 0.53 percent from 0.73 percent. Finance companies had adequate capital in hands, owned high-quality assets, sufficient provisions and ran a good business on the whole. As of the end of 2014, the industry-wide average capital adequacy ratio was 22.48 percent, up 1.3 percentage points year on year; and non-performing assets (NPA) outstanding amounted to 3.281 billion yuan, and the NPA ratio was 0.12 percent. As of the end of 2014, China Huarong Asset Management Co., Ltd, China Great Wall Asset Management Corporation, China Oriental Asset Management Corporation, and China Cinda Asset Management Co., Ltd, on a group-wide basis, had total assets of 1752.964 billion yuan, a 54.10 percent increase from the beginning of the year; total owners' equity of 276. 605 billion yuan; total consolidated net profit of 38. 822 billion yuan, up 27. 50 percent from the beginning of the year ; and on a parent corporation basis, total assets were 1048. 352 billion yuan, up 52. 33 percent from the beginning of the year, total owners' equity was 204. 88 billion yuan and total net profits were 24. 919 billion yuan, up 24. 99 percent from the beginning of the year. As of the end of 2014, 30 financial lease companies in China (including one financial lease subsidiary) recorded total assets of 1281. 333 billion yuan, up 26. 55 percent from the year beginning, total liabilities of 1132. 899 billion yuan, total owners' equity of 148. 433 billion yuan and total net profit of 16. 42 billion yuan. As of the end of 2014, the average capital adequacy ratio of financial lease companies was 12. 43 percent, the average NPA ratio was 0. 71 percent, and the provision coverage ratio was 269. 96 percent, indicating there was still much room for risky business. Thanks to intact asset quality and sufficient capital charge, auto finance companies displayed a high risk-bearing ability. As of the end of 2014, the average capital adequacy ratio stood at 16 percent, and the NPA totaled 1. 328 billion yuan; the NPA ratio was 0. 38 percent, down 0. 03 percentage points year on year. As of the end of 2014, currency brokers had total assets of 671 million yuan and realized net profits of 142 million yuan. In the year, cumulative turnover of RMB brokerage was 58. 04 trillion yuan and that of foreign exchange brokerage was 6. 09 trillion US dollars. The trade turnover continued expanding, the products were more diversified and market recognition was heightened. As of the end of 2014, consumer finance companies' capital adequacy ratio was 22. 83 percent on average, its NPA was 354 million yuan and the NPA ratio was 1. 56 percent.

1. Made a Landmark Breakthrough in the Reform and Opening-up of the Banking Sector

A new breakthrough was made in private capital's access to the banking sector in 2014. The first five private banks completed preparations for start-up, and one of them started business. 14 privately-controlled non-bank financial institutions and 162 private-controlled rural banks came into existence. Private capital was more actively involved in the property right reform of rural credit cooperatives. The reform of the banking governance system was progressing. All major commercial banks formed inter-bank business units and 453 banks opened wealth management business units. Opening-up of the banking sector was broadened. The criteria for admission and RMB business applicable to foreign banks were loosened. The same market access standards applied to both Chinese and foreign banks. The pre-establishment national treatment plus negative list approach were adopted for the first time to expand opening-up to the Hong Kong and Macau banking sectors.

2. Made Achievements in Serving the Real Economy

By introducing a set of guiding opinions, the CBRC urged banking financial institutions to refine the differentiated credit policy, gave support to industrial restructuring and overcapacity mitigation in some sectors, lowered the financing cost of enterprises and stepped up financial services to those fields of importance to the economy and the society. The growth of loans to small and micro enterprises and to the agriculture, rural areas and farmers were not lower than the growth of total loans and the increment was no less than that in the previous year. New banking outlets were built in 49 towns, 2,308 urban communities and 318 clusters of small-and-micro enterprises community that had no financial institution around before. Universal coverage of basic financial services were realized in over 500,000 villages. Moreover, housing finance for redevelopment of shanty towns and residence and financial support to quake-hit regions in Yunnan and Tibet were also considered in making policy.

3. Defused Risks in Key Fields and Defended the Bottom-line of Non-occurrence of Systematic or Regional Risks

In 2014, risks hidden in steel trade, coal trade, copper trade, guarantee circle and guarantee chain were gradually released and as a result influenced bank credits, trusts, wealth management industry and shadow banking sectors. In view of this, the CBRC tightened control over credit risks in key fields, adopted a differentiated credit policy on industries with overcapacity, local government financing platforms and housing loans, and strengthened consolidated management of banks; refined classified supervision, permitted six banks to apply the advanced capital measurement approaches and launched innovative capital replenishing instruments such as preferred shares. In the meantime, the CBRC took initiative to prevent and defuse hidden risks in non-credit assets and off-balance sheet activities and kept a close eye on the liquidity risks, technical risks, external risks and operational risks in commercial banks.

4. Disclosed More Information, Streamlined Administration and Delegate Power

In 2014, the CBRC strictly followed the requirements in *Regulations of the People's Republic of China on the Disclosure of Government Information and Key Tasks in the Disclosure of Government Information* (2014), considered the facts of supervisory work of the banking sector, and used itsofficial site as a portal of information disclosure to the public. The CBRC refined the working mechanism and substantiated the content of government information disclosure, updated the public on supervisorywork of the banking sector in a timely, active and complete manner, enhanced the transparency of supervisory work, deepened the public's understanding of supervision of the banking sector and heightened its ability to discharge its supervisory duties lawfully. At the same time, the CBRC abolished and delegated some approval items and released the *Notice on Matters Concerning Streamlining of Administration, Delegation of Power and Improvement in Market Access*. Some matters that used to need mandatory approvals were administered on the basis of reporting. Reimposing these approval requirements under new names or titles was banned. The preset target for streamlining was attained.

5. Strengthened Consumer Protection

The regulation of the conduct of bancassurance by commercial banks and service prices was improved. 2014 Financial Knowledge Month was organized to strengthen consumer rights protection.

6. Involved in International Financial Supervision Reform and Stepped up in International Communication and Cooperation among Regulators

The CBRC attended conferences of Financial Stability Board, meetings convened by central bank presidents and monetary authority officials, and Basel plenums on several occasions in 2014. The CBRC signed MOUs with five foreign regulators, namely, the central bank of Ghana, Sweden Financial Supervisory Authority, the central bank of Mongolia, the Superintendency of Banking and Insurance of Peru, and the central bank of Qatar, and inked the *Agreement on Cooperation and Exchange of Information in Bilateral Regulation of Overseas Client Wealth Management by Commercial Banks* with the Financial Markets Authority of France, the *Agreement on Division of Supervisory Duties for Opening of Branches of Chinese Banks in the UK* with the Prudential Regulation Authority of the UK, and held talks with its counterpart in the USA, Canada, Hong Kong SAR and Taiwan. In addition, the CBRC hosted the 18th International Conference of Banking Supervisors (ICBS) in Tianjin from Sep. 22 to 25, 2014.

7. Optimized the Supervisory System of Non-bank Financial Institutions

The trusts sector played a dominant role among non-bank financial institutions. There was a landmark development in the governance system, the so called *Eight Mechanisms, and Eight Duties* were newly proposed in 2014. [1] In 2014, with the beginning of the New Normal era of the Chinese economy, the trusts sector faced profound changes in the competition and development landscape, and strategic opportunities and challenges aroseconcurrently. Requested and supervised by the CBRC, trusts companies have adapted themselves to the New Normal, improved both growth quality and efficiency, and performed the proposed *Eight Duties* earnestly. The CBRC discussed and amended the *Notice on Adjusting the Calculation Base of Net Capital of Trust Companies*, *Guidelines for the Regulatory Rating* and *Classification of Trust Companies* (Revised), *Administrative Measures for Trust Registration*, and *Guidelines for Due Diligence of*

---

[1] The Eight Mechanisms are complete corporate governance mechanism, product registration mechanism, classified operation mechanism, capital constraint mechanism, social responsibility mechanism, restoration and response mechanism, industry stability mechanism and supervisory rating mechanism. The Eight Duties are fiduciary duty, broking duty, claim duty, accounting duty, institutional duty, shareholder duty, duty of the industry and regulatory duty.

Trust Companies, and set up the trust security fund and its management body. The supervision of other non-bank financial institutions was also steady and effective. The industries performed soundly without material risky events.

(iii) Policy Review and Outlook

Speaking of the supervisory work done in 2014, first of all, the CBRC combined international standards with domestic practices consistently, upheld the supervisory philosophy of Manage Legal Persons, Manage Risks, Manage Internal Control and Improve Transparency, enforced all international rules strictly, applies capital, leverage ratio, liquidity and other supervisory indicators, adopted more prudential standards in some fields, including raised core tier-1 capital and leverage ratio requirements, applied regulatory capital to all banking financial institutions, and always assured compliance with the definition of Qualifying High Quality Liquid Assets. In the meantime, as China's banking sector was skewed towards credit business, the CBRC enforced quantitative supervisory requirements for liquidity and high-value degree of concentration and framed a consistent supervisory approach, Accurate Classification—Sufficient Provisioning—Reliable Profit—Adequate Capital. Some simple yet effective supervisory indicators such as loan-to-deposit ratio and provision coverage ratio were used consistently. Second, the CBRC combined macro prudence with micro prudence and structured a macro-and-micro prudential regulation framework. A supervisory system that covered all types of institutions, business activities, senior management and corporate governance shaped up. Moreover, the CBRC learnt a lesson from the recent global financial crisis, strengthened dynamic supervision, raised regulatory capital adequacy ratio and NPL provision ratio, sharpened countercyclical supervision skills, intensified coordinated supervision among the banking sector, the securities sector and the insurance sector, drived cross-sector and cross-border supervisory cooperation, and defended the bottom-line of non-occurrence of systematic or regional risky events. Third, supervision by institution and supervision by function were combined. In terms of supervision by institution, the principle of Life Cycle Coverage was applied and the supervisory process applicable to different types of institutions was comprised of market access control, off-site supervision and on-site examination, which were interdependent. In terms of supervision by function, supervisory organs concentrated on some specified fields, such as financial innovations, IT system, and consumer protection, were set up to promote intensive and specialized supervision. Fourth, risk monitoring and serving the economy were combined. While tightening supervision and risk prevention, the CBRC always placed a high emphasis on guiding the banking sector and other financial institutions to serve the real economy, to better support those important yet weak fields that concerned the national economy and the people's livelihood and to serve the real economy more efficiently.

The guidelines for supervisory work of the CBRC in 2015 are described as follows: to seek growth amid stability, to improve growth quality and efficiency, to adapt to the New Normal of the economy, to press ahead with the reform and opening-up of the banking sector, to drive the rule of law in the financial sector, to tighten financial risk management, and to heighten the ability to serve the real economy. Detailed tasks will be done as follows.

First, improve the quality and efficiency of financial services. Pertinent financial services of high added-value will be provided to the real economy by taking advantage of the strategic opportunity arising from deepened international economic ties and transformation and upgrade of the national economy. The CBRC will support implementation of national strategies, boost industrial restructuring, promote inclusive finance and do its best to lower the financing cost of the society.

Second, enforce risk prevention and control responsibilities, and tighten detection and precaution against client credit risk, collateral value volatility risk, liquidity risk, operational risk and social financial risk.

Third, deepen the reform and openup of the banking sector and other non-bank financial sectors. Private capital is encouraged to get involved in all sorts of banks and other financial institutions by varied means. The reform of the management architecture and supervisory system of the banking sector and other non-bank financial sectors will be pushed forward. The financial service infrastructures will be enhanced.

Fourth, drive the rule of law in the banking sector and other non-bank financial sectors, consummate the legal system, improve enforcement and impose stricter punishment on illegal practices.

The year of 2015 is crucial to deepening the reform comprehensively and the year to witness the beginning of full implementation of the rule of law. On the basis of deep understandings of the new circumstances and the New Normal of reform and development of the banking sector, the CBRC will put forth its greatest effort to enhance the awareness of the rule of law, perfect the legal system of the banking sector, enforce the laws strictly, reinforce supervision and evaluation of law enforcement, defend the bottom-line of non-occurrence of systematic or regional financial risk, conduct supervision and operation according to the laws, modernize the governance system and ability of the banking sector, take financial services of the banking sector to the next level under the condition of the rule of law and boost sustainability of the economy and the society.

III. Highlights of Regulatory Policy of the CSRC[①]

(i) Highlights of Regulatory Policy of the CSRC in 2014

Table 6 – 3   Regulatory Policy of the CSRC in 2014

Date	Description of Policy	Issued by
Jan. 3	*Rules for the Information Disclosure and Reporting of Companies Offering Securities to the Public No. 21—General Regulations for the Internal Control Evaluation Report*	CSRC, MOF
Jan. 12	*Measures for Strengthening the Regulation of Offerings of New Shares*	CSRC
Jan. 21	Beijing hosted 2014 National Work Conference on Securities and Futures Supervision. CSRC Chairman and Party Secretary Xiao Gang addressed the participants on promoting the transformation of supervision	CSRC
Feb. 25	*Specifications for Overall Risk Management of Securities Companies and Guidelines for Liquidity Risk Management of Securities Companies*	Securities Association of China
Mar. 21	*Decision to Amend Measures for the Administration of Securities Issuance* and *Underwriting and Decision to Amend Interim Provisions on the Public Sale of Shares by Shareholders in Initial Public Offerings*	CSRC
May. 14	*Administrative Measures for the Initial Public Offerings (IPOs) and Listings* on the *Growth Enterprise Market* and *Interim Administrative Measures for the Issuance of Securities of Listed Companies on the Growth Enterprise Market*	CSRC
Jun. 23	*Administrative Measures for the Acquisition of Non-listed Public Companies*	CSRC
Jun. 26	*Guidelines for Risk Management of Fund Management Companies*	AMAC
Jul. 4	*Several Opinions on Reforming and Implementing Delisting Arrangements for Listed Companies (Draft for Comment)*	CSRC
Jul. 18	*Interim Measures for the Supervision and Administration of Integrity in the Securities and Futures Markets (Draft for Comment)*	CSRC
Aug. 21	*Interim Measures for the Supervision and Administration of Privately-Raised Investment Funds*	CSRC
Aug. 31	*Decision to Amend Five Laws, Including the Securities Law of the PRC and the Insurance Law of the PRC*	The 10th meeting of the 12th NPC Standing Committee
Sep. 12	*Guidelines for the Performance of Duties of Independent Directors of Listed Companies*	China Association for Public Companies
Sep. 19	The revised *Interim Measures for the Supervision and Administration of Integrity in the Securities and Futures Markets* was promulgated	CSRC

---

① Written by Wang Xin.

Continued

Date	Description of Policy	Issued by
Oct. 15	*Opinions on Reforming and Implementing Delisting Arrangements for Listed Companies*	CSRC
Oct. 17	*Memorandum of Understanding between the CSRC and the SFC on Strengthening of Regulatory and Enforcement Cooperation under Shanghai-Hong Kong Stock Connect*	CSRC
Oct. 31	*Notice on Tax Policies for Shanghai-Hong Kong Stock Connect Pilot Program and Notice on Temporary Exemption of Enterprise Income Tax for QFIIs and RQFIIs in Respect of Gains Derived from Transfer of Shares and Other Equity Interest Investment in China*	MOF, SAT, CSRC
Nov. 19	*Rules on Asset Securitization of Subsidiaries of Securities Brokers and Fund Management Firms*	CSRC
Dec. 26	*Notice on Participation of Securities and Futures Brokers in the New Third Board*	CSRC

Source: Collected by the research group.

(ii) Review of Regulatory Policy of the CSRC in 2014

1. The Registration System Reform has Taken Big Strides

In his address to the executive meeting of the State Council held on Nov. 19, 2014, Premier Li Keqiang called for a plan for the registration system reform of stock issuance, cancelling requirement for continued profit-making before stock issuance and lowering bar for listing of small and micro and innovative businesses. An express low-value refinancing mechanism is proposed for the capital market and equity crowd-funding is piloted. The stock issuance registration reform taskforce, founded under the leadership of the CSRC as required by the central government, with members including the central bank, the Legislative Affairs Office, the CBRC, the CIRC and the Legislative Affairs Commission of the NPC, had completed the draft plan for the registration system reform, and would submit it to the State Council before the end of November, CSRC spokesman announced on Nov. 28, 2014.

2. The New Round of the Delisting System Reform has Started

On Oct. 15, 2014, the CSRC officially promulgated *Opinions on Reforming and Implementing Delisting Arrangements for Listed Companies* (the Opinions). The Opinions are formulated to refine delisting arrangements in five aspects, that is, to improve voluntary delisting arrangements for listed companies, specify and implement mandatory delisting arrangements for companies with major violations, implement mandatory delisting indicators with regard to market trading and financial performance, improve supporting arrangements in relation to delisting procedures, and strengthen protection of lawful rights and interests of investors of delisted companies. Delisting arrangements form an essential component of the capital market. Without an effective delisting mechanism, it would be impossible to allocate resources in the securities market in a reasonable and effective manner, or to propel restructuring and upgrade of the industries. Continued efforts to reform, perfect and enforce delisting arrangements can enhance the functionality of the capital market, motivate market players, make the market more competitive, foster survival of the fittest, penalize major offences against the laws, promote rational investment, and protect the legitimate rights and interests of investors, especially small-/ medium-sized ones.

3. Supervision over Integrity in the Securities and Futures Markets is Tightened

On Sep. 19, 2014, the CSRC unveiled the amended *Interim Measures for the Supervision and Administration of Integrity in the Securities and Futures Markets*, wherein the CSRC is explicitly required to launch an Internet-based platform exclusively for the purpose of information disclosure about breaches of laws and integrity. The platform will provide a centralized and public access to information regarding major breaches of laws and integrity committed by market players, including administrative sanctions, market bars and disciplinary punishments. The amendment has also adjusted the validity period of information concerning breaches of laws and integrity in the integrity records. Records of general breaches of laws and integrity have a validity of 3 years, while records of major violations such as administrative sanctions, market bars and criminal penalties have a validity of 5 years. [1]On Dec. 26, 2014, the securities and futures markets integrity data query platform went live officially. The public may visit the platform to find out breaches of integrity by market players, such as administrative sanctions, market bars and disciplinary punishments.

4. Regulatory and Enforcement Cooperation under Shanghai-Hong Kong Stock Connect has Begun

Oct. 17, 2014 witnessed the signing of *Memorandum of Understanding between the CSRC and the SFC on Strengthening of Regulatory and Enforcement Cooperation under Shanghai-Hong Kong Stock Connect* (the MOU). Thereby, the institutional arrangements for cross-border regulatory cooperation between mainland and Hong Kong authorities under Shanghai-Hong Kong Stock Connect are completed. Signed by CSRC Chairman Xiao Gang and SFC Chairman Carlson Tong, the MOU is organized into seven parts: (1) the purpose of regulatory and enforcement

---

① CSRC website: The CSRC amended *Interim Measures for the Supervision and Administration of Integrity in the Securities and Futures Markets* todiversify integrity constraints, http://www.csrc.gov.cn/pub/newsite/zjhxwfb/xwdd/201409/t20140919_260634. html, visited on: Mar. 1, 2015.

cooperation and the validity of the MOU; (2) alerts and exchange of investigatory information; (3) procedures and arrangements for investigatory assistance and joint investigation; (4) use of information, including scope of use and confidentiality of information in enforcement cooperation; (5) arrangements for service of documents; (6) arrangements for mutual assistance in execution of orders under Shanghai-Hong Kong Stock Connect; (7) miscellaneous arrangements, including investor compensation, publication of information, consultation and regular liaison, and internship, training and secondment programmes for enforcement staff.

5. *Interim Measures for the Supervision and Administration of Privately-Raised Investment Funds* (the Interim Measures) have been Released

The Interim Measures set out five arrangements. First, the registration and record-filing system is all-inclusive. Second, qualified investor is clearly defined. Third, private fundraising rules are specified. Fourth, rules governing investment operations are enumerated. Fifth, discriminative self-regulatory and regulatory arrangements targeting different types of privately-raised funds are mapped out. The Interim Measures prepare the legislation ground for formulating and refining the policies intended to boost privately-raised funds, especially venture capital funds, and may prompt the finance and tax authorities and the industry and commerce administration to refine the finance, tax and business registration policies applicable to privately-raised funds, so as to foster growth of privately-raised funds, and allow them to make important contribution to robust running of the multi-level capital market, optimum resource allocation and strategic restructuring of the economy.

6. Policies Concerning the New Stock Issuance Reform are Refined

On Mar. 21, 2014, the CSRC disclosed the *Decision to Amend Measures for the Administration of Securities Issuance and Underwriting and Decision to Amend Interim Provisions on the Public Sale of Shares by Shareholders in Initial Public Offerings*, to go further with the new stock issuance reform. Following is an outline of the decisions. First, optimize the existing share transfer system, loosen the restriction on the use of funds raised as appropriate and intensify information disclosure on proper use of funds raised. Second, promote good practice of offline inquiry and pricing. Offline investors must hold non-restricted shares with market capitalization at a minimum of 10 million yuan. Third, better meet the subscription need of small- and medium-sized investors. The ratio of offline to online clawback will be raised. In cases where valid online subscription exceeds 150 times of the offered shares, no more than 10% of the shares in public offering should be reserved for offline subscription, with the rest being clawed back online. Fourth, strengthen supervision over rationing. Regulatory requirements shall be enforced. A ban on placing shares to related parties is added. Lead underwriters are prohibited from placing shares to any institution or individual that is involved in sponsorship, underwriting or any other type of partnership. Fifth, tighten ongoing and subsequent supervision. In cases where violations or abnormal circumstances are detected following stock issuance and underwriting, issuers and underwriters shall be ordered to suspend or terminate the offering of shares, while an investigation into relevant matters shall be going on. [1]

(iii) Policy Review and Outlook

In 2014, the securities market of China experienced unprecedented regulatory reform and many new policies and arrangements were introduced. The reform is intended, on one hand, to pave the way for the rollout of the registration system by changing the new stock issuance system and the delisting system, and on the other hand, to drive regulatory change by intensifying supervision over integrity in the securities market and imposing severer penalties on malpractices and crimes. In 2015, regulatory policies for the securities market are expected to deepen the reform and innovations and give first priority to accelerate regulatory change; drive the registration system for stock issuance; whip a multi-level equity market into shape; boost the private raising market and optimize the issuance system of private raising, to foster sound growth of privately-raised funds; relax access control over the securities and futures services sectors with good timing; optimize the Shanghai-Hong Kong Stock Connect; and tighten risk control and address law offenses and defaults properly.

IV. Highlights of Regulatory Policy of the CIRC[2]

(i) Highlights of Regulatory Policy of the CIRC in 2014

Table 6 –4   **Regulatory Policy of the CIRC in 2014**

Date	File Name	Issued by
Jan. 7	*Notice of the CIRC on Matters Concerning Investment of Insurance Funds in Shares of GEM Listed Companies*	CIRC
Jan. 8	*The CIRC and the CBRC jointly released the Notice on Further Regulating the Sales Conduct of Bancassurance Business of Commercial Banks*	CIRC, CBRC
Jan. 17	*Notice of the CIRC on Releasing Life Insurance Disability Evaluation Standards and Codes*	CIRC

---

[1] CSRC website: The CSRC refines policies concerning the new stock issuance reform, http://www.csrc.gov.cn/pub/newsite/zjhxwfb/xwdd/201403/t20140321_245900.html, visited on: Mar. 1, 2015.

[2] Written by Liu Xueqing.

Continued

Date	File Name	Issued by
Jan. 23	Notice of the CIRC on Strengthening and Improving Supervisory Ratios for Use of Insurance Funds	CIRC
Jan. 23	Decision of the CIRC to Amend Provisions on Qualifications of Directors, Supervisors and Senior Managers of Insurance Companies	CIRC
Jan. 29	Notice of the CIRC on the Regulation of High Cash Value Products	CIRC
Feb. 14	Decision of the CIRC to Amend Implementation Measures for Administrative Licensing of the CIRC	CIRC
Feb. 19	Guidelines for Reputational Risk Management of Insurance Companies	CIRC
Feb. 27	Notice of the CIRC on Abolished Administrative Approval Items	CIRC
Feb. 28	Notice of the CIRC on the Regulation of Depositing Insurance Funds in Banks	CIRC
Mar. 5	Notice of the CIRC on Matters Concerning Involvement of Foreign Insurance Companies and Their Affiliates in Reinsurance	CIRC
Mar. 21	Administrative Measures for Acquisition and Merger involving Insurance Companies	CIRC
Apr. 2	Notice of Authorizing CIRC Branches in Beijing and Other Cities to Pilot Supervision over the Use of Insurance Funds	CIRC
Apr. 4	Decision of the CIRC to Amend Interim Measures for the Administration of Use of Insurance Funds	CIRC
Apr. 4	Notice of the CIRC on Issuing Rules for the Preparation of Solvency Reports of Insurance Companies—Questions and Answers No. 21: Convertible Subordinated Bonds	CIRC
Apr. 9	Notice of the CIRC on Issuing Rules for the Preparation of Solvency Reports of Insurance Companies—Questions and Answers No. 22: Securities Investment Funds and Asset Management Products	CIRC
Apr. 14	Notice of the CIRC on Issuing Rules for the Preparation of Solvency Reports of Insurance Companies—Questions and Answers No. 20: Minimum Capital for High Cash Value Products	CIRC
Apr. 15	Decision of the CIRC to Amend Administrative Measures for Equity of Insurance Companies	CIRC
Apr. 24	Notice on Regulating Interbank Business of Financial Institutions	PBC; CBRC, CSRC, CIRC, SAFE
May 5	Notice on Matters Concerning Investment of Insurance Funds in Collective Trust Schemes	CIRC
May 19	Information Disclosure Rules for Use of Funds by Insurance Companies No. 1: Related Party Transactions	CIRC

Continued

Date	File Name	Issued by
May 26	*Notice on Checking up on and Regulating Evaluation and Appreciation of Investment Properties of Insurance Companies*	CIRC
Jun. 22	*Rules on Internal Control and Compliance Scoring for the Use of Insurance Funds*	CIRC
Jun. 24	*Urgent Notice of the CIRC on Regulating Development and Sales of Insurance Products by Property Insurance Companies*	CIRC
Jun. 24	*Notice of the CIRC on Issuing Rules for the Preparation of Solvency Reports of Insurance Companies—Questions and Answers No. 23: Investment in Blue Chips with Funds of Existing High-interest-rate Policies*	CIRC
Aug. 10	*Several Opinions of the State Council on Promoting the Modern Insurance Service Industry*	State Council
Aug. 12	*Notice of the CIRC on the Annulment of Some Regulatory Documents*	CIRC
Sep. 16	*Notice of the CIRC on Strengthening the Administration of Reinsurance Ceded of Property Insurance Companies*	CIRC
Sep. 23	*Notice of the CIRC on Issuing Rules for the Preparation of Solvency Reports of Insurance Companies—Questions and Answers No. 24: Trust Schemes*	CIRC
Sep. 28	*Interim Measures for the Administration of Non-insurance Subsidiaries of Insurance Companies*	CIRC
Oct. 17	*Notice of the CIRC on Matters Concerning Investment of Insurance Funds in Preferred Shares*	CIRC
Oct. 17	*Guidelines for Five-Tiered Risk Classification of Insurance Assets*	CIRC
Oct. 24	*Notice of the CIRC and the CBRC on Regulating the Insurance Asset Custody Business*	CIRC, CBRC
Nov. 14	*Opinions of the CIRC on Strengthening Insurance Consumer Rights Protection*	CIRC
Nov. 15	*Notice of the CIRC on Tightening Regulation of Sales of Non-insurance Financial Products*	CIRC
Dec. 4	*Guidelines for Consolidated Supervision over Insurance Groups*	CIRC
Dec. 5	*Notice of the General Office of the CIRC on the Pilot Run of Jurisdiction-based Supervision over the Use of Insurance Funds*	General Office of CIRC
Dec. 8	*Notice of the CIRC on Administrative Approval Items to Be Cancelled or Adjusted*	CIRC
Dec. 12	*Notice of the CIRC on Matters Concerning Investment of Insurance Funds in Venture Capital Funds*	CIRC
Dec. 24	*Statistical Rules for Insurance Retirement Communities*	CIRC

Source: Collected by the research group.

(ⅱ) Review of Regulatory Policy of the CIRC in 2014

1. Complete Research and Development of Backbone Technical Specifications and Get the Second-generation Solvency Supervision System into Shape

In conformity with the trends of economic globalization and the reform of China's insurance, market, the CIRC has taken the initiative to explore the way and mode of solvency supervision reform, with a view to empower the insurance sector to prevent and defuse risks and boost sustainable growth of insurance. In April, 2012, the CIRC started working on China Risk Oriented Solvency System ("C-ROSS"), the second-generation solvency system. On May 3, 2013, the CIRC unveiled China Risk Oriented Solvency System Conceptual Framework (the Framework). Then, China completed top-level design and set the goal of C-ROSS, established a three-pillar framework and formulated a set of basic technical specifications for C-ROSS. In 2014, the CIRC went further with C-ROSS. Throughout the year, the CIRC introduced a whole set of 17 consultative documents on supervisory rules. Following many rounds of industrial tests, including sample test, solution test, parameters test and calibration test, the backbone technical specifications for C-ROSS have been finalized and a solvency supervision system well suited to the characteristics of the Chinese market has shaped up.

The whole set of backbone technical specifications for C-ROSS consists of 17 supervisory rules: 9 quantitative supervisory requirements forming the first pillar, 3 qualitative supervisory requirements forming the second pillar, and 3 market discipline mechanisms forming the third pillar, plus one article on solvency reporting and one on the supervision of insurance groups. These interconnected rules form an organ supervisory framework.

The first pillar consists of 9 quantitative supervisory requirements. To be more specific, Article 1 about available capital specifies rules on the evaluation of admitted assets, admitted liabilities and available capital of insurance companies, as well as capital classification standards. Article 2 about minimum capital specifies the rules on the composition and measurement of minimum capital of insurance companies. Article 3 about valuation of liabilities of life insurance contracts specifies valuation principles for provisions of life insurance contracts of life insurance companies and reinsurance companies for solvency supervision purposes. Article 4 about insurance risk minimum capital (non-life insurance undertakings), Article 5 about insurance risk minimum capital (life insurance undertakings) and Article 6 about insurance risk minimum capital (reinsurance companies) set out rules on the measurement of minimum capital for life insurance, non-life insurance undertakings of insurance companies and reinsurance companies, respectively. Article 7 about market risk minimum capital prescribes for the measurement of market risk minimum capital of insurance companies. Article 8 about credit risk minimum capital prescribes for the measurement of credit risk minimum capital of insurance companies. Article 9 about stress test sets out the solvency stress test system of insurance companies and specifies the stress test methods and requirements.

The second pillar consists of 3 qualitative supervisory requirements, detailed as follows. Article 10 about integrated risk rating (classified supervision) prescribes for a comprehensive evaluation of the overall solvency risk of insurance companies and proposes a supervisory mechanism combining quantitative and qualitative approaches to make supervision more effective. Article 11 about solvency risk management requirements and assessment principles sets out a supervisory framework for assessing insurance companies' solvency risk management capability, wherein risk management is indexed to capital requirement. That is to say, the capital requirement can be lowered for those companies with strong risk management capability, and vice versa. This approach can motivate insurance companies to heighten their risk management capability consistently. Article 12 about liquidity risk specifies consistent liquidity risk supervisory requirements, liquidity risk supervisory indicators and cashflow stress test system for property insurance companies and life insurance companies and lays a complete liquidity risk safe net.

The third pillar consists of 3 market discipline mechanisms, described as follows. Article 13 about solvency information disclosure specifies rules on solvency information disclosure, and requires insurance companies to disclose solvency information on a quarterly basis, improve solvency transparency and reinforce the binding force of market discipline. Article 14 about exchange of information on solvency creates and consummates an exchange of information mechanism among the supervisor, insurance consumers, investors, credit rating agencies and media, to allow market stakeholders to monitor and restrain the behaviour of insurance companies. Article 15 about insurance company credit rating specifies the credit rating framework of insurance companies, to allow credit rating agencies to contribute to risk prevention.

Besides the aforesaid provisions, Article 16 about solvency reporting and Article 17 about the supervision of insurance groups involve the content of all of the three pillars. Article 16 specifies rules on solvency reporting, wherein the reporting system mainly comprised of annual reports currently is changed to one that is mainly comprised of quarterly reports. In this way, the CIRC is able to discover, give warnings of and address risks in the industry as early as possible. Article 17 about the supervision of insurance groups broadens the definition of group supervision, and as a result insurance (holding) groups and all kinds of implicit or hybrid insurance groups are also subject to supervision. The quantitative supervisory requirements, qualitative supervisory requirements and market discipline mechanisms also apply to insurance groups, marking a concrete step forward in terms of the supervision of solvency of insurance groups.

As mentioned previously, the CIRC organized several rounds of industrywide quantitative tests. The test results prove C-ROSS outperforms the first generation counterpart in risk identification, with a better-designed risk framework, and is able to measure and reflect all risks in the insurance sector in a scientific, accurate and complete manner.

Next, the regulator will launch and put into operation C-ROSS officially and refine the supporting arrangements accordingly. C-ROSS will have positive effect on China's insurance sector, when it is completed and put into operation. First, enhanced solvency supervision can impose compulsory constraints on insurance companies, so as to prompt insurance companies to change the way of extensive development, drive transformation and upgrade, improve the quality and efficiency and foster sustainable growth of the insurance sector. Second, C-ROSS pegs risk management capability to supervisory capital requirement, which can motivate insurance companies to heighten their risk management capability consistently and then sharpen the core competitive strength of the insurance sector. Third, the implementation of C-ROSS can help insurance companies use their capital more efficiently, and boost the insurance sector's appeal to social capital. Fourth, C-ROSS, as a supervisory framework developed by the Chinese financial regulator independently, can help China gain power in international insurance rules making and heighten the influence of China's insurance sector on the international arena.

2. Press Ahead with the Reform of Use of Insurance Funds, and Attach Equal Importance to Streamlining of Administration and Delegation of Power and to Risk Control

In 2014, regarding the use of funds, the CIRC followed the supervisory philosophy of Lift control over the frontend and Control the backend, and spurred market activity, tightened risk prevention and improved the ROI of insurance funds by pressing ahead with the reform, streamlining of administration and delegation of power, widening investment scope, simplifying supervisory investment ratio, giving support to innovations and promoting good investment practice. To be more specific, the CIRC introduced these policies in 2014.

First, widen investment scope and promote good investment practice. On Jan. 7, 2014, the CIRC released the *Notice on Matters Concerning Investment of Insurance Funds in Shares of GEM Listed Companies*, giving permission to investment of insurance funds in shares of GEM listed companies officially. On Oct. 17, 2014, *Notice of the CIRC on Matters Concerning Investment of Insurance Funds in Preferred Shares* gives details on investment of insurance funds in preferred shares. On Dec. 12, 2014, in the *Notice on Matters Concerning Investment of Insurance Funds in Venture Capital Funds*, the CIRC approved of investment of insurance funds in venture capital funds, in support of start-ups and small and micro enterprises. Thanks to these constructive moves of the CIRC in 2014, a wider choice of investment options is now made available to insurance funds. In the meantime, the CIRC has also tightened constraints on all kinds of investment behaviours to prevent investment risk. On Feb. 28, 2014, the CIRC released the *Notice on the Regulation of Depositing Insurance Funds in Banks*, in a bid to put to rights some hidden risks and problems in bank deposit activities of some insurance companies, such as non-transparent operations, defective disciplines, vulnerable risk management and misappropriation by others. On Apr. 24, 2014, the CIRC, together with the PBC, CBRC, CSRC and SAFE, jointly released the *Notice on Regulating Interbank Business of Financial Institutions*, with a view to assure proper dealings between financial institutions. On May 5, 2014, the CIRC issued the *Notice on Matters Concerning Investment of Insurance Funds in Collective Trust Schemes*, which is intended to refine the requirements for internal control over investment of insurance funds in collective trust schemes, regulate investment behaviour and take precautions against investment risk when insurance funds are used.

Second, simplify supervisory ratios and meet market needs. On Jan. 23, 2014, the CIRC promulgated and implemented *Notice on Strengthening and Improving Supervisory Ratios for Use of Insurance Funds*, introducing a new set of supervisory ratios that are "based on classification of insurance assets, operated by multiple supervisory ratio ladders and supplymented by discriminative supervision and supported by dynamic adjustments". Under the new framework, assets are classified into five categories, namely, liquid assets, fixed-income assets, equity assets, immovable assets, and other financial assets. Then on the basis of asset classification, a ceiling on the supervisory ratio of total investments, as well as degree of concentration, is set for each category. With that, the supervisory ratios governing the use of insurance funds in China are now basically on a par with the international common supervisory practices. Meanwhile, the supervisory ratios are supported by dynamic adjustments. The regulator may adjust the policies flexibly depending on latest market developments to meet reasonable market needs. On Apr. 4, 2014, the CIRC released the *Decision to Amend Interim Measures for the Administration of Use of Insurance Funds*, wherein the supervisory ratios of use of insurance funds are revised.

Third, found the Insurance Asset Management Association of China and accelerate the market reform. On Sep. 4, 2014, the Insurance Asset Management Association of China (IAMAC) was founded. IAMAC is an important fruit of the market-oriented reform of the insurance sector and marks a significant institutional innovation in the change of supervisory approach to insurance asset management. IAMAC, when it functions properly in its service, innovation and self-regulatory role, can push forward the market-oriented reform of use of insurance funds, protect the interests and boost growth of the industry, monitor market risks, preserve market order and foster sound development of the industry.

Fourth, pilot delegation of supervisory power and build an effective supervisory ladder. On Apr. 2, 2014, the CIRC released the *Notice of Authorizing CIRC Branches in Beijing and Other Cities to Pilot Supervision over the Use of Insurance Funds*. On Dec. 5, 2014, the *Notice of the General Office of the CIRC on the Pilot Run of Jurisdiction-based Supervision over the Use of Insurance Funds* came out. It is clearly stated in the document that the CIRC branches in Beijing, Shanghai, Jiangsu, Hubei, Guangdong and Shenzhen are authorized to exercise some supervisory powers over the use of insurance funds. The term of reference is specified as follows: first, monitor risks in the use of funds by small-/medium-sized insurance companies and the status of and risks associated with infrastructures, equity and immovables in which insurance funds are invested under their jurisdiction; second, delegate supervision over investment competency assessment of insurance firms under their jurisdiction on an item by item and step by step basis, according to the supervisory requirements for the pilot CIRC branches and available resources; third, coordinate insurance funds to support transformation and upgrade of the local economy and policies for financial innovation. In the meantime, infrastructures, equity and immovables in which insurance firms have made investment in the pilot regions must be subject to risk supervision by the pilot CIRC branches. The use of funds by insurance corporations operating in the pilot regions must also be subject to risk supervision by the pilot CIRC branches. These moves can step up supervision over the use of insurance funds, build an effective supervisory ladder, intensify risk supervision, create a multi-level supervisory framework for the use of insurance funds, and prevent systematic and regional risks effectively. Meanwhile, the market-oriented reform and innovation concerning the use of funds can also benefit therefrom.

Fifth, tighten risk control and defend the risk bottom-line. In 2014, the CIRC continued to tighten risk control over the use of funds, while promoting market-based use of funds. In the year, the CIRC unveiled *Rules for the Preparation of Solvency Reports of Insurance Companies—Questions and Answers No. 22: Securities Investment Funds and Asset Management Products*, *Rules for the Preparation of Solvency Reports of Insurance Companies—Questions and Answers No. 23: Investment in Blue Chips with Funds of Existing High-interest-rate Policies and Rules for the Preparation of Solvency Reports of Insurance Companies—Questions and Answers No. 24: Trust Schemes* in succession, with a view to specify solvency recognition standards applicable to a wide range of products invested by insurance companies, such as securities investment funds, asset management products and trust schemes, strengthen solvency constraints on investment behaviours, defend the risk bottom-line and assure robust performance of the market. On Jun. 22, 2014, the CIRC released *Rules on Internal Control and Compliance Scoring for the Use of Insurance Funds*, to launch a quantitative supervision approach to internal control and compliance risk associated with the use of insurance funds. On Oct. 17, 2014, the CIRC introduced *Guidelines for Five-Tiered Risk Classification of Insurance Assets*. By classifying and evaluating the risks in assets invested by insurance firms, the CIRC seeks to instruct insurance firms to step up integrated asset risk management, discover problems in the use and management of insurance funds timely, improve asset risk management of insurance firms, allow insurance funds to be used more efficiently and heighten asset quality.

3. Unveil the Strictest Ever Rules on Bancassurance and Put the Bancassurance Sector in Order with a Comprehensive Approach

Insurance distribution by banks and post offices has boomed in recent years and as a result, the premiums and assets of the life insurance segment have swelled. Meanwhile, insurance distribution by banks and post offices is still at an early stage and entails many problems, such as extensive development, improper business mix, misleading sales practices, misconduct of business, and a jump in surrender value. The public has a lot of complaints about bancassurance, for example, certificates of deposit changed into insurance policies, products sold to the wrong consumers, incomplete product introduction, and unreliable client information, just to name a few. In view of this, the CIRC and the CBRC have always placed a high premium on bancassurance supervision. As early as in 2010, the CBRC issued the *Notice on Further Strengthening the Sales Compliance and Risk Management of the Bancassurance Business of Commercial Banks*. In 2011, the CIRC and the CBRC jointly launched *Regulatory Guidelines for the Bancassurance Business of Commercial Banks*. Then, the CIRC and the CBRC jointly released the *Notice on Further Regulating the Sales Conduct of Bancassurance Business of Commercial Banks* (the Notice on Regulating Bancassurance) on Jan. 8, 2014, with a view to regulate the sales of bancassurance, put the bancassurance market in order and foster healthy growth of the industry.

The Notice on Regulating Bancassurance requires commercial banks to have a system to assess the demand and risk tolerance of policy applicants, and recommend appropriate products based on the assessment results. Some special client segments, such as low-income urban and rural residents and the elderly, must be well protected and products sold to these people should be ordinary products with definite insurance benefit. Automated underwriting by the system and drawing policies on the spot are forbidden. Manual underwriting by insurance companies is mandatory. During manual underwriting, the suitability of insurance products in question, policy application and signature must be double checked. Whenever an insurance product sold involves indefinite benefit and high premium, the policy applicant must be asked to sign his or her name on the Acknowledgement of Risk page before the policy application is accepted.

In order to guide insurance companies to adjust their business mix, bring into full play the pivotal function of insurance, and change the business model of bancassurance, the Notice on Regulating Bancassurance requires insurance companies and commercial banks to develop risk-proof and long-term-savings insurance products. The sum total of premium income that commercial banks derive from distribution of accident insurance, health insurance, term life insurance, whole life insurance, annuity insurance maturing in no less than 10 years, endowment life insurance maturing in no less than 10 years, property insurance (excluding investment-oriented insurance provided by property insurance companies), guarantee insurance and credit insurance must account for a minimum of 20 percent of total premium income derived from bancassurance business.

To root up misleading sales practices and other misdeeds, the Notice on Regulating Bancassurance puts forwards supervisory requirements for the sales behaviour of banks and post offices. The cooling-off period of bancassurance products is extended to 15 days from 10 days. The Notice on Regulating Bancassurance also requires clearly differentiating insurance contracts from banking documents and putting in place visible and unequivocal risk warnings, and the content of risk warnings for insurance products for wealth management purpose, such as participating insurance, unit-linked life insurance and universal life insurance, is specified. The existing provisions, "Commercial banks must not allow insurance companies to second staff members to their premises" and "Commercial banks are disallowed to distribute at their premises insurance products of more than three insurance companies", still apply. The Notice on Regulating Bancassurance requests banks to tighten the management of their sales team and forbids the sale of unauthorized insurance products, or alteration or retention of client data. Insurance companies and commercial banks must handle complaints and surrender applications properly.

On Jan. 29, 2014, the CIRC issued the *Notice on the Regulation of High Cash Value Products*. Since high cash value products are mostly distributed via banks, the move to rein in high cash value products will also have certain impact on bancassurance.

These two supervisory documents are promulgated to strengthen the protection of consumer rights, instruct insurance companies and commercial banks to fine-tune their insurance business mix, boost proper, healthy and sustainable growth of bancassurance and allow banks to provide better services and achieve win-win. In particular, the new rules on bancassurance may benefit those insurance companies with banking shareholders. The impact of the new rules on traditional large-sized insurance companies and value-oriented foreign companies is limited, while small-/medium-sized insurance companies highly dependent on the bancassurance channel are adversely affected. Life insurance companies of all kinds are readjusting their product mix and channel development strategy circumstantially. Generally speaking, the undiversified product mix of bancassurance is changing and the bancassurance channel is losing market share to new channels such as Internet, telephone and WeChat insurance sales channels.

4. Set the Deeds of Insurance Intermediaries to Rights and Assure Sustainability of the Insurance Intermediaries Sector

Insurance intermediaries have become an indispensable part of the insurance market in China. As of the end of 2013, there were 2500-odd insurance intermediaries, 200, 000-plus part-time insurance agents and more than three million insurance salespersons in China. Insurance intermediaries have made historic contribution to the reform and development of the insurance sector and become an indispensable part of the insurance market, by perfecting the insurance industrial chain, enhancing the efficiency of insurance resource allocation, improving insurance services and forging a tie between consumers and insurance companies. Generally speaking, insurance intermediaries in China are still at an early stage. Some problems have built up and some deep-rooted problems and contradictions remain unresolved. In order to deepen the reform of the insurance market and drive sustainable and sound growth of insurance intermediaries, the CIRC launched a countrywide campaign to whip the insurance intermediaries market into shape (the campaign) in 2014.

The near-term goal and long-term goal of the campaign are defined. The near-term goal is to, through a sweeping campaign, identify and defuse hidden risks, resolve acute problems in the insurance intermediaries market, purify the market environment, and put the market in order within a short period of time. The long-term goal is to deepen the reform, promote innovations, straighten out the mechanism of the insurance intermediaries market, form a scientific and appropriate market system, a set of open and transparent market rules, and a sound and orderly competition regime, and boost healthy and sustainable growth of the insurance intermediaries sector.

The campaign is carried out in five phases. At phase 1, fieldwork is done to glean basic facts. The regulator, insurance companies, insurance intermediaries and associations of the industry work together to conduct a general survey of the insurance intermediaries market, encompassing development of institutions, human resources, business performance, institutional arrangements, and risk exposure, and find out the status quo, basic characteristics and main problems of the market. At phase 2, the market order is restored. Based on the existing problems and risks in the market, those institutions and individuals that are found to have offended the laws and regulations in the general survey shall be kicked out or punished or ordered to behave themselves. At phase 3, the reform goes into more depth. In view of the deep-rooted contradictions built up in the insurance intermediaries market, a clear reform roadmap is drawn up and innovations are driven, to meet the requirements for clear-cut mechanisms and legal relations, higher efficiency and stronger service capability. The insurance intermediaries' market system and self-regulatory system are optimized based on market-oriented principle. The reform of the insurance marketing system is pushed ahead in terms of organization setup, incentives and daily management. The part-time insurance agent system is perfected and the responsibilities of insurance companies for management and control are reinforced. The access and exit management of insurance intermediaries is improved and corporate governance and internal control are strengthened. Information technology is enhanced to improve supervisory efficiency. At phase 4, rules and mechanisms are established. The insurance intermediary system is improved step by step. The business rules and supervisory provisions are repealed, amended or newly promulgated as appropriate in a timely manner. Thus, the fruit of the campaign is institutionalized to form long-term mechanisms. At phase 5, a summary is made to see if there is any room for improvement. The jobs done in the previous four steps are reviewed and a report is circulated with a summary of experience. Mistakes and omissions, if any, are corrected. Next steps to deepen the reform and further development are considered.

In the year, the insurance sector acted on the premade arrangements, whipped the intermediaries market into shape, improved market order, defused risks, and laid a solid foundation for sustainable growth of the insurance intermediaries market.

5. Promulgate Measures for M&A and Perfect the Market Access and Exit Mechanism

M&A and reorganization are effective tools for enterprises to integrate resources and realize quick growth and important ways to adjust and optimize the industrial mix and improve the quality and efficiency of growth. In recent years, thanks to openup of China's insurance sector to both domestic and foreign capital, the number of insurance companies has increased consistently, business management and performance have shown divergent trends, and insurance companies of different motives and sizes have been actively involved in a wide range of M&A activities. In order to boost and regulate M&A activities of insurance companies, the CIRC released *Administrative Measures for Acquisition and Merger Involving Insurance Companies* on Mar. 21, 2014, effective as of Jun. 1, 2014.

M&A activities in the insurance sector fall into two major categories, M&A of insurance companies and M&A by insurance companies.

Administrative Measures for Acquisition and Merger Involving Insurance Companies specify the policies applicable to M&A of or by insurance companies and encourages all kinds of high-quality capital at home and abroad, especially private capital, to invest in the insurance sector. First, the restriction on the source of funds is loosened as appropriate. The provision, "A shareholder is disallowed to make investments in an insurance company with bank loans and non-self-owned funds of other forms", in *Administrative Measures for Equity of Insurance Companies*, is superseded. Now investors are allowed to resort to M&A loans, among other financing means, subject to a cap at 50 percent of total consideration. Second, the eligibility criteria for shareholders are loosened. Investors may not comply with the requirement for a track record of three-year investment in insurance companies. Third, the ban on acquisitions in the same business is lifted. The provision, "Where two or more insurance companies are controlled by the same entity or by each other, they shall not engage in the same type of insurance business which involves conflict of interest or competition", in *Administrative Measures for Equity of Insurance Companies*, is also superseded. Instead, acquirers are allowed to control two insurance companies engaged in the same type of business upon the completion of the acquisitions.

Administrative Measures for Acquisition and Merger Involving Insurance Companies lay down moderate supervisory measures, while encouraging M&A by or of insurance companies. First, all parties to M&A deals involving insurance companies have an information disclosure obligation and specialized intermediaries shall provide services independently. Second, a transitional period and an equity lockup period are stipulated for acquisitions, to assure sustainable and robust performance of the acquired insurance companies. Third, necessary punishments against malpractices such as misrepresentation and shareholding on behalf of others are laid down.

This is another important move taken by the CIRC to practice the decisions and policies made on the Third Plenum of the 18th Central Committee of the CPC and to bring into play the decisive role of the market in insurance resource allocation, and also marks initial achievements in perfecting the access and exit mechanism of the insurance market.

6. Unveil Top-level Institutional Arrangements and Strengthen Insurance Consumer Rights Protection

In 2014, continued efforts were made to make claims easier and put misleading sales practices to rights, crack down on any form of infringement on consumers' rights and interests, investigate into complaints and disputes, spread insurance knowledge and strengthen integrity. In the meantime, the CIRC released *Opinions on Strengthening Insurance Consumer Rights Protection* (the Opinions) on Nov. 14, 2014, to map out top-level arrangements for insurance consumer rights protection.

The Opinions represent a top-level arrangement and a directive document for insurance consumer protection in China, by basing the content on the reality of insurance consumer rights protection in China, drawing upon the principles of consumer protection specified by international insurance supervisors and international experience in financial consumer rights protection, citing existing laws and regulations, defining the guiding principles, basic rules, targets and policy orientation of insurance consumer rights protection, and proposing main tasks and concrete measures.

The Opinions highlight insurance companies' primary responsibilities for insurance consumer protection, feature the combination of preventive and ongoing protection, accentuate supervisory transparency and emphasize the importance of synergy between competent authorities and social communities.

Regarding problems in insurance products that consumers are highly concerned about, the Opinions require insurance companies to formulate contractual rights and obligations and determine product rates in a fair and appropriate manner. With respect to the widely complained-about misleading sales practices, insurance companies are requested to set up a discriminative sales mechanism based on product properties and risk tolerance of consumers, and sell the right products to the right consumers, so as to uproot misleading sales practices. Regarding difficulty in claims, insurance companies are ordered to settle claims in a timely and fair manner. As for the safety of client data, insurance companies are expected to keep consumer data safe and sound. Using any consumer information obtained by unlawful means that to conduct any business activity or reap any illegal proceeds is forbidden. Altering consumer data in any way or by any means is banned.

In the meantime, the Opinions step up sanctions against any infringement upon consumer rights and interests. The regulator is required to tighten enforcement, keep a close eye on the market, and reinforce the responsibilities of executives of insurance companies for management and control. Insurance companies shall put in place an internal accountabilitymechanism to pursue the persons who are held responsible directly or indirectly.

The promulgation and enforcement of the Opinions will improve insurance consumer protectionhenceforth.

(iii) Policy Review and Outlook

Xiang Junbo, Chairman of the CIRC, announced in his address to National Insurance Regulation Work Conference held on Jan. 26, 2015 that insurance supervision will be concentrated on three reforms and three key tasks while continuing to do well in daily supervision jobs in 2015.

Three reforms are detailed as follows. First, get further with the reform of the premium rates of auto insurance, universal life insurance and participating insurance. The reform plan for commercial auto insurance will be firstly piloted in six provinces and cities, Heilongjiang included, upon the approval of the State Council, and will then be rolled out countrywide when conditions are right. The reform of universal life insurance premium rate has been kicked start officially, to be followed by the reform of participating insurancepremium rate. Life insurance premium rates are expected to be liberalized totally before the end of 2015 if possible. The reform of accident insurance pricing mechanism is explored. Second, implement C-ROSS. The insurance sector will go into the transitional period of C-ROSS in 2015. During the transitional period, insurance companies are expected to submit both the first generation and second generation data. The first generation system is applied as prevailing supervisory standards. The official switch from the old system to the new system will be carried out in a flexible and practical manner depending on running status and preparedness of the industry during the transitional period. Third, deepen the market-based reform of the use of insurance funds. More weight will be given to serve the real economy, formulate well-targeted supportive policies, channel insurance funds into the elderly care and health service industry, and encourage direct investments in new-type urbanization, redevelopment of shanty towns, technical companies, small and micro enterprise, and strategic emerging industries. An industrywide insurance asset trading platform and asset custody center will be built on a market-based running mechanism, to activate the existing insurance assets, enlarge and strengthen the insurance asset pool and sharpen the core competitive strength of the industry.

Three key tasks are described as follows. First, pursue the inspection of insurance institutions designed to "strengthen internal control, strengthen external supervision, combat malpractices and combat crimes", and create an effective mechanism to rein in misdeeds and prevent risks according to the decisions and arrangements made by the State Council. Second, proceed with amendments to the *Insurance Law*, and develop a directive document for driving the rule of law in the insurance sector, in accordance with *Decision on Some Major Issues Concerning Comprehensively Promoting the Rule of Law*. Third, establish two assessment systems of insurance companies concerning business performance and insurance services, to motivate insurance companies to provide better services, heighten consumer satisfaction and improve supervisory efficiency.

References

［1］ PBC：Financial Statistics in 2014.

［2］ PBC：All-system Financing Aggregate Statistics in 2013, All-system Financing Aggregate Statistics in 2014.

［3］ PBC：Chinese Monetary Policy Implementation Report of 2014Q4, February 10, 2015.

［4］ CBRC：Supervisory Statistics in 2014.

［5］ CBRC：CBRC 2014 Annual Report.

［6］ Xue Ruifeng, Yin Jianfeng：Private Banking：Institutions, Products and Supervision, Beijing, Social Sciences Academic Press, 2015.

［7］ Wang Boying：A Report on the Wealth Management Market in 2014, *CCB News*, March, 2015.

［8］ China Trustee Association：A Review of China's Trust Sector in 2014, Jan. 2013.

［9］ Chen Wenhui：The Framework and Implementation Roadmap of China Risk Oriented Solvency System, *China Finance*, 2015 (5).